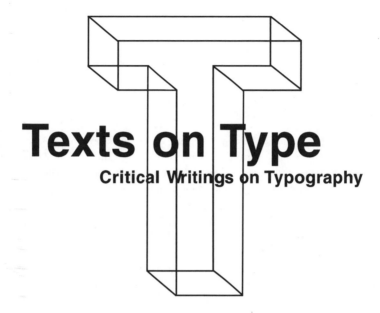

Texts on Type
Critical Writings on Typography

Edited by
Steven Heller and Philip B. Meggs

ALLWORTH PRESS
NEW YORK

05   04   03   02   01   5   4   3   2   1

Published by Allworth Press
An imprint of Allworth Communications
10 East 23rd Street, New York, NY 10010

Cover design by James Victore, Inc.

Page design by Jennifer Moore
Typefaces used in this book are credited as follows: Helvetica, designed by Eduard Hoffman and Max Miedinger; Bembo, modeled on faces by Francesco Griffo and designed under the supervision of Stanley Morison for the Monotype Company in 1929; Cheltenham, designed by Bertram Grosvenor Goodhue; Zapf Dingbats, created by Hermann Zapf; and Cuba, designed by Pablo Medina.

Page composition/typography by SR Desktop Services, Ridge, NY

Library of Congress Cataloging-in-Publication Data
Texts on type : critical writings on typography / edited by Steven Heller and Philip B. Meggs.
       p.   cm.
    Includes bibliographical references and index.
    ISBN 1-58115-082-2
    1. Type and type-founding.   2. Graphic design (Typography).   I. Heller, Steven.
  II. Meggs, Philip B.
  Z250.T365   2001
  686.2'24—dc21   2001018211

Printed in Canada

[Contents]

[Foreword]

By Steven Heller

The graphic signs called letters are so completely blended with the stream of written thought that their presence therein is as unperceived as the ticking of a clock in the measurement of time. Only by an effort of attention does the layman discover that they exist at all. It comes to him as a surprise that these signs should be a matter of concern to any one of the crafts of men.

—W.A. Dwiggins, Direct Advertising, 1919

ther than speculation about how many angels fit on the head of a pin, could anything be more arcane than a discourse on typefaces? The only difference between the former and latter is that average people, generally speaking, are more fascinated by the viability of angels than the reality of type. W.A. Dwiggins, who coined the term "graphic design," asserted that typecast letterforms are so inextricably wed to written language that the public routinely takes them for granted. And rightly so. Even in the current personal computer era, where the word "font" is familiar and typefaces are accessible to all, type is still not a common a subject of conversation. Except, that is, for those who are passionate.

Dwiggins was indeed passionate and obsessed with the art and craft of type. He once wrote that "to be concerned with the shapes of letters is to work in an ancient and fundamental material. The qualities of letterforms at their best are the qualities of a classic time: order, simplicity, grace. To try to learn and repeat their excellence is to put oneself under training in a most simple and severe school of design."

For those who design or compose letterforms, type is an article of faith. For the true believer, a classic typeface embodies ideals of truth and perfection. But as Dwiggins astutely observed, "By a remarkable paradox the one person who should not be called upon to perceive the fine qualities of the shapes of letters is the person who reads them. . . . If any single character presents itself to his attention as a single character, the process of reading is disturbed." Then it is the passionate and obsessive user of type who is duty-bound to examine its every nuance and critically address its very essence—if only to unburden the reader of such concerns.

The closest that the average person will come to lengthy reading about type are sections in manuals about downloading fonts onto computer hard drives. Otherwise, there is little impetus for the layman, indeed even for most graphic designers, to read type analyses or lore for pure enjoyment. Nonetheless, there is no shortage of aficionados who enjoy contemplating the minutiae; likewise, there is no dearth of essays concerning the intricacies of type. Moreover, such writing is neither trivial nor involuted. In fact, the best texts on type are fascinating exegeses on the art and craft—history and practice—of this lingua franca. For anyone involved in transforming words into print (or on the screen), learning how type functions, or why certain faces perform better than others, or how letterforms have come to embody various meanings and moods, is as necessary as understanding operating procedures. Although one can naively play around with typefaces, invariably those without a grounding in the history, aesthetics, and function of typography are doomed to be as clumsy as those writers who lack a grasp of grammar and syntax.

In recent years type has become more overtly integrated into mass communications. What was once a rarefied profession has experienced widespread adoption, starting as early as elementary school, through the use of user-friendly page-making programs. The computer has also made custom fontography easy while basic PC type bundles have democratized the overall practice by enabling access to thousands of specimens. As a byproduct, the rules concerning legibility and readability have been challenged, and the tenets governing type have been seriously questioned. Although this convention-busting is not entirely detrimental to the field, ignorance of true standards is indeed a problem.

Just because one can easily mutate and distort typefaces, even with momentarily pleasing results, does not guarantee an intelligent piece of typography. In fact, it usually promotes dubious principles that demand serious scrutiny. Although maintaining a body of critical essays on type and typography does not insure the practice of sound aesthetics, it is, nonetheless, a reminder, particularly in this age, that type is not a slave to caprice and whim. The purpose, in part, of this anthology, including myriad texts on different aspects of type design and typography, is to reinforce the idea that type is not some ad hoc collection of letters, like so many rubber slugs in a children's rubber stamp kit, but a venerable communications form rooted in historical precedent.

The study and practice of type is not as arcane as one might think. While some of the essays in this book are decidedly aimed at the serious typophile, most neither require advanced journeyman training nor a terminal degree in design to appreciate and learn from them. Although the editors have mainly scoured trade journals and professional periodicals, these essays do not comprise a ghetto of arcana shut off from the average type user. Since type is indeed the vernacular of mass communication, these texts on type are fundamental commentaries on what is truly the commonplace.

[Introduction]
Critical Writings on Typography

By Philip B. Meggs

ypography inspires passion. The magnificent orchestration of forms in a beautifully crafted type font; the unlimited possibilities of spatial syntax; and the meticulous attention to detail in a well-set page are attributes causing many graphic designers and printers to become fanatical about their craft. A vast divergence of opinion exists in the typographic community, whose members range from unyielding traditionalists to unbridled advocates of the shockingly new. A ceaseless parade of unprecedented fonts and page designs makes once progressive ideas seem ossified, making the dialogue about typography passionate and often controversial.

In the motion picture, book publishing, and fine arts arenas, critics monitor, evaluate, and explain new material. Conversely, although typography permeates the lives of everyone, until recent years it has remained an anonymous force in society. Before the computer revolution of the last two decades, most lay persons were totally oblivious to typography. It remained the exclusive domain of a small group of professional practitioners and trades persons. Like physicians whose prescription pads dictate the dispensing of billions of dollars of prescription pharmaceuticals each year, type professionals controlled an entire industry for the presumed benefit of all.

An apt metaphor for the evolution of typography might be found in a relic from the industrial age. After building enormous pressure in its pistons, a steam locomotive finally manages to jerk its wheels into motion and move thousands of tons of steel forward a fraction of an inch. Slowly inching along, it gradually gains speed, until it is hurling down the track with such vigorous momentum that it takes a half mile or more to stop. Typography has seen a similar expansive momentum. Technology, aesthetics, and cultural change have propelled this once rarefied craft into a rapidly changing activity practiced with varying degrees of accomplishment by millions of people.

Compositors controlled type during the four hundred years of handset metal type, then layout artists became important when hand-set display type was combined with machine-set type from keyboard-operated Linotype and Monotype machines in the 1880s.

The nature of type professionals changed markedly as the nineteenth century yielded to the twentieth century. Designing typefaces and composing pages was largely the province of punch-cutters and compositors trained in industry. Technological advances—such as automatic punch-cutting machines that cut punches from drawings, and machine-set text—spurred a shift to typeface designs and page layouts based on drawings by artistically adept individuals. These changes occurred just as a revival in printing and typography was underway.

The leader of the English Arts and Crafts Movement, William Morris, is the pivotal figure largely responsible for a remarkable reinvigoration of typeface design. His Kelmscott

Press inspired an interest in recapturing the quality of late Medieval and Renaissance printing; Morris used hand presses to imprint types emulating designs by past masters on handmade papers. His efforts inspired a tiny but ardent group of practitioners to reexamine earlier typography and printing.

During the first half of the twentieth century, a very small number of passionate scholars and historians established a body of connoisseurship and disseminated information helpful for effective practice. Even then, there were fears about falling artistic and technical standards due to more accessible technology and unschooled practitioners.

A critical dialog took place within the cadre of literate printers, typographers, book, and typeface designers. Little magazines popped up to provide forums for discussions. With names like *Alphabet and Image, Fleuron, Paper and Presses Illustrated Monthly, Pica,* and *PM* (for Production Manager), these periodicals usually had modest press runs and brief lives. The ardor of their editor and/or publisher was frequently the primary fuel available to keep them running, sometimes barely remaining financially viable.

These publications were joined by coverage of typography by the more mainstream graphic-arts press. Periodicals including *Inland Printer* (now published as *Printer's Ink*) and *American Printer* routinely offered monthly columns and articles about typography. These provided the unschooled with basic information about typographic refinements and advocated standards of quality in a field where routine and mediocre work was still the norm. Advertising and promotional specimen booklets from typefoundries offered another outlet of information. These sometimes lacked a critical editorial intent, for their overriding goal remained advocacy for the sponsoring manufacturer's typefaces.

Throughout this literature, a concern for typographic niceties and aesthetics recurs. Fundamental concerns, such as getting typesetters to take the time to kern misfit characters, or use appropriate leading, occupied those who took to their typewriters in an effort to improve the craft.

Alongside critics hammering away at basic issues during the first half of the century, several titans emerged. Among traditionalists whose passion and scholarship helped shape classical typography, Englishman Stanley Morison looms large on the horizon. Morison achieved a level of connoisseurship about matters typographic comparable to the great historian of painting, Bernard Berenson. Morison's anthologies of historical types presented well-designed specimens to the English-language audience. He edited four of the seven volumes of the *Fleuron,* establishing viable approaches to typographic criticism. As typographical advisor to many firms including Lanston Monotype Corporation (British) and the *Times of London,* he initiated many new and revival typefaces. Morison's essay "First Principles of Typography" (page 170) appeared in the final volume of the *Fleuron* in 1930, then was published in small book form in 1936. Absolute in its dicta but sometimes ambiguous about specifics, "First Principles of Typography" offered a canon of beliefs for others to accept or reject. Morison suffered assaults from distracters who questioned whether a critic not directly involved in typographic composition should be dictating to the professionals.

One curious note is Morison's contention about typography being "the efficient means to an essentially utilitarian and only accidentally aesthetic end." This disparagement of the aesthetics of type seems strange for several reasons, coming from a man who devoted his career to upgrading the quality and availability of typefaces. Excellent typographic craft in alignment, finish, and optically adjusted spacing improve both legibility and aesthetics.

While aesthetics might be accidental in vernacular and unschooled lettering, fine typography has benefited from a lengthy tradition of artistic concerns. From its earliest decades in the 1400s, this stemmed from long apprenticeships, a body of criticism, and the use of typographic artistry as a marketable commodity—first to differentiate books from other printers' editions of the same title, then in the sale of fonts.

Typeface design has always been a core concern in the literature about type. Indelible contributions to our understanding of historical typefaces were made by the American printer and scholar, Daniel Berkeley Updike, whose 1937 two-volume *Printing Types: Their History, Form, and Use* is a definitive study of old style and Renaissance fonts. Updike achieved a rare level of aesthetic bigotry, rejecting all innovations of the Industrial Revolution, including sans serif and slab serif types, as aberrations unworthy of consideration or use by serious typographers. Updike's narrow-minded stance did nothing to mar his definitive documentation and assessment of pre-Industrial Revolution typefaces by Jenson, Garamond, Caslon, and other masterful designers.

Critiques of new fonts as well as revivals of earlier typefaces has long been a staple of the typographic dialog. Essays discussing revivals of Garamond and Baskerville, the arrival of new (and at the time of their release, radical and unproved designs) twentieth-century sans serifs such as Futura and Univers, and experimental fonts such as Matthew Carter's Walker helped shape the look and feel of typography in successive decades. The weight of past controversies often stalk the type critic. When Jerry Kelly evaluated the newly released Adobe Garamond font (page 54), he surely understood the status of Beatrice Becker Warde's study of Garamond and its derivatives, as well as the rabid hostility many type experts held toward phototype-era Garamonds designed in the 1970s.

The traditions of typography were strongly challenged in the years between the world wars when the modern art movement turned its attention to the problems of typographic communications. Leaders of the modern design movement, especially Laszlo Moholy-Nagy, Herbert Bayer, and Jan Tschichold, were quite adept at arguing their case for a rejection of tradition and embrace of a new functionalism and aesthetic. Essays by early pioneers of the modern movement contributed to the world-wide acceptance of modern typography.

Drawing from the breakthroughs of Constructivism and de Stijl movements, the German Bauhaus design school became a center for launching modernist typography. Laszlo Moholy-Nagy's three essays (page 108) about modern typography are a call to arms, vigorously advocating clarity of communication, embrace of the machine ethic, and innovations based on emerging technology. His former student, Herbert Bayer, was more the practitioner and less the theorist; his essays (page 110) focus upon the practical realization of modernist theory.

The overnight conversion of Jan Tschichold—from traditional calligrapher and designer of symmetrical layouts using historical letterforms to the leading advocate of modernism—occurred after he visited the 1923 Bauhaus exhibition. He proved to be the most influential of modernists, because he not only argued for its validity but used his articles and books to teach a generation of designers and compositors about asymmetric typography, sans serif fonts, and geometric construction of the page. His seminal 1928 book, *Die neue Typographie,* codified the new approach with clarity and unrelenting advocacy. The section titled "The Principles of the New Typography" excerpted here (page 115) provides a logical yet impassioned argument for the new approach.

The firestorm of criticism unleashed by modernism resulted in a verbal war which went nowhere, for the inroads of modernism in advertising and corporate design could not be stayed, while traditional approaches using serifed types and a stately symmetry continued to exist, especially in book typography. As far as the wider world was concerned, modernism and traditionalism existed side by side with each other *and* a ceaseless parade of fashionable decorative and novel types designed to provide style and a contemporary aura to commercial messages. But to the typographic antagonists, modernism versus tradition was serious business. Traditionalists such as Frederic Goudy (pages 16, 149, and 218) actually believed modern layouts with bold contrasts, thick ruled lines, off-center balance, and elemental sans serif were disconcerting and ugly. Modernists including Douglas C. McMurtrie (page 143) and Paul Rand (page 154) were convinced that the stale and dated symmetrical placement of old-style type was an outmoded expression inappropriate to the modern technological age.

Artistic struggles are seldom limited to disagreements about what constitutes the noble virtues of beauty and truth. Opposing artists and designers wrestle to control the aesthetic future of the culture. Underlying the conflict are concerns about economic survival: Who will get the work?

When modernists attacked four centuries of typographic tradition as unresponsive to contemporary aesthetics and technology, victory could mean dominance over the visual syntax of graphic communication in a society whose steady transformation into an information-based culture was as relentless as its transformation from agrarian to urban life. Significant economic stakes were involved, for the prevalence of modernism over traditionalism would determine whether modernist or traditionalist designers became magazine and advertising art directors and received lucrative commissions for trademarks and package designs. Typesetting firms and typefoundries were vulnerable as well, for work flowed to firms whose arsenal of fonts contained the typefaces heavily specified by designers.

It is not surprising to find traditionalists and modernists vigorously defending their positions. Modernism has been so potent a force in twentieth-century design that even in the century's waning years, eminent designers including Mr. Keedy (page 159) have written eloquently about the need to confront and question modernism. He became a spokesman for designers seeking liberation from the modernist underpinnings of their education and practice. Advanced technology, an increasingly global culture, and changing social conditions prompted designers to seek new forms for a new age.

Disseminating information to promote more informed typographic practice has occupied many writers about type. Typographic education has been uneven over the past hundred years. Although many graphic-design curricula provide a thorough grounding in typography, many more do not. Some programs at technical institutes and community colleges offer lackluster production training, while many art schools emphasize experimentation without an accompanying understanding of the timeless principles underlying traditional and modernist typography. This has created a desperate need by many practitioners for basic information ranging from typographic conventions to an understanding of the principles of legibility.

Many writers bring clarity and ardor when expressing their beliefs about appropriate practice. Beatrice Warde, a tireless crusador for typographic excellence, advised on selecting typefaces (page 193). An American scholar working as assistant librarian at the

American Typefounders Company (ATF) library, she had garnered international attention for her research on Garamond type. Meanwhile, Josef Müller-Brockmann advanced the imperative need for organization using geometric grid structures (page 198) and William Golden insisted that designers always be true to his dictum, "Type is to Read" (page 210). David Ogilvy, who commanded one of America's largest advertising agencies in the 1950s, offered a blueprint for reader-friendly type (page 215).

Metal type's long reign ended with photographic typesetting processes of the 1960s; during this period the field of graphic design rapidly expanded as designers specified and ordered typography to use in paste-ups for offset printers photographic plate making operations.

Yet another radical transformation in typographic practice occurred in the 1980s when digital typography from computers and laser printers empowered individuals to set type on their personal desktops. Frenetic experimentation and innovation sprang to life as professional designers gained hands-on access to the tools for production and marketing of their own typeface designs. Young designers challenged the dominant cartels of large machinery and font companies, democratizing an entire sector of the communications industry. Experimental and eccentric fonts whose audacious designs might never get past the marketing committees of the large type firms are sold directly by their creators via the Internet.

Television, cinema, computer interfaces, and video games created an expanding need for type in motion; almost simultaneously, powerful work stations and software enabled individual designers to create kinetic effects formerly reserved for high-end systems only available to major television networks and national advertisers. The rapid expansion of the Internet during the 1990s provided yet another venue for animated letters.

Critical writing about type proliferated in volume and intensity during the digital era. Typeface designers including Rudy VanderLans (page 223) and Tobias Frere-Jones (page 228) hammered out position papers on their computer keyboards. Graphic designer Jessica Helfand (page 235) ruminates about the nature of electronic typography, while Peter Hall (page 260) contemplates the nature of dancing and moving type on cathode ray and silver screens. It is business as usual in the land of letterforms, and the usual has been quite spirited for over a century now.

The wellspring for typography's enduring vitality is human passion. A passion exists for letterforms, dynamic arrangements, history, and technique. It provides the motivation for innovative and experimental new fonts, unprecedented page designs, and critical writing. Throughout history, this passion for the aesthetic and civilizing aspects of typography has propelled this critical aspect of human endeavor forward, and it will continue to do so in the new millennium.

Aesthetics: On Form and Expression

Found Poetry: The Dude Typographers

By Alastair Johnston

s a letterpress printer, I've long been fascinated by the specimen books in which type manufacturers display the range of types and illustrations they offered. Beginning in the nineteenth century, the voice of the mostly anonymous printers whose job it was to compose the specimens began to show through. Since their only brief was to fill the pages with appropriate type, the texts often show an amusing mix of wit and nonsense, as well as references to current events.

One of the first to explore fully the type specimen book as a poetic vehicle was Thomas MacKellar. In 1867 MacKellar took over the L. Johnson firm, the oldest established typefoundry in the United States. A few stanzas—choice morsels from the want ads, circulars and fliers that make up much of the Johnson books—will convey a sense of the peculiar MacKellar humor:

FASHIONABLE EVENING PASTIMES.

Lambskin & Wolfsnap's Social

Hypocritical Delineations.

Admission Restricted.

Character Systematically Dissected.

The spirit of Charles Dickens pervades MacKellar's cast of characters: Mr. Justice Hogg, Mr. and Mrs. Billetdoux Turtledove, Sam Growler, John Barbecue, Mordecai Discount, P. Nipping Fyle, J. Censor Mentor and the happy honeymooners Jedediah Dumpling Honeyheart and Amarilla Lambkin Tendersoul. The glory of MacKellar in full bore is portrayed in this advertisement, suitable for the personals column:

To Women of Means, of any Pedigree!

Charles Harry Augustus Mellowtongue, Esquire, Bachelor and Gentleman,

The Pride of Fashionable Tailors,

Offers Himself to the Highest Bidder, Spinster

or Widow, under Fifty Years of Age.

His Accomplishments are Billiards and Dancing.

Ten Thousand a Year Indispensable.

Within twenty years, MacKellar's style—an ur-form of gonzo—was widely imitated, and each American foundry had its resident wag at the composing stand, parodying headlines and advertising claims, free-associating on the firm's faces. The typesetters at the Marder, Luse foundry of Chicago show they have assimilated all the techniques of sound newspaper reportage and editorializing in their specimen books of the last quarter of the nineteenth century:

LATE NEWS FROM THE SANDWICH ISLANDS.
Labor Market Quiet; Breadstuffs Heavy;
Missionaries Steady.
Highly Important Information, if True!

That the compositions are off the cuff is proved by the frequent typos as well as by their clear stream of consciousness, as seen in this 1892 bulletin from the Palmer & Rey foundry in San Francisco:

Long Continued Crisis in the Balkans
GIGANTIC FAILURE OF COLONIZATION
IN CENTRAL AFGHINASTAN
Somewhat Dubious & Unreliable Diplomatic Information

The types themselves were often discussed, if not wholly recommended, in the specimen texts:

This Pretty Letter Kerns not and therefore Breaks not. Very Useful
and Beautiful Type Cast on Standard Pica Body no Kerned Letters
to Bother the Operator and Break and Ruin the Fount.
All complete.

❖

A JUMBO CASE
Where Sleepers Dwell!
For Poster Printers

Many of the compositors responsible for these texts were "tramps"—footloose craftsmen who wandered from town to town looking for work. As described in *The Inland Printer* (April 1889), the transient printer was "certain to be pretty well up in his information touching on the leading questions of the day, and is ever ready to engage in a controversy, it making no material difference whether the subject is one of theology or politics, or on matters dramatic, musical or pugilistic." Judging by specimens such as this from Palmer & Rey, our compositor took a jaundiced view of politics that is remarkably up to date:

LEGISLATIVE MEASURES FOR LENGTHENING THE TERM
OF DEMOCRATIC PRESIDENCY TO 2345678 CENTURIES
WONDERFUL REPEATING APPARATUS
ten thousand majorities manufactured to order
OMNIPOTENCE OF MONEY-BAGS

❖

MIDNIGHT TO MORNING
LARGE MINORITIES MADE SMALL MAJORITIES
GLORIOUS BALLOT

The compositors were also quick to pick up new jargon. They adopted (and cited in their specimens) such trendy monikers as "Dude" and "Mugwump."

HONOR THE DUDE KING ordered the Cincinnati (1888) specimen. "Dude," according to the Oxford English Dictionary, was a term coined about 1883, meaning exaggerated fastidiousness in dress, speech, and deportment, even to the extent of affecting Englishness. Doubtless the fastidious tramp printer had mixed feelings about this fellow. Benton-Waldo's 1893 book tells us that the Dude is someone to reckon with, particularly when Priapus raises his head: **MAIDENS BEWARE FOR THE Impecunious Dude Stalketh Abroad in Tight Fitting Raiment**

"Mugwump," another recent neologism, was originally a term for boss or great man (occurring in Eliot's Massachusetts Bible), but by the 1880's was applied to undefined or non-party-line politicians, what today we'd call the Perot Factor. Eugene Field, a true poet among printers, celebrated the Mugwump in a verse written in 1885 in the style of Edward Lear:

A year ago and his plumes were red
As the deepest of cardinal hues,
But in the year they've changed, 'tis said,
To the bluest of bilious blues!
In the words of Benton-Waldo:
MUGWUMPS ARE PLENTY
Their Wants are Many and All they Require
now is the Earth $12

Barnhart Brothers & Spindler's 1883 book includes some remarkable poetry in great primer gothic extra condensed:

Chromoplastitudes & Chloroplastidesems
Boltesmanaz and Crossmannerism

234 Exaggerated Ginflingers Flopperdoesing 789
And, in double small pica lightface gothic:
HIFALUTIN CODFISH NABOBS
Such Dyspeptic Grumblers Grabbing Swindlers
75 UNWORTHY OF THOUGHT 24

Turning the pages of these books, you can see how often the choice of text reflects the types themselves, and catch the delight of the compositor when the straightforward idea mutated into witty nonsense—a moment when no shadow fell between the inspiration and the act of composition, when poetry flowed from the unconscious straight to the printed page.

From the *New York Times* (July 21, 1996).

Old and New Fashions in Typography

By Talbot Baines Reed

s artists, the printer and the letter-cutter are responsible to their generation. We live in the midst of a violent reactionary movement against dullness and conventionalism of all kinds. The artist has his three courses. He may sell himself slave to his public, and go wherever he is driven. He may set himself stubbornly to stem the torrent and fall a martyr to his conservatism; or he may strive honestly to control, even while following, the popular movement, and with his clearer artistic knowledge to direct it along lines of moderation and good taste.

My object, however, is not to deal with this matter, important and interesting as it is. The fashions to which I wish to call your attention are those belonging to the Roman character in typography, that is to say, to the type in which books are printed. I propose to take a brief historical survey of the changes through which the character has passed in the hands of various artists, and of those forms of it which at different times have competed for the distinction of realizing the perfect model.

I must remind you at the outset that the perfect model of a letter is altogether imaginary and arbitrary. There is a definite model for the human form. The painter, the sculptor, the architect, have their models in nature. But the man who sets himself to make an alphabet has no copy but that left him by former artists. He knows that the symbol which denotes the sound "I" must be perpendicular, and that which denotes the sound "O" must be round. But what should be the height of the "I" in proportion to its width, how the extremities of the stroke should be finished, on what particular arcs and parallels his "O" is to be erected—on all, that is, which pertains to the *fashion* of his letter—he has no absolute standard. His own eye must furnish the criterion. If the work of those who have gone before satisfies the criterion, he copies it. If it comes short, he corrects it.

What, then, is this criterion? It consists, I venture to think, primarily in the legibility of the character, and secondly in its beauty. It may be urged that the two are inseparable, and I am prepared to admit that, as a rule, the truest beauty in art is that which suggests utility. But it is possible for the two to exist without one another. A boot, for instance, may be beautiful in shape and finish, but unless it fit the wearer it is of little worth. An arrangement of lines and curves and angles may be beautiful in itself, but unless it suggest a form it is valueless. And the more clearly and definitely it suggests that form the more we admire it. Type that is not legible, and in the case of books and newspapers easily legible, however elegant its lines, however delicate its execution, is not good type. So that the artist of letters finds that his first test of an excellent letter is its legibility, and the second—which may easily be a consequence of the first—its grace and beauty.

When we inquire what constitutes legibility in type, we are confronted with numerous interesting speculations and theories. Artists, mathematicians, architects, and doctors have, in turn, tried to lay down rules on the subject. Geoffroy Tory, the Parisian printer, sought to derive the capital letters from the goddess IO, the two letters of whose name furnished the perpendicular and the circle from which every letter was to be constructed to measurements proportion to the form of the human body and visage.[1] Fantastic as the theory was, Tory's rules, in the master hands of his disciple Garamond, produced, as we shall see, one of the finest models of type in Europe.

Albert Durer made a serious effort to bring the alphabet under rule and compass; but his proportions were better suited to the sculptor than the typographer. Nor did the ingenious systems of the Spanish orthographists, Yciar and Lucas, contribute much to the ordering of the Roman letter in print. Moxon in our own country tried to reduce the popular Dutch letter of his day to mathematical rules, with conspicuous failure. The French Academy took the unruly symbols in hand, and produced a standard of form which they tried to fix by Royal decree. Lastly, in our own day, eminent oculists have studied the question with a view to determining to what extent type may be modified so as to spare the sensitive organ to which it appeals. The valuable memoir on this subject recently contributed by the eminent French eye doctor, Dr. Javal, deserves special attention. His argument for a reform of the alphabet is based on admirable theories; but what he really proves, when he comes to give practical form to those theories, is, to my mind, the futility of attempting to subordinate typography to mere laws of hygiene. Dealing with each letter separately, he practically destroys the harmony which at the present time—to lay minds at least—is a main element in the legibility of type, and corrects the alphabet into a form which would try the eyes and temper of readers as much, if not more, than it does in its present unregenerate state. Dr. Javal's theories, however, are full of suggestion as to what are some of the broad tests of legibility in type. What he points out is this:

1. That the eye is, after all, the sovereign judge of form.
2. That, in reading, the eye travels horizontally along a perfectly straight line, lying slightly below the top of the ordinary letters. So that the width of a letter is of more consequence than its height, and the upper half of it than the lower.
3. That, in reading, the eye does not take in letters but words, or groups of words.
4. That type which by its regularity of alignment, its due balance between white and black, its absence of dazzling contrast between thick and thin, by its simplicity and unobtrusiveness, lends itself most readily to this rapid and comprehensive action of the eye, is the most legible.
5. And that such type, as I hope to demonstrate by some illustrations, is on the whole the most beautiful.

Before proceeding to a brief historical survey of the different epochs of the Roman character in typography, I must detain you for a moment with one or two definitions necessary to a clear understanding of our subject.

I show you some letters of an enlarged size, forming the word

Manly

There is a capital letter and four small, or, as they are called, lowercase letters. Of these, two—the *a* and the *n*—occupy what is called the line of the letter. The *l,* like the capital

M, rises above the line. The *y* descends below it. The space between the top of an ascending sort and the bottom of a descending sort marks a full size of the "face" of the letter. Turning now to the capital letter, you will see that it consists of thick and thin lines, also of certain fine cross strokes at the extremities of these lines, called "serifs." The serif may be flat, that is, forming exact right angles with the perpendicular lines, or it may be the base of a triangle produced by the expansion of that line at its extremity; or it may be bracketed or joined to the lines by curves. These serifs are not confined to capitals, but are used to finish the straight strokes of the lowercase also, being attached of course in the same manner as they are to the capitals.

I ask your attention to these points, because, as we shall see, not a few of the fashions of the Roman letter have been imparted by modifications either in the thickness and thinness of the letter strokes, the length or shortness of the ascending and descending sorts, or in the length and method of attachment of the serifs to the main lines of the letter.

Coming now to the earliest appearance of the Roman letter in typography, I need scarcely remind you that, as regards the form of their characters, the first printers were absolutely unoriginal. They adopted, as was most natural, the common writing hand of their country as their model. Their aim, in the first instance, was to simulate as closely as possible the manuscripts of their national scribes. It did not enter into their scheme to improve upon their copy, still less to strike out a line of their own. Their hope of profit consisted in successfully deluding their readers into the belief that the new books were written books, produced by a swifter and cheaper process than the laborious pencraft of the scribe. Consequently they followed their copy painfully and rigidly, reproducing all the scribe's mannerisms, his archaisms, his pedantries, even his blunders. The German inventors of 1450 printed in blackletter, not from choice, but from necessity—to avoid detection in a hazardous enterprise. And in like manner, fifteen years later, the first Italian printers, in the monastery of Subiaco, although Germans,[2] and naturally more familiar with the Gothic form, had no choice but to make their first types in close imitation of the characters used in the Italian manuscripts of the day—that is, of the Roman characters.

They had beautiful models to work by. Caligraphy had just then touched its high-water mark, and some of the productions of the Italian scribes are specimens of rare beauty. If the first types of the Roman press are indifferent and crabbed in point of form, it is not the fault of the copy, but of the craftsmen who, wedded to Gothic ideas, failed to do proper justice to what, to them, was a foreign model. The first page of the *Subiaco Livy* will show you how imperfectly the spirit of the round national character was at first caught, and how difficult the artists found it to discard entirely their German prejudices. Still we may regard with reverence the first appearance in print of a type destined to become the dominant character of typography—the character whose fortunes, good and ill, it is our business to follow.

The manner of the scribes was better caught by Sweynheim and Pannartz when they removed their press to Rome, as also by many of their immediate successors.

For a few years the Roman letter remained in an immature and experimental stage, struggling on the one hand to free itself from the foreign features imported into it by the monks of Subiaco, and on the other to emancipate itself from its thraldom to the scribe. It was not till John and Vindelin de Spira took it in hand, in 1469, that it can be said to have emerged fully from the semi-Gothic into the pure Italian character. Even the

Venetian artists fell short of the standard given by the scribes. They gave roundness and clearness to the form, and improved the capitals, but they left the lowercase somewhat ragged and irregular, and lacking in proportion.

Itaꝗ ab Homeri magni eloquentia coſero me ad uera præcepta

Facsimile of Jenson's Roman Types (1471).

It is easy to account for the difficulty which the early printer would experience in engraving his first alphabet. The manuscript, however neat and regular, would have no two letters exactly alike. In the same page there might be twenty capital *M*s. Of these, one might be broader than the others, and one narrower. Some might be shorter, others taller than the average. Some might be exactly upright, others a little off the straight. In some the middle angle might dip to a level with the foot, in others it might barely descend halfway. The printer would have to select one and only one of these as his model, and having produced it in type, adhere to it throughout. If, for instance, he selected a narrow *M* with a short middle angle, all his *M*s would be of this kind. The free hand of the scribe would be reduced at once to the stiff regularity of the typographer. If the models were well selected, the appearance of the printed page would be neater and more precise than the manuscript—albeit less spirited. If, on the other hand, poor models were taken, or those models badly produced, the defects would recur with painful precision; offending the eye in print far more than in the written page.

Thanks to uneven casting, bad inking, and rough press work, many of the earliest types presented irregularities among themselves that produced in illusory resemblance to writing—an illusion which has more than once puzzled students of early printing not acquainted with the extraordinary variations which the same types, imperfectly cast or badly worked, are capable of exhibiting in print.

Indeed, experimental Roman types like those first used in Paris, or by the mysterious printer of the "R bizarre," or John of Westphalia in Holland, show most of the irregularities of the scribes without their brightness. Nor was it till the printer emancipated himself from the writer, and began to model letters for himself, that the art emerged from its experimental stage, and entered upon its brilliant classical epoch.

The pioneer of the classical Roman letter was Nicolas Jenson, of Venice, a specimen of whose type is shown. The beauty of his performance was so universally acknowledged at the time that he received the unmerited credit of having invented the Roman letter. His merit was rather that he selected the best letters of the best models, and brought them, with an artist's touch, in subordination to the rules and requirements of typography. His letters are round and clear. The white of the interior (the "counter") is sufficient to give an appearance of lightness, but not so open as to give the body marks an appearance of weakness. The alignment is beautifully regular without being painfully trim. The ascending and descending letters are well proportioned to the size of the ordinary letters. The serifs are gracefully triangled, so as to combine strength and elegance. The character has plenty of individuality without forfeiting its simplicity; notice particularly the round sorts of the lowercase, such as the *c, e,* and *o,* and the oblique top serifs of such letters as the *b, l, m, n.*

Jenson's models were destined to achieve European fame. In his own country the celebrated Aldus used them, putting into them—the capital letters especially—even more
freedom and grace than his master. Aldus was able to be bold as well as elegant. His
heavier Roman is often massive and dignified; it lacks, perhaps, some of the grace of his
earlier efforts, but the rugged, well-balanced letter, faithful still to the Italian model, is
eminently readable.

Abroad, there was at first some hesitation adopting the new Italian letter. The most
popular prejudice, especially among the religious orders which most affected printing, ran
in favor of the Gothic; and in Paris, where, as we have seen, an early form of the Roman
was introduced, it became necessary for the first printers to abandon their earliest
attempts in favor of the more familiar type. When, however, they came to adopt the
Jenson fashion, they put it to brilliant service. Geoffroy Tory, as we have seen, took upon
himself to reduce the capital letters of the alphabet to an artistic system, and his pupil,
Claude Garamond, at that time commissioned by the king to furnish types for the royal
printing house, entered with feeling into his master's precepts.

Garamond's Roman became the model type of Europe. It is the work of an able
punch-cutter. The clean cut and finish of each letter was an advance on anything
which typography had yet achieved, while the regular alignment—or, as typefounders
with term it, justification—of the font bears evidence that letter founding as well as
letter engraving had already come of age. The combination of strength and grace in
the form of the letters is admirably balanced. Garamond's fine strokes have a definite
thickness, and his triangled serifs are eminently calculated both to resist wear and
retain their clearness.

The Stephens of Paris, Plantin at Antwerp, John Day in our own country—three of the
greatest printers of that golden age—all owed their inspiration, if not their actual types, to
the French genius. Garamond's pupil, Le Bé, is said to have furnished Plantin with a magnificent Roman which made his press so famous. And in the typography of the equally
famous Elzevir press the influence of the Parisian artist is clearly discernible. The Elzevir
types were cut by Christophel Van Dijck, who preserved to a considerable extent the general form of Garamond's letter, compacted it into the trim and businesslike form which
adapted it so well for the special work of the Dutch typographers. It is a letter for use first
and ornament next. The strokes are strong, the serifs short and well triangled, and the contrast between thick and thin is reduced to a minimum. Van Dijck's round letters are perhaps
open to the criticism that they appear somewhat small beside the square, a defect which is
always apparent unless the punch-cutter cuts these particular sorts a trifle large in gauge. It
may also be urged that, for simple legibility, the ascending strokes of the Elzevir tall letters
are too tall. The Dutch type was presently to take its turn as the prevailing fashion.

Previous to that, however, we must notice that the Parisian fashion had been adopted
in England with conspicuous success by John Day, the only typographer of note in the
sixteenth century of whom we can boast. He certainly had no native model from which
to copy. Pynson's type, the earliest in England, had almost certainly come from a rough
disciple of the Venetian school in France, and after him no one had done anything
towards improving the character. Day, however, was a typefounder as well as a printer, and
his fine Roman letter, especially in its larger sizes, nobly redeems the English typography
of his century from almost unmixed reproach. Day treated the letter as Plantin did, boldly
and vigorously, not wholly without originality.

In one other British press the Garamond type made a brilliant appearance—that of the Huguenot printer, Vautrollier, whose Latin testament of 1754 is perhaps as good as anything produced in his day. Unfortunately for our boasting, both printer and type came from abroad.

Before quitting this epoch, I must call attention to one other fashion which has a claim to be included among the classical models of the Roman letter of Europe. The printers of Basle early achieved a great reputation for their excellent typography. In the matter of the Roman letter, they were to some extent original. Whether with an eye to the picturesque, or in deference to a northern predilecton for Gothic forms, Froben adopted for his fonts a curious mannerism, not altogether unknown before his day, which consists in thickening the round sorts—for instance, the *o*—not at opposite sides of the letter, but obliquely. The font is what typefounders would call cut "on its back," an effect which relieves the general appearance from commonplace, while interfering comparatively little with its regularity or grace, or—in Froben's case at any rate—with its legibility. Froben's fashion was copied, sometimes exaggerated, by other northern printers.

I have now described the four early classical fashions of the Roman letter; beginning with Jenson, taking new shape under Garamond, receiving precision from the Elzevirs, and enjoying a little unconventional liberty at the hands of Froben.

We have now to turn to a less agreeable epoch, an epoch of backsliding and degradation, when the sense of beauty in typography gave way to sordid economy and dull utilitarianism, when printers forgot to be original, and readers suffered patiently whatever print might be imposed on them.

Even France, with a Royal patronage of printing, and an Academy of Sciences to furnish it with models, fell off from the excellent models of Garamond to the more monotonous and less artistic types of Grandjean and Sanlecques. In Holland, the Elzevirs themselves allowed their work sometimes to become slovenly and dull. Germany stolidly relapsed into a gross form of her national blackletter. And England, without an artist to help us, distracted by civil wars, manacled by privileges and monopolies which stamped out competition and ambition—with bad ink, bad paper, bad presses, bad workmen, drifted back year by year, till she could hardly boast a Roman font worth the name. Day's letter, indeed, held its own, and reappeared occasionally; but for the rest, we sold ourselves, typographically, body and soul to the Dutch. The average specimen of English seventeenth century printing is a melancholy study. The Bibles, the broadsides, the classics of the day, compete with one another in grossness. Any merit which a font may have possessed was obscured by bad casting, or a continued use of types after the face was worn down by age, serifs broken, and the counters of the letters clogged with ink.

The Dutch influence became increasingly marked towards the close of the seventeenth century, at a time when, in its own land, it was sinking to decay, and wasting its energies in an attempt to become microscopic. The Oxford University Press was furnished with Dutch matrices. Moxon, a typefounder who attempted to apply mathematics to the Roman character, wrote enthusiastically of the Van Dijck letter; but his own specimens are a dismal commentary on his own incapacity to copy his models. English printers bought their type from Holland direct; and as late as 1713, a leading Scotch printer, James Watson, boasted that he had nothing but Dutch letter in his office.

In this third epoch of the Roman letter—the epoch of the decline and fall—there is no new fashion to record anywhere that is not either commonplace or coarse.

The renaissance of English—and I might almost say of European—typography dates from the establishment of William Caslon as a letter-founder in 1720. Caslon's Roman was modeled on the best form of the Elzevir letter. It is bold, regular, and clear; the fine lines retain a distinct thickness, while the thick are redeemed from the uninteresting clumsiness of the degenerate Dutch school. His serifs, moreover, while somewhat more delicate than those of the Elzevirs, are strong and durable.

A great merit of Caslon's letter was that it was truly justified, that is to say, every letter was cut not only as an individual, but as one of an alphabet, every member of which must harmonize and range, and be closely related to every other. This feature had been lamentably lacking in the period of the decline. Caslon's brilliant success, no doubt, was mainly due to the excellence of his models; but much of it was due to the care with which he justified and cast his fonts. Not only did he study the relation of one letter to another in the same alphabet, but in producing his different sizes he carefully preserved the uniformity of the series, so that a printer desiring to use two sizes of type in his work, might be sure of the same style of letter in both sizes—a luxury he had rarely been able to count on in dealing with the Dutch founders.

Here I should like to correct a common fallacy with regard to the gradation of type sizes. It is assumed that a perfect series of Roman fonts may be produced by taking the letters of one particular size, and reducing or enlarging other sizes from it in exact geo-metrical proportion. This is a mistake. In reducing from a large size to smaller, while the width of the letter follows the strict proportion, the height of the ascending letters undergoes a slightly increased diminution, while the thickness of the fine strokes and ser-ifs is usually reduced at a less ratio than the thick. The width of a letter is far more essen-tial to its legibility that its height; and from Caslon's day it came to be a special merit of the English Romans—as contrasted with those of the French—that the height of the ascenders was somewhat curtailed, without reducing the fullness of the ordinary face of the letter.

The new English fashion gave the *coup de grace* to the Dutch, and naturally provoked many imitators. The most distinguished of these was Baskerville. What he attempted, and succeeded in doing, was to refine the serifs and thin strokes, so as to bring into stronger relief the thick, preserving at the same time roundness and openness of the Caslon model. The effect was showy and attractive, and when printed, as his books were printed, in bright ink on a highly glazed paper, the result was very brilliant. The fault about it, and what caused the fashion to be comparatively short-lived was that it was too brilliant. It dazzled and fatigued the eye, and was too delicate to wear. Artistically, Baskerville's type is one of the most beautiful we have had. But it was ahead of its time, and English printers and readers, after looking at it admiringly for a few years, called meretricious, and went back to Mr. Caslon. Baskerville achieved a *postmortem* success in France, whither his types were transferred, and appropriately used for the great Kehl edition of the brilliant Voltaire. The fashion survived for a long time in France, where, till comparatively recently, it was held to be a merit in an old style type, intended for fine work, to be known as "after the manner of Baskerville."

In England, meantime, up to nearly the close of the last century, the Caslon Roman held its ground. The great artist's apprentices kept closely to their master's models, with a tendency perhaps to lighten the face. His Scotch rivals had already made the character famous in the admirable works of the Foulis press; and others, like Frys, who began in avowed imitation of Baskerville, found it incumbent on them to revert to the older and more popular fashion.

This security was suddenly disturbed by the rising fame of the Italian typographer Bodoni, whose magnificent productions became the envy of European printers. Bodoni's style was a marked departure from the old classical models. He sharpened his fine lines and thickened his heavy lines simultaneously, thus producing a strong and dazzling contrast. Added to this, he lengthened both his ascending and descending sorts, and finished up his straight strokes with a very fine unsupported horizontal flat serif. The regularity and precision of his work are remarkable; the type, exhibited as it was in luxuriously printed specimens and wide margined pages, made a deep impression on England, where for a short time ensued a competition for his services. One or two English books were, as a matter of fact, produced at the Parma press, and by one of those mysterious caprices of fashion, the popular taste veered completely round in favor of the new Roman. The Caslon letter for the time was doomed. At enormous sacrifice the old punches and matrices of the English founders were discarded, and a race ensued for the production of the modern Roman. Perhaps the new style is seen to best advantage in the productions of the Bulmer and Bensley presses.

De gustibus non est disputandum. To many eyes the modern fashion lacks all the graciousness and dignity of the old. Its straight hard serifs, its stiff interiors, its harsh contrasts of thick and thin, more than nullify the passing advantage of exact lining and delicate finish. But apparently no remorse for the abandonment of the old style was felt at the time; the public was well pleased with the new style, and with one accord deserted the old.

A change of equal importance was in progress abroad. France, the land of revolutions, had long since broken away from the traditions of Garamond. As early as 1693, a commission of experts was appointed by the French Academy to inquire into and draw up rules for the best form of the Roman character, for the use of the Royal Printing-office. It is much to be regretted that M. Jaugeon's report and drawings—the result of this interesting inquiry—only exist in manuscript. His letters were designed on a highly elaborate geometric system in a square subdivided into 2,304 small squares. It is doubtful whether they were an improvement on the letters already in use. The outcome of the inquiry, however, was the reformed "King's Roman," cut by Grandjean, and continued by Alexandre. It is noteworthy that Grandjean, although consulted by the commissioners, declined to regulate his alphabet entirely by the mathematical rules laid down for him. He referred his models to the supreme tribunal of the eye, and probably produced a far more satisfactory letter than had he worked slavishly within the confines of his 2,304 minute squares. His chief modification of Garamond's type was the substitution of a flat for a triangular serif, the straightening of the hitherto oblique top serif, a more marked contrast between thick and thin, and the addition of the unseemly double serifs to the ascenders, and the cross mark on the *l*—badges of the Royal proprietorship of the type.

Luce, who came half a century later, ruthlessly elongated the alphabet, shortened and fined down the flat serifs to a reprehensible extent, restored the oblique serif of Garamond (but too late to be of much use) and gave an air of general cramp to what was before generous and distinguished. Luce, in some of his fonts, carried this narrowing process still further, increasing the height as he contracted the width, and produced a type, highly praised by Fournier and other *savants* of the day, which was styled *poétique.*

Firmin Didot, who followed, succeeded in reshaping the Roman into something like its old proportions; but in doing so he extinguished the last spark of the antique, and produced the trim, sleek, gentlemanly, somewhat dazzling fashion, which has since, I venture to think in degenerate forms, continued to rule in French typography. To complete the evolution from Garamond to the modern French, we have the alphabet of M. Marcellin le Grand, narrow and stiff, and with due respect to foreign taste, unpleasing to English eyes.

Here, then, with Didot, we close the epoch of the renaissance. It began with Caslon; Baskerville followed, but did not supplant the old master; what Baskerville failed to do Bodoni achieved; and he and Didot between them killed the old-style, and left us our modern Roman.

The epoch which ensued, occupying the first half of the present century, was, so far as the Roman character is concerned, an epoch of respectable commonplace. But unlike epochs which preceded it, it ended better than it began. The new Roman was barely established as the prevailing fashion, when a vulgar taste for fatter faces asserted itself. The demand was promptly responded to by the founders of the day, Robert Thorne leading the way.

These fashions—passing fashions, happily—represented a reactionary movement against the tendency to lighten and refine the Bodoni Roman to forms of excessive fineness. The rise of the newspaper press, and the introduction of steam machinery, made it necessary to cast types in much harder metal than hithertofore, so as to defy the ordeal of the new process. In this metal it was discovered that the serifs and fine lines were capable of the most delicate treatment, and the founders of the day entered on a competition for the sharpest and finest of effects. It also came to be a consideration with printers how much could be "got in" in the line, and the compositors' tariff began to exercise considerable influence on the style of the Roman letter. The tendency developed itself, particularly among the Scotch founders, to condense the letter after the French style, and the Scotch letter in its day achieved considerable favor. It was neat, and clear, and delicate, and "got in" considerably more than the ordinary style. The English founders, however, resisted the innovation, and adhered to the rounder forms as more readable and better calculated to retain their clearness. Clearness was not, however, the main ambition of the punch-cutters. The applause bestowed upon the productions of some of the famous London printers about 1820, notably those of the Bulmer press, fired their emulation to dazzle the public eye. They prided themselves on the exquisite fineness of their hair lines, the graceful sweep of their curves, the *crescendos* and *diminuendos* of their round letters. But all the while they were drifting away from the canons of easy legibility. It may be a pleasant sensation to some people to be dazzled, but the majority of readers prefer more homely and restful effects. The old artists of the classical school were never egoists. Egotism has been and remains responsible for many of the defects of modern typography.

We come, finally, to our last epoch—the present. It was ushered in, about 1845, by the revival, under the auspices of Mr. Whittingham, of the Caslon old face. The old master, thought to be dead and buried, sprang again to life as potent as ever. I need scarcely remind you of the result of this revival both at home and abroad. Side-by-side with the new and improving Romans of the letterfounders appeared fonts cut after the antique, with all the superior finish of modern workmanship. Founders did not venture in their reproductions to copy all the strong lines of the old models, but embellished their "mediævals" with the delicate tapers and hair lines of the modern school. The typography of the last half century owes a great deal to this opportune return to the past; and the continued favor of the old styles, I venture to think, is a hopeful sign for the future.

For newspapers, and for a great deal of bookwork, the mediæval is no doubt unavailable. Indeed, under present conditions, the Roman must, of necessity, form the staple character of typography; and in its present serviceable forms is likely to hold the field for a good while yet. It is the work-a-day letter. The old-style is the *lettre-de-luxe.*

In conclusion, I venture, as a humble member of my ancient art and craft, to remind you that the typefounder does not profess to be the educator of the printer and his readers, but their servant to command. It is for the reading public, in large measure, to determine what shall be the future of typography. If it be content to read hardly where it might read easily, if its taste runs towards vulgar ornaments or meretricious display, if it too easily tolerate bad type, or even good type badly printed, it will not fail to get what it wants. If, on the other hand, it demand simplicity, and grace, and legibility, I doubt not it will obtain them. *Simplex munditiis* is a motto for Roman letters as well as for Roman maidens.

I take it as a hopeful sign that the aesthetics of typography are at the present time being studied by men of artistic taste and authority. The result cannot fail to be of benefit. For printing, in all its career, has followed close in the wake of its sister arts. When they have flourished, we have had our most beautiful books; when they have declined, printing has gone down below them. It is a bad day in the history of any art when it becomes a mere trade, and the "Art which preserves all other arts" should by all means be saved from that calamity.

15

---

[1] Edward F. Strange in "Alphabets" says Tory's book is "at once the most useless, most curious work on lettering in existence."

[2] Sweynheim and Pannartz.

From *Ars Typographica* 1, no. 3 (Winter 1920).

Art in Type Design

By Frederic W. Goudy

he increasing interest in lettering and printing types and the greater appreciation of fine printing on the part of readers has suggested it might also be interesting if an experienced designer of types should set down somewhat of the mental processes that lead to the production of a new typeface.

The revival of printing which began in the 1890s has had a very marked effect on both commercial and book printing of today, bringing to light specially designed types for private use, which in turn have served as models or suggestions for other types for general use.

The question as to the sources of future types as yet undrawn demands an answer, whether it is better to reproduce or adapt for present-day printing the historic types of the older masters of type cutting & typography—those types that have withstood both use and abuse of years—or to attempt the creation of newer forms more suited to the changed conditions of today.

The course first suggested does not appeal to the writer as the right road to real progress. Our admiration for the work of masters should not lead to the absolute idolatry which would prevent new essays in the field of type design. On the other hand the fine old types should suggest a continued train of perceptions and ideas which the designer may employ that will aid him to create new expressions of beauty and utility, at once advancing growth and development by keeping his work in healthful motion, lifting it up and driving it on and preventing unwholesome stagnation. The work of the older masters is now a noble heritage of every reader; to tamper with the monumental type-forms of those early printer-craftsmen can make them only commonplace & ordinary. Under their hands the forms evolved naturally, the emanations of the spirit in which they worked; to reproduce them today is merely to give the shell, as it were, of a body forsaken by the soul of life.

When tradition is renewed and advanced into our own times personal expression is made possible. The old forms were simple; the meaningless lines or excrescences upon which so many modern designers, without ability to reach the higher beauties, rely, in their endeavor to conceal their lack of genius or taste, were never present in the types of the golden age of typography.

The insatiable demand for novelty in printing is giving us, just now, a senseless and ridiculous riot of "beautiful atrocities." Former products of ignorance and eccentricity are revived and new designs even more bizarre are contributed to present day printing. The efforts of the few (who retain their sanity) to prevent printing reverting to the innocuousness of the last century are rendered difficult and of little avail by the inundation of freak types.

There is no harm in "novelty," indeed, novelty keeps things fresh and alive; but the novelty which harks back to the extraordinary ugliness of earlier gross and bizarre forms will soon bore and disgust the thinking spectator. Worse yet, is the imitation of novelty quite plainly in evidence among advertisers seeking striking effects. So many of the "new" offerings are merely old things "newly" advertised.

Morris said, "You may be sure that any decoration is futile and has fallen into at least the first stage of degradation when it does not remind you of something beyond itself, of something of which it is but a visible symbol." The same thing is true of types. One shudders at the result of an attempt to apply this formula to a number of recent type offerings.

New type-forms must, of course, conform to the spirit and ideals of the present, but it does not follow that freaks or caprices of fickle fashion are controlling factors. Contemporary considerations are governed by environment and conditions of life and not by the vagaries of fashion. We may still carry on the fine traditions of the past while respecting the prejudices of the present and new types based on classic models may still express artistic individuality. They must not, however, be too personal. When our new types present unassuming simplicity; freedom from eccentricity, a manly earnestness and strength; when too, they express careful thought in every detail, legibility, beauty, and simple grandeur, they may indeed prove monumental.

When designers begin to think consciously of technical limitations and attempt to comply more completely with mechanical conditions, their designs tend to draw away from artistic standards in the pursuit of the utilitarianism gradually arrived at. To meet the demands of utility and preserve an aesthetic standard is a hard problem.

In 1920, when the Monotype Company asked the writer of these lines to serve as its Art Director and design new faces for use on the Monotype machine he was faced with this same problem. Could he, without sacrifice of the ideas for which he stood, design within the mechanical limitations of the machine?

For years there has been a tendency on the part of writers on typography to maintain that to accommodate types to the limitations of composing machines, was necessarily to debase them, to deform them. Did those writers say truly or did they jump at conclusions not warranted by facts? And with regard to new designs—could they be made for use on the Monotype and still retain the individuality of the designer?

The writer never had been identified with the fantastic or trivial in his work as a designer; could he carry on those principles which he believed sound, or must artistic considerations give way to commercial necessities? He did not believe so. Of course, all existing types could not necessarily be put on the machine without modifications, since they were of varied design not always good, but the machine did not for that reason preclude the presentation of new faces that would require no deformation or degradation from good tradition in their design and individual handling. After seven years of close association with the Monotype organization he finds he can truthfully say that no sacrifice of his ideals has at any time been necessary. The limitations imposed, like those of poetic meter, add to the beauty and interest of all good work produced within them as long as those limitations are not made an excuse for failure to employ the independent good taste and intelligence that good work requires.

In 1923, Alfred Pollard, Keeper of Printed Books, King's Library, British Museum, in a review in the *Library,* a magazine for bibliographers and bibliophiles, said of an issue of

"Monotype" set entirely in Monotype Garamont type that "the result is to prove once again that the most beautiful results can be obtained from modern labor saving devices, when these are devised and applied with fine craftsmanship. . . . The types, roman and italic, are beautiful in themselves." "Praise from Sir Hubert is praise indeed." In short, the designer of types should not think of letter shapes as mere abstract arrangements of line and form; instead, they should bring to him some reminder of their origin, of the beauty and freshness of the necessity that created them, some message of the relation of art to practical life. The drawings must be clear, elegant, and strong, nothing loose or vague, no finesse of design, all quiet, inevitable & great-minded. Art in type design is then, the spirit the designer puts into the body of his work, not merely the shape his work takes; art is the evidence of his seriousness, the intrinsically right-principle in the making of things—it harmonizes man's work with nature.

The type designer's work will not be so much a mere drawing of letters, but rather something growing naturally into being, well defined and vividly alive.

From *A Bibliography of the Village Press* by Melbert B. Cary, Jr. (New York: The Press of the Woolly Whale, 1938).

The Modern Type Family

By Charles Brodie

If prizes were offered for the largest family in the world, first award would have to go to Mr. and Mrs. Modern Type. Certainly no other family album anywhere can boast of some eleven hundred pages as does the American Type Founders specimen book. However, as would be natural in so large a collection of offsprings, there is a wide variance of quality and ability among these type children. Some of them have made themselves indispensable in their scheme of things, while many of them might just as well never have been born. As a matter of fact, we in the advertising game are, or should be, concerned with but very few of that vast brood.

Probably the daddy of them all, and the most versatile, is Caslon Old Style—dear old Caslon O. S.—who suffered a serious relapse a few years ago, but who today is hale and hearty and very much on the firing line. A real, true friend, he has saved our skins on many occasions, rising admirably to meet an emergency. Firm, stanch, loyal, with becoming grace and dignity, bespeaking an efficiency second to none. Of Caslon we may say, "He always does his job and does it well."

Second place in our affections should go to Bookman. Not as dignified or regal as his brother Caslon, but every bit as efficient in his task. Just a plain, blunt fellow with a round, full face, honest and convincing, who goes about his work in a businesslike manner without frills or furor. The advertising world is better for his presence.

Then we have Bodoni—a cold, reserved, austere member of the family who always wears his frock coat and high silk topper. Educated abroad—in Italy to be exact—snobbish and a bit intolerant, yet withal, not a bad chap when you know how to handle him. He is the kind of a fellow you hesitate to call on, but when you do you may be assured that he will lend himself as wholeheartedly as his cold nature will allow. Truly, the blue-blooded aristocrat of the family.

Garamond Old Style, a rather recent acquisition to the Modern Type family, belongs to the female side of the house. Deliciously feminine and delightfully graceful—really a great credit to the family. Artfully elusive and dainty enough in her appeal to warm the cockles of any advertising man's heart. At the present time she is very popular, and deservedly so.

Goudy Old Style is also one of the ladies, and while Miss Garamond has stolen some of her popularity, she is still very much in demand. A little severer in form, perhaps, but very beautiful, combining feminine grace and dignity in a degree that makes her a great favorite with those a bit more conservative.

In Goudy Bold and Garamond Bold we have two perfect gentlemen, well bred and dignified. Goudy Bold is a bit the stronger of the two, but both are clean cut, strong in character and efficient. Their voices are deep and resonant, and when they speak they command undivided attention and respect. Their positions as two of the leading lights in the Modern Type family have been well earned and are a just reward.

There is another youngster in this big family who deserves special mention, and that is Cooper Black. Just a new arrival, but a great, big, husky fellow who makes a lot of noise and promises to be the ballyhoo man of the lot. Rugged and good natured, with a powerful voice, he has already made a place for himself which he is likely to hold for many a day without fear of competition.

We can not leave this interesting family without a word in passing about a much criticized but faithful old friend—Cheltenham Bold. A bit of an ugly duckling today perhaps, but he had a big job and he did it well. Honest, strong, and efficient, there is still many a task that he can handle, and in all probability will make himself heard again before his demise.

These are by no means all the important offsprings of this illustrious and huge family, but we do think they are the ones of whom Mr. and Mrs. Modern Type can be proudest. There is, in addition, Miss Kennerley, who has beautiful features and is molded along much the same lines as Sister Goudy, for whom she is often mistaken by those who do not know them well. Mr. Scotch Roman, too, is another interesting and good looking specimen. In the past few years he has lost a great deal of his former popularity, but he is still to be seen around town and eventually will no doubt regain much of his lost prestige.

One or two other members of the family like Century and Cloister, who are most efficient and dependable, might also be mentioned, but the hundreds of other freaks and misfits of the type world should have been thrown to the waves while the bugler played taps over their watery graves.

From the *Inland Printer* 77, no. 5 (August 1926).

An Existential Guide to Type

By Karrie Jacobs

he advertisement for Hyundai is set in what looks to be a Garamond—let's call it Garamond Bold Sanforized. And the letters in the headline, "Most cars in our price range have around 50,000 miles on them." are awfully cozy. They are more intimate with one another than decency and the conventions of typesetting allow. Focus for a moment on the word "range." The *n* with its thick, hard serif is kicking the *g* in the groin. And the *a* is a two-timer; on one side it nuzzles the *r*'s teardrop-shaped finial with its own upper stroke, and on the other side the *a* plays footsy with an *n,* hooked lower finial rubbing against ample serif.

The tightness of the set on this ad is obvious—it's right there in black and white—but before Type 1987 I never would have noticed. At Type 1987, a conference held in New York's Grand Hyatt Hotel last October, a geographically diverse mix of typographers, typesetters, typeface designers, art directors, and representatives of typesetting-equipment manufacturers spoke out on every conceivable subject related to the use of mechanically reproduced letterforms.

The fashion for tightness was given particular attention, denounced regularly and with great vigor as an evil, a detriment to the integrity of letterforms, an enemy of legibility (the clarity of the individual letters) and readability (how easily the characters work in concert). Rules were being broken, those that dictate the relationship between the proportions of a given letter and the whiteness around it, an equilibrium between the space within a letter and the space without.

Advertising agencies were to blame, cried distraught type aficionados. When you send copy to your typesetter it comes back too tight because typesetters have been conditioned by the agencies. Tightness of set was denounced in the sort of jeremiads others might reserve for skyscrapers that cast long shadows or incinerators that emit PCBs.

Now I can see the tightness because I know it's there. Everywhere. But I'm not personally incensed. It's just not my cause. I mean, Madison Avenue routinely bowdlerizes all aspects of our culture. There's no reason to expect that the niceties of letterspacing would be exempt. I only bring up the tightness issue because it's a perfect example of a heightened awareness (in this case mine) springing type from its quiet, contextual role.

The great paradox of type is that it is at once omnipresent and diaphanous. Type, camouflaged by the meaning of the words it forms, is invisible. The text and the type—it's a perceptual conundrum, like the one about the forest and the trees.

I'm not professing indifference to the anatomy of letterforms or the characteristics that distinguish one typeface from another. When I concentrate on examining letters rather than on reading them, I can see the insouciant twist of a Palatino *y*'s descender, the open, hungry maw of a lowercase Souvenir *e,* and the nicely tapered stems of a Bembo *m.* But letters, regardless of the grace of their individual forms, are designed, *rigorously* designed, to work collectively as words, and the abstract shapes of words, unless we are unable to read, are superseded by their definitions. If readers generally don't pick up on the differences between one typeface and another, it's because the face itself is transparent. Only the message is obvious.

Certain things work best when we are unaware of them. For example, it's only in the most extreme and unpleasant circumstances that we must pay heed to the beams that support the floors on which we walk or the mechanics of our city's water-supply system. Letters on the printed page are like that. If the design of a typeface, a text face, demands attention, there's a problem.

Type 1987 was sponsored by the Type Directors Club of New York and starred the world's best known living alphabet makers, including Herman Zapf, designer of Optima, Palatino, and Zapf Book; Adrian Frutiger, designer of Univers, Meridien, and Frutiger; Ed Benguiat, designer of ITC Souvenir, ITC Panache, and ITC Benguiat; and Matthew Carter, designer of Bell Centennial, ITC Galliard, and Bitstream Charter. Type users and fans of every variety participated as panelists, speakers, or simply as members of a very vocal and articulate audience.

In the garish, mirrored, and pseudocrystal-festooned carnival-of-the-nouveau-riche milieu of Donald Trump's Hyatt, a gathering of those obsessed with the subtlest of details was staged. It was a conference about the nuances of line—the thicks and the thins, the angles and the curves, the edges hard and soft, the white areas corralled by ink. Here was a long weekend dedicated to the quantum mechanics of the printed word, the molecular structure of the language, and it had the potential to be as dry a dry night of barhopping in Salt Lake City.

But it wasn't.

Type 1987 transcended its specialized subject matter because the issues that were raised time and time again, often vehemently, were and are central to every aspect of every kind of design. Technology. The demands of the marketplace. The relentless urge to modernize. The siren song of trendiness. All of these things impact the shape and style of our ABCs as much as they impact architecture or the way we equip our kitchens.

Every stage of a typeface's life cycle was discussed, from the inception, the first inkling a designer has that there is something to be done with the alphabet that hasn't yet been done, to the conversion of a letterer's drawings into a state-of-the-art type font, to the published uses of a face as advertising, signage, or text.

How letterforms are treated between the time they are drawn (with pen and ink or on a computer screen) and the time they appear on the printed page was a subject brought up many times during the conference. Control was the issue. Do type designers have any control over how their output gets used, should they have control, and do they care? Some designers were sanguine, others fatalistic; at least one was, in one instance, nauseated.

During a panel discussion called "My God, What Do They Want?" about the relationship between type designers and type users, several creators of typefaces expressed resignation. Once the ink is dry on their drawings and the face is marketed, it's as much under their control as a child who has grown up and gone away to college.

"When I finish a face, I forget it," declared Adrian Frutiger. "I only see how good or how bad it gets used."

"Typography is not a police state," reasoned Matthew Carter. "No way can we control it. I'm tickled to see my faces used at all. My bête noir is people who draw curlicues on my script faces."

More troubled by the ways his type (or what passes for his type) gets used, Herman Zapf spoke about encountering a pirated version of his face, Palatino on a brochure for the hotel where the conference was held: "You need no scrambled eggs, no food for the rest of the day," he said. "Your stomach is so upset. It's a poor use of letterforms. Somebody copied my letterforms. If they did a good job it might be OK. The proportions are clumsy, there are additional characters you've never done that don't fit into the concept. This version has nothing to do with my original design."

All of the things that impact the designs of letterforms were debated. Historic faces resurrected and revamped for contemporary usage raised hackles, as did metal types "cleaned up" when digitized for use in computerized typesetting equipment. Adjustments, it seemed, were endemic . . . and controversial.

Early in the conference, at a panel discussion called "A Critical Look at New Typeface Design," Paul Hayden Duensing, the type critic for *Fine Print* magazine, spoke out against the practice of digitizing historic faces: "Digitizing Janson is like playing Bach on synthesizer," Duensing decreed, referring to the face that was first cut in seventeenth-century Leipzig.

"Bastardizing our heritage," is how Sandra Kirshenbaum, editor of *Fine Print* and also on the panel, described the process.

And there was a somewhat stagy but by and large earnest debate between conference organizer Roger Black, the former *Newsweek* art director who is currently designing a travel magazine for the high-concept clothiers Banana Republic, and designer Paula Scher, a New York partner in the firm Koppel and Scher who is well known for her playful use of historic influences and her full-throttle delivery of strong opinions. The subject was the International Typeface Corporation (ITC), a company organized in the early 1970s by design-community pillars like Aaron Burns and Herb Lubalin to license contemporary typefaces, combat piracy, and distribute royalties to those who deserved them. "Resolved: That ITC Is the Best Thing that Ever Happened to Modern Typography" was the point to be argued. Black was pro. Scher was con.

Black, boosterish as a vice-principal or a camp counselor, painted a picture of the late 1960s as a sad time in the world of type: "Foundries were dying. One by one all of the sources of typography for the last century were gone. We found our great old friends were not available to us. What we were getting were copies of old faces forced into new sizes, new raster patterns."

He lauded ITC's type library, the almost universal availability of ITC faces, their publication of the quarterly magazine *U&LC,* and even their interpretations of historic faces: "ITC's Garamond is a peculiarly contemporary Garamond," Black opined. "It's not a bookish Garamond."

As the focus of her end of the debate, Paula Scher, not coincidentally, chose Garamond, a face first cut in the sixteenth-century Parisian workshop of Claude Garamond but recut and sharpened sixty years after Garamond's death by Jean Jannon. Garamond in its many variations is one of the most used faces today and one of ITC's top three sellers.

"I can't disagree with 90 percent of what Roger says," prefaced Scher. "But redesigning old faces makes them [ITC] open to criticism." She showed two slides, one of ITC Garamond and the other of a Garamond out of a Linotype book. Two of Garamond's hallmarks, the peculiarly high waist of the lowercase *e* and the dainty loop of the lowercase *a,* had been normalized a bit, rounded out slightly, by ITC for their Garamond. "The problem with the new form is it's called Garamond and it's not Garamond," argued Scher.

"We know they know better," she continued. "I'd like them to take it back, *admit* it, write about it. . . . ITC Garamond is the most popular face in the U.S. I used to hate it, but I've seen it so much I don't even know if I hate it anymore."

The loop of a small *a,* the counter of an *e.* They are tiny things, the smallest of small potatoes. But the whisper of difference between the *a* of one Garamond and the *a* of another, the precise angle of a serif, the ligature that allows two *f*s to stand next to each other in a word—these tiny factors are what a typeface is about. Minute details give each letter its distinctive form, and the forms of individual letters give a printed page its color, the texture of lights and darks, the pattern of alternating thickness and thinness that varies from typeface to typeface. As nitpicky as Scher may have sounded, she wasn't being a crank. She was getting to the heart of the subject.

So much of the talk at Type 1987 concerned the permutations of letterforms, the bending of letters, the unconventional settings, and the alterations made in traditional typefaces for myriad reasons that I began to question what I believed to be true about type. I started to get ontological. I asked myself, "What exactly is a typeface?"

I know that the name given to a face—Futura, for instance—is really the family name, and the family encompasses a variety of faces: Futura Light, Futura Light Italic, Futura Medium, Futura Heavy, Futura Extra Black, Futura Heavy Catalogue, Futura Extra Black Condensed—all of these weights and styles are typefaces in the Futura family. But that's not what I mean.

A typeface is distinguished by the tiniest of elements, but if those elements are changed, even a little, for whatever reason—the cleaning of a few crotchets from an old face to make it suitable for reintroduction as a contemporary face, the easing of certain angles to make a face more sympathetic to the popular 300 dot-per-inch resolution laser printer, the addition of a couple of lines to make a face into a trademark for a particular brand's advertising—is it still the same typeface? Is it still a member of the family? Should it be? Given that all the aforementioned practices are commonplace and the very elements that make a typeface identifiable can be altered, then what exactly is a typeface?

Physically, artistically, practically, are typefaces what they used to be or are they something less concrete? Or have typefaces always been mutable? Is it possible that because typefaces are disseminated more widely now than ever before and because our methods of storing information are much more sophisticated now than ever before, type is actually *less* in flux today than it was in the days when letters were cast in solid, invincible metal?

A gulf, made wide by time and technological momentum, has opened between the day when type was a chunk of metal you could hold in your hand or toss like a stone and today, when type is as insubstantive as a ghost. Letterforms are ethereal, invisible, a mathematical arrangement of digital bits. *Bits.* For each letter the computer says yes or no, or more accurately black or white, thousands of times.

And in a way the digitization of type is perfectly logical. After all, what is a letter on the printed page but a binary equation of black and white?

What emerged at Type 1987 was a confrontation between the purists and the technoids: designers, small-press operators, and miscellaneous type fundamentalists insisted that letterforms have degenerated since the extinction of hot type. They argued that the only true typefaces were on sturdy chunks of lead alloy placed squarely, shoulder to shoulder, on a galley, allowing no real flexibility in spacing and offering no opportunity for setters and renegade art directors to go astray. No reshaping or reproportioning the letters. No squeezing, no bending, no overzealous kerning, no fooling around.

The computer enthusiasts, on the other hand, exuded optimism and boasted of a world full to overflowing with more and *better* faces. They conceded that letters may once have been blurred, stretched, and misshapen by flaws in early photo-lettering and computer typesetting systems (systems that, for example, reduced and enlarged type photographically to a great range of sizes from one or two size of fonts, wreaking havoc with proportion) and that computers allowed typographers a freedom that simply didn't exist in the days of metal type: the freedom to overstep the bounds of taste. They argued that any messes made by slightly sophisticated technology would be mopped up in the future by very sophisticated technology.

So what is type? The question turns out to be more appropriate and the answer less obvious than it would appear.

For instance, what exactly is it that the International Typeface Corporation supplies to its customers? Well, they give permission to companies that manufacture typesetting equipment—Linotype, Compugraphic, Berthold, etc.—to offer ITC typefaces like ITC Bookman, ITC Avant Garde Gothic, or ITC Galliard to their customers, the type shops, for use on their machines. Type shops purchase the font for a given face and pay the typesetting-machine company the asking price plus a $30 royalty, which goes to ITC. (On photocomposition machines the font was a filmstrip with all the letters, numbers, and symbols for a given size of typeface on it, and now, for digital machines, the font is in the form of a floppy disk encoded with the numerical information needed to produce letterforms.) What do those equipment manufacturers actually, physically receive from ITC when they license a face? Sometimes absolutely nothing.

ITC buys original typefaces from designers or commissions adaptations of historical faces. They have a review committee chaired by ITC's executive vice-president, Allan Haley. Other members of the review board include one of ITC's founders, Aaron Burns; Colin Brignal, the type director for ITC's parent corporation, Esselte Letraset, in London; Cynthia Hollandsworth, who heads a design studio that develops typefaces; and Erik Spiekermann, a German type and graphic designer known for, among other things, writing *Rhyme & Reason: A Typographical Novel*.

The board evaluates unsolicited submissions and discusses what sorts of typefaces ITC should commission. "A large degree of our faces in the past were sort of like choosing strawberries. We get them in and we say, that's a good one, that's a bad one, that's a good one," notes Haley in an interview at ITC's New York headquarters.

The board has begun to take what Haley describes as a "more pro-active" role, discussing what sorts of typefaces would fill needs in the marketplace or in ITC's library. Haley offers an example: "With all of these things, with laser printers and such, so many people are now sending letters that are set in type. You get a letter that's in Palatino or you get a letter that's in Souvenir. At first we thought that was kind of neat. After looking at it you realize there are some good places for laser printers, but to put type in letters maybe isn't the best thing to do. They tend to look like brochures or catalogs rather than letters. So we're talking with a number of designers to create a typeface that is something better than a typewriter face and yet doesn't look like a full typographic face." ITC, like other developers of typefaces, is trying to capture the new market, the desktop publishing market, the business people for whom buying a typeface for their office equipment is a new concept. Haley sees this better-than-typewriter face as part of an educational process, an initiation into type. "It's sort of a step for someone up to using full typography."

Another face the ITC board might commission is a sans serif that doesn't "lack humanity." They're talking about getting a designer to overhaul Edward Johnston's London Underground type or Eric Gill's Gill Sans, two similar and quite famous faces dating from 1916 and 1928 respectively.

When evaluating a design the board first reacts to a face's beauty. Then comes a debate about tricky distinctions: Their goal is to find a typeface that is "sufficiently different from other typefaces that an unsophisticated user would readily distinguish it from other designs. Yet, another requirement is that the design not be so unique that its usability is impaired. There's a fine line between unique and overpowering, a line to be approached but not crossed."

Once the board has decided that the face in question is beautiful and different enough to be told apart from existing faces but not dramatically so, they analyze a face's value as a text face—the way the letters sit together on the page, its readability and legibility. A designer must submit the word "hamburgerfonts" in capital and lowercase letters in four weights of roman and italic letters. After a successful "hamburgerfonts" test, the designer is paid to draw a *complete* alphabet of roman and of italic letters, numerals, punctuation marks, and accents, which ITC uses to create text samples.

If a face survives the successive levels of scrutiny, it may become one of the four type families that ITC releases each year. The face's designer then draws the two most extreme weights in both roman and italic, the lightest and the boldest. ITC sends those weights off to URW, the German maker and operator of type-digitizing equipment. URW creates from the weights provided as many intermediary weights as are desired. The computer interpolates, thickening the letters' strokes and adjusting the proportions as the typeface family grows. Between the designer's "Light" and "Heavy," the computer draws a Book weight, a Medium, a Demi, perhaps an Extra-Bold. Hundreds of characters now exist that the type designer didn't draw.

The interpolation of type weights seems like a miracle to some type designers and a scam to others. Ed Benguiat is a prolific New York designer whose lines have a peculiarly idiosyncratic way of swelling and bending, whose looped letters are often unusually voluptuous. He is appalled by the idea of drawing on a computer ("because a computer doesn't have a heart") but is warming ever so slightly to the idea of having a high-powered electronic draftsman in Germany draw his medium and demi-bold weights. "I don't like it, but they do it. . . . And I watch them."

Benguiat notes, "I used to spend a year drawing a typeface. Now, with URW doing it, I can spend six months and they can draw the ones in between."

So what does ITC supply to those typesetting-equipment firms that license their typefaces? "What they used to get was black stuff on white paper," answers Haley. "Prints that allowed the Linotypes of the world to make a font."

That's clear-cut and easy to picture. ITC gives its licensees big black-and-white glossies of all the characters. Except that's not necessarily what they do anymore. "So what they buy is a trade name," Haley adds. "A trademark name and a proven brand-name product is really what they're buying."

But the product. What then is the product? Does it have a corporeal form or is it just a nonsubstantive something that gets passed from ITC to "the Linotypes of the world" to the multitudes of type shops to the consumers of type? Is type a virus, spreading far and wide without a medium, without weight?

Well, yes, in a way it is.

Says Haley, "Physically they get nothing that they can put their hands on. If they do their own digitizing we can supply them with analog artwork, prints of the letters. Companies like Xerox, IBM to some degree, do their own digitizing, so we would supply them with the product they need to create a font.

"With Adobe, which makes the fonts for the Apple Laser Writer, there is no physical thing which passes between us and Adobe. They license faces from us. They have a contractual agreement with us. They say, we want to put ITC Souvenir on this printer, what is the royalty? We negotiate the royalty and that's all. They buy digital data from Bitstream or Linotype or URW."

Then it is like a virus? "With new designs it almost is," admits Haley.

The historical continuum of type from raised letters on metal blocks to the winking of a microchip is embodied by the Cambridge, Massachusetts, headquarters of Bitstream, a company that is described by its principals as a digital-typefoundry.

Bitstream's location seems to be a consciously symbolic choice. Yes, it's in the part of Cambridge adjacent to the Massachusetts Institute of Technology, one of many high-technology firms nourished by the proximity of so much scientific brilliance. But it's housed in a corner of an old brick building that once was the home of the Athenaeum House printers, and a statue of Athena, patinated and wise, stands on the roof surveying the Charles River. Matthew Carter, whose own career as a type designer spans the transitional period from the wane of metal through photocomposition and into digital, and who is the son of a type historian Harry Carter, was one of the company's founders and is its vice-president of design. He designs his own faces and oversees all the work that has to do with the typefaces themselves. And Carter, perhaps more than anyone else, seems to straddle the two sensibilities present in the type trade; he is a type buff who has also made a point of appreciating and understanding the metamorphoses. In the lobby of the Athenaeum House, in what is now an arcade of sorts, Carter points out where the inky printing presses once labored, where the doors once opened to allow the delivery of hunking rolls of paper.

At Bitstream you don't see much paper or ink. And the type they design is geared toward the compact printers of desktop systems rather than the big presses of traditional publishing.

I imagine that real typefoundries—the places where punch-cutters hewed letters from steel, where matrices were formed from copper, where type itself was made of lead— were loud, hot, smelly, noisy places. Bitstream, the digital foundry, is characterized by a palpable hush, a steady white noise, and quiet lighting. The main work area is a large, high-ceilinged room full of men and women working intently in the glow of oversize terminals typical of Computer Aided Design (CAD) systems. It feels as if the electronic impulses used to code alphabets were also in the air, enriching and charging the atmosphere like domesticated lightning.

What they actually do at Bitstream is connect-the-dots. These new-age type designers spend their time producing legible forms by inputting key points of each letter's exterior and letting the computer program they work with fill in the interior. They digitize.

Bitstream was founded in 1981 to make type for the growing field of electronic word-processing systems, systems that both upgraded the kind of type used in office situations and provided an alternative to hiring a typesetter when something fancier than IBM Selectric type was needed.

"The reason we started the company is that companies coming into this business, laser-printer manufacturers or personal computer manufacturers or whatever, need type," explains Carter. "And for competitive reasons that aren't hard to imagine, the older established typesetter manufacturers were very reluctant to license type to what they saw as competitors."

Bitstream was uniquely positioned as the only major manufacturer of type that wasn't in the business of manufacturing typesetting equipment. Bitstream makes typesetting software but not hardware. They create bitmaps.

A bitmap is a structured collection of dots, a guide to exactly where each dot goes when a printer prints a letter. Each letter has its own bitmap. Each letter in each point size has its own bitmap because larger characters require more dots than smaller characters. This is a lot of information for a computer's memory to store. What Bitstream has done recently is issue a product called Fontware, which allows someone with a desktop publishing or word-processing system to specify a type family (any family within Bitstream's library), a point size, a weight, and a style (roman or italic), and further to specify what kind of screen or printer will be displaying or spitting out the type. Fontware then supplies a correctly proportioned outline for that face and point size and formulates the necessary bitmaps. All of this information is stored on a floppy disk, which can be thought of as a font. (In the days of metal type, the word font was used to describe a collection of all the letters, symbols, and figures that would be needed for a specific typesetting job. Now it simply refers to a typeface in a given point size contained in some way: on a filmstrip, on a disk, in a computer system's memory as a file.)

If Bitstream is issuing a design, historic or contemporary, that was first drawn or printed on paper, they take the analog version, the familiar black on white, and mark strategic points on the letter, then scan the drawing with an electronic "puck." The letterform, as it appears on the screen, is then corrected by manipulating those points. At a Bitstream work station you might find a resident type designer transfixed by a mosaic of electronic tiles that closely resembles the letter *g*. Slowly, judiciously, the designer turns one tile on and another off, trying to correctly imply the smooth curves of the letter's ideal form. The object of this game is to approximate the letter in such a way that a computer-linked printer will respond by assembling a tight raster (the parallel scanning lines put out by a laser printer) configuration that, to the naked eye, looks like a solid blackletter rather than a jagged arrangement of dots.

Here we have come back around to the issue of technology's impact on the integrity of type. How well does a bitmap impersonate a letter? The answer varies depending on the resolution of the printer and, more than that, on whom you ask. At Type 1987 there were people who would look at a *Q* or *B* generated by a laser printer and see the Odessa Steps. They complained of angular jots where angular jots shouldn't be. Others claimed that the ultimate result of typefaces, particularly the classic ones, being digitized was an unfortunate breed of perfection. Little quirks and peccadilloes of early faces were being cleaned up in the same way that historic buildings are cleaned up by renovation. Something is gained and something is lost.

On the other hand, Bitstream may actually be incorporating typographic quirkiness on their design agenda. A Bitstream brochure claims, "Existing typefaces that have been distorted over the years to fit out-of-date typesetting technologies have been reexamined and restored to their true form."

Carter's career began in the 1950s when he served an unofficial apprenticeship at a typefoundry in Holland, and his early experiences with metal type gave him a broad perspective on the issue of technology and type. "The reason I'm glad at the end of a day that I spent that year working in the traditional techniques is that it demystified them for me," says Carter.

Carter denies that metal type had an "indefinable quality" that subsequent type technologies lack. "I don't feel that everything ground to a halt at the end of metal type," Carter remarks. "I think that there is no real truth to materials."

Does a type designer attuned to the current technology (whatever the current technology happens to be) let his knowledge of that technology's limitations and attributes play a role in design? For Carter the answer is yes. And the answer is also no.

"Consider the difficulty of designing a typeface: Let's rate it ten on a scale (of one to ten). By difficulty I mean the things that are always difficult about a type design or always important about a type design—making all the letters look as though they're the same size, spacing them right, getting the rhythm of it, the weight, and all those things. I would say that the technical consideration, whether you're doing this for digital techniques or cutting it in steel or engraving it in stone, rates about two or three on the same scale."

Carter is well aware of the eccentricities of the laser printer, the fickleness of the raster: "That coarse resolution of the vertical-horizontal axis of the raster means that there are some faces that it doesn't really do very well," he admits.

Typefaces, according to Carter, that are not quite perpendicular to the horizontal scanning of the raster, those that list to one side or the other by several degrees, are liable to be marred by the laser printer. "That's hell," Carter explains, "because you get very coarse steps up the letters where it crosses from one raster line to the next.

"Similarly, there are typefaces that have very slow curves, very flat curves. There again, because of the coarseness of the raster, it's hard to reproduce them well."

Carter has designed faces that are beautiful (Snell Roundhand, a cursive, but not a florid one); exactingly practical (Bell Centennial, the telephone-book face); and faces that are both aesthetically motivated and apt. Charter, for instance, is specifically designed to perform well at 300 dots per inch, the resolution of a common laser printer.

Carter explicates: "It's a rather simple letterform. It's uncluttered, uncomplicated. It's a serif type, so it already has a degree of complication. It's simple partly for the reason that various kinds of curves don't lend themselves to laser-printer resolutions. If you could avoid them it's probably no bad thing to do that. Also it's rather economical in digital data to store. That's not always a very important point, but sometimes there are constraints on computer memory when it comes to storing fonts. And because of certain simplicities in the way Charter is drawn, it minimizes the amount of digital data that is actually needed to represent that typeface.

"I had in mind the kind of printing that gets done within businesses, even this one. We've got it on all the laser printers here. So it's sort of readable and unfancy and straightforward."

While technical concerns may be low on Carter's scale of design difficulty, they are a consideration. At the same time he warns against tailoring typefaces to whatever equipment is in vogue: "If you aim a typeface at a particular technology, you're really designing a self-obsoleting typeface.

"When I first got involved in photocomposition in the early 1960s, at that stage of the technology it was very common to use as an image source a spinning disk, a negative disk which was rotated within the machine. The way you captured characters was to expose them photographically with a very fast flash of light. But in those days the flash lamps weren't really fast enough to freeze the letter. So you'd have sort of a trailing edge, a smudge, on the letters as they appeared on photographic paper, and this tended to clog up letters, like cap *W*'s or *M*'s, which had oblique lines meeting at rather acute angles. So we used to try and avoid that by opening these angles up and doing various tricks in drawing the letters to hide the effects of this sort of halation.

"The next thing that happened was some bright engineer speeded up the flash time or put a filter in the optical part and corrected it. Suddenly all these letters, which did indeed go partway toward compensating for the imperfect technology, looked very strange when perfectly reproduced. So there you are. You've obliged the engineers by trying to solve a problem, but the engineers are smarter than you in the end and they fix it themselves and that's happened to me so many times. . . ."

When Paula Scher stands at the Podium and accuses ITC of undermining type's heritage, she's not simply quarreling with the fact that they've redesigned traditional faces. The larger problem is that ITC faces have a way of muscling out the faces from which they were adapted. ITC faces are widely and intensively distributed to the manufacturers of every brand of type-setting equipment. In the largest of cities, a designer has a great many type suppliers to choose from. If she doesn't want an ITC Garamond, she can get a Berthold or a Linotype version. But in a one-typesetter town, the odds are that the local type shop will offer mainly ITC faces. The distinctions between Garamonds then become moot. ITC Garamond *is* Garamond.

Distribution is one issue; taste is another. Historicists like Scher are acutely sensitive to classic typefaces being remodeled by contemporary design clichés, whether of the simple-is-good ethic or the decorative style associated with the "New York School" designers like Lubalin, Benguiat, or Glaser. Today's clichés are omnipresent and infuriating, but the clichés of the past are either endearing or invisible to a contemporary critic.

It's not nostalgia exactly that colors our vision of past design but an absence of critical context. What has survived from the past—whether it's a type design, an advertising poster, or a piece of industrial design—exists in a vacuum. It has been jettisoned from its cultural context. A typeface from a hundred years ago is a time traveler, so we don't always question its credentials, we don't ask whether it's the best of its day. We like it because it's here. And we don't want the survivors of the past to be corrupted by the present.

Actually, Allan Haley alluded to this problem: "We get accused of having a look, an ITC look. When we first created typefaces there were a group of designers that worked for us or with us that came out of the New York advertising, lettering school. They had a look. We came out with typefaces that had a feel to them, a look to them that was successful." ITC became a magnet for a certain sensibility, success feeding on success. Says Haley, "It kept repeating on itself."

Nonetheless, Haley insists that ITC *is* conscientious about conserving the history of type and argues that the adaptations ITC markets are consistent with that history: "Type design," Haley contends, "is a history of adapting. Garamond adopted his designs from Manutius, and Plantin adapted his designs from Garamond, and Times Roman is based on Plantin. It's all there. It's been traditional with the industry. Helvetica is based on Akzidenz. Grotesk is based on. . . ."

Several years ago ITC hired type designer Tony Stan to redraw Goudy's University of California Oldstyle, a typeface Frederic Goudy created in the late 1930s for that university's press. The differences between the original and revised roman faces is slight—there is something about the quality of the line—but certain italic letters—*U, Q, Z*—are clear departures in Stan's family, which was dubbed Berkeley Oldstyle.

"University of California Oldstyle was done in metal type and several years later Monotype brought it out only in metal," says Haley. "We always liked that design—that was some of Goudy's better work—but it was a very small family and you really couldn't use it and couldn't get to it, so we went to Tony Stan and asked him if he could create a face with the feeling of that face. If you had Berkeley Oldstyle on one side of the room and University of California on the other and you couldn't look at them at the same time, you might say, 'Well, they're pretty much the same face'; but if you put them side by side they're very different."

The transformation of University of California Oldstyle to Berkeley Oldstyle can be read as a case of ITC playing fast and loose with type's heritage, but ITC didn't invent this strategy. For instance, the *Times* of London back in 1930 instructed Stanley Morison, typographical adviser to the Monotype Corporation and the Cambridge University Press, to draw a modernized version of the typeface Plantin, one with sharper serifs. Morison did this and spawned Times Roman.

ITC adapts a face rather than replicates it for the same reason the *Times* of London remade Plantin—to make a face of their own. With ITC, though, it goes deeper. The company was founded by contemporary type designers to supply fashionable new faces to a voracious advertising industry and, moreover, to guarantee income from their own designs. If ITC reproduced an unadulterated version of a venerable face, a face in the public domain, how could they call such a face an ITC face? How could they demand a royalty for it? They couldn't. So ITC, if they are to issue anything but brand-new original faces, are bound to recast whatever they touch.

Still, if adaptation is unquestionably part of the history of type design, why all the fuss? Perhaps it has something to do with the rate of change. The newest technologies speed up the process of drawing typefaces. An alphabet can be originated or reconfigured at a CAD station at twenty minutes per character. Maybe even faster. Alphabets used to take years to draw (and still do for most designers), and drawing was the snappy part back when type had to be cut into steel punches and molds had to be made before type could be cast. Adaptations happened but they took years to execute. There were natural, physical, chronological limits to change. Adaptations can take place in a matter of weeks now. Hell, they can happen overnight. Computers *exist* to allow manipulation of data. Now that type is nothing but data, numbers for the crunching, it can be a chameleon, remade for every situation. Digital faces can come from nowhere, and spread like the flu. Put a typeface on software for Apple, for IBM, for their respective clones, and it can reach saturation in no time.

So what is a typeface? Under laws in this country and in much of the world, a typeface isn't protected by copyrights; only the name of the typeface can be registered. Because Linotype has kept the name Helvetica on a short leash, one finds this most ubiquitous of typefaces listed as Helios or Triumvarite in the Compugraphic type book or Swiss in Bitstream's roster. It is confusing: the pedigree of the faces themselves, the question of origin, of ownership, the varying names. And then, the advertising agencies. Theoretically, the way to get a new typeface to catch on is to get it used in a major advertising campaign. Once a typeface has debuted in one high-profile ad, it's safe for all the other agencies to pick up on it. But major advertisers aren't content to have a signature typeface. They have to alter that face to make it truly their own. "Some of them just thumbprint stuff," says Haley, meaning they lop off a serif or stretch a descender. Others distort a face. Apple uses a condensed ITC Garamond, but they tamper with it electronically so that it looks like nobody else's ITC Garamond.

So what is a typeface? The question gets harder to answer the more you know.

Maybe Ed Benguiat provides the best answer in his metaphoric way. He's explaining why typefaces designed on computers aren't, to his way of thinking, really typefaces, saying that computer design often involves recycling and repeating letter strokes: "On a computer, when you have an *I,* an *H,* that stroke, you say, 'OK, we'll use that stroke here, we'll use it there. We'll use it all over.'" Benguiat, who was a jazz drummer before he started drawing the alphabet, talks as though the two disciplines were one. And perhaps they are. "It's just like a bing-bing-bing-bing . . . ," he says, hitting the table with a steady, monotonous beat. "You know, rhythm is type. This isn't rhythm. That's nothing more than a tap. The minute you have this—" he adds a second beat with his other hand, "then you're cooking. The idea is that type has a feeling, and if it doesn't have that feeling it just goes. . . ." And here Benguiat makes a noise that defies accurate transliteration. "If it doesn't have that feeling it just goes blaaaaahhh."

A typeface, then, is rhythm. The beat of the written language, the stride of letters marching across a page.

Matthew Carter defines type in another way, a way I particularly like because it assumes an alliance between the creator of letterforms and the writer of words. It is always heartening to a writer when someone involved in typography remembers that there is a relationship between form and content: "There are very few things you can say to distinguish type from other kinds of industrial design," Carter remarks. "One of them is that we design letterforms, obviously. That's what we draw, but the real product is words. We don't know how those letterforms are going to be combined linguistically. And essentially we have to make them so they can be combined randomly in any combination. It's when the thing gets into words, gets printed, that's the proof of it. That's when it's doing its job. So there's a funny sort of remove. You're designing something but you have no control over how it's actually used. We are really word designers, but we can't be."

From *Metropolis* (April 1988).

Criticism: Type as Discourse

A Plea for Authentic Type Design

By Hermann Zapf

I am an artist who has been designing types for many years. As we all know, to make a living as a freelance designer, you have to work hard with your mind as well as with your hand. For you to want to earn at least enough money to dress your wife nicely, feed your children every day, and live in a house where the rain doesn't come through the roof onto your drawing pad.

As long as you are creative, as long as you are in good health, everybody thinks you cannot have problems of any real importance. But type designers do have problems.

I have, in the past, designed several successful typefaces. To make one type family, you have to spend several months on each alphabet. This investment of time, the designer hopes, will be repaid bit by bit over time in the form of royalties. But some people claim that all alphabets are in the public domain, so the creative work of a designer is something that can be freely copied; and in fact there is no copyright protection for alphabets, most conspicuously in the U.S. By copying typefaces, a smart businessman can make money without investing a nickel in the design or paying anything to the original designer. What is generally accepted as a fair arrangement in the fields of music and literature is, strangely enough, not yet accepted in a creative art like type design.

The copyright laws in many countries are outdated. A revision of some parts of the U.S. Copyright Law of January 1, 1978, is necessary, for it does not take into account video, PCs, photocopiers, or even low-resolution designs used by laser printers. Copyright protects the creator of a piece of art during the lifetime of an artist, plus fifty years thereafter.

Type designs have so far not been included in U.S. copyright laws. Some protection is offered to them by the Universal Copyright Convention (UCC), and by the Berne Convention. But the latter has never been signed by the U.S.

Assume, for example, that Leonard Bernstein conducts a special performance of his *West Side Story* for Columbia Records. This performance is released under the Columbia label and, as a consequence, royalties accrue to Bernstein. If someone copies this record and sells it at a cheaper price (for he avoids the expense of royalties), would this not be a gross injustice to Bernstein? In fact, would it not actually be illegal?

Pirates don't spend money to develop and introduce unknown or new faces, by which they might further the art of type design. Instead, they go after proven, successful types, make a profit on them, but never use their profits to commission new ideas, as is customary practice in honest business. These people are Alaska-cool and emotionally unconcerned about the rights of artists.

None of the copied alphabets offered in specimen books under the bizarre description "similar to" has ever been given away to printers or typographers for free. At least I have never heard of such a generous offer. Do we know of any companies producing alphabets just to further truth and better global understanding, or to spread moral values?

There are a lot of variations of my typefaces around for which I am not responsible. Without my approval, they are sold by big companies, sometimes under strange names. Typographers and users should therefore examine very carefully what kind of original type or poor copy they order. And they should know that the copyist does nothing creative at all; he is exploiting an artist's work.

But these days, besides the piracy of alphabets, we face another problem. Unfortunately, many people—even professionals—don't see the differences between the details of a good original typeface and a sloppy copy in low resolution. The visual sensibility of many of our contemporaries is becoming more and more deadened by all the poor—sometimes primitive—letterforms they absorb, day by day, in low resolution on PCs, VDTs, computer printouts, and even television.

Type designing is connected with printing, often called the "black art." Are we a disadvantaged minority within the graphic arts community, our rights unacknowledged and ignored?

People who would rather not respect the property rights of a type designer—his creative work—apparently expect the designer to be a kind of philanthropic dreamer devoting himself to mankind. In their eyes, he is a cow to milk. These very people, however, would never accept the notion that *they* should work for several months for the benefit of the public without any reward.

Let me end with an anecdote that expresses my situation, for I probably hold the world's record for the most type designs copied without permission.

At one time I had neighbors who grew apples commercially. I also grew apples, and I had spent a great amount of time and money in cultivating my trees. As a result, I developed some unique varieties unobtainable elsewhere. Occasionally, my neighbors would sneak over and pick my apples in order to sell them. Their own apples were merely ordinary, while mine were of the "Palatino" and "Optima" variety. Before long, I realized what was going on. "What do you think you're doing?" I said to them. "You can't take my best apples. That isn't right." "But apples are apples," they retorted. "They depend on the sun and the rain and the rich soil. All that comes from the Good Lord." I was unconvinced. My problem was that I had no fences or any other protection around my property.

The International Typeface Corporation in New York, founded in 1970 by Aaron Burns, licenses alphabets. Since I began to work for this firm, I have gained support and an ITC fence around my property, my ITC alphabets. ITC sells types—both mine and those of other designers—to their customers around the world. And everyone receives his fair share of the profits for his specialty.

I do not intend to have anyone steal my apples ever again.

From *Print* 40, no. 6 (Nov/Dec 1986).

The Obscene Typography Machine

By Philip B. Meggs

t a recent Washington AIGA meeting, editors from four major design publications held a panel discussion. One of the shills in the audience asked, "Do the design magazines establish design trends, or do you merely follow and report about them?" After all of the editors replied that they weren't too interested in stylistic trends or the latest fashion, one editor commented that the one *real* trend that everyone in the room should watch closely is the increasing importance of computers in graphic design. Most designers who have overcome their computer phobia and learned computer-assisted design have become mesmerized by its possibilities. Text can be poured into columns, PMS match-color backgrounds can be changed instantly to try different color combinations, and type size and style can be changed at will. For thousands of organizations with publications budgets too small to afford design and typesetting services, desktop publishing allows a significant upgrade of routine printed material ranging from internal company publications to public-school study guides and church bulletins. But this wonderful new tool that is revolutionizing graphic design has its dark side.

Unfortunately, the ease of computer use puts potent graphic capabilities into the hands of people who are devoid of any esthetic sense about typography and have little or no understanding of the most basic principles of design. Powerful new software programs including Aldus Freehand and Illustrator 88 give the designer (or moron, as the case may be) the power to flip, rotate, stretch, or bend typography with the click of the mouse button. This permits some of the most obscene type-forms ever devised or imagined. Certainly, distortion can be a useful and innovative design tool when handled with sensitivity and intelligence, but we are seeing type distorted in violation of everything that has been learned over the past 500 years about making functional and beautiful letterforms. Newspaper advertisements are a major source of grotesque typographic distortion, as headlines are stretched or condensed to fit with about as much grace as a fat lady squeezing into a too-small girdle.

A principle from perceptual psychology is that when identical rectangles are placed on the page with one in a horizontal position and the other in a vertical position, the horizontal rectangle will appear heavier, even though it is identical to the vertical form. A typeface designer spends hours refining his strokes, shaving horizontal forms until they appear to have the same thickness as the vertical form.

Everyone who takes an introductory typography class learns that if a letter composed of curved strokes such as an O is the same height as a letter composed of vertical strokes such as an *E,* the O will appear too small. Typeface designers optically adjust circular forms, which must extend slightly above the capline and slightly below the baseline to appear correct.

One reason a typeface is considered a masterpiece is because the designer achieved optical harmony in adjusting the size and proportion of the parts—not mathematically, but esthetically and perceptually. Frederic W. Goudy's Goudy Old Style, Adrian Frutiger's Univers, and John Baskerville's Baskerville: these typefaces are honored as great tools of communication and works of art because a virtuoso designer poured heart, soul, and countless hours of work into creating harmonious relationships between letterforms.

Suddenly in 1988, anyone with a Macintosh or other computer and a $495 software program could wreak havoc on these beautifully crafted forms. Consider the four versions of Helvetica Medium, executed on a computer and outputted from a Linotron 100 at 1270 dots per inch. The top setting is normal type, reasonably close to the original font created by Max Miedinger and Edouard Hoffman thirty years ago, allowing for some alteration when converted to a specific digital output device. The second version was produced by grabbing the corner of the type with the mouse and squeezing it down into a shorter version, and the lower versions were produced by grabbing the corner of the type with the mouse and stretching it into taller, condensed versions. The computer is a dumb robot, totally ignorant of the principles of perception mentioned earlier. In the lower versions, the horizontal strokes were stretched wider, while the vertical strokes maintained their original width. The result is grossly misproportioned letterforms. The optical adjustment of the *O* and *S* is exaggerated, making them seem too tall for the other letters. We are seeing typography approach this level of obscenity as students, neophytes, and even experienced designers, berserk over the new toy, violate well-drawn letterforms without bringing compensating values of expression or form to their work. Goudy and Baskerville must be spinning in their graves, and Frutiger and Miedinger must be quite depressed to see their artful letters, created as an act of love, destroyed by those who either cannot see or simply do not care.

One impact of this new graphic software relates to what is becoming known as Deconstructivist typography, whose integrated whole is taken apart. While some of the practitioners of this new typographic movement exhibit great sensitivity and originality, others are merely flitting through the collection of graphic procedures available with the new software. . . . Operations that formerly required painstaking cut-and-paste work, such as setting type in an oval or along a curved baseline, can now be performed instantly by drawing an oval, a circle or a meandering line, typing in the text, then clicking the mouse on the word "Join" in the menu. The oval, circle, or line instantly becomes the baseline of the type. These graphic devices provide a vocabulary of instant clichés, executed as simply as snapping one's fingers. Often, these techniques are used, not for thoughtful communicative or expressive reasons, but simple because they are there. The problem for designers exploring the elastic typography and/or the Deconstructivist sensibility on a computer is, "What do you do for an encore?" As with most specialized tools, a computer-graphics program permits one to do a limited number of things very efficiently, but only operates within a fixed range of possibilities. Its innovative graphic techniques will become old and tired very rapidly as more and more people hop on the bandwagon, transforming graphics that originally appeared fresh and innovative into hack work.

Another problem with all this graphic power is that tremendous capability is put into the hands of people who don't know an ampersand from a hole in the ground. A newsletter recently crossed my desk with each column of type linespaced differently, because the novice desktop publisher discovered that the page-layout program would permit automatic leading to fit the column depth. Columns in 10-point Times Roman with no leading were adjacent to other columns set in 10-point Times Roman with about 25 points of leading between the lines. Text columns were justified, producing gaping holes in each line of type due to poor wordspacing. He or she was too naïve about typography to realize how the inconsistent wordspacing destroyed legibility and the tonal quality of the page.

Although equipment manufacturers and software developers have made modest efforts to educate their users about the rudiments of design through little booklets explaining effective page layout or newsletter design, complete with case studies of redesigned publications with notable improvements, a new generation of unschooled graphic designers—editors, public-relations agents, secretaries, and other do-it-yourself desktop publishers—are totally ignorant of the rudiments of publication design and typography. Adobe, the company that developed the PostScript software that transforms crude bitmapped type on the computer screen into refined high-resolution output, publishes excellent materials. Some software tutorials address design issues, but do it poorly. More must be done. There should be an ethical responsibility on the part of companies that put powerful tools into the hands of uninformed people without educating them about the proper use of these tools.

The obscene typography machine can also be the sublime typography machine. Professional designers can explore new creative possibilities and spend more time developing concepts and designing and less time laboriously executing their work. As this technology becomes available in third-world nations, their efforts toward education and development can take quantum leaps forward as a result of the economy of desktop publishing. The computer-graphics force is now with us, but its dark side must be controlled; otherwise, the obscene typography machine is going to inflict unimagined graphic atrocities upon the public.

From *Print* 43, no. 5 (September/October 1989).

Type Is Dead: Long Live Type

By Matthew Butterick

ype designers tend to be a nervous lot, with reason. Especially in the U.S., type design in the last ten years has been increasingly an undertaking for the brave, the masochistic, or the independently wealthy. Lack of copyright protection for type designs has resulted in unscrupulous companies profiting from cheap imitations, while the proliferation of desktop publishers has made fonts even more popular to pirate than QuarkXPress.

Now we are witnessing the emergence of a purely digital visual culture: users are taking their doses of typography on screen as well as on paper. Type and graphic designers alike are viewing this development with the proverbial cautious optimism. Typography is inexorably moving into the digital realm, going from design to output without pausing to rest on a sheet of paper. Should designers be excited or alarmed?

The ATypI conference is the largest annual gathering of type designers; the theme of last year's conference in Barcelona was "Into the Type Net." When I received the flyer in the mail, I was slightly bemused ("type net"?) but curious, so I pressed on:

"The analog and linear alphabet is dead—long live digital text and type in space and time! . . . [The 1995 conference] will cast an eye on the present and future of interactive type and its relationship with the image in an expanding virtual-visual environment . . . ATypI welcomes people . . . who are interested to support communicative design aspects within the information society."

I still have no idea what this means. Even disregarding the linguistic kinks that may have cropped up in the translation from the original Spanish, phrases like "interactive type" and "virtual-visual environment" are vapid techno-portmanteaus. But ATypI can't be blamed; these kinds of terms are endemic to the current discourse on digital design.

Something big is definitely happening, but most prognosticators about the digital future seem to be uncomfortable saying that life will be anything but bigger, better, and faster for everyone. It's clear that type designers and those who design with type will not be so fortunate. Ironically, current technology has made text more important than ever, but the same technology has conspired to further erode the value of quality typography.

The sole bit of good news is that text rules the digital frontier, because it is compact to load, easy to create, familiar to use, and compatible with all computing platforms. The popularity of the World Wide Web has shown that text is still a vital medium, and though it's less flashy than pictures, sound, and video, it offers the best bang for the bandwidth. And if text is alive and well, so should typography be: after all, there can be no visual representation of text without type, and the proliferation of text in a new medium would imply the necessity of new design solutions. More work for type designers, more work for typographers—the birth of a type renaissance! Right?

No. The jubilance that type makers should rightly feel has been cut by the grim realization of the workings of the software industry. Once, those who made type also controlled the means of production—in the days of hot metal, the choice of a Monotype versus a Linotype caster was similar to the choice of Macintosh versus Windows. Each platform had its strengths and foibles, but if you needed type, you chose one and stuck with it. A hot metal caster was a sort of operating system for type, and the matrices were the software that worked with it. This continued through the ages of phototypesetting and early digital typography, where proprietary systems meant proprietary fonts, and proprietary fonts meant type makers could still maintain control over font production and access.

But when type technology became commingled with personal computing technology, things changed. At that point, the ability to make and use type became available to anyone with a computer, along with the newfound ability to make speedy, accurate, and untraceable pirate copies. This was better for users of type, but much worse for type designers. Type has had to relinquish the power of its own proprietary barricades. Many of the improvements in type functionality introduced on computers have caused a decline in type designers' quality of life. Moreover, the goals of interoperability and data exchange will continue to be antithetical to type's long-term aesthetic and economic viability.

For example, one brass ring for which Apple, Adobe, and others have groped recently is the portable digital document—a document that can be viewed and printed with its formatting intact, without needing the software that created it. These schemes have typically been riddled with unstable engineering and other difficulties. But let's take apart the problem: consider a page-layout document containing images and formatted text. Text is certainly portable, and formatting can be made into a series of tags; images can be converted to a variety of platform-independent bitmap formats. All that's left are the fonts! The handiest thing would be to encapsulate the fonts into the document, but this would be tantamount to saving users the trouble of pirating the fonts themselves. Adobe's scheme at one point was to retain metric files of hundreds of typefaces in the software so that a reasonable facsimile could be built when the document was opened. Uncountable programmer-hours have doubtless been spent to preserve the type designer's livelihood, but the result is products that can't quite do what they claim. Surely more than one software company has thought, why can't the fonts just be free so we can copy them?

Microsoft, with typical bravado, was the only company willing to act on that principle. Several years ago, Microsoft began to create its own type library. At first there were special font packs; then fonts showed up in other products. Now, it's rare that a box goes out the door without new typefaces in it. Microsoft is probably one of the largest publishers of typefaces in the world, and it has also built font embedding into its operating system, for use in any sort of document. Nevertheless, users who are receiving dozens of free fonts may not see much point in paying for more.

Typographers who are wincing should stop reading now—that's nothing compared to the culture of the Internet. On the surface, Internet users look like the most fertile new group of type consumers: a giant new demographic suffering from an acute case of dreadful typography (Times and Courier are used almost exclusively). However, the language of Internet typography (HTML) allows for no explicit typeface choices, and only a handful of different sizes. Worse, much of the software that can be used for browsing the Internet is free. If users don't have to pay for an industrial-strength Web browser, why will they pay for a font, of all things? (As this issue goes to press, Microsoft has just released

Matthew Carter's Verdana, a type family commissioned expressly for use in Web browsers—and it's available from their site for free.) Then there's the taste issue: I'm sure most graphic designers have had a client who insisted on a job being set only in Times, Palatino, or Courier. Now you have 15 million clients who feel the same way.

The undeterred typographer might still bravely withstand these slings and arrows and elect to create the consummate on-screen text typeface. Sadly, one's design choices at the level of the 12-point bitmap are limited to determining how to render the curve of the lowercase *s*. It seems safe to speculate that there are no more than eight mutually distinguishable 12-point text faces, all of which had been discovered by 1985. It's a field with limited growth potential at best (Matthew Carter notwithstanding).

Some of the blame for the current dismal situation can be put with Apple, Adobe, Microsoft, Quark, and their ilk. All have had the opportunity to improve typography by enhancing software or hardware, but they have pursued it with little vigor. Certain developments (anti-aliased type) have been slow in coming, others (QuickDraw GX) have been overhyped, and others still (high-resolution displays) don't seem to be on anyone's task list. These improvements wouldn't just make typophiles happy; they would benefit anyone who has to experience type on a screen—i.e., anyone who owns a computer. Given the continuing importance of text to computers, it's surprising type technology has been stagnating.

But the best consolation may be that print will never die. Part of the current anxiety seems to stem from the idea that print will disappear in the face of the putatively superior on-screen technology. It's not true. The experience of reading off an illuminated phosphor will never compare to thumbing through the Sunday *Times*. This isn't romantic atavism, it's a simple matter of a screen not being able to provide the density of information that the eye can efficiently comprehend. A printed text is also easier for us to navigate because we can manipulate it in a direct, physical, and familiar way.

Type, typography, and the printed word have been a phenomenal success for 500 years and there's no reason for that to change. Though the situation for on-screen type will improve, it will never evolve to such an extent that readers will stop wanting to read printed type. Sadly the goal of preserving quality typography in the digital sphere is at odds with many trends in personal computing and the Internet. But the printed word is, and will remain, as irreplaceable to readers as it is to typographers.

From *AIGA Journal of Graphic Design* 14, no. 3 (1996).

Designing Hate: Is There a Graphic Language of Vile Emotion?

By Steven Heller

hat typeface says "nigger?" What logo denotes kike, chink, spic, or wop? Are there design conventions for expressing racism? Can hate be well designed?

In a sense, Adolf Hitler was a brilliant art director, for he etched hate into the minds of millions. He took credit for the design of the Nazi party emblem, the swastika, a benign ancient symbol before he, or the others who also claim credit for its creation, transformed it into a trademark of malevolence. Hitler's Ministry of Information, a uniquely German government body composed of media experts organized around the model of the modern advertising/public relations agency, was responsible for mythologizing the state and interpreting its racist policies aesthetically. Architectural, environmental, and graphic design were key to this process. Grandiose buildings at once dwarfed the individual and symbolized the omnipotence of the state. Spectacular environments (including rallies, pageants, and festivals) unified the masses into a mammoth body. Heroic graphics provided visual signposts that directed the masses toward ideological truth. And since one of the principal truths of Nazi ideology was anti-Semitism, part of the Ministry's graphics were aimed at its official propagation.

The Nazis developed derisive verbal and graphic symbols to cast suspicion on, and ultimately dehumanize, its enemies. Some were more overt than others—the Germans were masters of euphemism—but all promoted hatred. Graphic design played a key role in the systematic racist propaganda targeted at Jews, Gypsies, Poles, and Slavs, and a ministry department was dedicated to developing graphics that would efficiently communicate this message. The most diabolically effective visual weapon was the metamorphosis of Jews into vermin. The caricatured exaggeration of stereotypical physical characteristics resulted in the symbol of the Jew as rat. When combined with other malicious cartoon types, such as the rapacious banker or the mongrel Hebrew, as well as the whore and pimp, the verminous Jew, as seen in newspapers, on placards, and in films, became the paradigm of German revulsion.

The graphics of hate, however, were practiced in Europe long before the Nazis. Anti-Semitic imagery dating from before the eighteenth century was common in prints and paintings. Yet, without justifying them, these were often political or social commentaries that spoke more of a deep-seated social intolerance than the virulent strains of criminal hatred exhibited by the Nazis. It was the Nazis who masterminded the aesthetics of hatred and so set standards for its continued practice.

If a graphic designer were commissioned today to design hate, Nazi-influenced imagery would inevitably be used. German Fraktur type (as opposed to other medieval gothics, such as Old English) still evokes iron-fisted authority. The words **Alt!**, **Verboten!**, and **Jude!** are frightening when spelled out in these letterforms. Actually, anything set in Fraktur, even the most harmless words and phrases, takes on a decidedly ominous look.

When the Nazis took power in 1933, propaganda minister Josef Goebbels briefly outlawed Modern sans serif type for official use. Calling it a "Jewish invention," he returned to Fraktur, only to revoke this decision some years later, when pilots complained that airplane tail markings set in Fraktur were too difficult to read. But if Fraktur doesn't connote hate well enough, then the swastika says it all. Rather than being merely a charged national symbol, the swastika became an odious icon that retains the ability to strike fear or revulsion in many. When used or adapted today by members of rightist fringe groups, it is a symbol of defiance, racism, and hatred. So, too, are the nefariously brilliant supplementary images in the Nazi visual identity. The twin lightning bolts, the logo of the SS, like the various twisted arrows and crosses of kindred fascist parties, evoke unmistakable symbolic connotations.

Certain American icons are similarly loaded. The hooded robe of the Ku Klux Klan is a living logo or garment *parlant*. Based on the habits of medieval religious orders, the hooded robe was adopted after the Civil War to symbolize white supremacy. The logo for the KKK, a slabbed cross with a diamond bull's-eye inset with a drop of blood, may not be as geometrically precise, or as aesthetically pure, as the swastika, but there is no mistaking its meaning. The logos for the KKK and other American fringe groups have ominous characteristics stemming from a mixed marriage of Christian and pagan iconography— crucifixes and death's heads, black against blood-red color fields. There are, of course, benign Christian symbols that include hearts and crowns, as well as images depicting sacrifice, but they are ennobled by time, popular perception, or the nuance of composition. Even if the KKK logo were not associated with the burning cross, that drop of blood would still indicate a violent ideology.

Symbols of power and violence are common in the lexicon of hate. They are drawn from, and often misuse, ritualistic symbols of the past. The most hackneyed, though no less powerful, are the shooting lightning bolt from mythology, the thrusting arrow from antiquity, and the gunsight from weaponry. Alone or together, they indicate that force is not a threat but a linchpin of belief. While the wearers might argue that these emblems are no different from the patriotic patches for government military units (indeed, during World War I an orange swastika on a red field, symbolizing good luck, was the emblem of a decorated American infantry unit), the fact that many of these American hate groups are paramilitary underscores the threatening nature of their symbols.

In addition to the overt signs, hate and its cousin intolerance are often tritely designed as well. *Der Sturmer,* the most loathesome of Nazi periodicals, was designed like any other newspaper, following the pre-Bauhaus convention of central-axis composition of Fraktur and other Germanic serif faces. While its typography was somewhat neutral, its headlines extolled Aryan superiority over "Jew trash." Similarly, American right-wing magazines of the 1920s and 30s also used conventional printing styles. The *KKK Kourier* was as deceptively bland as many of the left or centrist journals of the day; it did not even display the KKK logo on the front page. *Liberation,* the weekly journal of Aggressive Patriotism, was

43

elegantly composed, its logo suggesting a heraldic influence typical of many traditional journals. Its interior format was staid and quiet, but like *Der Sturmer,* its venom against Jews, Catholics, and blacks was to be found in its text.

Hate is perhaps most effective when designed according to middlebrow standards. The Germans did not entertain design extremes, partly because racist decrees had to gain widespread, matter-of-fact acceptance. Their official policy of hate could not be construed as an anomaly, and commonplace design fostered a favorable public response. However, during the 1930s another reason that hate literature conformed to convention was that printing demanded standardization. These constraints were actually in the best interest of racist groups, whose goal was to influence mainstream opinion. Breaking tight design strictures was ultimately possible with the introduction in the sixties of cheap offset printing. Through underground newspapers, the left proved that the printing and design media could be harnessed for distinctive, emblematic graphics, but the old-line right did not follow suit, fearing an association with the youth movement. In recent years, however, as new and younger hate groups—notably the skinheads—have emerged, the need to distinguish ideology and message has resulted in an increased number of graphics. The Macintosh has, of course, facilitated this expression.

WAR, the tabloid of the White Aryan Resistance, a hate group founded by Tom Metzger of Fallbrook, California, is not going to win any design awards, but it is a vivid example of how the tools of commonplace graphic design are used in the service of hate. This right-wing underground publication has taken on the ad hoc look of the former left-wing underground press; self-conscious design is rejected in favor of the neat "fit." Whatever default typeface and column width will get the message across is used without regard for nuance. In fact, its real visual distinction comes through the advertisements. The images and symbols of violence and power shown in these ads are veritable icons of hate. Posters with burning swastikas, heroic mounted Klansmen, and bloody daggers are understandable to all, and frightening to many.

While euphemism may take the sting out of unpleasantness, and neutrality can be subversive, ambiguity does not really help further the cause of malevolence. Therefore, the design of hate must be painfully obvious, relying upon tried-and-true symbols and icons that cannot be misconstrued, for they embody a history that cannot, and should not, be ignored.

From *AIGA Journal of Graphic Design* 12, no. 2 (1994).

A Post-Mortem on Deconstruction?

By Ellen Lupton

heory" and "graphic design" have always been a problematic union. Perhaps because graphic design is often approached more intuitively than intellectually, theory is rarely an explicit part of design practice. When theory does emerge as a topic among designers, it often serves to name a new style, a current stock of mannerisms. A conspicuous example of this surfacing of theory is the circulation of "deconstruction" within the graphic design community.

The term "deconstruction" was coined by the philosopher Jacques Derrida in his book *Of Grammatology,* published in France in 1967 and translated into English in 1976. Deconstruction became a banner for advanced thought in American literary studies, scandalizing departments of English and French across the country. Deconstruction is part of the broader field of criticism known as "post-structuralism," whose theorists have included Derrida as well as Roland Barthes, Michel Foucault, Jean Baudrillard, and others. Each of these writers has looked at modes of representation—from alphabetic writing to photojournalism—as culturally powerful technologies that transform and construct "reality."

In the mid-1980s, graduate students at Cranbrook were reading various post-structuralist works, finding in them analogues for their own ideas about communication. Meanwhile, artists, architects, and photographers in art schools and studios across the country were connecting similar texts to visual practice. "Deconstructivism" catapulted into the mainstream design press with MoMA's 1988 exhibition *Deconstructivist Architecture,* curated by Philip Johnson and Mark Wigley. MoMA used the term "deconstructivism" to link contemporary architecture to Russian Constructivism, whose early years were marked by an imperfect vision of form and technology. The MoMA exhibition found a similarly skewed interpretation of Modernism in the works of Frank Gehry, Daniel Libeskind, Peter Eisenman, and others.

The phrase "deconstruction" quickly became a cliché in design journalism, where it usually has described a style featuring fragmented shapes, extreme angles, and aggressively asymmetrical arrangements. This collection of formal devices was easily transferred from architecture to graphic design, where it named existing tendencies and catalyzed new ones. The labels "deconstructivism," "deconstructionism," and just plain "decon" have served to blanket the differences between a broad range of design practices and an equally broad range of theoretical ideas.

I take a narrower view of deconstruction. Rather than viewing it as a style, I see it as a process—an act of questioning. In Derrida's original theory, deconstruction asks a question: how does representation inhabit reality? How does the external appearance of a thing get inside its internal essence? How does the surface get under the skin? For example, the Western tradition has tended to value the internal mind as the sacred source of soul and intellect, while denouncing the body as an earthly, mechanical shell. Countering this view is the understanding that the conditions of bodily experience temper the way we think and act. A parallel question for graphic design is this: how does visual form get inside the "content" of writing? How has typography refused to be a passive, transparent vessel for written texts, developing as a system with its own structures and devices?

A crucial opposition in Derrida's theory of deconstruction is speech versus writing. The Western philosophical tradition has denigrated writing as an inferior, dead copy of the living, spoken word. When we speak, we draw on our inner consciousness, but when we write, our words are inert and abstract. The written word loses its connection to our inner selves. Language is set adrift. Grammarians, schoolteachers, and other priests of verbal correctness have long bemoaned the inaccuracies of the alphabet—its inability to consistently and concisely represent the sounds of speech. In written English, for example, the function of a letter pair such as *ph* is woefully at odds with our expectations of how these letters behave individually. Herbert Bayer's "fonetic alfabet" (1958–60) attempted to reform this situation.

The Latin alphabet is supplemented by a range of conventions with no relation to speech at all. Spacing, punctuation, the styles of letterforms, the conventions of page layout—these are non-phonetic devices that the alphabet now depends on. Writing is not merely a bad copy, a faulty transcription, of the spoken word. Writing has, in fact, changed the way we think and talk.

A work of design can be called "deconstruction" when it exposes and transforms the established rules of writing, interrupting the sacred "inside" of content with the profane "outside" of form. Modernist typography has long engaged in such structural games, from the calligrammes of Apollinaire, which use typography as an active picture rather than a passive frame, to the experiments with simultaneous overlapping texts produced within the "New Typography" of the 1970s and '80s.

Such self-conscious explorations of language and design within the context of Modernism are matched by numerous developments within the "vernacular" field of commercial publishing, which since the early nineteenth century has expanded the limits of classical book typography to meet the needs of advertising and popular media. The early nineteenth-century display face called Italian deliberately inverted the anatomical parts of the "modern" letterforms that had been formalized in the late eighteenth century. The neoclassical fonts of Didot and Bodoni epitomized the tendency to view typography as a system of abstract relationships—thick and thin, serif and stem, vertical and horizontal. The designer of Italian turned the serifs inside out, demonstrating that the forms of letters are not bound by the authority of divine proportions, but are open to endless manipulation.

Within the context of philosophy and literary theory, deconstruction is just one question among many that emerged out of the body of critical ideas known as post-structuralism. Roland Barthes's theory of "mythology" looks at how images validate key beliefs in modern culture—such as "progress" or "individualism"—making ideologically loaded concepts seem like natural and inevitable truths. Graphic design can reveal cultural myths by using familiar symbols and styles in new ways. A typeface such as Barry Deck's Template Gothic, based on an industrial stencil, calls into question the values of polished perfection commonly associated with technology. Deck calls his typeface "an imperfect typeface for an imperfect world," countering utopian beliefs in technology as social savior or corporate notions of technology as law and order.

It has recently become unfashionable to compare language and design. In the fields of architecture and products, the paradigm of language is losing its luster as a theoretical model—we no longer want to think of buildings, teapots, or fax machines as "communicating" cultural messages, in the manner of post-Modern classicism or product semantics. Yet the link between language and typography is quite different from the link between language and three-dimensional objects, because typography is so close to the language. In fact, typography is the frontier between language and objects, language and images. Typography turns language into a visible, tangible artifact, and in the process transforms it irrevocably.

For the design fields, "deconstruction" has been reduced to the name of a historical period rather than an ongoing way of approaching design. Derrida made a similar point himself in a 1994 interview in the *New York Times Magazine,* when asked if he felt that deconstruction was losing credibility in the academic world, he answered that deconstruction will never be over, because it describes a way of thinking about language that has always existed. For graphic design, deconstruction isn't dead, either, because it's not a style or a movement, but a way of asking questions through our work. Critical form-making will always be part of design practice, whatever theoretical tools one might use to identify it.

From *AIGA Journal of Graphic Design* 12, no. 2 (1994).

Rumors of the Death of Typography
Have Been Greatly Exaggerated

By Peter Fraterdeus

avian Tabibian, humanist scholar and restaurateur, dismissed me as "one of those computer addicts" when I tried to laud him on his "Twilight of Humanism" talk at last year's Aspen Design Conference (he saw *designOnline* on my name tag). "But," I said, as he turned away, "I'm a card-carrying humanist—here, look, I've studied Petrarch's handwriting; I write with goose quills and was a letterpress printer way before it was hip to deep-emboss logos from your Mac LaserWriter output . . ."

I tried to tell him that I agreed with his analysis of the Internet. At least, it was one of the most colorful and provocative descriptions I had heard: "The bastard child of the necrophiliac father War and the shameless whore Entertainment." That stopped the murmur in the big tent for a second. I think most people just figured he was some kind of academic with a socialist agenda, and never gave it another thought. I, on the other hand, found his definition the high point of the conference, particularly after listening to Mr. Four-Million-Dollar-Video-Studio and Mr. Think-and-Get-Rich and the general run of "Business is Good Business" corporate design apologists.

There are still some of us who do believe that the purpose of design is to help make a better world. Perhaps we are those who take seriously the relationship between the culture and the cultural workers whose artifacts help to define the culture. See *www.dol.com/worldstudio.*

The Jet Ski as Cultural Attack Weapon

In northwestern Washington state there is a quiet corner of Puget Sound that has taken a giant step toward balancing the all-pervading mechanophilia that seems to overwhelm our society, and all too often, our better judgment. This small community, which depends on its peace and quiet as a special quality to attract vacationers, has banned Jet Skis in the entire portion of the Sound under its jurisdiction, saying that the constant buzz of these obnoxious watercraft and their loud-mouthed and inconsiderate riders traveling back and forth across the waterfront have destroyed the tranquility of the area, which is a natural treasure and a commonwealth of the community. Of course, the Jet Ski industry won't take this lying down! They're already in court claiming a constitutional right to "interstate travel" and so forth, arguing that "you can't fight progress." It seems that the predominant culture is largely made up of terminally immature kids who are forever rebelling against their eternally authoritarian elders. Of course, things are no different in the culture of typography.

Degenerate Type—Signifyin' Nuthin'

"[Degenerate type is] a form of canned cynicism which will doom its perpetrators to a special room in hell where lovely little children of all races, creeds, and religions are eternally bathed in gentle rosy and amber glows, singing *It's a Small World After All*. There's no legitimate typographic reason to create an alphabet which looks like it leaked out of a diaper."

—P.F. lecture notes for ATypI, Barcelona 1995

Trash type is proud of being the worst student in the class. As if it were more "legitimate" to create ugly little malformed splotches in Fontographer than to attempt to draw the platonic nature of the alphabet from its essential causal form into a well-reasoned and deliberated family of symbols. Please, I'm not getting personal here. Some of my favorite people are making trash type these days. It seems to be the only thing small foundries can even sell! But we don't have to accept that these are anything more than accidental expressions of a techno-sociological transition.

"Letters are programs, not results of programs."

—Erik van Blokland

"Letters are things, not pictures of things," says Eric Gill. Perhaps the "fontography" buffs (sorry Macromedia, it's a generic term now!) and "fontographists" are really just making pictures of things. The difference between a fontographist and a type designer is simple enough. Ask a fontographist to draw a three-inch high roman S with a pencil, without tracing. Soon enough, you'll know if there's any real knowledge of the shapes of letters there (although even many type designers don't know the true subtleties of these forms).

Mangling Caslon and calling it a typeface is not what type designers do. Maybe it's what font designers do, but then who cares, since apparently anyone with a PC and a pirated copy of Fontographer can be a "font designer." It's time for someone to say, "The friggin' emperor's got no friggin' clothes on!" Nonetheless, graphic designers can't seem to get enough of these fonts. It's apparently related to the fact that in our Jet Ski society, no one can get enough novelty to satisfy that *itch,* that craving for the next one. And since our visual circuits are so overloaded with snap, crackle, and buzz, people don't even notice letters anymore, unless they jog our deepest reptile-brain fears of death and decay.

A bicycle ad in the *Chicago Reader* is lettered in a decaying, crumbling font, generating a deep subconscious response in me that says, "These letters represent some kind of danger. I'd better pay attention." As if they've just been run over by an eighteen-wheeler, and I'm still in the middle of the highway. And of course, with the hundreds of millions of dollars spent, since the earliest days of advertising, on detailed psychological research to determine exactly what makes people buy, we can be sure that these fonts have caught the attention of the marketing people, who see their vast potential.

"The grunge face Burner has been accused of being illegible, but this feature is built in intentionally. Graffiti as an artform is a way of expressing your message to those who will care to read it. Many of the pieces seen on subways and the like are overlooked every day by people who do not care to take the time to read. Burner allows the reader to become part of the message by forcing him or her to understand the type in order to get the message."

—*http://users.aol.com/penultimate/chroma.html*

The wave of trash type and grunge "typography" is just that—a wave. The sound of it crashing on the beach of long-term typographic structure is not the sound of the whole beach being washed away. There is nothing more pretentious, to my view, than the designers (or worse, the purveyors) of trash type claiming that their wares are responsible for "changing the nature of legibility." For as in language, while the styles and vernacular shift with the seasons, the underlying grammar and structure change very slowly indeed.

The question, at this juncture, seems rather to be whether there's any lasting value to the "new typography." In fact, as graphic design is really a fashion industry, one can't dispute that the new tools have widely broadened the palette for typographic designers. But there seems to be an unfortunate paucity of brilliant, clear hues. Instead, we are faced with an overabundance of murky industrial corruptions and mutations rendered mechanically possible by Fontographer. I suppose it really comes down to simple Newtonian (Isaac, that is) physics, where it is noted that it's much harder to create order than to create chaos. Chaos is the inevitable expression of the loss of order.

In our typographic universe, sociological and personal chaos find expression in letterforms often artlessly drawn and mechanically rendered. Of course, there are exceptions, and if you browse through the list of foundries at Chris MacGregor's online font foundries Web page *(http://users.aol.com/typeindex/)*, you will find among the chaff some remarkable and useful designs being produced by small font offices around the world.

The nature of typographic design will change more in the next eighteen months than it has since the birth of printing, as design for online environments becomes more widespread and its strengths and limitations are tested and developed. The Web browser is the new "codex"—somewhere between a scroll and a folio, it challenges designers to think in a new dimension. The technological discussion about online fonts is starting to take shape, and unfortunately, it is again an afterthought, arriving after the camel has left the corral. However, the inclusion of some form of designer control over on-screen fonts is inevitable, and with it considerations of moving type, random type, hyper-spaced type. Through it all, the underlying issues of proportion, structure, and legibility will remain.

Good typography is in no danger of disappearing on the Net. Clear visual signs are a highly developed and widely understood method of message transmission, and if a typeface doesn't serve this purpose, it will quickly evaporate. There will always be market forces seeking to bypass the rational mind with the use of jumbled and degenerate typography, but it seems the argument is not with type design, but, indeed, with consumerism. However, if the folks in Puget Sound win their battle, there may still be hope, and with it, the potential for a rebirth of quiet places in the world, and a return to clarity, elegance, and skillful drawing in typography and type design by the turn of the millennium.

From *AIGA Journal of Graphic Design* 14, no. 3 (1996).

American Gothic

By Rick Poynor

he process by which particular typefaces come to embody the look, mood, and aspirations of a period is mysterious and fascinating. It cannot be predicted with any accuracy and no single designer can will it to happen, but somehow a typeface will look fresh, unexpected, precisely attuned to the moment—and a consensus emerges. Eventually, with repeated applications in less and less appropriate contexts, the face becomes exhausted, incapable of inducing the required *frisson* and falls into disuse, until such time (it may well never happen) when it is revived.

In Britain, such a fate has overtaken the angular post-constructivist type designs of Neville Brody, Zuzana Licko, and Max Kisman. By a curious paradox (helped along in Brody's case by himself) these faces, once so urgently new, are judged less "contemporary" than san serif stalwarts that one might have supposed to be irredeemably passé.

Now, just a year or two into the 1990s, comes a typeface so far removed from the unbending geometries of the 1980s that it evokes an authentic sense of what the art critic Robert Hughes called "the shock of the new." The uses it has found give a good sense of flavor—from the soundtrack album for Wim Wenders's new science fiction film *Until the End of the World,* to a flyer announcing a season called *Towards the Aesthetic of the Future* at London's Institute of Contemporary Arts.

Template Gothic, designed by CalArts graduate Barry Deck, might set a boffin-like brow towards the future, but it also maintains an affectionate toehold on the past. Tony Arefin, a British designer who was one of the first to use the face, compares its effect to the street market/super-building contrasts of *Blade Runner:* "It has a mixture of low-tech with high-tech." The low-tech, we know from Deck's account, comes from the typeface's origins in a stencilled sign he saw in his local laundromat. On this level, he suggests, it is a "homage to the vernacular." The irregular, tapering strokes, thickened junctions, inconsistent weight and lopsided rhythm combine to suggest letters afflicted by what the designer calls the "distortive ravages of photomechanical reproduction." Created digitally with the type design program Fontographer, the face embodies a post-modern narrative on the methods of character-generation it supersedes.

Template Gothic's "high-tech," too, is impeccably post-modern. This is a playful reminder (and revision) of the future as it was imagined in the 1950s—an organic age of kidney dish-shaped tables from which the straight line and the right angle have been expelled. These are fuzzy forms—suggestively vague rather than robotically exact—to match the dawning era of fuzzy logic. Deliberately "imperfect," though oddly lucid, Template Gothic is sufficiently malleable to withstand the most casual designs. There is no way of knowing how it will look in five years' time, let alone fifty. For now it is one of the most interesting and original new faces we have.

From *Eye* (June 1992).

Anatomy: Understanding Typefaces

Adobe Garamond: A New Adaptation of a Sixteenth-Century Type

By Jerry Kelly

hough often questioned, the practice of adapting early types for contemporary use has been quite common during the past century. The revival of the art of fine printing begun by William Morris in 1891 and continued by C. H. St. John Hornby at the Ashendene Press (established 1894) and T. J. Cobden-Sanderson and Emery Walker at the Doves Press (established 1900) emulated the qualities of the best early printed books— all-rag handmade paper and gutsy handpress printing— while copying or adapting of some of the best letterforms of the fifteenth century. The second wave of modern fine printers—Updike, Rogers, Meynell, Morison, Mardersteig, and others—allowed machine printing and some machine-made paper to enter into the equation, but on the whole still favored modern revivals of earlier typefaces.

By the late 1920s, however, fine printers began to use some modern designs: Updike installed Jan van Krimpen's Lutetia type in 1927 and Stanley Morison's Times New Roman in 1939; Burce Rogers also used Lutetia, as well as Goudy Newstyle and other modern fonts; Meynell employed a wide variety of newer types, including Perpetua, Goudy Modern, Times New Roman, Lutetia, and others.

Particularly important to the aesthetic values of twentieth-century typography is the work of Stanley Morison at the British Monotype Corporation (not to be confused with the American Lanston Monotype Corporation). Morison was retained by the firm in 1922. He began a programme of revivals of historic types, the first of which was a so-called Garamond. Some of the revivals were quite unheralded at the time, such as Poliphilus (originally cut in 1499 and recut by Monotype in 1923) and Bembo (first cut in 1495 and recut in 1929). New types were also commissioned by Monotype, including Perpetua, issued in 1929, and Times New Roman, issued in 1932.

Occasionally, some typographers have questioned the use of historic resources for modern purposes. Jan van Krimpen wrote, "I need hardly say here once more that I am no friend of copying or even adapting historical typefaces."[1] Hermann Zapf has expressed similar views on this point, saying that "we need new concepts, not historical copies."[2] Early in his career, Jan Tschichold went so far as to say that the modern sans serif style is "so simple and clear that it is by far the best all-purpose type for today and will remain so for a long time to come."[3]

Yet all three of these great typographers used historical revivals to some extent. Jan van Krimpen was deeply involved in Monotype's revival of the Van Dijck type;[4] an impressive twenty-seven of the one hundred book designs Hermann Zapf selected for inclusion in his bibliography use a historical revival as the main text type;[5] and Jan Tschichold eventually reversed his earlier statements, writing in 1952 that "the only really good types are those that have stayed close to the major incarnations of the classical patterns."[6]

Quibus principiis pofitis, deorum ethnicorum numina ita traducit, vt
ex fcintillæ illius fulgore patrias tenebras animaduertiffe omnino vi-

*dũ typographici correctoris munus meditarer) neque,fi facere licuiffet,mar-
go capere quæ addenda erant potuiffet. Quinetiã contingebat interdum vt*

Quibus principiis pofitis, deorum ethnicorum numina ita traducit, vt
ex fcintillæ illius fulgore patrias tenebras animaduertiffe omnino vi-

*du typographici correctoris munus meditarer) neque ,fi facere licuiffet ,mar-
go capere quæ addenda erant potuiffet. Quinetia contingebat interdum vt*

Quibus principiis pofitis, deorum ethnicorum numina ita traducit, vt
ex fcintillæ illius fulgore patrias tenebras animaduertiffe omnino vi-

*du typographici correct oris munus meditarer) neque, fi facere licuiffet, mar-
go capere quæ addenda erant potuiffet. Quinetia contingebat interdum vt*

Quibus principiis pofitis, deorum ethnicorum numnia ita traducit, vt
ex feintillaeillius fulgore patrias tenebras animaduertiffe omnino vi-

*du typographici correct oris munus meditarer) neqve, fi facere licuiffet, mar-
go capere quoe addenda erant potuiffet. Quinetia contingebat interdum vt*

A comparison with the original of various roman and italic types based on Garamond or Jannon. FIRST AND SECOND BLOCKS: the
Parangonne of the Stephanus Plato; THIRD AND FOURTH BLOCKS: Adobe Garamond; FIFTH AND SIXTH BLOCKS: Sabon; SEVENTH AND
EIGHTH BLOCKS: Monotype Goudy Garamont, series 248.

Type Revivals

This is not the place to discuss the relative merits of reviving historic types. Suffice it to
say that a survey of the typographic arts of this century proves that historical revivals are
here to stay—and among the historic types, none has inspired more modern versions than
the roman fonts of Claude Garamond. In this century, his types have been the design
model for "Garamond" fonts from ATF, Deberny & Peignot, British Monotype, Stempel,
Ollière, Mergenthaler Linotype, Ludlow, Simonici, Typoart, and ITC, as well as Lanston
Monotype's Garamont, Mergenthaler Linotype's Granjon and Estienne, and Sabon. The
latest addition to the line is Adobe Garamond.

The evolution of the Garamond design model is fascinating and complex. In 1926
Beatrice Warde, writing under the pseudonym Paul Beaujon, published one of the most
important articles in twentieth-century type studies. In "The 'Garamond' Types: Sixteenth
& Seventeenth Century Sources Considered,"[7] she definitively proved that most of the
modern types then claiming Garamond's fonts as a direct model were in fact based on
Jean Jannon's early seventeenth-century types. Ironically, Warde concluded that George W.
Jones's Linotype Granjon—which didn't even bear the "Garamond" appellation—most
closely emulated the sixteenth-century orginal. Stempel's Garamond was called "a pleas-
ant and practical old-face" marred only by its truncated descenders,[8] which Giovanni
Mardersteig later had lengthened.[9]

Since Warde's review of nine Garamond revivals, many others have appeared, including Jan Tschichold's Sabon and Tony Stan's ITC Garamond. Sabon, which in its foundry version first appeared in the 1966 Trajanus Presse edition of *Tristan und Isolde,* is notable for going back to the original Garamond for its inspiration. It eschewed Jannon's mannerisms which had become so deeply associated with the "Garamond" name, but was severely influenced by some unusual technical restraints: a group of German master printers had commissioned Tschichold to design a type which would be identical in its Monotype, Linotype, and foundry versions—a typographic first.[10] The design therefore had to conform to the Linotype machine's inability to cast overhanging letters (or, in the terminology of metal type, "kerns"), had to have an italic of identical width to the roman, and had to conform to the Monotype machine's eighteen-unit width system. In addition, modern printing equipment and size ranges called for more open counters and generous widths of individual letters, resulting in a lowercase *a* in composition sizes which Garamond would not recognize as his own. It is a shame that the more elegant *a* drawn by Tschichold for 14-point and larger sizes was not adopted in any of the various phototype versions. It is illustrated on page 155 of Alexander Lawson's *Anatomy of a Typeface.*[11] Incorrectly labeled Linotype Sabon, it is actually the more elegant and historically accurate foundry version. The Tschichold drawing for the larger foundry sizes also retains many of the other nuances and niceties of the sixteenth-century model which make it far superior to the smaller sizes; note, for example, the elegant ear on the *r,* the narrow *s,* and the more generous descenders and refined drawing of the capital *M, R,* and *T.* The figures are among the most elegant ever issued.

While there is much to praise in Sabon roman, there is little relationship between its italic and either Garamond's or Granjon's sixteenth-century italic fonts. The limitations of Linotype's duplex matrix system, where a lowercase italic *o* or *a* must match the width of a roman lowercase *o* or *a,* were too much for even so skilled a typographer as Tschichold to overcome. Again, the phototype companies procured the text-size version of Sabon italic instead of adapting the design for 14-point or larger, which is far better. Still, even the larger italic is far from its ancestry, and the lack of a tail on the *j* and *f* was a technical concession that would have been unnecessary in photocomposition.

Such criticisms aside, Sabon remains an excellent type based on Garamond's work. Tschichold was on the right track in ignoring other revivals and going back directly to the sixteenth-century original, but the technical limitations of late metal machine composition were a tremendous hindrance to authenticity.

In contrast, ITC's Garamond is an aberration of Jannon's aberration of Garamond's types. Generally speaking, most of the photocomposition "Garamonds" are slavish copies—technical limitations, misdrawings and all—of metal copies of Jannon's copies of Garamond's types. They are so many generations removed that little, if anything, of the original design is left. They would be unrecognizable to any sixteenth-century printer familiar with the types of Garamond.

It was left to Robert Slimbach and Adobe Corporation to go back directly to proofs of the authentic Garamond types and redraw them for the Postscript digital format. The result is what I would unequivocally rate as the closest replica of the sixteenth-century original ever made. No other Garamond-inspired type comes as close in proportion, refinement of drawing, evenness of fit, and general elegance of appearance.

ABCDEFGHIJKLMNOPQ
RSTUVWXYZÄÖÜ
abcdefghijklmnopqrstuvwxyz
ßchckfffflfft&äöü
1234567890 1234567890

The Stempel foundry version of 36-point Sabon (metal type), reduced here. The drawings of the larger sizes of foundry Sabon are quite different from the text sizes.

An enlargement of a letterpress specimen of Garamond's original Vraye Parangonne roman type, under which Robert Slimbach has made drawings for Adobe Garamond. (From a reproduction in the Adobe Garamond specimen book.)

Slimbach astutely anchored his Garamond design to the 1592 specimen sheet of the Egenolff foundry, which displays several sizes of Garamond's types; of those, Slimbach chose the *Parangonne* for his model.[12] The decision to use a sixteenth-century source was made despite the fact that occasionally in this century authentic Garamond sorts have been cast from the original (albeit incomplete) matrices which survive at the Plantin-Moretus Museum in Antwerp. Showings of modern castings appear in *The Journal of the Printing Historical Society 1* (1965), H. D. L. Vervliet's *Sixteenth Century Printing Types of the Low Countries,* and elsewhere.[13]

These modern proofs show the type sharper and leaner than Claude Garamond would have anticipated—or desired. Far more ink was required to print metal type with crude sixteenth-century presses onto irregular handmade paper than is needed with our modern

The 1592 Egenolff-Berner specimen sheet showing types by Garamond, Granjon, and others.

cylinder presses and evenly formed, machine-made paper. Garamond would have taken the anticipated "ink squeeze" into account when cutting his punches, thereby cutting them thinner than he wanted the finished strokes to appear. Had Slimbach based his design on these modern, perfectly printed proofs, the result would have been a typeface that was too thin.

Optical Scaling

In metal type manufacturing, new molds or matrices needed to be made for every size of type to be cast. Once a typefounder created the matrices for, say, a 10-point font, there was no possibility of casting 12-point or even 11-point type from those mats unless one wished to cast the same size letter on a different body size. Since new punches or matrices were required for each size, punch-cutters would subtly adjust the letterforms for dif-

quickly margins of error widen unless

quickly margins of error widen unless

The top line shows Monotype Bembo (metal type) 18-point, actual size, from the Monotype desk specimen book. The line below shows 8-point Monotype Bembo (metal type) from the same source enlarged to the same line width. Note the wider proportions, heavier stroke and serif width, and shorter descenders.

Caslon's   a g s

Caslon's   a g s

A comparison of 36- and 48-point Caslon, both metal foundry versions cast from the original matrices. Note the vast differences in the drawing of the "same" typeface.

ferent sizes in an effort to create the most beautiful and legible type possible. Smaller types would be slightly wider, with heavier hairlines and serifs and more open counters. The larger sizes could have longer ascenders and descenders and more refined drawing that incorporated nuances which would be lost in the smaller sizes.

The idea of taking one "design" or ideal shape of each letter and optically adapting it for various sizes, i.e., forming one unvarying style in a range of sizes, is a relatively new one. Early punch-cutters, Garamond included, would cut a Cicero to a specific style they had in mind, and then go on to cut a Gros Romain to what might have been a somewhat different ideal. Over the course of years that ideal may have varied, and even two types cut back-to-back were sometimes in quite a different vein. Types made by a particular punch-cutter had inevitable similarities due to the fact that they were cut by the same hand, just as there are certain similarities among Goudy's types, or Dwiggins's, or van Krimpen's—or, for that matter, Matisse's paintings, or Klee's. The practice of rendering a range of scaled sizes from one model is a relatively new phenomenon, and it was not the goal of Garamond or Granjon or Griffo. Even as late as William Caslon's types, or Walbaum's roman, there are differences between sizes which clearly derive from something other than a concern for optical scaling. Surely a type manufacturer with Caslon's skills and standards did not cut a 36-point *a* so different from that in the 48-point size while trying to make them the same. (Compare also the 36-point *R* to the 30-point, the 18-point *C* with the serifs top and bottom and the 16-point version with only a top serif, etc.)

In Claude Garamond's time each size was cut in what we today would call an individual style. Only in modern times did the idea take hold of cutting one style, such as Bembo, in a wide range of sizes. We have become so used to having a complete range of sizes available to us that we take it for granted; indeed, it is a necessity for any typeface to succeed today. With few exceptions, when metal typefounders created a series of one style they optically compensated for different sizes by creating several slightly modified master drawings. Goudy's later types, which he cut pantographically from his own hand-cut patterns,[14] often followed only one master pattern and suffered accordingly. The British Monotype Corporation used different drawings for every two point sizes, and the Stempel foundry in Frankfurt most often used three distinct drawings for one style—one for 12-point and below, one for 14- to 24-point, and one for the larger sizes.

¶ Quis credidit Auditui noſtro: uelatum eſt, Et aſcendit ſicut virgult

The largest size of Garamond's roman types shown in the 1592 Egenolff specimen. Note the thinness of the type and the extremely long ascenders and descenders.

In the early days of photocomposition, a similar three-master system was tested. Due to time, increased error factor, and expense, it did not catch on. If "Joe's Type" could photo-set Garamond for $15 a page from one master, but "Dave's Type" charged $17 a page for using three masters, Dave would probably get less work than Joe. Similarly, Dave's night foreman might have forgotten that the daytime crew left the 12-point master in the machine when he had a job to set in 24-point, thereby creating an inferior job that would not match Dave's other 24-point composition. With the new generation of digital composition computers, it would be desirable if a preprogrammed "multiple-master" system could scale type optically and automatically "on the fly." Even so, the inevitable slight additional cost would still be present, and who could say if the marketplace would bear that cost in return for the extra quality.

For the past few decades, one master has been the norm for computer composition. Some successful types have been created taking one size of a sixteenth-century design and creating a single master for use in digitally generated multiple sizes. Matthew Carter's Galliard design is directly based on Robert Granjon's Gros Cicero type of around 1560.[15] The italic is based on Granjon's unusual Ascendonica—one of his most unique italics, bearing little relationship to the other sizes he cut.

For his roman model, Slimbach chose the Vraye Parangonne (or approximately 18-point) size in the 1592 Egenolff-Berner specimen. It is one of six romans on that sheet attributed to Garamond, the others being designated "Granjon." All of the Garamond types shown on this specimen are probably from his mature period.[16] The Vraye Parangonne is one of his finest roman types and one of his last; it was followed only by a titling font he did not complete before his death in 1561. Garamond's larger types— approximately 30-point and above—have a thinness which was in vogue in the sixteenth century, but would not translate well into smaller sizes. Since his smaller types—12-point and below—would inevitably be most distorted by the primitive presswork of his time, the medium range of sizes—the Parangonne, Gros Text, and St. Augustin—would serve best as models for modern adaptation. Of these, Garamond's Parangonne roman is as good, if not better, than the others. Mixing forms from assorted sizes would have been unwise since, as discussed above, Garamond did not look on these fonts as different sizes of one "design," but as unique expressions of the roman letterform.

It is possible to criticize certain details of Adobe Garamond. While the *g* is pleasant enough, a more open-countered, accurate form could be rendered; the shading of the upper left of the *e* is slightly too light; some of the italic swashes would have been better omitted (we do not need a swash variant for every majuscule). Nonetheless, Adobe Garamond is the most accurate derivation of Claude Garamond's types done to date and a significant addition to the world's typographical resources. In fact, some of the face's less immediately obvious features contribute substantially to its beauty and utility, and bear discussion.

Special Fonts

In the 1960s, '70s, and '80s there was a marked decline in the number of types available with old-style figures and genuine small caps. This decline actually started over a century ago, but accelerated—probably due to some shortsighted economic rationale—in the last thirty years. Modern figures have become so commonplace that just recently an accomplished designer asked me if Bodoni had ever cut old-style figures; ironically, Bodoni only cut old-style figures and never cut modern lining figures. John Bell issued the first modern figures in 1788.[17] They were not universally accepted by any means, but have proven a useful addition to the printer's resources. Many types cut in this century, whether revivals of historic designs which did not originally have modern figures (i.e., Bembo, Garamond, Janson, Bodoni, and Baskerville) or new designs, offered both modern and old style figures. In time, founders and machine composition companies began to sell modern figures with their fonts by default, only offering old-style figures by special request (i.e., ATF Garamond, Bauer Bodoni, Palatino, etc.). With Hermann Zapf's Optima type, old-style figures were drawn and cut in one size but never issued.[18]

True small caps, with weight, proportion, height, and serifs designed to harmonize with the lowercase, also suffered a decline in the last few decades. While Zapf's Palatino, released in 1950, had small caps available, his other types, including Optima and Melior, did not. In the phototype era, techniques were devised to photographically alter the width and size of a font's capital letters, but this created a poor substitute for true small caps.

Adobe Systems includes both old-style figures and small caps in its "Expert" collections (available at additional cost). It is to be commended for offering these and other typographical niceties for many of its fonts.

If small caps and old-style figures are a rarity in today's type market, titling fonts are practically unheard of. In metal type, the presence of the shoulder below the baseline—necessary on both capital and lowercase letters to leave room for the descenders—made it difficult to use the capital letters from a font for initial letters: the shoulder would often not allow the line below to fit closely enough. Either the shoulder could be filed or sawed off—making that piece of type difficult to use next time it was set in a regular line of text—or special sorts could be cast on a smaller body without the shoulder. These special fonts were called titling types, since they were intended for use as titles or initials only, not for text composition.

It was possible to take the capitals from a regular font and cast them on a smaller body to create a titling font, as with Caslon Titling, or a new drawing could be made specifically for an all-cap alphabet, as was the case with Dante Titling, Weiss Titling, Castellar, Carolus, Michelangelo, and so on. Augustea is an unusual instance of a type originally cut as a titling series which had a lowercase added later.

For Adobe Garamond, Slimbach has created a titling alphabet slightly lighter in weight, with more delicate serifs. Not surprisingly, the font bears a resemblance to Garamond's Canon capitals. Adobe Garamond Titling is a welcome addition to a designer's typographic palette. It is worth mentioning that these capitals should never be used in the smaller sizes, where they will look weak and the serifs will begin to disappear. Unfortunately, in the Adobe Garamond specimen book, the complete alphabet is only shown in a small size, which makes it appear unattractive.

ABCDEFGHIJKLMNOPQRSTUVWXYZ
abcdefghijklmnopqrstuvwxyz & 0123456789

ABCDEFGHIJKLMNOPQRSTUVWXYZ

1234567890&   0123456789

ABCDEFGHIJKLMNOPQRSTUVWXYZ
&0123456789Æ

ꜳ e rꞧꞇꞇ ꜳ n z Q ꝯꝯ ꝥ

ABCDEFGHIJKLMNOPQRSTUVWXYZ
abcdefghijklmnopqrstuvwxyz
1234567890&

ABCDEFGHIJKLMNOPQRSTUVWXYZ
abcdefghijklmnopqrstuvwxyz
1234567890&

ABCDEFGHIJKLMNOPQRSTUVWXYZ
abcdefghijklmnopqrstuvwxyz
1234567890&

ABCDEFGHIJKLMNOPQ
RSTUVWXYZ&ctstv

A display for some of the fonts released in the Adobe Garamond family. From top to bottom: roman capitals, miniscule, and modern figures; true small capitals, old-style roman and italic figures; titling capitals and figures; swash roman sorts and ornaments; italic capitals, miniscule and figures; simi-bold roman, simi-bold italic; and swash italic capitals.

The use of historical models for typefaces has been common in this century. Several types survive as punches or matrices in their original form. The earliest of these is proba- bly a roman of the fifteenth or sixteenth century presently in the archives of the Enschedé typefoundry.[19] Among other punches still in existence are those for the so- called Janson series, Baskerville, Bell, and Caslon. In addition to these types, many others have been "recreated" in the twentieth century: Jenson's, in the form of Cloister, Eusebius, and Centaur; Griffo's romans, as Poliphilus, Bembo, and Griffo; Granjon's, as Plantin and Galliard; and Garamond's, to name just a few. Even when we are fortunate enough to have extant punches for early types, these designs often require modification to meet the technical requirements of modern printing equipment and typecasting meth- ods, particularly machine composition, which imposes myriad technical requirements on letterforms. With digital composition and offset lithography the changes in reproduction are far greater than before, while the flexibility of photocomposition frees typefaces from many of the restraints of metal typography.

et tu reuerſi ſumus ; ut de Aetnae incendi- is interrogaremus ab iis, quibus notum eſt illa nos ſatis diligenter perſpexiſſe ; ut ea tandem moleſtia careremus; placuit mi hi eum ſermonem conſcribere´ ; quem cum Bernardo parente habui paucis poſt	tu reuersi sumus; ut de Aetnae incendi- is interrogaremus ab iis, quibus notum est illa nos satis diligenter perspexisse; ut ea tandem molestia careremus; placuit mihi eum sermonem conscribere; quem cum Bernardo parente habui paucis post

A reproduction from the Aldine edition of Bembo's *De Aetna* (1495) and the same lines set in Monotype Bembo. (From the Officina Bodoni of *De Aetna* (1967).

It has become apparent that revivals of earlier types are here to stay, and why not? As long as types are handsome, useful, and adaptable to modern printing, we should welcome them. Neither should we discourage original type designs, which are as much an expression of our own time as Garamond's were to his. The fact that we can enjoy Shakespeare today doesn't mean we should cease to create new literature; conversely, we should not stop reading Shakespeare just because new books are being published. In the same way, fine new types and historical revivals can happily continue to flourish side by side.

Whenever a letter based on a historic source is redrawn, particularly when it must conform to specific technical requirements, its contours need to be adapted. The first decision is the selection of a model on which to base the new version—a decision that can always be called into question. Many more decisions follow which can be decided in any number of ways. It's a familiar story: if you have five different type designers in a room, they would probably render five different Garamond Parangonnes. It is interesting to note that one of the most successful modern revivals, Monotype Bembo,[20] strays relatively far from its model, Griffo's 1495 roman for Aldus Manutius. The fact that it is far from an exacting copy of the original does not make Bembo a less successful font; it may even be a more useful type because of the changes made from the Renaissance model.

With Adobe Garamond, Robert Slimbach has recreated Garamond's Parangon roman and one of Granjon's italics. (The combining of Garamond's roman with Granjon's italic has become standard.) Slimbach has captured the flavor of the true Garamond type better than any of the adaptations made to date. Adobe Garamond is a valuable addition to today's type repertoire, and it is already enjoying widespread popularity for a variety of uses from fine books to ephemeral advertisements.

[1]Jan van Krimpen, "On Preparing Designs for Monotype Faces" *Matrix* 11 (1991): p. iii of insert facing p. 128.

[2]Hermann Zapf, *Hermann Zapf and his Design Philosophy* (Chicago: Society for Typographic Arts, 1987), 39.

[3]Jan Tschichold, *Asymmetric Typography* (New York: Rheinhold Publishing Co., 1967), 28.

[4]See Jan van Krimpen, *On Designing and Devising Type* (New York: The Typophiles, 1957).

[5]Hermann Zapf, *Ein Arbeitsbericht* (Hamburg: Maximilian Gesellschaft, 1984), 84–114.

[6]Jan Tschichold, *The Form of the Book* (Point Roberts, Wash.: Hartley & Marks, 1991), 16.

[7]Beatrice Warde, "The 'Garamond' Types: Sixteenth & Seventeenth Century Sources Considered" *Fleuron* 5 (1926): 131–79.

[8]Warde, 176.

[9]*Specimens* (New York: Stevens-Nelson Paper Co., n.d.), SN90.

[10]Ruari McLean, *Jan Tschichold: Typographer* (Boston: David R. Godine, 1975), 114.

[11]Alexander Lawson, *Anatomy of a Typeface* (Boston: David R. Godine, 1990), 155.

[12]*Adobe Garamond* (Mountain View, Calif.: Adobe Systems, Inc., 1989), 6–7.

[13]H. D. L. Vervliet, *Sixteenth Century Printing Types of the Low Countries* (Amsterdam: Menno Hertzberger & Co., 1968), 66.

[14]Frederic W. Goudy, *Typologia* (Berkeley: University of California Press, 1940), 98.

[15]Matthew Carter, "Galliard: A Modern Revival of the Types of Robert Granjon," *Visible Language* 19 (Winter 1985): 77–97.

[16]John Dreyfus, ed., *Type Specimen Facsimilies 1* (London: Bowes & Bowes and Putnam, 1963), 3.

[17]Stanley Morison, *John Bell* (Cambridge: Printed for the author at the University Press, 1930), 18.

[18]See numbering of notes in Hermann Zapf's *Manuale Typographicum* (Frankfurt: Z-Presse, 1968) for showing of Optima old-style figures.

[19]See *A Roman Type of the XVth Century* (Haarlem: Enschedé, 1926).

[20]*A Miscellany of Type* (Andoversford, Eng.: The Whittington Press, 1990), 124.

Modern Style with a Human Face

By John D. Berry

 obert Slimbach has taken on one of the harder tasks in type design: making a text type in the modern style. The result is his latest Adobe typeface, named for the seventeenth-century astronomer Johannes Kepler.

"My intention with Kepler," says Slimbach, "was to make a practical and expansive multiple-master typeface family, one that retained the structure of modern style forms, but with a humanistic tone." By humanizing his modern design with calligraphic details and carefully modeled strokes throughout, he has taken the essentially rational structure of a modern face and given it a bright friendliness that only a few modern types have achieved before. (The results are visible all around you in this magazine, which has adopted Kepler as its text face beginning with this issue.)

Kepler is not Slimbach's first foray into designing a modern typeface, but there's no doubt that it's his most successful. Slimbach is a talented calligrapher and a student of typographic history who delights in using this background to create digital type that speaks in a full range of voices, including the quiet, unalloyed voice of straight text. As one of the core type designers at Adobe, Slimbach has also designed Adobe Garamond and Utopia, the versatile Minion and Jenson, the calligraphic Poetica, Sanvito, and Caflisch Script, and, collaborating with Carol Twombly, the generically useful sans serif Myriad. You can see a lot of similarities between Kepler and his earlier Utopia typeface, but Kepler is rounder, more open, and it flows better in text.

"Modern" in typography doesn't mean new; it means a style that evolved in the late eighteenth century, new compared to the "old style" roman types of previous centuries. Modern typefaces were drawn and cut at the end of the Enlightenment, in the era of revolution, reflecting not only new technologies in printing but also the neoclassical trappings of Napoleon's Imperial France. The most famous designers of modern types were Bodoni in Italy and the Didot family in France; their types, in one form or another, are still in use today.

Modern typefaces have an almost architectural structure, with a vertical stress (rather than the oblique stress of old style type, which came from the angle of the hand while writing with a broad-nibbed pen) and a great deal more contrast between the thick lines and the thin lines within each letter. The most severe of the modern faces, especially those of Firmin Didot, have serifs with no curve at all joining them to the letter's stem: just a straight line athwart the end of the stroke. With enough space around them, as in the famous typographic manual of Giambattista Bodoni, these letters can look exceptionally elegant: cool, graceful, technically precise, and very regular in their arrangement.

Denied the space they need, however, modern typefaces lose all their elegance, looking cramped, confusing, like a tangled thicket. Because so many of the upright strokes are heavy and thick, while many of the horizontals and curves are light and thin, the reader's eye picks out the uprights first, and a badly spaced line of modern type can look like a picket fence. This is a built-in problem with modern typefaces, even the less rigorous, more homey and friendly ones like Bell and Bulmer.

Slimbach brought his calligraphic experience to bear on the problem. "For all the precision I intended with Kepler," says Slimbach in an essay in the specimen book that accompanies the fonts, "I didn't want to make a type that was mechanical looking." He began by sketching out alphabets on paper, trying out different possibilities. "I gave the roman letters a slightly technical appearance, as with traditional modern-style alphabets, but with a graceful quality reminiscent of written forms. By softening harsh features and giving the letters a hint of old-style proportion and calligraphic detailing, I was able to give the typeface added warmth." He then created an italic that would harmonize with the roman but stand out from it for emphasis. "The italic lowercase has a mix of angular and soft features, along with a substantial slope, which gives it a dynamic quality." Once the sketches were done, he scanned and digitized them. Then began more than a year of testing, refining, and extending the fonts into the full multiple-master ranges of weight, width, and optical size.

While Slimbach wanted to soften Kepler and make it lively, he had to keep a tight rein on his calligraphic exuberance so that he wouldn't compromise Kepler's usefulness as a text face. "A typeface intended for continuous reading shouldn't have eccentric elements that draw attention away from the author's message," Slimbach says. Kepler's calligraphic aspects are subtle: a slightly tapered stem here, a flick of an italic serif there. It speaks in an even, technical voice, but with a lilt. The shape of the letters is round and sturdy, even in the steeply sloping italic. The counters are open, even in the heaviest weights. At the tiniest text sizes, Kepler still has a distinctive character.

Slimbach used the possibilities of multiple-master technology to give Kepler an enormous possible range of typographic expression. The width and the weight axis both extend very far: from condensed to extended in width, and from light to black in weight. Those alone would create a wide range of variation, but the optical-size axis adds another dimension by giving you size variants from the sparkling 72-point master all the way down to a stoutly legible 5-point master. The delicate hairlines of this modern design stand out at display sizes, but when you use the face at text sizes—using an instance of the optical-size axis in the text range—the hairlines are thickened a bit, just as they would be in metal type, for optimum reading. The letters also get a little wider, and a little more widely spaced, at the smallest optical sizes. Since you can also control the width of the letters through the width axis, you can create any combination of sturdiness and width that you like.

The lightest weights show the typeface's character most strongly, because the bright "action" of the curves and stems is less complicated by the swelling and narrowing of the thick and thin strokes. Condensed widths maintain their legibility surprisingly well, never looking cramped at text sizes. Only the extended width starts to look a little extreme; it's hard to imagine using the extended instances for text, although for a few words of display, or for a few very long lines of text at large sizes, they might work fine. Because the shape of the counters changes as the width increases, extended versions of Kepler need a little more leading than narrower ones. The vertical counters of the narrow letters contrast with the horizontal white space between lines, making it easy to read them, but the more horizontal counters of the wide letters blend in with the visual space between the lines.

Kind Face

Here's a sample of Kepler's 535 weight, 575 width, and 72 optical size, set at 72 points.

Along with the regular roman and italic, Slimbach has given Kepler a full set of swash italic caps, plus a slightly modified lower case, with simplified upper serifs on some letters. While too many of the swash caps have identical swashes (which defeats their intent), some, like the *A* and *M,* are quite distinctive.

Although Kepler is obviously intended as a text face suitable to a broad range of uses, it's quite distinctive in display, too. The refinements of the optical-size axis make Kepler sparkle as a display face. Try a very large display size (condensed if need be) in a fairly light weight to accompany normal-weight text.

In addition to letters, the Kepler type family includes a huge collection of type ornaments. There are, in fact, three separate fonts just for ornaments: one of fleurons and swashes, one of geometric patterns, and one of abstract floral and leaf-like designs with a few more geometric patterns thrown in for good measure. Most of these ornaments are meant to fit together as borders or solid tapestries.

Kepler is a big typeface—technically as well as typographically. It comes on several disks, and when you install it, it takes up a lot of real estate on your font menu. Like Adobe Jenson, Kepler uses more advanced technology than earlier multiple-master fonts, so it requires the latest (or near-latest) versions of software like ATM (Adobe Type Manager) and Adobe's downloader utility. These are included with the fonts.

Running the installer is easy, and it ensures that you've got the latest software on your system. It's slightly annoying, though, since the installer automatically puts the fonts where it thinks they should be (on the Mac, it installs them in the Fonts folder inside the System Folder, which may not be where you want them if you're using a font-management utility such as Suitcase or Master Juggler). In addition, the installer forces you to restart your system—and if you're installing both Kepler and Kepler Expert, that means restarting twice.

Since Kepler has so many possible variations, not all of the ones you might expect to be pre-built as primary fonts are. (Primary fonts are the variants that come ready to use and that correspond to traditional weights and styles: for instance, Semibold or Regular Condensed. You can have a perfectly usable font family by sticking to nothing but the primary fonts, never creating your own custom instances.) The primary fonts in Kepler are mostly different weights in the normal width at the 10-point optical size, which are very useful for text; they also include the regular weight of the normal width at 72-point optical size, for display, plus condensed and extended versions at 10-point size.

In some ways, the freedom of digital type design, and especially that of multiple-master fonts, is like the freedom that designers of metal type found in copperplate engraving: suddenly the constraints that forced type into narrow channels are gone, and the possibilities become much wider. This freedom made the modern typefaces what they were two hundred years ago, and it makes Robert Slimbach's Kepler what it is today.

From *Adobe Magazine* (Spring 1997).

Mrs. Eaves

By Zuzana Licko

can't remember when I first encountered a type specimen that had been printed by letterpress, or even if this experience preceded my knowledge of phototype technology. However, I do remember vividly, being shocked by the great difference between letterpress type and phototype, especially when comparing specimens of what was supposedly the same typeface design.

What impressed me was not so much the fact that there was a difference; it's expected that different technologies will yield different results. What surprised me was that this difference was so uniquely uniform. Phototype font revivals consistently had an uncanny polished tightness, as though they sought to reproduce the original lead typefaces in some previously unattainable perfection, sometimes with such tight spacing that letters would practically touch; a very difficult task in lead. Perhaps it was their newly-found achievability that made these characteristics desirable at the time. Rarely did designers seek to capture the warmth and softness of letterpress printing that often occurred due to the "gain" of impression and ink spread.

Digital font revivals merely extended the quest for perfection introduced by phototype. This evolution is particularly strange in light of the fact that the development of type manufacturing technology has increased freedom of expression by reducing the mechanical restrictions on the form of type. One might imagine that these technological developments would in fact have also increased the variety of interpretations on the past, instead of reducing them. Ever since then, I have contemplated trying my hand at reviving an "old favorite" in a manner that challenged the common, preconceived method of interpreting the classics.

When selecting a typeface for revival, I recalled reading in various sources that Baskerville's work was severely criticized by his peers and critics throughout his lifetime and after. From personal experience, I could sympathize.

One recurring criticism of Baskerville's type addressed its "sterile" quality. D. B. Updike, in his book *Printing Types of 1922,* wrote, "As we look at Baskerville's specimen-sheets, the fonts appear very perfect, and yet somehow they have none of the homely charm of Caslon's letter. It is true that the types try the eye. Baskerville's contemporaries, who also thought so, attributed this to his glossy paper and dense black ink. Was this the real fault? The difficulty was, I fancy, that in his type-designs the hand of the writing-master betrayed itself, in making them too even, too perfect, too 'genteel,' and so they charmed too apparently and artfully—with a kind of finical, sterile refinement."

Much of the criticism Baskerville received for his work was fueled by type snobbery and professional jealousy, as is illustrated in the following passage from the book *Letters* by James Hutchinson: "There's the story that Benjamin Franklin, in a letter to Baskerville, told him of a practical joke that he, Franklin, had played on a critic of Baskerville's types. The critic said that Baskerville's types would be 'the means of blinding all the readers in the nation owing to the thin and narrow strokes of the letters.' Franklin gave the critic a specimen of Caslon's types with Caslon's name removed, said it was Baskerville's and asked for a specific criticism.

The critic, an author whose book was printed in the same Caslon face, responded at great length about the faults he felt were very apparent in the type. Before he had finished, he complained that his eyes were suffering from the strain of reading the text."

Sadly, because the proliferation, and consequently the assimilation, of new typefaces occurred at a much slower pace in his time than it does today, Baskerville missed the good fortune, which many "envelope-pushing" type designers enjoy today, of having his work appreciated during his lifetime. Baskerville's work has in retrospect been classified as the ultimate transitional typeface, being pivotal between old style typefaces, and the modern typefaces that followed. Similarly, from a practical standpoint, Baskerville has achieved the status of a respected text face consistent with today's reading preferences. This illustrates once again that readers' habits do change in time and are influenced by repeated exposure to particular typefaces, more so than by any measurable physical characteristics of the typefaces themselves.

In my rendition of this classic typeface, I have addressed the highly criticized feature of sharp contrast. To a great degree, the critics were wrong; it did not prevent Baskerville from becoming assimilated as a highly legible text face, and in fact, the high contrast between stems and hairlines became quite desirable, as is apparent in typefaces such as Bodoni, which followed in the lineage. However, the criticism did make me wonder about possible alternatives. Thus, I was prompted to explore the path not taken. After all, the sharp contrast evidenced in Baskerville was new at the time of its creation due to recent developments in printing and paper-making technologies. In his pursuit of "perfect" printing, John Baskerville developed ultra-smooth and brilliant white papers, as well as intensely black printing ink. In fact, as D. B. Updike suggests in the previous quote, the contrast achieved through the use of these papers and inks probably contributed to the criticism of his work more than the design of his typefaces. Ultimately, it may have been merely the fascination of meeting these technical challenges that made this pursuit so desirable at the time, and its proliferation in our era is merely a perpetuation that remains largely unquestioned.

An aspect of Baskerville's type that I intended to retain is that of overall openness and lightness. To achieve this while reducing contrast, I have given the lower case characters a wider proportion. In order to avoid increasing the set-width, I reduced the x-height, relative to the cap-height. Consequently, Mrs. Eaves has the appearance of setting about one point size smaller than the average typeface in lower case text sizes.

I realize that certain aspects of this revival probably contradict Baskerville's intentions, but my point in doing so is to take those elements from Baskerville that have become familiar, and thus highly legible, to today's reader, and to give these my own interpretation of a slightly loose Baskerville that may be reminiscent of a time past.

This typeface is named after Sarah Eaves, the woman who became John Baskerville's wife. As Baskerville was setting up his printing and type business, Mrs. Eaves moved in with him as a live-in housekeeper, eventually becoming his wife after the death of her first husband, Mr. Eaves. Like the widows of Caslon, Bodoni, and the daughters of Fournier, Sarah similarly completed the printing of the unfinished volumes that John Baskerville left upon his death.

From *Émigré Catalogue* (1998).

An Examination of Egyptians

By Ruari McLean

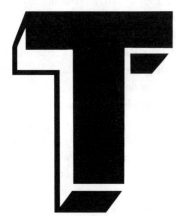

he first definition of the Egyptian letterform appears to be that of the Irishman who is said to have declared in 1806 that the thin strokes of these characters were exactly the same size as the thick ones.[1] Any attempt at a more academic definition might prove merely pedantic and less exact, but we may note that in 1825, soon after the first Egyptian was introduced by English typefounders, Hansard in his weighty *Typographia* opined that the new letterform was "a typographical monstrosity." In our own time the prototype and its many derivatives have met a wide range of critical opinion. The *Fleuron* ignored them. Updike wrote that he agreed with Hansard's century-old opinion (adding a chilling footnote concerning one of the plagues of Egypt.)[1] It has been left to a later critic, less knowledgeable perhaps, but bolder than these authorities, to find merit in the Egyptians. Extravagant virtues, in fact; for, after adjudging the Egyptian face to be "the most brilliant typographic invention of the nineteenth century," Mrs. Nicolette Gray[2] went on to claim that it formed "perhaps the most complete and concise expression of the dominant culture of its brief period; more inspired than contemporary paintings, combining the elegance of the furniture, and the weight of the architecture, and the color and precise romance of Bulwer Lytton."

Vindication indeed for a type so long confined to the æsthetic wilderness!

The origins of the Egyptian letterform are undoubtedly involved with the history of signwriting during the late eighteenth and early nineteenth centuries. Until late in the eighteenth century signwriters had usually based their letterforms upon available type designs. We see the typographical influence of Van Dyck, Caslon, and Baskerville upon fascias, signboards, and other lettered announcements now preserved in town halls, churches, museums, and other buildings. During the early nineteenth century, however, signwriters began to break away from these models and to become more adventurous, particularly in the employment of decorative alphabets. Callingham, in his *Manual of Signwriting*,[3] states that the Egyptian style of lettering was first used by signwriters towards the close of the eighteenth century, and, although generally antipathetic towards letterfounders, he charitably suggests that the initial approach to the Egyptian and the sans serif letterforms might well have been made by Mr. Caslon in 1785, in a font of roman letters, measuring three inches in height.[4] These letters, he claims, were undoubtedly the largest that had ever been made at this period. The thin strokes were enlarged proportionately with the thick, and the type, which was known as thick Roman, would now probably be known as Clarendon. This type, although possibly in part a precursor of the Egyptians, would certainly not now be included within that nomenclature. The actual invention of the letterform cannot definitely be attributed to any one designer, or even to signpainters rather than typefounders, although it was most probably the work of the former.

Two letterforms (actual size) from five (EPSOM) first shown in *A Specimen of Large Letters,* published by William Caslon in 1785, and to which James Callingham attributed the origin of Egyptian types.

Five Lines Pica Antique

Four Lines Pica Antique

Two Lines Small Pica Antique

Two Lines Nonpareil Antique

The first specimens of Egyptians shown by any typefounder.

In 1820 William Thorowgood issued a specimen book showing the state of Robert Thorne's stock at the time of the latter's death earlier that year. This specimen made the first reference to "Egyptian types", and included pages from Thorne's own specimen settings, prepared for issue as a type specimen. The largest size was the six line pica, shown here actual size (compare with the reduction opposite).

In his 1821 specimen Thorowgood showed five pages of Egyptians. These pages are reproduced (much reduced) on this page and below; they included extra sizes cut after Thorne's death, and formed the most comprehensive specimen of Egyptians marketed by any founder at that time. The Egyptian Open specimen was amongst the earliest versions of this popular form of decorated letter.

Egyptian letterforms would certainly come more naturally to the brush than to the chisel, graver, etching-needle or pen; it is also more suitable than most letterforms to be made in wood or to be cast or molded for shop fronts and other architectural uses.

Egyptian types, as we recognize them today, were not introduced by English typefounders until 1815, when Vincent Figgins first showed specimens of four Antique alphabets, all titling, in the following sizes: five-line pica, four-line pica, two-line small pica, and two-line nonpareil. Mrs. Gray mentions a Double Pica Antique and a Shadowed Antique, but these do not appear in the 1815 Figgins' specimen, although a Fat Face Shadowed or Inshade appears on the same page as the Antique innovations. Thorne was credited by contemporary typographic historians (such as Hansard) with having invented Egyptian, as well as the Fat Face, London Jest Book of 1806 mentioned by Updike, and applied to signboard lettering. The first use of the word for slab serif type is probably in Thorne's auction list of 1820. Thorowgood, his successor, was for some time the only founder to use the name. Others called the new letterforms Antique. To add confusion, the early sans serif types were called English Egyptian on their first appearance, in the Wm Caslon IV and Blake, Garnett specimens (1816 and 1819). Sans serif lettering is still called Egyptian by Chancery Lane law writers, as Mr. Morison has observed.[5] Only gradually did the name Egyptian become associated more firmly with slab serifs, and the name Grotesque with sans serifs.

The name Ionic seems to have appeared first in Blake and Stephenson's specimen of 1833 and for some time Ionic was synonymous with Egyptian, but usage has slowly defined Egyptian as a heavy slab-serif letterform with certain differentiations between thick and thing strokes. Ionic, in its smaller sizes, has been a popular newspaper face and was used for the *Times* before the introduction of Times New Roman. Clarendon appears to have been first used as a type name by Besley in 1845, for a type rather similar to Ionic; it survives today as a generic name for bold versions of the Ionic letterform.

Quousque tandem abutere, Catilina, patientia nostra? quamdiu nos etiam furor

ABCDEFGHIJKLMNOPQRSTUVW
ABCDEFGHIJKLMNOPQRSTUVWXYZ
Ionic

ABCDEFGHIJKLMNOPQRSTUVWXYZÆŒ &,;:-'!.
THE DIRECTORS OF THE EAST INDIA COMPANY.
Ionic Open

The Ionic types, introduced by Blake and Stephenson in 1833, bore certain resemblances to the earlier Egyptian types, although there was much greater contrast between stroke and serif. From 1820 on, typefounders produced a variety of decorated Egyptians. Among these, versions of Open Egyptians were extremely popular. A selection from type specimen books of the 1830s is shown opposite. The most reprehensible was the so-called Caslon Italian, introduced in 1821, which Hansard castigated as "a typographical monstrosity."

Signwriters had been content to label the characters they had evolved as "block" letters. The name Egyptian, the innovation of Thorne, and but slowly adopted by the rest of the letterfounding fraternity, probably came from the current vogue amongst the educated class of patrons, and the craftsmen who worked on their behalf, for so-called Egyptian motifs and manners derived (despite the martial enterprises of Napoleon against England) from the influence of French contemporaries and the Empire extravaganza. In architecture and furniture design this influence was particularly marked. The furniture designers, Thomas Hope and George Smith, were amongst the liveliest of these English imitators; and the latter, writing of Baron Denon, who had been the principal archæologist on Napoleon's staff during the Egyptian campaign, notes that the introduction of these novelties "gave a new life to a taste for the [Egyptian] style of embellishment." Typefounders, as business men, were as quick to capitalize the vagaries of æsthetic fashion as are their descendants today.

These Egyptian letterforms may be seen upon buildings throughout this country, particularly in those towns in East Anglia or the West Country where much early nineteenth-century architecture remains, and in the North, where, for example, many of the street names in Chester and Liverpool are in Egyptian. Such titles or notices, often made in raised brass or wooden characters, sometimes in stucco relief, or cast-iron, frequently antedate Figgins' Antique of 1815. Perhaps Callingham was just when he claimed, somewhat sharply, that "there is not sufficient ground for the assumption that makers of printers' type lead in introducing new designs and styles in lettering."

The variety in metal and wood, number, size, weight and novelty of these early Egyptians was impressive. Mrs. Gray lists forty variations between 1815 and 1847 and it is probable that many more were shown in typefounders' specimen books of that unselfconscious era. Unfortunately, few of these specimen books remain. The designs which were evolved between these years form a fantastic gallery, against which the Egyptian revivalists of our own day can assemble but a pallid progeny. Examples of certain of these types are shown in accompanying reproductions.

The Egyptian types were widely used. They formed a suitable typographical medium for much of the period's John Bullish printing. They were bold, assertive, with few airs and graces. They were more than a touch vulgar. In their lighter weights and versions

Egyptian Ornamented

Egyptian Open

Antique Open

74

Egyptian Open

Egyptian White

Italian

they might have "the color and precise romance of Bulwer Lytton," but mainly they were the carriers of commercial names or messages, the injunctions of the Law and the Parish Council, the titles of Seven Dials broadsheets, Drury Lane theatre bills, circus and auction notices and the myriad other examples of ephemeral printing with which an increasingly industrial age wished to advertise its wares and wants. That the type was well used was due simply to the fact that printers of the day, as Mr. Holbrook Jackson[6] has said, "got on with their jobs, meeting the requirements of their times as well as they knew how," rather than that they were consciously trying to produce good typography.

Within a decade of the opening of the Victorian era, however, the popularity of the Egyptians had seriously declined. Although still used frequently by the many jobbing printers who helped to popularize and publicize the products of the developing Industrial Revolution, they no longer occupied first place in the typefounders' specimen books and sheets. The innumerable variations of Tuscan, Perspective, Heraldic, and Ornamented offered far greater novelty and ingenuity for customers' money, and gradually took pride of place over the less-fashionable Egyptian. Almost a century was to elapse before the day of the slab serif returned.

That day returned with a flourish even more emphatic than that which had attended the earlier heyday of the letterform. Within a span of five years, from 1929, almost every typefounder in Europe had produced an individual variation on the Egyptian theme.

Memphis from Stempel began this unholy pageant in 1929, and was marketed in this country by Caslon. Ludlow claims to have produced Karnak in 1930 in the United States and to have had a version in this country by the following year. Beton, which was the most ubiquitous of the early Egyptian revival types, had a resounding success. No other similar type from a founder had a comparable éclat. Luxor came from Ludwig and Mayer in 1931, Rockwell (medium weight) from Monotype in 1933. Cairo was the Intertype version of the fashion in the U.S.A. and reached England in 1934. Stephenson Blake were slow into the fray, delaying the issue of Scarab until 1937. This was the last, although variants upon the Rockwell Medium prototype continued to be issued by Monotype from time to time.

The worth of these revivals is debatable. They were essentially a German innovation following much the same progress as the revival of sans serif during the same years from the same sources. These revivals sprang primarily from an energetic breakaway on the part of German artists and designers (led by such figures as Count Kessler, Anna Simon, E. R. Weiss, Rudolf Koch, Paul Renner, who themselves were inspired by William Morris and Edward Johnston) from the long tradition of domination by Fraktur. The breakaway was violent and its results had that quality of violence often deemed an essential feature of competitive advertisement display. In England and America, advertising agency art directors and typographers seized upon these types as typographical novelties and, without examination, used them in their booklets, advertisements, and magazines. The types continued to be fashionable in Britain and the United States after Hitler's decision that the German nation should revert to Fraktur as a typographical demonstration of nationalistic resurgence and unity. The use of Egyptians in America and Britain was fostered by German typefounders as a sound economic proposition until the outbreak of the recent war.

Now, with that war as an excuse and hiatus, we may look back and compare the designs evolved during the two periods. The comparison is wholly favorable to the earlier designs, which have greater originality, vitality, and character. Such a comparison also inevitably provokes the query why none of these earlier designs was resuscitated during the latter Egyptian revival. In retrospect it appears that English typefounders were either stampeded into adopting inferior designs or were insufficiently aware of the treasure within their own archives. Thus Monotype adopted Rockwell, a dull font with few prepossessing characteristics, based upon designs prepared and marketed by the Lanston Monotype Corporation of New York; Caslon (for D. Stempel) marketed Memphis, which is a better design than Rockwell but not an outstanding success; Stephenson Blake introduced Scarab, perhaps the least favored of all the Egyptians of the thirties. Yet both

ABCDEFG: IJKLM
Cairo (Intertype)

ABCDEFGHIJKL
Karnak (Ludlow)

ABCDEFGHIJKLMN
Beton Light (Bauer, Frankfurt-am-Main)

ABCDEFGHIJKLM
Rockwell Medium (Monotype)

ABCDEFGHIJKLMNOPQR
Memphis Medium (Linotype)

ADBCEFGHIJKLM
Scarab (Stephenson Blake)

A selection from designs which appeared during the 1930s in an Egyptian revival, sponsored chiefly by advertisement designers. The vogue was begun by the immediate success of the Stempel Memphis.

Monotype and Stephenson Blake held designs, types, and matrices of designs superior to the rigid, geometrical Beton or any of its companions in the Teutonic spate. England, with a rich repository of original specimens evolved by Regency architects, signwriters and letterfounders, had neglected a heritage, had turned instead to the copyists of her own tradition and inevitably suffered loss. For the Egyptian revival in England there was, unfortunately, no designer able to deal with the situation as expertly as Eric Gill dealt with the twentieth-century revival of the sans serif.

[1] *Printing Types, Their History, Forms and Use,* D. B. Updike. (Harvard University Press, 1922).

[2] *Nineteenth-Century Ornamented Types and Title Pages.* Nicolette Gray. (Faber and Faber, 1938).

[3] *Signwriting and Glass Embossing: A Complete Practical Illustrated Manual of the Art.* James Callingham. (Simpkin Marshall, 1871).

[4] Probably the 199-line pica shown in *A Specimen of Large Letters,* by William Caslon, 1785, and referred to by Berry and Johnson.

[5] *Catalogue of Specimens of Printing Types by English and Scottish Printers and Founders* 1665–1830. W. Turner Berry and A. F. Johnson (Introduction by Stanley Morison). London 1935.

[6] *Fleuron,* No. 2, 1924.

From *Alphabet and Image,* no. 1 (London: Spring 1946).

Lead Soldiers

By Paul Shaw

"Writing systems are political, and typography is just as rich a source of cultural insights as gastronomy."
—Otl Aicher

 lackletter type is often seen as an anomaly unique to Germany, an anachronism from the Middle Ages that perversely continued to exist into the twentieth century. In this view, it is the complete antithesis of modernism in typography as exemplified by the Bauhaus and the New Typography of Jan Tschichold. Its retrograde status is further confirmed by the widespread association of blackletter with the Nazi regime that closed down the Bauhaus and forced Tschichold and other avant-garde designers to flee Germany. However, those very same Nazis later banned blackletter and officially promoted roman type in its stead. This was, in the opinion of printing historian S. H. Steinberg, "the one good thing Hitler did for German civilization." Thus, the history of blackletter type in the twentieth century and its role in the debate on modern typography is more complex—and far more interesting—than generally realized. What follows is a look at how German designers tried to reconcile their nationalist blackletter heritage with the cosmopolitan realities of the modern industrialized world.

There are four principal varieties of blackletter type: textura, rotunda, Schwabacher, and fraktur. All are modeled on medieval calligraphic scripts. Textura is based on northern European calligraphy, while rotunda is its southern European counterpart. Schwabacher and fraktur, derived from bastarda scripts, are particularly German forms of blackletter.

The first Western book printed from movable type, Johannes Gutenberg's 42-line Bible of 1455, was set in textura. Although roman types began to appear as early as 1465, blackletter—often identified with the vernacular and emerging nationalism—was a significant presence throughout Europe for another 250 years. In the 1700s, it was increasingly marginalized as roman type became the norm for commerce and culture. Only in Scandinavia and German-speaking countries did blackletter continue to remain in everyday use—often alongside roman. But by the beginning of the twentieth century, Scandinavia had gone over to the roman camp, leaving the new nation of Germany as the principal standard-bearer for the blackletter tradition.

Despite the prominence of blackletter, roman type had always been present in Germany. The dual-script tradition was constantly in flux, influenced by shifting intellectual currents in Europe and subjected to the vagaries of nationalist politics, especially those tied to the ever-changing relationship between Germany and France. It was strong in the latter half of the nineteenth century. Blackletter was identified with the Lutheran strain of Protestantism, German culture and literature, and the German language. In contrast, roman was identified with other languages, as well as science, industry, and technology. Thus, scientific works printed in roman existed alongside *belles lettres* and Bibles set in blackletter. In advertising, commercial packaging, and newspapers, the two scripts were often used together, because blackletter provided more visual impact than roman for headlines and for copy requiring emphasis.

As the nineteenth century came to a close, Germany was in the midst of an unprecedented industrial expansion, accompanied by equally grand political and military ambitions. Cultural upheaval followed. This tumult was reflected in the wild diversity of typefaces issued by German foundries between 1890 and the outbreak of World War I. During this period, the dual-script tradition increasingly came under scrutiny.

Nationalists looked to blackletter as a visible manifestation of German identity. The connection was succinctly explained by H. Weizsäcker: "A script belongs to its nation as much as its language. It pertains—like language—to the most original manifestations of its thought, feeling, and will. Therefore, it is a part of the national character, a part of that through which and for which the nation has developed. We Germans enjoy the privilege of having a script which not only complies to all these general features but which in addition has an abundance of beautiful forms and carries within it a uniquely German artistic sensibility." In response to this nationalist feeling, some foundries reissued classic blackletter types, such as Alte Schwabacher, while others released new interpretations such as Liturgisch (1906) by Otto Hupp (1859–1949), a textura based on the fifteenth-century types of Peter Schoeffer.

Many designers and artists, inspired by the English Arts and Crafts movement or the Art Nouveau *zeitgeist,* questioned the relationship between blackletter and roman. Some sought to modernize blackletter, others to overthrow it. And still others searched for a type that would combine the best aspects of each script. Among the hybrid typefaces that emerged from this pre-World War I ferment were Eckmannschrift (1900) and Behrens-Schrift (1901). Painter Otto Eckmann (1865–1902), a leading member of the Jugendstil movement, created Eckmannschrift as a protest against both overly decorative fraktur typefaces and the "petrified" forms of roman letters. His design, an outgrowth of his Art Nouveau brush-lettering for *Die Woche,* was an attempt to wed the warmth and vitality of blackletter to the easy legibility of roman. Behrens-Schrift, based on pen-lettering—a new idea at the time—was a similar effort by architect Peter Behrens (1868–1940) to fuse the two scripts into a single German type.

Between 1900 and the beginning of World War II, German type designers tried to contemporize or modernize blackletter in numerous ways: by stripping it of excess ornamentation, simplifying its structure, adapting roman proportions, reducing it to its skeletal essence, reconstructing it from fundamental geometric units, subjecting it to a grid, and stylizing it. Sometimes two or more of these approaches were used in combination.

Many of the new blackletter typefaces that emerged between 1900 and 1940 were heavily influenced by the revival of broad-pen calligraphy that had been sparked by the Arts and Crafts movement at the turn of the century. Many prominent German type designers used their calligraphic expertise not to re-create historic designs, but to devise new ones that would maintain a link to the past. Leading the way was Rudolf Koch (1876–1934). Deutsche Schrift (1910), his first major type design, eschewed decoration in favor of the expressive power of simple pen-made forms. Julius Rodenberg pointedly remarked that it was a blend of textura and Schwabacher, "not a bastard of antiqua [roman] and gothic." Koch's Maximilian (1914), a textura designed to celebrate the four hundredth anniversary of the Reformation, was considered a "big step towards clarity and simpleness." It was accompanied by a set of roman capitals called Maximilian Antiqua. Later, Koch took the idea of Maximilian and Maximilian Antiqua further, mixing roman and uncial capitals with a blackletter lowercase in Wallau (1925–30), Peter Jessen-Schrift (1926), and Offenbach (1930–34). Wallau is a rotunda, while Peter Jessen-Schrift and Offenbach are minimalist texturas. The first two were designed in the 1920s and became popular with the Nazis.

E. R. Weiss (1875–1942), a calligrapher, painter, and book designer, created Weiss Fraktur (1908) as a simplified blackletter with roman proportions. He perceived it as a modern counterpart to Unger Fraktur (1793) and Jean Paul Fraktur (1794), both classico-romantic attempts to imbue fraktur with the clarity of roman. Weiss later created Weiss Kursiv (1924), a rare blackletter italic, as a companion.

In the 1920s, modernist designers, in a search for a fundamental alphabet, reduced roman letters to their skeletal forms, applied them to a Cartesian grid, and built them out of basic geometric units. Although very few blackletter types were created in these ways—their paucity can probably be explained by the still vital calligraphic tradition underlying blackletter at the time—those that were are fascinating for what they reveal about the differences and similarities between blackletter and roman forms.

When roman letters were reduced to their basics, the result was experiments like Herbert Bayer's Universal Alphabet—based on circles and straight lines—or geometric sans serif types such as Erbar, Futura, and Kabel. In blackletter, this approach inevitably led to designs such as Light Lehmann Fraktur (1920) or Anglo-Gothic and Lettres Angulaires, two nineteenth-century non-German texturas.

The De Stijl lettering of Theo van Doesburg and Vilmos Huszar are prominent examples of roman grid-based alphabets. A fascinating blackletter counterpart is Johannes Type (1933) by Johannes Schulz, a design with fascist overtones. Its identity as a blackletter is only revealed by the form of a few key letters such as *W* and *h*. These letters, as well as the long *s* and the esszett (ß, or double *s*), betray fraktur origins. Otherwise, the implacable logic of the grid forces both roman and blackletter characters into similar shapes.

The geometrically based modular alphabets of Josef Albers, Joost Schmidt, and Paul Renner in the 1920s were anticipated several centuries earlier by Albrecht Dürer, who in 1525 proposed a constructed textura on a modular. Dürer's alphabet differs from a Cartesian grid-based blackletter in employing diagonal units as well as horizontal and vertical ones. In order to reproduce a pen-made letter, Dürer also had to add some non-modular strokes to achieve the proper form for several letters. A twentieth-century variation on Dürer's idea is, surprisingly, an American design, American Text (1932), by Morris Fuller Benton (1872–1948).

The modernist experiments of the Bauhaus and the New Typography were conducted in the same years that Art Deco was flourishing. Gotika (1934), designed by Hungarian-born Imre Reiner (1900–1987) and described as a new ornamental type when it was issued, could be called an Art Deco textura. Its roots lie in nineteenth-century texturas like Fette Gotisch.

Of all the methods for bringing blackletter into the twentieth century, the most common was to strip the letters of their historical decoration and to straighten out their complex curves. Calligraphers Like Rudolf Koch and E. R. Weiss had been exploring this path for several decades. But in the early 1930s, designers seeking minimalist texturas appropriate for a technological age rejected calligraphy in favor of geometry. The result was typefaces such as Element, Tannenberg, and Deutschland, three type families whose release coincided with the Nazi rise to power in 1933. These and several other contemporary type designs have been labeled *schaftstiefelgrotesk* (jackboot sans serifs) by critics of fascism. *Schaftstiefelgrotesks* represent a rigidly simplified form of textura, shorn of decoration, that differs not only from traditional texturas but from twentieth-century interpretations such as Offenbach or Weiss Gotisch (1936). Bearing no trace of the broad pen, they lack personality and warmth. Their status as "Nazi types" is a matter of contention since there is a distinction to be drawn between the design of a typeface, its marketing, and its use.

The first of these *schaftstiefelgrotesks* was Element (1933), created by Max Bittroff (1890–1968). Friedrich Friedl has called it "the first and only constructivist Gothic face," clearly separating it from Tannenberg and the others. He sees it as the antithesis of the "homage to handicrafts from Offenbach or [the] scroll-like script from Leipzig that were officially encouraged by the [Nazi] state." It was promoted by the Bauersche Gießerei as a modern blackletter, a natural face for the New Typography: "Thus, the typographer welcomes the appearance of Element, a type by Max Bittroff whose crystal-like purity can only be compared to such a modern typeface as Futura. Such letters are required for the necessary constancy of change, the organic evolution of typography." Unlike other *schaftstiefelgrotesks,* the Element family includes a set of minimally decorative initial capitals.

In contrast to Element, the type specimens for Tannenberg (1934)—designed by Erich Meyer and named for the Battle of Tannenberg—confirm its militaristic associations, both in words and images. The cover of one brochure proclaims: "Words set in the bold Tannenberg stand strong and uniform, clear and powerful, a convincing expression of a new German determination." In another brochure, the traditional metaphor of type as twenty-six soldiers of lead is ominous in light of political events in the 1930s: "We are Hans Gutenberg's followers!/The letter is our weapon and our defense!/We carry the word everywhere!/Printed paper has wondrous strength!/We move the world!" The symbolism of Tannenberg has continued into the 1990s, as neo-Nazis have used it to affirm their heritage and antifascists have used it critically.

The marketing of Deutschland (1934) was even more blatantly nationalist. One type specimen used the same militaristic metaphor as Tannenberg: "Germany marches! Everyday thousands of soldiers in rows and units of Deutschland type leave the machines at our typefoundry. Many hundreds of thousands have already entered print shops all over Germany. There they function as soldiers of German advertising."

Formally, *schaftstiefelgrotesks* are a logical extension of the modernist impulse to rationalize letters as applied to textura. In this, they are uncannily similar to the blackletter calligraphy executed by Jan Tschichold in the mid-1920s. But the marketing and use of these types has ineradicably branded them as symbols of Nazi ideology, regardless of the intent of their designers.

At the same time that *schaftstiefelgrotesk* types were being marketed, calligraphically-trained type designers were attacking the problem of creating a legible, contemporary blackletter from a different angle. They followed the suggestion made by Heinrich Wallau in the 1870s to look to rotunda as the solution to the conflict between fraktur and roman. The result was Wallau by Koch, Weiss Rundgotisch (1938) by Weiss, Kühne-Schrift (1939) by Hans Kühne, one of Koch's students, and Ballade (1938) by Paul

Renner (1878–1956). Like Wallau, Weiss Rundgotisch offered both roman and simplified rotunda capitals. In contrast, Ballade Kühne-Schrift mated rotunda lowercase letters with simplified fraktur capitals.

The various experiments with the form of blackletter—including the *schaftstiefelgrotesk* types—during the first four decades of this century came to an abrupt end when, in January 1941, Hitler's secretary Martin Bormann issued a circular letter, decreeing that all future printing for the state had to be carried out in roman. The use of fraktur (meaning all forms of blackletter) was forbidden on the grounds that it was based on "Schwabacher Jewish letters." Albert Kapr, author of Fraktur, comments, "Were stupidity or race hatred the motives for this measure? The most important reason for discarding the national form in printing policy was to enable the military orders of the occupying German forces— which had at this time subjugated half of Europe—to be read by the oppressed nations." Regardless of the motive, this decree effectively ended the German dual-script tradition in favor of roman.

Thanks to Peter Bain for his insight on many aspects of the twentieth-century blackletter, and Peter Lasch for his translations from the German.

From *Print* 52, no. 4 (July/August 1998).

Futura

By Alexander Nesbitt

he opportunity to discuss the history, form, and use of Futura is a project dear to my heart.

I have long felt that Paul Renner, the designer of the face, was far too little known to students and professional typographers in the United States. To my mind he has been very much underrated. Other German graphic artists, Rudolf Koch for example, have commanded our entire interest, to the point of being slightly overrated.

Renner was born in 1878. He attended the art schools of Berlin, Karlsruhe and Munich; and started his career as a painter—the statement in one American book that he was an architect is erroneous. His first important job was as a book designer for the Georg Müller publishing company, a well-known Munich firm.

Paul Renner has always been active in typographical education. He has written extensively for graphic arts journals and is the author of four books which come to grips with many of the aesthetic and practical problems that concern the printer. These are not to be had in English translations; and they are therefore little known in this country. Renner's credo as a teacher may be expressed in the following translation of one of his remarks: "As difficult as it may be, there is little else we can do except to train or teach each individual who is in any way connected with letters or typography to become an independent and self-sufficient judge of quality." From 1926 to 1933 he was the director and moving spirit of the Munich School for Master Book Printers; although this school did not really function until 1927. The National Socialist regime removed him because he spoke and wrote sharply against the turn of events. It is impossible, if we are to cover our subject adequately, to record any further biographical details. The reader may be assured, however, that the reasons Futura became—under its various guises—the most used advertising display letter lie largely in the character of its creator.

The history of the serifless letter is not too complicated. These two pages should be sufficient to clear up at least one fairly false hypothesis and indicate the course of development up to the present. The hypothesis is the one which suggests that the sans-serif letter of today was based on Greek inscriptional letters of about the fifth century B.C. It is only necessary to point out that the Greeks had no minuscule alphabet, to damage this argument severely. The illustration of Renaissance capitals shows sans serif letters that were used on medals; but this usage too is a long way from the proper foundation on which to base a type like Futura. To my mind, the most difficult part of the design of such a face lies in the lower case. The solution to this problem could only come about gradually, over the centuries; and in the end it was a specific type-design project that could only be worked out in strict reference to the techniques and usage of the present day.

Capitals taken from Renaissance medals. Reproduced from Frank Chouteau Brown's *Letters and Lettering.*

ABCDEFGHIJKL
MNOPQRSTU
VWXYZ

abcdefghijklmn
opqrstuvwxyz
123456789

The sans serif letter designed by Edward Johnston for the *London Underground,* 1919. It is still used on cars, posters, and signs.

    There were, of course, earlier sans serif types. Such a type appeared for the first time in a specimen sheet put out by William Caslon IV in 1816. This was a font of capital letters, not a successful type as far as can be judged. There was no follow-up until about 1832, when Vincent Figgins and William Thorowgood cut sans serif faces, which had a lower case and were more popular. Figgins called his type a "sans surryphs;" Thorowgood used the name "grotesque." Both of these terms are in use today: grotesque is used on the con-

W CASLON JUNR

LETTERFOUNDER

tinent for letters without serifs in general; England inclines toward a double usage; we have not used the word grotesque until quite recently, when the current mode for expanded display types was started.

At this point it is best to define exactly what is meant by sans serif as a classification. To me, the normal face—Futura book—is representative. It is a design in which the capitals have classic proportions, and in which the lower case is based mostly on traditional minuscule patterns. The capitals are not even widths; and the lower case is far from a picket-fence proposition in respect to spacing and arrangement. Superficially viewed, the strokes are all the same width; and the text page presents a rather neutral, uncontrasting effect, quite even in tone and texture. This definition rules out the "gothics, which are based on a different design principle.

The sans serifs as defined made little impression throughout the rest of the nineteenth century; typographically the style remained a dud. In the 1920s though, the post–World War I period, there were experiments, innovations, and revolutions all over Europe. Nowhere, perhaps, were these experiments and changes more interesting to us in the typographical sense than in Germany. Here, in the 1920s, there was great dissatisfaction with tradition—there was a definite turning away from the past, from anything associated with the war and the defeat. All things that seemed new were eagerly accepted and tried out. Added to this was what Stanley Morison has noted as the greater willingness of the German craftsman to experiment with letters. In the course of these experiments the sans serif letter received a full treatment.

There has been some wrangling about who first had the idea of a sans serif letter of the Futura design. Some consider that Edward Johnston's "Underground" alphabet of 1919 gave the first impetus. This may well be a part of the answer. Rudolf von Larisch had also been using a sans serif letter, all capitals usually, to teach the practice of turning the pen to his writing classes in Vienna. The principles of both Von Larisch and Johnston had wide influence in the teaching of lettering in Germany.

It is much more probable that the idea of creating such a type as Futura was inspired by the new use of the old grotesque types—gothics as we know them—in the evolving functional typography. That plus experiments at the Bauhaus by Herbert Bayer and others, plus the efforts of many individual artists and designers to shed the old snake-skin of tradition, began to give the printed page the clean, precise look which they felt the typography of the disillusioned post-war world should have. Among the latter group was Paul Renner, the designer of Futura.

He began his sketches for a sans serif type in 1924. The Bauer Foundry became interested in the letter and did preliminary trials in 1925. It was not until two years later that Futura reached the market; all of the "bugs" had been worked out of it by that time. This is the reason it has displaced all its rivals as the definitive sans serif design—much copied and imitated.

Renner was a man not only capable of devising Futura but also of using it. He was altogether alert to the various theories of aesthetics and art that had passed over Germany

ORIGINAL FUTURA

light   ABCDEFGHIJKLMNOPQRSTUVWXYZ
abcdefghijklmnopqrstuvwxyz 1234567890

book   ABCDEFGHIJKLMNOPQRSTUVWXYZ
abcdefghijklmnopqrstuvwxyz 1234567890

medium   ABCDEFGHIJKLMNOPQRSTUVWXYZ
abcdefghijklmnopqrstuvwxyz 1234567890

demibold   ABCDEFGHIJKLMNOPQRSTUVWXYZ
abcdefghijklmnopqrstuvwxyz 1234567890

bold   ABCDEFGHIJKLMNOPQRSTUVWXYZ
abcdefghijklmnopqrstuvwxyz 1234567890

The weights of Futura are indicated above; the weights for which an oblique was cut are set in it; there is a medium condensed, a bold condensed and a Futura display.

A section of the tenth exercise from *Unterricht in Ornamentaler Schrift* by Rudolf von Larisch.

in succeeding waves. The influences of expressionism, constructivism, suprematism, dadaism, and non-objectivity he had felt and absorbed some twenty years before America knew much about them.

Certainly in discussing the introduction of Futura into the United States one must consider the typographic style that was floated in with it. The illustrations on the pages before you will help to explain a few of the stages in the development of that style. It was

An early experimental phase of the Futura design compared to the finished type. Renner's sketches above—the type below.

the new style as much as the new type that had such a great effect on American advertising typography. Those of us who are of sufficient age can remember this occurrence; and we can recall the weird efforts of our own unschooled and innocent compositors to create something like it.

The early influences on this developing functional typography were constructivism, suprematism, and dadaism; all of which are evident on these pages. Renner foresaw that any new typography would get a bit out of hand at first. He pointed out that it was based partly on the new painting and partly on the new architecture; having, therefore, a split in its basic motivation which would have to be mended. This was because the kind of painting involved—cubist, dadaist, non-objectivist—which influenced the typography, was a sort of ghost production as he put it, completely devoid of all purpose or rationality. In the architecture Renner saw the best chances for working out a really related and rational typography.

One of Renner's great dislikes was period typography. On that subject he expressed himself as follows: "The print shop is not a costume shop. It is not our task to clothe each literary content in a period costume; we must see to it that it receives a garment that suits the style of our time. We want a living typography, not a typographic theater or masquerade."

Period typography is, of course, partly a matter of style and partly of type design. Since we have considered the style in as much detail as these pages will allow, some of Renner's ideas on type design may be expressed at this point. He felt very strongly that there was no longer any valid reason why types should always resemble the early models, which were based on broad-pen writing and produced by hand-cut punches. Types, he maintained, were reading symbols and that we were gradually leaving the older conception of written symbols behind. Therefore, a new and beautiful type style was only possible through the direct and functional use of all our present mechanical equipment for producing type.

86

It was not Renner's idea to toss all period types into the hell-box; he simply wanted a reestimate taken of where we stood in typographical history; he did want a line drawn under our two-thousand years of letter development and wanted it summed up and then reduced to its common denominator again. He believed with Corbusier that we should start again at zero if necessary in order to clear the decks.

There are only these components to any printed job as he saw it: the purpose, the raw materials, and the techniques. Instead of using our present-day components he felt we were still playing around at being Jenson, or Simon de Colines, or Bodoni—when we should be simply ourselves with a clear and simple typography. There is much in his point of view that recommends itself to the contemporary designer; his thinking is as clean and as straight-forward as his Futura.

No story of Futura would be complete without some examination of its wide use as a display and text letter, often under other names and mostly as a linotype or monotype face. Intertype's Futura is, of course, the original Futura suited to the slug-casting machine. There can be little doubt that both Linotype's Spartan and Monotype's Twentieth Century lean very heavily indeed on the Futura design. Both companies abandoned earlier sans serif faces which were obviously inferior to Futura-Metro in the first instance and Sans Serif in the second. ATF, too, tried Bernhard Gothic and then went over to the foundry variety of Spartan. There is no question that the original Futura won the long and hard-fought battle of the sans serifs.

There are various reasons for the dominant use of the Futura design as a display and utility letter: it is a really well-designed face without bad optical illusions; it has a large character count; it contains, as a family, probably the greatest range of well-related weights and variants of any one face; it offers foolproof reproduction in all processes.

If anyone is in doubt about the position of the Futura style in advertising or printing in general, he might consult the surveys made by Eugene Ettenberg and Professor Thomas Blaine Stanley, in the *American Printer* of December, 1950 in the first case and in *Printer's Ink* of November 14, 1952 in the second. Both analyses show that the sans serif faces as a class are well up at the top of advertising and printing type usage. A careful examination of the figures in each case reveals that such type has no rival for display use. The Bauer firm had an early Futura publicity slogan which, translated, said, "A type conquers the world." This was more prophetic perhaps than they meant it to be.

From the Type Directors Club talks held in New York in the Spring of 1953.

Univers: A New Sans Serif Type by Adrian Frutiger

By Emil Ruder

here is a spate of new printing types at the present moment. A similar situation existed between the two wars once the break necessary for recuperation had come to an end. Modern technical devices (electrotypes, punching the matrix by means of the pantograph, microscopic controls) are continually increasing the speed at which fonts can be produced. The question, however, is whether this progress in the mechanics of typefounding is equaled by the visual aspect, the design of the type.

The majority of the new types are not intended to last. Printers and designers can all name types which have become visually outmoded long before they are technically worn out. Every press works with one or more standard typefaces and a comparison of the short-lived fashionable printing types with them reveals the curious fact that the former, almost without exception, are products of the present time, while the standard typefaces belong to the past. They are classics of their kind, dignified and ennobled by centuries of use: Caslon, Garamond, Baskerville, Janson, Plantin, Fournier, Bodoni, Didot, and Walbaum. It almost looks as though our own age is only attracted by the ephemeral and avoids the standard typeface, because of the fundamental visual problems and permanent values it involves.

A Swiss type designer, Adrian Frutiger (a pupil of Alfred Willimann of the Zurich School of Industrial Design), has been working in Paris in the atelier of the Fonderie Deberny et Peignot on a new sans serif typeface. This is of extreme interest for it comes at a time when it seemed beyond the bounds of possibility to hope for the realization of a project which demanded so much determination on the part of the designer if he were to surmount the overwhelmingly difficult problems involved. Instead of adhering to conventional principles of construction the designer of "Univers" has made use of forms which permit a rich interplay of visual effects. In order to emphasize the visual character of the letters the larger sizes are much varied, the strokes, where they are joined, are slightly conical in shape, the free end is somewhat thickened, the other end attenuated, to lighten the effect of blackness and to prevent smearing during printing. The height of the capitals is also slightly varied. When the narrow end of a stroke marks the height of a letter (*H*) the capital is larger than when the broad end of a stroke is uppermost (*E*). The condensation of some of the letters and the expansion of others is noticeable to a greater degree. The upper parts of *g, m, n, p, q,* and *u* are condensed while the lower parts of *a, b, d,* and *u* are expanded. The *c* is made narrower than the *o* because the greater amount of white makes it seem optically as broad as the *o. n* and *u* are not the same in width. The *u* is narrower, for as the opening occurs at the top of the letter the white is more dominant than in the *n* which is open at the bottom.

Frutiger's method of allowing for all twenty-one sizes from the beginning is quite new. The starting point and the most important cut in a font in the norm (12 pt.) and all the other sizes are usually developed from this, for all further possibilities are contained in 12 pt. Until today it was customary to issue a type font in a few sizes only and to prepare additional sizes according to the success of the first cuts.

The different sizes are numbered. Number 55 is the norm. The various large sizes are indicated by tens, the different widths and heights by single numbers. Odd numbers signify roman, even numbers italic.

The font "Univers" was prepared in the first place for the electric composing machine "Lumitype," which was evolved in the workshops of Deberny and Peignot. In the "Lumitype" the matrices of the traditional composing machine are replaced by a plate onto which are deposited eight rows of letters and punctuation marks arranged in a circular formation, altogether sixteen different sorts, which can be used in twelve different sizes. Altogether therefore 17,280 letters and punctuation marks are always at the disposal of the machine. The plate rotates on a horizontal axis within focusing range of a camera and the image of the letters is projected onto a film by means of an electric current.

After several decades of restless groping after something worthwhile this new sans serif font gives reason for rejoicing, especially in the way in which the designer has resolved the formal and technical problems involved.

From *Neue Grafik* 2 (July 1959).

Sideshows in the Evolution of the Alphabet

By Jerry Kelly

n the history of literacy, an extremely significant development (credited to
the Phoenicians) was the use of a visual mark to represent a sound of spo-
ken language, rather than a complete idea. Earlier systems had relied upon
pictographs or ideograms to represent complete ideas or things. While the
new system required far more written strokes to represent a thought than
the earlier systems did, since most words would require many characters, it
also meant that far fewer characters would need to be learned. For example, Chinese—a modern pictographic alphabet—requires well over two
thousand characters to be memorized, while English has twenty-six characters to be learned, which in an almost infinite number of combinations can
represent the most complex ideas.

Pictograms were adapted to form the early phonetic alphabets (as in
"alpha/betas," or ABCs). The letter *A* began as a stylized ox, but became the symbol for
the first sound in the Phoenician word for "ox;" *B* was a stylized floor plan representing
"house," *M* was a stylized symbol representing water, and so on. All these letterforms were
originally pictograms representing entire words, but were adapted to phonetic use to
stand for sounds instead. In many cultures, both ancient and contemporary, these symbols
do a remarkable job of representing all possible sounds in a language, and thereby all possible words. For example, today for Italian or German the Roman alphabet of twenty-six
characters is almost perfect in its ability to represent the spoken language.

However, some languages have not developed as neatly as Italian or German. In these
other instances spelling has evolved in such a way that the twenty-six symbols for sounds
do not consistently represent a unique sound, but instead can represent several sounds.
The most notorious example of this is in English, where a single character (such as *y*) can
represent totally different sounds (as in "try" or "you"). In this troublesome language there
are also many sounds that are represented by more than one letter (*th* forms a unique
sound). Some sounds have just the opposite problem, where different alphabetic symbols
can represent the exact same sound: the *y* in "try" represents exactly the same sound as *ie*
in "lie." It can get very confusing to the uninitiated. So English has a far from precise system of using symbols to represent sounds. This certainly adds to the difficulty of learning
the system, and for this reason and other (perhaps even just a sense of tidiness?) several
attempts have been made to develop a system of symbols that accurately represents all the
spoken sounds in English. (Reformers have conducted similar experiments in other languages as well.) These systems take two basic forms. Most commonly there have been
attempts for centuries to modify our Roman alphabet to represent the forty or so sound
units upon which all words in English are built, or otherwise change the accepted alphabetic arrangement. The other method would be to develop a new, distinct set of symbols—perhaps not even based on any previous alphabet—to depict each of these sounds.

Throughout the history of printing numerous attempts have been made by spelling
reformers, often in collaboration with type designers, to adapt typefaces to phonetic

requirements. The earliest attempt in English was probably the thirty-four-character Alphabetum Anglicum. Another early experiment, and certainly one of the best known attempts at changing letterforms, is the alphabet Thomas More appended to his most famous work, *Utopia,* in 1516. However, More's reform was totally imaginary and somewhat facetious, concerning itself solely with changing the forms of our letters, not the sounds they represent, and it is therefore out of the scope of the reading/phonetic proposals we are considering.

A fascinating experiment in phonetic alphabetical reform from earlier in this century (and, in my opinion, the most aesthetically successful since the Arrighi/Trissino collaboration of the sixteenth century) was the modified alphabet used by Robert Bridges, Britain's poet laureate, in the volumes of his essays published by the Oxford University Press. Bridges had the good fortune to be assisted in the development of his new font by Stanley Morison, on of the giants of typography in this century. As a typographical adviser to the British Monotype Corporation, Morison was in an extremely advantageous position to work with Bridges on his alphabet. His program of typeface development at Monotype, based mainly on well-chosen and carefully manufactured revivals of historical types, but also a sprinkling of original modern designs such as Eric Gill's Perpetua and Joseph Blumenthal's Emerson, was well established by the time he began working with Bridges on his font in 1927. Morison, an expert in typographic history and an admirer of Arrighi's italic type, chose his own adaptation of Arrighi's third type, made by Monotype in 1923 and christened "Blado" (after Arrighi's printer), as the basis for the Bridges phonetic alphabet.

It is a sound premise to use an italic rather than a roman design for adaptation to a phonetic usage. Roman letterforms are ultra-conservative, to the extent that variants common in the early years of printing, such as *h* with a round right stroke, or *p* with a line through the descender, are now considered jarring. However, we still readily accept alternate forms, such as *g* or *g*, *a* or *a*, etc. Morison exploited these acceptable alternate forms in creating the additional symbols Bridges needed for his phonetic alphabet. The result is one of the most successful experiments in this direction. The Bridges alphabet can be read fairly easily in the normal manner, while still delineating a wider range of sounds required in English through the use of alternate forms. Morison himself, often a severe critic of his own work, thought well enough of the type to include a reproduction of it as plate 345 in his monumental survey *The Typographic Book 1450–1935.*

There has also been much experimentation in this century, much of it avant-garde in nature, with combining the standard roman font of twenty-six lowercase and twenty-six uppercase letters. Lucian Bernhard, Herbert Bayer, Paul Renner, Bradbury Thompson, Charles Peignot, and others have all designed alternative types based on our Roman letters, but with changes radical enough to be deemed a variant alphabet. Bradbury Thompson's alphabet consisted of basically combining uppercase and lowercase forms (totaling fifty-two characters) into one alphabet of twenty-six letters, which he called the Monalphabet. In 1944, inspired by Bayer's work in a similar vein, Thompson set an entire issue (no. 145) of *Westvaco Inspiration for Printers* in a Monalphabet based on Futura. Four decades later, in 1988, Thompson acknowledged that "critics today may view the Monalphabet experiment as a futile waste of time," but nonetheless he believed it "an idea that remains to be tested and played with" (*The Art of Graphic Design,* Yale University Press, 1988, page 37).

William Addison Dwiggins, the famous American type designer, also experimented with combining a mixture of upper and lowercase letters with unusual characters in an alternative version of his Winchester typeface. He began dabbling with this new alphabet, which avoided ascenders and descenders, in 1942. By 1946 the type was ready. It was used only in a few unusual pieces designed by Dwiggins himself, and in some promotional materials for Mergenthaler Linotype (which produced the font). An interesting essay in what Thompson called Monalphabet design, and one of the few that sees any use at all today, is A. M. Cassandre's Peignot type of 1937. This font, which is serifless but has stressed weight to the strokes like Lydian or Optima, was produced by the Deberny and Peignot foundry in Paris. Occasionally one sees it used today for very specialized typography, although almost never for running text. (Readers may remember it as the typeface used in the title captions for the *Mary Tyler Moore Show*.)

There have also been more radical attempts at modifying the symbols used to represent sounds in English. Surely the most revolutionary in modern times was the Shaw Phonetic Alphabet competition. In his will, George Bernard Shaw instructed his executors to offer a reward of £500 for a totally new set of characters, not based on any previous alphabets, to represent all the sounds in the English language. Some thought this to be Shaw's last sarcastic joke, and indeed this aspect of his will was contested. However, in 1958 a committee selected a compromise submission, incorporating a system developed by Kingsley Road to which they appended aspects of three other entries. In 1962 Penguin Books published an edition of Shaw's *Androcles and the Lion* with English text in roman letters and the Shaw phonetic alphabet on facing pages. This was the only book ever printed in the type.

The most thorough and serious attempt to reform the phonetic aspects of the marriage of the Roman alphabet with the English language was made by Sir Isaac Pitman. At its height it was claimed that the Pitman alphabet (called ITA, or International Teaching Alphabet) was used in over ten thousand schools. Monotype Ehrhardt with special ITA characters added was a particularly handsome example of this alphabet, and appeared in many of Monotype's specimen books.

Surely no one would want to stand in the way of anything that would make reading (and, by extension, learning) easier. However, the forms of our letters are so well established that any attempt to modify them results in deterioration, not enhancement, of comprehension. One can rightfully question whether there is any need for reform. To my knowledge no studies have been done comparing the difficulty of learning English, whose system of spelling is woefully inadequate from a phonetic viewpoint, to learning a totally phonetic alphabet such as Italian. I would guess that to the facile mind of a young child there is negligible difference between totally phonetic and semi-phonetic languages, even if older, less receptive minds find English more difficult. The attempts at alphabet reform throughout the centuries make interesting sideshows in the evolution of our alphabet and language, but I think it is fairly safe to say the current forms of our twenty-six letters will be around long after the already rusting fonts of Pitman, Shaw, Thompson, and others have disappeared.

From *The AIGA Journal of Graphic Design* 15, no. 2 (1997).

The Space Between the Letters

By Moira Cullen

n March this year, Matthew Carter traveled to the Walker Art Center in Minneapolis to present the results of a revolutionary experiment in museum identity. The British-born, Boston-based type designer was the Walker's first and only choice to craft a new typeface that would communicate its "multi-voiced" mission. Turning many a head, Carter told the museum's executive board that with his proposal the institution's identity would be conveyed not by a logo but through a family of letterforms with variant horizontal rules and "snap-on" serifs—themselves characters in the font that would transform a single, simple typeface into polyphonic voice. "Think of this typeface as Laurie Anderson, John Cage, Aretha Franklin, Merce Cunningham, and Tom Jones crammed into one pair of pants," explained an accompanying billboard.

Most institutions—corporate, cultural, or otherwise—are dedicated to stability. Immutable, impersonal preserves of constancy, they exist to persist—to standardize practices, secure ideologies, sequester aberrations, or sustain the flame. Bound by hierarchy and conformity, their relevance eroded by their distance, they speak in monotones of clipped cohesion as the gap widens between them and the pluralistic world outside their doors.

Not so at the Walker, whose monthly calendar proclaims: "Open to interpretation. Closed Mondays." Founded in 1879 to house the eclectic collection of a prominent timber tycoon, Walker Art Center established early its intent to be more than a polished showcase for culture's artifacts. Through an ambitious program of public exhibitions, educational activities, and workshops, the Walker today has surpassed its regional roots to distinguish itself internationally among the foremost purveyors of contemporary visual, performing and media arts. "Bruce Nauman," Duchamp's Leg," "In the Spirit of Fluxus"—Walker-organized exhibitions circulate to museums nationally and abroad from Boston to Barcelona, Cologne and Basel to Madrid. The performing arts program—the largest of any museum—has featured musicians, composers, performers, and choreographers such as John Cage, Philip Glass, Laurie Anderson, and Meredith Monk; writers William Burroughs, Toni Morrison, and Jorge Luis Borges; and video artists and film-makers Jean-Luc Godard, Jonathan Demme, and Chantal Akerman. "We're not cornflakes," says design director Laurie Haycock Makela.

Also unique is the Walker's long-time commitment to contemporary design. Having hitched its visual identity to an ascendant International Style at the end of the Second World War, the museum has since contained its multiplicity of media and audiences in variations of a Modernist aesthetic—sans serif type, white space and an ordered grid. "The Walker set up the paradigm for Modernist institutional identity," says Haycock Makela. "We've spent the last several years loosening up and undoing it [replacing a stolid Franklin Gothic, Helvetica, or Univers with the subtle lilting curves of DIN]. Now it's time to pull it together in a new way."

The retirement in 1989 of design director Mildred "Mickey" Friedman and her director husband Martin after a twenty-year regime brought new priorities to light: financial circumstances had changed, audiences had grown ethnically and culturally more diverse, and the content and context of contemporary art had become increasingly difficult to convey. The Walker, like many other institutions, needed to realign itself with changing times. "Connect to the New" became the rallying cry for an extended mission that emphasized communication, internationalism and experimentation. One of the means to convey this to the public was through a new identity—something less authoritarian, more expressive, with enough flexibility and character to describe the museum in understandable yet remarkable ways. "When Laurie proposed that Matthew design a new typeface that would reflect our new mission," says director Kathy Halbreich, "I jumped on it with great pleasure."

But typography as identity? The idea is not new—corporations and magazines routinely commission signature fonts, while cultural institutions, with varying degrees of success, have considered typography part of their signature style: Musée d'Orsay's Didot, Seattle Art Museum's Bodoni, and Centaur, the titling font designed in the 1920s by Bruce Rogers for New York City's Metropolitan Museum of Art. Haycock Makela's inspiration came from a previous exercise. She had commissioned Carter, Ed Fella, and Emigre's Zuzana Licko each to design a typeface for the Winter 1993 issue of the Walker's highly regarded but now defunct journal. Licko's "neo-folk" Quartet, Fella's vernacular Out West on a 15 Degree Ellipse and Carter's Sophia, its lyric ligatures inspired by sixth-century Greek letterforms, all supported her sense of a "shared impulse among a new generation of digital type designers to humanize and ornament letterforms." It was then that she and Carter began to discuss what a typeface for the Walker might be.

"We began with the idea that a typeface could be an identity—a font rather than a logo—that would run through the system like blood," says Haycock Makela. What happened next was an extraordinary collaboration that crossed generations, gender, and state lines, between the fifty-seven-year-old Carter on the East Coast (see *Eye* no. 11 vol. 3) and Haycock Makela's studio at the Walker in America's northern heartland. Along with Haycock Makela—a Los Angeles native, veteran of Rhode Island School of Design and Cranbrook Academy of Art, and design educator (Otis/Parsons and CalArts)—the other featured players were Matt Eller, a twenty-something senior designer and self-described "Iowa farm boy," and Santiago Piedrafita, a young Brazilian graduate from the Pratt Institute who after a year's internship recently joined the staff. Communicating by phone, FedEx, and fax, the group created a virtual shared space that linked the evolving design to individual screens. "It was fantastic," says Carter. "I'd send them trial fonts and they'd send me back ten used in different ways." Adds Halbreich, "It was the most amazing experience to have a mind like Matthew's in our cyber-midst."

For his part, Carter was immediately intrigued by the Walker project, not for financial gain (all rights revert to him after three years), but for its experimental appeal. "I've been doing this kind of thing now for forty years, so it's rather unusual to find something new. But it was such a cool job, I really wanted to do it." What excited him most was the opportunity to make a typeface for a controlled environment—essentially a laboratory— where a limited number of designers (only three or four) would be using the font on a restricted range of materials. "I realized that I could do things I wouldn't dream of doing with a retail face which has to be plug in and play. In this case, I could leave much more of how the typeface could be used to the user. I had absolute confidence that the designers at the Walker would not only use it in ways I had foreseen, but would probably find ways of their own that I hadn't."

Which is exactly what happened. According to Carter, the original brief was "incredibly loose"—no mandatory typographical directives to make it warm and furry," just a few words from the director over a glass of wine in her backyard: "Not too jagged, please, Matthew." "Undoubtedly she was having a nightmare of rioting pixels, but it's not my style," Carter muses. "I probably said 'not too nervous'," claims Halbreich, who admits her concern that a typeface that mirrored the Walker's complexity might end up "looking like a stew instead of a menu of opportunities. In the end Matthew with Matt and Laurie developed a menu. But that was the risk." This was the first project of its kind under her tenure and Halbreich was very aware that the Walker's continued support of the practice of good design was imperative. "Corporate America," she acknowledges, "understands that its future lies in research and development and the artistic community can't forsake that either. That's what this project was—R&D."

Indeed, the story of Walker the typeface (as it was named by executive decision) is unique as much for how it was made as for what it is. According to those who use it, Walker is a concept, not just another interesting face. Carter began with three ideas—all sans serifs—to launch the discussion. By condensing one he tapped the vestigial notion of discretionary serifs, which he tracked out, exploded and treated as separate characters, later dubbed "snap-ons." (He had wanted to call them "deputy serifs" but reconsidered because it sounded too much like the "font police.") Haycock Makela fell in love with the snap-on concept but the Walker was uncomfortable with the style of the font and began to look at a second face that in comparison appeared less unusual. At the same time Haycock Makela had begun a redesign of the monthly calendar, moving from a dense 5.5″ × 7″ tri-fold to an 11″ × 17″ sixteen-page tabloid with lots of room to "move and groove." It was the calendar that provided the context which provoked the final design.

The designers began dropping the trial fonts into their layouts and faxing them to Carter, who concurred that in use the favored face was too informal (and a bit too Tekton). Instead he suggested that what was needed were "some good strong sans caps" that could work with DIN. Putting his three earlier ideas aside, he began again, this time designing a deliberately sturdy, quite unexceptional set of capitals. "I think of them rather like store window mannequins with good bone structure on which to hang many different kinds of clothing," says Carter.

He also revisited the idea of "snap-ons" in five flavors—Egyptian slabs of different sizes, symmetricals, curved brackets, and thin triangular forms—that responded to the idea of inflection, mutability, and tones of voice. Carter remembers warning the designers that because the serifs were independent characters they would unstick, even disintegrate, when tracked out. "Frankly, they didn't seem too fazed by that," he says.

Seeing the font in use on the calendar prompted Carter to produce another variant—horizontal rules (overlines, underlines, or "train tracks" that bind the letterforms, leaded or stacked) after noticing the Walker's preference for standing baseline type on an illustration's edge. But it was Eller who came back with the recommendation for an italic. "Brilliant," says Carter. "It was my dream. I was feeding them stuff, and they gave me back better than I gave them. It was symbiotic."

One wonders when any of the Walker's designers had time to experiment. Straddling the line between an in-house service and a creative laboratory, the eight-person Walker studio handles a staggering workload—on average forty projects a week, four to ten publications a year and ten exhibitions in two-month cycles. Each programming strand has its own identity, with requirements for programs, banners, signage, and other event support in addition to membership and educational materials.

What does Eller, as user and contributing designer, think of the new font? "It's totally Franklin Gothic for 1995," he quips. "What Matthew has done is take a basic Pepsi logo-type of a font and give you endless possibilities." He proceeds to put Walker through its paces. "Here it is in its plainest form—strong and girthy, scale is its friend." Down comes a menu of options that reads simply "Over, Under, Both" to key the horizontal rules. "You can stumble into some pretty neat things." And the serifs? "Five different ones like brothers and sisters in the same family give just enough variety. They allow you to fill in the negative spaces or make a ligature out of anything." He adds, "I just found this yesterday—ligaturing *os* like race car fonts." Shift, option, click. "Or you can delete the letterform and leave just the serifs. It's a formatic language, totally transmutable."

Though not for amateurs, Walker works as a straight font in default mode, its alter egos and multiple personalities encoded as optional extras in the normal Macintosh keyboard. Carter eliminated the # sign and other little-used characters, replacing them, character for character, with serifs keyed to "shift, option" or "shift" commands. Recognizing that variant characters are often more easily placed than found on the keyboard, he annotated all the programmed combinations on a handy, easily memorized chart.

Surely there must be something Walker doesn't do? "I wish there was an incredibly feminine characteristic, some Snell Roundhand (also a Carter-designed face) flowery swoop that connected on to the hardcore letters," says Eller. But he quickly adds, "You can make some incredibly beautiful forms. Here it is being real girly. The coolest thing for me is that it's all about the space that doesn't really exist—the real estate in between—which makes you much more aware of each letter and where it exists. Each word is unique." Piedrafita chimes in, "You're not typesetting a font, the font is created in the process of designing the piece." In Walker the serifs are the ultimate connectors, the antithesis in type of a Modernist apartheid. Each character holds its own frame but an inspired or decisive stroke can will the letterform to nuzzle its neighbor or extend an arm or leg across the white divide.

Could Walker present too many possibilities? The designers agree that because it is so subjective it carries a high illegibility quotient. Yet curiously, they report, it seems to activate a self-correcting principle. "You can put gold lamé on this thing and discofy it with all the options until you're totally disgusted, but then you pull back," explains Eller. Haycock Makela is quick to point out that Carter, who is the master of correctness, did not dictate a correct way for its use, adding, "He's waiting for us to fall into its wierdnesses and idiosyncrasies." The tweaking continues.

Considering its novelty, Walker's public debut has been somewhat low key. In June 1995 the Walker unleashed its redesigned monthly calendar, sent to all members and distributed on site, which featured the new typeface. The exhibition in the lobby that described the face and the process by which it was created had been up since March, to coincide with Carter's presentation to the board which preceded a packed reception for the local design community who shuddered with delight when told about serifs that snap on. And September marked Walker's color debut—a steely metallic blue-green centered italic on the institution's new letterhead—that when stacked next to its predecessors, Franklin Gothic and DIN, made, Haycock Makela acknowledged, a "deliberate salute" to the museum's sans serif history.

The museum's designers are obviously enthralled by Walker's seemingly endless possibilities, but what about those who have not experienced the pleasure of its use? So far, according to Halbreich, there have been no "monstrously negative comments," while the bookstore reports inquiries (they suspect from other designers) as to whether the typeface is for sale (it is not). Random samplings about the success of the new identity drew many a blank stare. "They don't have to know it's a new font," says Haycock Makela, "but are they drawn to it, does it create a certain distinction for them, does it irritate them in a way that is good, or are they simply saying 'Oh, that Walker'?"

Of course, this is only the beginning. Walker's potential for communicating personalized messages to the multiple audiences in the museum's niche markets has yet to be fully tapped. How will Walker voice the idiosyncratic inflections and simultaneous identities required by an African-American photographer's exhibition, an Indian dance troupe, the annual Dyke Night extravaganza, and family weekends in the sculpture garden? "We've all learned to become very sensitive to audience," Haycock Makela remarks.

Education is the secondary goal driving the Walker's typographic identity project. Regarded as another way to "Connect to the New," the typeface, the way it was made and its use are intended to help audiences understand the conceptual and technical realities of type design in the digital age. In the next phase of the project, Walker will be joined by a new character named Mr. Al Phabit—"a nationally distributed kids' activity-learning-alphabet-digital fun guide"—inspired by Haycock Makela's four-year-old daughter, who like many children her age is learning not by picking up a pencil but by pecking on keys. "Most children's alphabet books are about matching letters to sounds," says Haycock Makela. "Mr. Al Phabit talks about the look of the letters—a big belly *B*, for instance."

The controlled simplicity of one audience, one image may have been everything in the Modern age, but times have changed. Ahead lies complexity not consistency, a future fragmented and far from uniform. In the Walker project, the computer, that much maligned tool, in the hands of a master and several passionate designers has produced an extended typeface that embodies the peculiarities and precision of a highly personalized voice. Unity need no longer be misconceived as conformity. Like the brushed aluminum letters set in artist Lawrence Weiner's own font on the brick of the Walker facade, as individuals, institutions, communities, and cultures we are but "bits and pieces put together to present a semblance of a whole."

From *Eye* 19 (1995).

Movement: Defining Modernism

From De Stijl to a New Typography

By Kees Broos

et us define the word "typography" here as the deliberate use of letters, in the broadest sense of the word. The user can be printer, typographer, architect, poet, or painter. The materials are not restricted to those of the type case or typesetting machine, but encompass every suitable medium from linoleum to electronic news marquees and from a tile tableau to television. It is important that the user be aware of the shape and function of each letter and consequently of the expressive potential in the design and arrangement of letters and text opened up to the reader and the viewer.

Roughly speaking, the use of letters can have two entirely different purposes. The first one is summarized in Beatrice Warde's adage: "Printing Should Be Invisible."[1] Here, typographic arrangement is subservient to content; its principal requirements are clarity and optimum legibility. The autonomous material presence of the letter and its substance—printer's ink on paper, paint on wood—should be as discrete as possible in relation to the substance of the text. The typographer is definitely in the service of the writer. The second purpose is practically opposed to the first. Here, typography has an autonomous function. Such typography emphasizes the visual potential of letter shape and the arrangement of text; symbolic, associative, and expressive possibilities of typography affirm the content of the text or weaken it.

Some of the painters and architects that founded the Dutch De Stijl group in 1917 have practiced typography in this latter sense. Their magazine *De Stijl* also kept track of similar typographical experiments by non-members. For those outsiders of De Stijl who experimented with typography, such as Paul van Ostaijen, H.N. Werkman, and Piet Zwart, De Stijl ideas were a challenge and touchstone. Beatrice Warde disapprovingly called them "stunt typographers;" Herbert Spencer classified them as *Pioneers of Modern Typography.*[2] One of those pioneers was the painter Theo van Doesburg, whose artistic and literary versatility and eclecticism were evident in his use of typography. As editor-in-chief of *De Stijl* he used at first a rather symmetrical, plane-filling typography, and later an asymmetric one, tending towards the principles of the functional "new typography." He used a less conventional typography in his dadaistic pamphlet *Mécano,* and in his collaborations with El Lissitzky and Kurt Schwitters. In van Doesburg's typographic works we encounter both his dadaist and constructivist sides.[3]

Typographically, the first three volumes of the monthly periodical *De Stijl* are not very remarkable. Its design is solid and seems to have been delegated by van Doesburg to the small printing house in Leiden where the monthly was produced. Only in the cover and in a few advertisements do we perceive some deviations from the classic typographical image. In the first issue the cover design is specially annotated: "The typographical ornament on the cover, between title and text, is by the Hungarian artist Vilmos Huszar. It is taken from a woodcut, which was intended to be pure visual art, but has been applied here in order to create an aesthetic harmony and unity with the printing."[4] Letters and image have been deliberately balanced with each other.

The design for the title "De Stijl," over the abstract composition, has sometimes been attributed to van Doesburg, but since the dimensions of the letters correspond exactly to those of the composition, we appear to be entirely justified in assuming that Huszar designed both.[5] Moreover, the fragmentation of the letter images fit perfectly well into the context of Huszar's paintings of that particular period. In a letter to the painter Bart van der Leck, some months later, he explained his point of view regarding the figure-ground problem in a painting. According to him, these should be "equivalent." "This is the same process I have used on the cover of *De Stijl,* namely: to give white and black equal value, without ground. You may agree or disagree with this method, but the point is to understand it from the perspective of a solely aesthetic solution."[6] This cover design shows, as much as his paintings from 1917, to what extent Huszar was wavering between van Doesburg's and van der Leck's ideas. The abstract representation shows an affinity to van Doesburg's *Composition IX,* 1917, while the letters of the title are more closely related to Huszar's own painting *Composition II,* 1917, in which he reduces tiny skating figures to small horizontal and vertical rectangles with white interspaces.[7] The problems in a painting, as experienced by Huszar in 1917, are reflected in the shape of the letters in the title De Stijl." The meaning of the words "De Stijl," as well as their shape embodied a program. When van Doesburg modified his ideas about visual art, these letters disappeared from the title and were replaced, starting in the fourth volume, by a more dynamic use of typographical resources.

Geometrical experiments with letter shapes and letter combinations were rather popular in the post–World War I years. The most prominent representative of this deliberately anti-classical typography was the architect H. Th. Wijdeveld who, in his luxuriously laid-out periodical *Wendingen,* founded in January 1918, devised extremely complicated typographical constructions with typographical materials. This made the design of *Wendingen* compatible with its contents and consequently the antipode of van Doesburg's austere *De Stijl.* In spite of this antithesis, both show a certain tendency toward systematizing and plane filling, which can be traced back to the work of the important but somewhat forgotten architect J. L. M. Lauweriks.[8] His "systematic design" of his periodical *Ring* (from 1908 on) considerably influenced such outsiders as architects, interior designers, and other letter designers, with "scant regard to the traditions of the printing industry."[9]

Theo van Doesburg designed monograms for his friends the poet Antony Kok and the architect J. J. P. Oud. These monograms were executed on graph paper. Gerrit Rietveld designed a monogram for the front of an Amsterdam jewelry shop, consisting of the capital letters *G, Z,* and *C,* inscribed precisely in a square. The architect Jan Wils, who belonged to De Stijl from the very beginning, signed his drawings from 1916 on with a geometric monogram consisting of rectangular blocks. In 1920, his then collaborator Piet Zwart used the Wils monogram in a design for a letterhead; this was the beginning of Zwart's career as a typographic designer.[10] Piet Zwart, who happened to be Huszar's neighbor, collaborated with him in designing furniture and interiors. The lettering of the drawings followed a pattern of squares, linked together, according to Wijdeveld's system; Zwart used the same principle in his designs for bookplates and printed matter for the Haagse Kunstkring (Hague Art Circle),[11] and in his geometric logos for the LAGA/IOCO Company, importer of rubber floors.

Wils, Huszar, and Zwart lived in Voorburg, a suburb of The Hague, which was also the residence of Cornelis Bruynzeel, founder of a woodworking industry, who was rather sympathetic to the young new art. He commissioned interior designs and exhibition stands from Huszar, Zwart, Klaarhamer, and van der Leck, and supported the first six issues of *De Stijl* with a full-page advertisement designed by Huszar. In a letterhead for Bruynzeel, Huszar used a geometric alphabet, and also for a cover of a portfolio of architectural drawings, published by the Haagse Kunstkring. This time the letters on the cover are solidly constructed and the abstract composition consists of distinct elements, just the opposite of the *De Stijl* cover. These letters are comparable to the basic, uppercase alphabet which van Doesburg made for his own use, on a basic pattern of 5 × 5 units. He maintained that one could arbitrarily distort the basic shape of a letter horizontally or vertically. This was absolutely contrary to classical typography in which the proportions of the basic shape are inviolate and wherein the letter can only be scaled up or down without distortion. His design for the cover of the periodical *Klei* (Clay), 1919, and the poster for the exhibition *La Section d'Or*, were based on this fundamental alphabet. By changing the basic square framework sometimes to a 2 × 3 rectangle and at other times to one of 5 × 4, he could squeeze long and short lines within a rectangular frame and at the same time construct a visually cohesive picture. Clear legibility was evidently relegated to secondary importance.[12]

Later, van Doesburg experimented very little with letter shapes themselves. When, in 1927, he designed type for the Cafe Aubette directory in Strasbourg, he reverted to his basic alphabet from 1918–1919.[13] Van Doesburg's alphabet, as distinct from the letters in the title of *De Stijl,* consists of letters which are compact, self-contained constructions.

The manner in which the image of the letters of the *De Stijl* title can be separated into elements is found most consistently in the work of Bart van der Leck. In 1919 he designed a poster for the Nederlandse Olie Fabriek (Netherlands Oil Manufacturing Company) at Delft, in which the destruction of the letter shape parallels completely what he was doing in his paintings. The round elements in the classic letter shape are reduced to linear shapes in his letters, but—and here he differs from Huszar—the diagonal is accepted as a matter of course, and the white background is much more prominent than in the more compact shapes of Huszar's letters.[14]

Although the client who commissioned the design did not have it printed, van der Leck continued to use this alphabet; at first in a poster for an exhibition of his own work at Utrecht and later—a lighter version—for wrapping and advertising material for the Amsterdam store Metz & Company. As late as 1941 he designed a bibliophile edition of one of Andersen's fairytales in this way. Van der Leck's letter shapes are not constructed according to a rigid pattern, but distilled from common letter shapes and subsequently interwoven into a homogeneous texture. The resulting loss in direct legibility is amply compensated for by the strong poetic element gained effortlessly through the artless childlike manner in which they are drawn.

Experiments with letter shapes that suggest a parallel with the principles of De Stijl remained few and far between. Gerrit Rietveld applied beautiful geometrically stylized letter shapes to some storefronts (G. & Z.C. jewelry shop, Amsterdam, 1920–22, among others), and as late as 1929, Huszar designed a cover for an issue of *Wendingen,* dedicated to Diego Rivera, in which he used his square letters from the Huszar/Zwart period. But eventually the geometric deformation of the letter image was abandoned, perhaps because this was too reminiscent of Wijdeveld's typography in *Wendingen.*[15]

The potential for the development of new letter shapes from a geometric basis was not realized in The Netherlands; in Germany it was to a certain extent: Herbert Bayer (*Universal,* 1925), Josef Albers (Stencil lettering based on three basic geometric shapes, 1925) and Kurt Schwitters (*Systemschrift,* 1927) made a few attempts in this direction, with varying degrees of success.[16] The visual artists and architects belonging to the De Stijl group reverted to using existing sans serif types, which, though dating from the nineteenth century, were nevertheless very well suited to the requirements of legibility and applicability to diverse media. Starting with the fourth volume the cover of *De Stijl* was constituted once more of existing "grotesques," but now in a new manner that considered the letter as a constructive element in the plane.[17]

In a short article about Rietveld's furniture, in the third volume of *De Stijl,* van Doesburg for the first time used existing type in an unusual manner: he employed different letter sizes in order to emphasize the meanings of his words.[18] In the next issue he went even further and published, in collaboration with Mondrian and Kok, a manifesto about literature in three languages. He wanted to ". . . give a new meaning and new power of expression to the words" and to ". . . create a constructive unity of content and form." Typography was one of the means he wanted to use to this end.[19] In the next issue his meaning was explained, when he published a series of poems, entitled "X-Images" under the pseudonym, I. K. Bonset. These poems had been created some years earlier under the title "Cubistic Verses," but here for the first time they assumed a typographical form. It was no longer the individual letter that created an "atmosphere" or "association," but rather the organization and scale of the letters and words on the page that accentuated the contents of the text and the meaning of the words. Thus the "X-Images" fit into a literary tradition that traces back to the "calligrammes" of Guillaume Apollinaire by way of futurist poetry to the concrete poetry of our time.[20]

Van Doesburg was aware that similar experiments with visual typography were underway in Belgium. The Belgian poet Paul van Ostaijen achieved even more fascinating results with his "rhythmical poetry" than had van Doesburg, but he was criticized ungraciously in *De Stijl.*[21]

So far, autonomous typography emphasized form and meaning. However, van Doesburg had, in his manifesto about literature, postulated that in poetry the word should be posed according to its meaning as well as according to its sound. In van Doesburg's work the "sound" element also assumes a shape through typographic means. He published his "Letter-Sound Images" in the fourth volume of *De Stijl,* with directions for correct performance. Here, too, he realized earlier ideas about the role of sounds in poetry, and gave a form to free, elementarist verse through his typography. These ideas related to those of Raoul Haussmann and Kurt Schwitters. In the second issue of his periodical *Mécano* (1922) van Doesburg published a sound poem by Haussmann and his "Manifesto on the laws of sound;" a "Sonata" by Kurt Schwitters appeared in *Mécano* 4/5. In his turn, Schwitters published van Doesburg's "Letter-Sound Images" in the first issue of his magazine *Merz.* Later, van Doesburg published sound poems by Til Brugman and Antony Kok in *De Stijl.*[22]

De Stijl's truly important contribution to typography came from abroad. It was the special issue *Of 2 Squares,* van Doesburg's adaptation for the Dutch public of the children's book by El Lissitzky, which had just been published in Berlin. This book gave an unequalled survey of all visual, associative, meaningful, and auditory possibilities that word and image—juxtaposed in tension—could bring out on the page.[23] Although the Dutch version was not as strong as the original in Russian, it did burst upon the scene like a thunderclap in a clear sky; it made a powerful impression by simultaneously breaking through many conventions because of its revolutionary and convincing notions about the visual potential of the printed book.[24] El Lissitzky's typographical version of Mayakowsky's volume of poems *For Reading Aloud* (Berlin, 1923), which demonstrated even more forcefully the creative use of existing letters and linear materials, resulted in enthusiastic support for his work among the European avant-garde.

When he visited The Netherlands in 1923—on May 23 he gave a lecture for the Haagse Kunstkring on New Russian Art—he met a younger generation, with whom he could discuss his typographical ideas: "The design of the book . . . must be in accordance with the strains and stresses innate in the contents."[25] Soon afterward we can see in the typographical work of Piet Zwart new dynamics and a more spontaneous use of letter and image; and van Doesburg too could not stand aloof from the strong effect of Lissitzky's visual typography. When he visited Kurt Schwitters in Hannover in 1925, he also met Kathe Steinitz, with whom Schwitters had previously collaborated on the children's books *Der Hahnepeter* (The Rooster) and *Die Marchen vom Paradies* (Fairytales of Paradise). She recollects that van Doesburg said, "Couldn't we make another picture book, an even more radical one, using nothing but typographical elements? Lissitzky had once designed a book of poems in a new typographical style. We would try the same method but make it entirely different."[26] Thus *Die Scheuche* (The Scarecrow) was born, the most sympathetic typographical experiment on which van Doesburg collaborated.[27] Schwitters realized the possibility of making these typographical experiments more commercially appealing through group publication. In 1927 he founded the Ring neuer Werbegestalter (Circle of New Advertising Artists). Four of the regular contributors to *De Stijl* became members of the Ring (Friedrich Vordemberge-Gildewart, Cesar Domela, Werner Graeff and Hans Richter). They were joined by Jan Tschichold, Piet Zwart, Hans Leistikow, and Walter Dexel. Van Doesburg refused to join. The new ideas found a wide and penetrating distribution through many exhibitions of the group and the publication, in 1928, of Jan Tschichold's influential handbook, *The New Typography*.[28]

De Stijl had been in part the source of inspiration for these ideas, in part their incubator, and finally, it had played a crucial role as irritating antagonist.

[1]Beatrice Warde, "Printing Should Be Invisible," in Paul A. Bennett (ed.), *Books and Printing* (Cleveland and New York: World Publishing Co., 1951); also: John Ryder, *The Case for Legibility* (London, Sydney, Toronto: Moretus Press, 1979).

[2]Herbert Spencer, *Pioneers of Modern Typography* (London: Lund Humphries, 1969).

[3]L. Leering-van Moorsel, "Annotations on Theo van Doesburg's Typography," in *Theo van Doesburg 1883–1931* (Eindhoven: exh. cat. Stedelijk Van Abbemuseum, 1968).

[4]It is a bit odd that the abstract composition on the cover was characterized as "typographical." This would imply that it had been put together from separate typographical constituents, such as brass squares and rules. The original print does not indicate anything of the kind. I suspect that the word "typographical" here means that the composition was not printed directly from a woodcut,

but from a line block after a drawing. Judging from the typography of the inside of De Stijl, the first five volumes of the periodical were printed by the same printing house in Leiden, which used T.M. Cleland's Della Robbia typeface. The exception is issue IV, 5, which was typeset in the Genzsch Antiqua (Fr. Bauer, 1907). It was printed by Dietsch & Brückner in Weimar, Germany, like the first four issues of the 1923 volume. Particularly in the sixth and seventh volumes, printed in Paris and Strasbourg, quite different typefaces are used for the text: Roman (VI, 6/7, 8;VII, 79/84,87/89); Light Bodoni (VI, 9); Cheltenham Old Style (VI, 10/ 11, 12;VII, 73/74–78, 87/89) and Baskerville (dernier numéro).

[5]Spencer and Leering-van Moorsel both cite van Doesburg as the designer of De Stijl's title lettering.

[6]R. W. D. Oxenaar, Bart van der Leck tot 1920—Een primitief van de nieuwe tijd (Utrecht State University, PhD diss., 1976), p 126. Yve-Alain Bois, "The De Stijl Idea" in his Painting as Model (Cambridge Mass., The MIT Press, 1990), p 101.

[7]Vilmos Huszar summarized both aspects in a painting dated 1916, which shows a variant of the cover picture in color, including the lettering of the title (Collection Gemeentemuseum, The Hague). The simpler composition of the color surfaces and the extension of the lower horizontal beam of the letter Y to the full width of the letter image—a correction which was applied to De Stijl's title page in the issue of August 1919—suggest that this painting has been dated at least three years too early.

[8]Hans Oldewarris, "Wijdeveld's Typography," in Forum, XXV, 1, 1975, p 3.

[9]Spencer, op. cit.

[10]Fridolin Müller, Peter F. Althaus, Piet Zwart (Teufen: Verlag Arthur Niggli, 1966), pp 15, 17. They incorrectly attribute Jan Wils' seal to Piet Zwart.

[11]This portfolio was published on the occasion of an exhibition dedicated to low-income housing in the Haagse Kunstkring, September 1919. The plates—after works by Granpré Molière, Dudok, and others—were drawn by Jan Wils; H. P. Berlage wrote the introduction.

[12]Haagse Kunstkring: Werk verzameld (The Hague: exh. cat. Haags Gemeentemuseum, 1977), p. 34. The Golden Section exhibition came from Antwerp in 1920 to the rooms of the Haagse Kunstkring.

[13]In 1922 his letters appear on a poster design for the "Kölner Messe" (Cologne Fair), which was reproduced in De Stijl, V, 12, 1922. Designer was Bauhaus student Egon Engelien, who, like Peter Röhl and Werner Graeff, had become a follower of Theo van Doesburg who had taught a "Stijl-course" in Weimar in the Spring of 1922. See: Kees Broos, Mondriaan, De Stijl en de nieuwe typografie (Amsterdam: De Buitenkant; The Hague: Museum van het Boek, 1994), p. 31.

[14]R. W. D. Oxenaar, Bart van der Leck 1876–1958 (Otterlo: exh. cat. Rijksmuseum Kröller-Müller, 1976), fig. T163. Bart van der Leck had previously employed geometrically styled letter shapes on his famous poster for the Batavierlijn (1915–16), designed for the shipping firm Wm. Müller & Co., Rotterdam. See: Marcel Franciscono and Stephen S. Prokopoff, The Modern Dutch Poster (Cambridge, Mass.: The MIT Press, 1987), nr. 35, and: Kees Broos and Paul Hefting, Dutch Graphic Design. A Century (Cambridge, Mass.: The MIT Press, 1993), p. 64.

[15]The Belgian periodical Het Overzicht (The Survey) used the same kind of geometric letters on the cover, designed and cut in linoleum by the painter Jozef Peeters (see numbers 7/8, 1921; 13, 1922; 19, 1913). He wrote about this work and the work of his colleagues Jos. Leonard, Karel Maes and Alf. Francken under the heading "Constructive Graphics:" "Whenever a graphic artist is asked to design the letter, he will need to adapt its form to the atmosphere of the literary work." (Het Overzicht 19, 1923, p. 111). The constructivist periodical De Driehoek (The Triangle), 1925–26, the successor of Het Overzicht, also uses letters that are a crossbreed between van Doesburg's and Wijdeveld's alphabets.

[16]Herbert Bayer, "Typographie und Werbsachengestaltung" (Typography and Advertising Design), in Bauhaus, Zeitschrift für Gestaltung (Bauhaus Design Journal), II, 1, 1928, p. 10. Josef Albers, "Zur Schablonenschrift" (On Stencil Lettering), in Offset, Buch und Werbekunst (Offset, Book and Advertising Design), 7 (Bauhaus Issue), 1926, p. 397. Kurt Schwitters, "Anregungen zur Erlangung einer Systemschrift. I–II" (Attempt to Achieve a Letter System), in Der Sturm (The Storm) XIX, 1,2/3, 1928. In a letter dated 27 June 1927, Schwitters asked van Doesburg to publish some of his

"letter systems" in the next issue of *De Stijl*. Van Doesburg did not comply. Kurt Schwitters, *Wir Spielen, bis uns der Tod Abholt* (We Play Until Death Picks Us Up), (Frankfurt/Main, Berlin, Vienna: Ullstein Verlag, 1974), p. 116.

[17]Examples of such a "commercial" letter type in architecture are Café De Unie (Rotterdam, J.J.P. Oud, 1924) and the Zaudy store (Wesel, Germany, G. Rietveld, 1928). Vilmos Huszar reverted to a common sans serif letter in his advertisement for Miss Blanche Cigarettes in *De Stijl*, VII, 79/84, 1927, p. 30. *De Stijl*'s new cover, with its open center and a composition constructed from the edge, deliberately deviates from axial typography in favor of a dynamic solution. The same thing happens in *De Stijl*'s stationery: the title shifts from top center to the left, and is balanced by a vertically placed text in the lower left. The changeover to a two-column format was explained by van Doesburg in *De Stijl*, IV, 2, 1921, p. 17, on purely practical grounds: the magazine could now be folded for mailing. Painter Piet Mondriaan in Paris had earlier sent suggestions and sketches for a new *De Stijl* cover in two colors to van Doesburg in a letter of August 5, 1920. Broos, *Mondriaan, De Stijl en de nieuwe typografie, op. cit.* p. 20.

[18]Theo van Doesburg, "The paintings of Giorgio de Chirico, and a chair by Rietveld," in *De Stijl*, III, S, 1920, p. 46.

[19]Theo van Doesburg, Piet Mondrian, Antony Kok, "Manifesto II of De Stijl, 1920—Literature," *De Stijl*, III, 6, 1920, p. 49.

[20]I.K. Bonset, "X-Images," *De Stijl*, III, 7, 1920, p. 57. Van Doesburg's poems have been reprinted—partly in manuscript, partly in their definitive typographical form—in I. K. Bonset, *Nieuwe woordbeeldingen. De gedichten van Theo van Doesburg. Met een nawoord van K. Schippers.* (New Word Images. Poems by Theo van Doesburg. With an epilogue by K. Schippers). (Amsterdam: Em. Querido, 1975). See Hannah L. Hedrick, *Theo van Doesburg, Propagandist and Practitioner of the Avant-garde, 1909–1923* (Ann Arbor: University Microfilms International Research Press, 1980), for an English translation of some of the poems, and an evaluation within the literary tradition.

[21]Van Doesburg reviewed Paul van Ostaijen's volume *Bezette stad* (Occupied City) (Antwerp: 1921) very harshly; "Literary: empty, hollow and inflated—a gross imitation of the French sport of literature," in *De Stijl*, IV, 12, 1921, p. 179, after he had already panned it in *Het Getij* (The Tide), VI, 1921, p. 25–29, as an imitation of Blaise Cendrars. Gerrit Borgers, *Paul van Ostaijen* (The Hague: Bert Bakker, 1971).

[22]Til Brugman, "R," in *De Stijl*, VI, 3/4, 1923, pp. 55–56. Antony Kok, "Nachtkroeg" (Nightclub), in *De Stijl*, VI, 3/4, 1923, pp. 55–56.

[23]El Lissitzky, "Van twee kwadraten" (Of 2 Squares), in *De Stijl*, V, 10/11, 1922. Yve-Alain Bois, "El L. didactique de lecture" (El L. teacher of reading), in *Avant-Guerre* 2, 1981, p. 57.

[24]The translation of the Russian text into Dutch naturally forced van Doesburg to change Lissitzky's typography in some places. He also changed the original vertical format of the publication in Russian (Berlin, 1922) to the oblong format in which *De Stijl* was published from the fourth volume on. This change caused the relation between text and illustrations to be drastically altered in some places. Lissitzky was clearly least happy with the addition, on the inside of the cover, of van Doesburg's own typographical composition of the words "Voor Allen" (For Everyone). This change was undoubtedly unavoidable, because it was practically impossible to translate Lissitzky's drawing, constituting p. 3, into Dutch. In any case, Lissitzky's widow expressed herself in the following negative terms: "By his changes, van Doesburg made the cover more commercial than Lissitzky's design had been." Sophie Lissitzky-Küppers, *El Lissitzky: Maler Architekt Typograf Fotograf* (Dresden: VEB Verlag der Kunst, 1967), p. 21. See also: Camilla Gray, "El Lissitzky's Typographical Principles," in *El Lissitzky* (Eindhoven: exh. cat. Stedelijk Van Abbemuseum, 1966), p. 20.

[25]L. Leering-van Moorsel, "The Typography of El Lissitzky," in *The Journal of Typographic Research*, II, 4, 1968, p. 323. Jan Tschichold, "Werke und Aufsätze von El Lissitzky" (Works and essays by El Lissitzky), in *Typographische Monatsblätter* (Typographic Monthly), Dec 1970, p. 1.

[26]*Ibid.*

[27]L. Leering-van Moorsel, in "Annotations on Theo van Doesburg's Typography," *op. cit.*, is of the opinion that the typography of *Die Scheuche* can be attributed completely to van Doesburg, because of a letter from van Doesburg to Käthe Steinitz, dated 16 April 1925. In this letter he pro-

poses detailed typographic corrections. However, from a letter from Schwitters to van Doesburg, dated 22 April 1925, we can conclude that those corrections were not incorporated into the book: "Mrs. Steinitz has departed. I have read your letter to her with the corrections, my dear Does. They came too late, the volume is ready. I hope to be able to send you the first copy today." (Schwitters, *Wir spielen bis uns de Tod Abholt, op. cit.,* p. 94.)

[28]Jan Tschichold, *Die Neue Typografie* (The new typography), (Berlin: Verlag des Bildungsverbandes der deutsche Buchdrucker, 1928).

This essay was first published in *De Stijl: 1917–1931. Visions of Utopia,* edited by Mildred Friedman (Minneapolis: Walker Art Center; New York: Abbeville Press, 1982). For this reprint, minor corrections were made and some of the notes were brought up to date.

The New Typography

By Laszlo Moholy-Nagy

ypography is a tool of communication. It must be communication in its most intense form. The emphasis must be on absolute clarity since this distinguishes the character of our own writing from that of ancient pictographic forms. Our intellectual relationship to the world is individual-exact (e.g., this individual-exact relationship is in a state of transition toward a collective-exact orientation). This is in contrast to the ancient individual-amorphous and later collective-amorphous mode of communication. Therefore priority: unequivocal clarity in all typographical compositions. Legibility-communication must never be impaired by an *a priori* esthetics. Letters may never be forced into a preconceived framework, for instance a square.

The printed image corresponds to the contents through its specific optical and psychological laws, demanding their typical form. The essence and the purpose of printing demand an uninhibited use of all linear directions (therefore not only horizontal articulation). We use all typefaces, type sizes, geometric forms, colors, etc. We want to create a new language of typography whose elasticity, variability, and freshness of typographical composition is exclusively dictated by the inner law of expression and the optical effect.

The most important aspect of contemporary typography is the use of zincographic techniques, meaning the mechanical production of photoprints in all sizes. What the Egyptians started in their inexact hieroglyphs whose interpretation rested on tradition and personal imagination, has become the most precise expression through the inclusion of photography into the typographic method. Already today we have books (mostly scientific ones) with precise photographic reproductions; but these photographs are only secondary explanations of the text. The latest development supersedes this phase, and small or large photos are placed in the text where formerly we used inexact, individually interpreted concepts and expressions. The objectivity of photography liberates the receptive reader from the crutches of the author's personal idiosyncrasies and forces him into the formation of his own opinion.

It is safe to predict that this increasing documentation through photography will lead in the near future to a replacement of literature by film. The indications of this development are apparent already in the increased use of the telephone which makes letterwriting obsolete. It is no valid objection that the production of films demands too intricate and costly an apparatus. Soon the making of a film will be as simple and available as now printing books.

An equally decisive change in the typographical image will occur in the making of posters, as soon as photography has replaced posterpainting. The effective poster must act with immediate impact on all psychological receptacles. Through an expert use of the camera, and of all photographic techniques, such as retouching, blocking, superimposition, distortion, enlargement, etc., in combination with the liberated typographical line, the effectiveness of posters can be immensely enlarged.

The new poster relies on photography, which is the new storytelling device of civilization, combined with the shock effect of new typefaces and brilliant color effects, depending on the desired intensity of the message.

The new typography is a simultaneous experience of vision and communication.

Originally published in *Staatliches Bauhaus in Weimar, 1919–23* (Munich, 1923). Reprinted by permission of Mrs. Sibyl Moholy-Nagy. This reprint was adapted from Richard Kostelanetz, ed., *Moholy-Nagy*, Documentary Monographs in Modern Art (New York: Allen Lane, 1974). Translation from the German by Sibyl Moholy-Nagy.

on typography

by herbert bayer

ypography is a service art, not a fine art, however pure and elemental the discipline may be.

the graphic designer today seems to feel that the typographic means at his disposal have been exhausted. accelerated by the speed of our time, a wish for new excitement is in the air. "new styles" are hopefully expected to appear.

nothing is more constructive than to look the facts in the face. what are they? the fact that nothing new has developed in recent decades? the boredom of the dead end without signs for a renewal? or is it the realization that a forced change in search of a "new style" can only bring superficial gain?

it seems appropriate at this point to recall the essence of statements made by progressive typographers of the 1920s:

previously used largely as a medium for making language visible, typographic material was discovered to have distinctive optical properties of its own, pointing toward specifically typographic expression. typographers envisioned possibilities of deeper visual experiences from a new exploitation of the typographic material itself.

they called for clarity, conciseness, precision; for more articulation, contrast, tension in the color and black and white values of the typographic page.

typography was for the first time seen not as an isolated discipline and technique, but in context with the ever-widening visual experiences that the picture symbol, photo, film, and television brought.

they recognized that in all human endeavors a technology had adjusted to man's demands; while no marked change or improvement had taken place in man's most profound invention, printing-writing, since gutenberg.

the manual skill and approach of the craftsman was seen to be inevitably replaced by mechanical techniques.

once more it became clear that typography is not self-expression within predetermined aesthetics, but that it is conditioned by the message it visualizes.

that typographic aesthetics were not stressed in these statements does not mean a lack of concern with them. but it appears that the searching went beyond surface effects into underlying strata.

it is a fallacy to believe that styles can be created as easily and as often as fashions change. more is involved than trends of taste devoid of inner substance and structure, applied as cultural sugar-coating.

moreover, the typographic revolution was not an isolated event but went hand in hand with a new social, political consciousness and consequently, with the building of new cultural foundations.

the artist's acceptance of the machine as a tool for mass production has had its impression on aesthetic concepts. since then an age of science has come upon us, and the artist has been motivated more than ever, to open his mind to the new forces that shape our lives.

new concepts will not grow on mere design variations of long-established forms such as the book. the aesthetic restraint that limits the development of the book must finally be overcome, and new ideas must logically be deduced from the function of typography and its carriers. although i realize how deeply anchored in tradition and how petrified the subject of writing and spelling is, a new typography will be bound to an alphabet that corresponds to the demands of an age of science. it must, unfortunately, be remembered that we live in a time of great ignorance and lack of concern with the alphabet, writing, and typography. with nostalgia we hear of times when literate people had knowledge, respect, and understanding of the subject. common man today has no opinion at all in such matters. it has come to a state where even the typesetter, the original typographer, as well as the printer, has lost this culture. responsibility has been shifted onto the shoulders of the designer almost exclusively.

in the united states the art of typography, book design, visual communication at large, in its many aspects, is being shelved as a minor art. it has no adequate place of recognition in our institutions of culture. the graphic designer is designated with the minimizing term "commercial," and is generally ignored as compared to the prominence accorded by the press to architecture and the "fine arts." visual communication has made revolutionary strides and real contributions to the contemporary world picture. yet, the artist-typographer represents a small number of typography producers compared to the output of the nation. their efforts must be valued as they keep the aesthetic standards from falling, and because they alone set the pace in taste.

there can be no doubt that our writing-printing-reading methods are antiquated and inefficient as compared to the perfection attained in other areas of human endeavor.

the history of our alphabet and any probing into its optical effectiveness expose a lack of principle and structure, precision and efficiency which should be evidenced in this important tool.

attempts have been made to design visually (to distinguish from aesthetically) improved alphabets. but redesigning will result in just another typeface unless the design is primarily guided by optics as well as by a revision of spelling. this, in turn, reveals the need for a clearer relation of writing-printing to the spoken word, a reorganization of the alphabetic sound-symbols, the creation of new symbols. the type designer is not usually a language reformer, but a systematic approach will inevitably carry him to a point where he will ask for nothing less than a complete overhaul of communication with visual sound.

however unlikely the possibilities for the adoption of such far-reaching renovation appears at the moment, revitalization of typography will come:

a. from the increased demands made on the psychophysiological apparatus of our perceptive senses;

b. from a new alphabet;

c. from the different physical forms that the carriers of typography will take.

the more we read, the less we see. constant exposure to visual materials has dulled our sense of seeing. overfed with reading as we are, the practice of reading must be activated. a new effort is needed to recapture and retain freshness. little known is the fact that the act of seeing is work, that it demands more than a quarter of the nervous energy the human body burns up. during waking hours your eyes almost never rest. in reading this article you must refocus as you skip from word to word. much energy is required for blinking and turning the eyeballs. more is needed by the tiny ciliary muscles to alter the shape of the crystalline lens for focusing. the effort of seeing contributes a large share to physical tiredness.

taking a closer look at present-day typographic customs, i make the following suggestions, believing that they offer immediate possibilities for both improvement and change.

visual research

"the eye seldom focuses for long on one point in a design. it flits back and forth from one element to another in haphazard sequence, unless the design is skillfully arranged to focus its orderly progress from one idea to the next. it is a vital part of the designer's job to make sure that the eye sees first things first and that it is made to dwell as long as possible on areas of special importance, such as the name of a product."[1]

graphic design will more than ever be determined by its purpose. the designer-typographer can find new impetuses from research in vision such as the above exemplifies.

universal communication

for a long time to come we will accept the existence of the different languages now in use. this will continue to pose barriers to communication, even after improved (possibly phonetic) writing methods have been adopted within all the languages. therefore, a more universal visual medium to bridge the gap between them must eventually evolve. first steps in this direction have, strangely enough, been made by the artist. now science must become a teammate and give him support with precise methods for a more purposeful handling of visual problems.

the book has been a standard form for a long time. a new spirit invaded the stagnant field of rigidity with the adoption of the dynamic page composition. an important extension was introduced with the recognition of supranational pictorial communication. with its combination of text and pictures, today's magazine already represents a new standard medium. while pictorial communication in a new sense has lived through a short but inspiring childhood, typography has hardly aspired to become an integrated element.

exploration of the potentialities of the book of true text-picture integration has only begun and will, by itself, become of utmost importance to universal understanding.

communication of selling

recently certain american national advertising pages have expressed a remarkable trend to planning. these pages contain and operate with a conglomeration of ugly, differently styled, contrasting or conflicting alphabets. the advertising agencies (no artist-designer's reasoning or taste could produce these pages) that produced this concept clearly must have been motivated by attention-getting-by-all-means aggressiveness and provocation. the result is irritation to the reader, who, therefore, reacts. this ignoring of aesthetics, in fact this twisting of unaesthetics into a function, provides a lesson to be learned. here is bad taste under the disguise of functionalism par excellence.

but new typographic life may come from such a ruthless technique, as is exemplified in many of america's "hard-sell" advertising pages. the reason for this speculation is that here typography clearly serves an intended purpose. the means by which the purpose is obtained are wrong and bear none of the aesthetic restraint that dominates much typographic thinking.

the narrow column

sizes of typefaces must be proportionate to the length of the line. the smaller the type, the shorter the line (for a standard measurement, 10 point typeface should not be set wider than 20 to 25 pica). adoption of the narrow column, which has proven itself to be considerably easier and faster to read, as newspaper readers can testify, would change the shape of the book. a "one column" book would be high and narrow, would not lend itself to binding on the long side, but might be divided into separate chapters in accordion folds collected in binders or boxes.

square span

tradition requires that sentences follow each other in a horizontal continuous sequence. paragraphs are used to ease perception by a slight break. there is no reason for this to be the only method to transmit language to the eye. sentences could as well follow each other vertically or otherwise, if it would facilitate reading.

following is an excerpt of a letter from "the reporter of direct mail advertising:" "square span" is putting words into thought groups of two or three short lines, such as

after a	you will	in easily	groups of
short time	begin	understood	words
	thinking		

you will	confusing	with	and
automatically	your	complicated	unnecessary
stop	sentences	phrases	words[2]

typewriters and typesetting machines would have to be adjusted to this method. text written in logical, short thought groups lends itself best. the advantages of grouping words support the theory that we do not read individual letters, but words or phrases. this poses a new challenge for the typographer.

text in color

black printing on white stock, because of its extreme opposites, is not entirely satisfactory. the eye forms complementary images. flickering and optical illusions occur, however minimized they may be in a small typeface. they can be reduced if the contrast of black on white is softened by gray printing on white stock; black printing on gray, yellow, light blue, or light green stock; brown, dark green, or dark blue printing on light colored stock. the colors of printing in relation to the colors of stock need not necessarily be chosen for harmonies; it is the power of controlled contrast that must be retained.

change of impact

furthermore, a great easing of reading is effected and freshness of perception is prolonged if a book is made up with a sequence of pages of different colored stock printed in various colors. which color follows another is less important than that the hues be approximately of equal value to safeguard continuity.

dr. w. h. bates has recommended a frequent shifting to aid in refocusing a fixed stare caused by the eye-tiring monotony of reading matter. the typographer can support this recommendation by the above change of impact through color.

new slaves

speculation into the future (perhaps not so distant) leads me to assume that methods of communication will change drastically.

the storage of books will be replaced by microfilms, which in turn will change the design of libraries. computing machines can already substitute for printed matter by storing knowledge. they will have any and all desired information available and ready when needed on short call, faster, more completely than research teams could, relieving and unburdening our brains of memory ballast. this suggests that we will write and read less and less, and the book may be eliminated altogether. the time may come when we have learned to communicate by electronic or extrasensory means. . . .

formalism and the straightjacket of a style lead to a dead end. the self-changing pulse of life is the nature of things with its unlimited forms and ways of expression. this we must recognize and not make new cliches out of old formulas.

---

[1]From a booklet *An Approach To Packaging,* Container Corporation of America, Design Laboratory, which makes extensive use of an ocular camera to check this aspect of the designer's work.

[2]Square span writing was developed by Robert B. Andrews, Dallas, Texas.

From *herbert bayer: the complete work,* edited by Arthur A. Cohen (Cambridge: MIT Press), 1984. Originally used as one of several introductory essays to an exhibition catalogue of the Busch-Reisinger Museum at Harvard University, Cambridge, for their exhibition Concepts of the Bauhaus, April 30–September 3, 1971.

The Principles of the New Typography

By Jan Tschichold

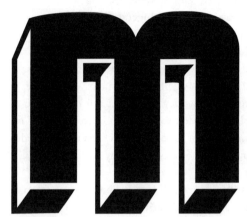odern man has to absorb every day a mass of printed matter which, whether he has asked for it or not, is delivered through his letter-box or confronts him everywhere out of doors. At first, today's printing differed from that of previous times less in form than in quantity. But as the quantity increased, the "form" also began to change: the speed with which the modern consumer of printing has to absorb it means that the form of printing also must adapt itself to the conditions of modern life. As a rule we no longer read quietly line by line, but glance quickly over the whole, and only if our interest is awakened do we study it in detail.

The old typography both in feeling and in form was adapted to the needs of its readers, who had plenty of time to read line by line in a leisurely manner. For them, function could not yet play any significant role. For this reason the old typography concerned itself less with function than with what was called "beauty" or "art." Problems of formal aesthetics (choice of type, mixture of typefaces and ornament) dominated considerations of form. It is for this reason that the history of typography since Manutius is not so much a development towards clarity of appearance (the only exception being the period of Didot, Bodoni, Baskerville, and Walbaum) as an embodiment of the development of historical typefaces and ornaments.

It was left to our age to achieve a lively focus on the problem of "form" or design. While up to now form was considered as something external, a product of the "artistic imagination" (Haeckel even imputed such "artistic intentions" to nature in his *Art Forms in Nature*), today we have moved considerably closer to the recognition of its essence through the renewed study of nature and more especially to technology (which is only a kind of second nature). Both nature and technology teach us that "form" is not independent, but grows out of function (purpose), out of the materials used (organic or technical), and out of how they are used. This was how the marvelous forms of nature and the equally marvelous forms of technology originated. We can describe the forms of technology just as "organic" (in an intellectual sense) as those of nature. But as a rule most people see only the superficial forms of technology, they admire their "beauty"—of airplanes, cars, or ships—instead of recognizing that their perfection of appearance is due to the precise and economic expression of their function. In the process of giving form, both technology and nature use the same laws of economy, precision, minimum friction, and so on. Technology by its very nature can never be an end in itself, only a means to an end, and can therefore be a part of man's spiritual life only indirectly, while the remaining fields of human creativity rise above the purely functional of technical forms. But they too, following the laws of nature, are drawn towards greater clarity and purity of appearance. Thus architecture discards the ornamental façade and "decorated" furniture and develops its forms from the function of the building—no longer from the outside inwards, as determined by the façade-orientation of pre-wartime days, but from the inside outwards, the natural way. So too typography is liberated from its present superficial and formalistic shapes, and from its so-called "traditional" designs which are long since fossilized. To us, the succession of historic styles, reactions against Jugendstil, are nothing but proof of creative incompetence. It cannot and must not be our wish today to ape the typography of previous centuries, itself conditioned by its own time. Our age, with its very different aims, its often different ways and means and highly developed techniques, must dictate new and different visual forms. Though its significance remains undeniable, to think today that the Gutenberg Bible represents an achievement that can never again be reached is both naïve and romantic rubbish. If we want to "prove ourselves worthy" of the clearly significant achievements of the past, we must set our own achievements beside them born out of our own time. They can only become "classic" if they are unhistoric.

The essence of the New Typography is clarity. This puts it into deliberate opposition to the old typography whose aim was "beauty" and whose clarity did not attain the high level we require today. This utmost clarity is necessary today because of the manifold claims for our attention made by the extraordinary amount of print, which demands the greatest economy of expression. The gentle swing of the pendulum between ornamental type, the (superficially understood) "beautiful" appearance, and "adornment" by extraneous additions (ornaments) can never produce the pure form we demand today. Especially the feeble clinging to the bugbear of arranging type on a central axis results in the extreme inflexibility of contemporary typography.

In the old typography, the arrangement of individual units is subordinated to the principle of arranging everything on a central axis. In my historical introduction I have shown that this principle started in the Renaissance and has not yet been abandoned. Its superficiality becomes obvious when we look at Renaissance or Baroque title pages. Main units are arbitrarily cut up: for example, logical order, which should be expressed by the use of different type-sizes, is ruthlessly sacrificed to external form. Thus the principal line contains only three-quarters of the title, and the rest of the title, set several sizes smaller, appears in the next line. Such things admittedly do not often happen today, but the rigidity of central-axis setting hardly allows work to be carried out with the degree of logic we now demand. The central axis runs through the whole like an artificial, invisible backbone: its raison d'être is today as pretentious as the tall white collars of Victorian gentlemen. Even in good central-axis composition the contents are subordinated to "beautiful line arrangement." The whole is a "form" which is predetermined and therefore must be inorganic.

We believe it is wrong to arrange a text as if there were some focal point in the center of a line which would justify such an arrangement. Such points of course do not exist, because we read by starting at one side (Europeans for example read from left to right, the Chinese from top to bottom and right to left). Axial arrangements are illogical because the distance of the stressed, central parts from the beginning and end of the word sequences is not usually equal but constantly varies from line to line.

But not only the preconceived idea of axial arrangement but also all other preconceived ideas—like those of the pseudo-constructivists—are diametrically opposed to the essence of the New Typography. Every piece of typography which originates in a preconceived idea of form, of whatever kind, is wrong. The New Typography is distinguished from the old by the fact that its first objective is to develop its visible form out of the functions of the text. It is essential to give pure and direct expression to the contents of whatever is printed; just as in the works of technology and nature, "form" must be created out of function. Only then can we achieve a typography which expresses the spirit of modern man. The function of printed text is communication, emphasis (word value), and the logical sequence of the contents.

Every part of a text relates to every other part by a definite, logical relationship of emphasis and value, predetermined by content. It is up to the typographer to express this relationship clearly and visibly, through type sizes and weight, arrangement of lines, use of color, photography, etc.

The typographer must take the greatest care to study how his work is read and ought to be read. It is true that we usually read from top left to bottom right—but this is not a law. . . . There is no doubt that we read most printed matter in successive steps: first the heading (which need not be the opening word) and then, if we continue to read the printed matter at all, we read the rest bit by bit according to its importance. It is therefore quite feasible to start reading a text at a different point from the top left. The exact place depends entirely on the kind of printed matter and the text itself. But we must admit that there are dangers in departing from the main rule of reading from the top to the bottom. One must therefore, in general, not set a following body of text higher than the preceding one—assuming that the arrangement of the text has a logical sequence and order.

Working through a text according to these principles will usually result in a rhythm different from that of former symmetrical typography. Asymmetry is the rhythmic expression of functional design. In addition to being more logical, asymmetry has the advantage that its complete appearance is far more optically effective than symmetry.

Hence the predominance of asymmetry in the New Typography. Not least, the liveliness of asymmetry is also an expression of our own movement and that of modern life; it is a symbol of the changing forms of life in general when asymmetrical movement in typography takes the place of symmetrical repose. This movement must not however degenerate into unrest or chaos. A striving for order can, and must, also be expressed in asymmetrical form. It is the only way to make a better, more natural order possible, as opposed to symmetrical form which does not draw its laws from within itself but from outside.

Furthermore, the principle of asymmetry gives unlimited scope for variation in the New Typography. It also expresses the diversity of modern life, unlike central-axis typography which, apart from variations of typeface (the only exception), does not allow such variety.

While the New Typography allows much greater flexibility in design, it also encourages "standardization" in the construction of units, as in building.

The old typography did the opposite: it recognized only one basic form, the central-axis arrangement, but allowed all possible and impossible construction elements (typefaces, ornaments, etc.).

The need for clarity in communication raises the question of how to achieve clear and unambiguous form.

BUCHVERTRIEB
G   M   B   H

»DAS POLITISCHE BUCH«

BERLIN-SCHMARGENDORF

13.12.1926.
B.H./Sch.

Centered layout using lightweight sans serif has no visual effectiveness
and reaches a "typographic low" for today (letterhead for a bookshop).

Above all, a fresh and original intellectual approach is needed, avoiding all standard solutions. If we think clearly and approach each task with a fresh and determined mind, a good solution will usually result.

The most important requirement is to be objective. This however does not mean a way of design in which everything is omitted that used to be tacked on, as in the letterhead "Das politische Buch" shown here. The type is certainly legible and there are no ornaments whatever. But this is not the kind of objectivity we are talking about. A better name for it would be meagerness. Incidentally this letterhead also shows the hollowness of the old principles: without "ornamental" typefaces they do not work.

And yet, it is absolutely necessary to omit everything that is not needed. The old ideas of design must be discarded and new ideas developed. It is obvious that functional design means the abolition of the "ornamentation" that has reigned for centuries.

The use of ornament, in whatever style or quality, comes from an attitude of childish naïveté. It shows a reluctance to use "pure design," a giving-in to a primitive instinct to decorate—which reveals, in the last resort, a fear of *pure* appearance. It is so easy to employ ornament to cover up bad design! The important architect Adolf Loos, one of the first champions of pure form, wrote already in 1898: "The more primitive a people, the more extravagantly they use ornament and decoration. The Indian overloads everything, every boat, every rudder, every arrow, with ornament. To insist on decoration is to put yourself on the same level as an Indian. The Indian in us all must be overcome. The Indian says: This woman is beautiful because she wears golden rings in her nose and her ears. Men of a higher culture say: This woman is beautiful because she does not wear rings in her nose or her ears. To seek beauty in form itself rather than make it dependent on ornament should be the aim of all mankind."

Today we see in a desire for ornament an ignorant tendency which our century must repress. When in earlier periods ornament was used, often in an extravagant degree, it only showed how little the essence of typography, which is communication, was understood.

It must be understood that "ornament" is not only decorated rules and printers' flowers but also includes all combinations of rules. Even the thick/thin rule is an ornament, and must be avoided. (It was used to disguise contrasts, to reduce them to one level. The New Typography, on the other hand, emphasizes contrasts and uses them to create a new unity.)

"Abstract decorations" which some foundries have produced under different names are also ornaments in this sense. Unfortunately many people have thought the essence of the New Typography consists merely in the use of bold rules, circles, and triangles. If these are merely substituted for the old ornaments, nothing is improved. This error is forgivable since, after all, all former typography was oriented towards the ornamental. But that is exactly why the utmost care must be taken to avoid replacing the old floral or other ornamentation with abstract ornaments. Equally the New Typography has absolutely nothing to do with "pictorial" typesetting (Bildsatz) which has become fashionable recently. In almost all its examples it is the opposite of what we are aiming for.

But it is not enough to dispense with ornament in order to create a meaningful form. We have already seen that even the old form that dispenses with ornament is ineffective because it is still based on the effect of ornamental types. The form of the old typography could be taken in at a glance, even though this does not correspond with the reading process. Even if I succeed in recognizing the outline of the type matter I have not really read anything. Reading presupposes eye movement. The New Typography so designs text matter that the eye is led from one word and one group of words to the next. So a logical organization of the text is needed, through the use of different type-sizes, weights, placing in relation to space, color, etc.

The real meaning of form is made clearer by its opposite. We would not recognize day as day if night did not exist. The ways to achieve contrast are endless: the simplest are large/small, light/dark, horizontal/vertical, square/round, smooth/rough, closed/open, colored/plain; all offer many possibilities of effective design.

Large differences in weight are better than small. The closer in size different types are to each other, the weaker will be the result. A limit to the number of type sizes used—normally three to not more than five—is always to be recommended. This has the additional advantage of being easier both in designing and in setting. Variations in size should be emphatic: it is always better for the headline to be very large the remaining text noticeably smaller.

It is vital that all contrasts, for example in type sizes, should be logical. For example, a forename should not have a much larger initial letter if the beginning of the principal name is not specially indicated. All form must correspond with meaning and not contradict it.

In asymmetric design, the white background plays an active part in the design. The typical main display of the old typography, the title page, showed its black type on a white background that played no part in the design. In asymmetric typography, on the other hand, the paper background contributes to a greater or lesser degree to the effect of the whole. The strength of its effect depends on whether it is deliberately emphasized or not; but in asymmetric design it is always a component. The New Typography uses the effectiveness of the former "background" quite deliberately, and considers the blank white spaces on the paper as formal elements just as much as the areas of black type. In this way the New Typography has enriched the art of printing by giving it a new medium of expression. The powerful effect in many examples of the New Typography depends directly on the use of large areas of white: white is always stronger than grey or black. Strong contrasts between white and black, in the form of type or rules, emphasize the white areas and greatly assist the total effect.

A common misunderstanding of what we are about can be seen when the area of white has been decided beforehand and the text compressed into it. It is equally wrong to suppose that areas of white are ever more important than the words of the text.

When the design of a piece of typography is looked at—and all typography has a design, of varying nature and quality—modern typography is distinguished by its formal use of the white and black areas. Of course, logically only the type is important.

The pursuit of greater effectiveness and clarity in the relationship between black and white areas often leads to a noticeable reduction of margins (always prominent in the old typography). In the New Typography margins often almost entirely disappear. Of course type cannot in most cases be set right up to the edge of the paper, which would hinder legibility. In small items of printed matter, 12 to 24 points are the minimum margin required; in posters 48 points. On the other hand, borders of solid red or black can be taken right up to the edge, since unlike type they do not require a white margin to achieve their best effect. Blocks too can be bled off the page provided the trim is accurate.

Color

In contrast with the old typography, in which color as well as form was always used decoratively, in the New Typography color is used functionally, i.e., the physiological effect peculiar to each color is used to increase or decrease the importance of a block of type, a photograph, or whatever. White, for example, has the effect of reflecting light: it shines. Red comes forward, it seems closer to the reader than any other color, including white. Black on the other hand is the densest color and seems to retire the furthest. Of the other colors, yellow, for example, is close to red, and blue to black. (We do not accept a "literary" identification of colors, for example, red=love, yellow=envy, as not being natural.)

We have today a strong feeling for light, therefore for white, which explains its importance in the New Typography. The liveliness of red corresponds to our own natures, and we prefer it to all other colors. The already strong contrast between black and white can be greatly enhanced by the addition of red. (This is admittedly not a new discovery: but we have perhaps made sharper use of this combination than the earlier typographers, who also much enjoyed using black-red on white, especially in the Gothic and Baroque periods.)

The combination of black-red is of course not the only possibility, as is often mistakenly supposed, but it is often chosen because of its greater intensity. Color should be used, in general, to help express the purpose of the work: a visiting-card does not require three colors, and a poster generally needs more than just black and white.

Pure red, yellow, and blue, unmixed with black, will generally be preferred, because of their intensity, but other mixed colors need not be excluded.

Type

None of the typefaces to whose basic form some kind of ornament has been added (serifs in roman type, lozenge shapes and curlicues in fraktur) meet our requirements for clarity and purity. Among all the types that are available, the so-called "Grotesque" (sans serif) or "block letter" ("skeleton letters" would be a better name) is the only one in spiritual accordance with our time.

To proclaim sans serif as the typeface of our time is not a question of being fashionable, it really does express the same tendencies to be seen in our architecture. It will not be long before not only the "art" typefaces, as they are sometimes called today, but also the classical typefaces, disappear, as completely as the contorted furniture of the eighties.

There is no doubt that the sans serif types available today are not yet wholly satisfactory as all-purpose faces. The essential characteristics of this type have not been fully worked out: the lowercase letters especially are still too like their "humanistic" counterparts. Most of them, in particular the newest designs, such as Ebar and Kabel, are inferior to the old sans serifs, and have modifications which place them basically in line with the rest of the "art" faces. As bread-and-butter faces they are less good than the old sans faces. Paul Renner's Futura makes a significant step in the right direction.

But all the attempts up to now to produce a type for our time are merely "improvements" on the previous sans serifs: they are all still too artistic, too artificial, in the old sense, to fulfill what we need today.

Personally I believe that no single designer can produce the typeface we need, which must be free from all personal characteristics: it will be the work of a group, among whom I think there must be an engineer.

For the time being it seems to me that the jobbing sans serifs, like those from Bauer & Co. in Stuttgart, are the most suitable for use today, because of their functionalism and quiet line. Less good is Venus and its copies, owing to the bad design of caps *E* and *F* and the lowercase *t* with its ugly slanted crossbar. In third place, when nothing better is available, come the "painterly" (malerischen) block letters (light and bold, etc.) with their seemingly gnawed-off edges and rounded finals. Of the roman types, the bold romans (the Aldine, the bold Egyptians), with their exact drawing, are best, as far as types for emphasis are required.

The essential limitation of this restricted range of typefaces does not mean that printers who have no or too few sans serif faces cannot produce good contemporary typography while using other faces. But it must be laid down that sans serif is absolutely and always better. I am aware that to lay down the law like this will offend the romantic predilections of a large part of the printing trade and the public for the old "decorative" faces. These old types can however from time to time find a new use in modern typography: for fun, for example in order to make typographical parody of the "good old days"; or as an eye-catcher—for example by using a bold fraktur *B* in the middle of sans serif—just as the pompous uniforms of Victorian generals and admirals have been degraded for flunkeys and fancy dress. Whoever is so attached to fraktur—this sixteenth-century clerk's type—that he cannot let go of it, should also not do violence to it by using it in modern typography where it can never be comfortable. Fraktur, like gothic and Schwabacher, has so little to do with us that it must be totally excluded as a basic type for contemporary work.

The emphatically national, exclusivist character of fraktur—but also of the equivalent national scripts of other peoples, for example of the Russians or the Chinese—contradicts present-day transnational bonds between people and forces their inevitable elimination.[1] To keep these types is retrograde. Roman type is the international typeface of the future. These important changes must come, since they express the actual spirit of our age and are required by the technical forms of the present and indeed the future.

As undesirable as fraktur are those roman types with extraordinary forms, such as script and decorated, like Eckmann and others. The details of these faces distract from the meaning and thus contradict the essence of typography, which is never an end in itself. Their use for parody, in the sense described above, of course remains legitimate.

As a bread-and-butter type today's sans serifs are only partially suited. A bolder face is out of the question because continuous reading matter in bold sans serif is not easy to read. I find the best face in use today is the so-called ordinary jobbing sans serif, which is quiet and easy to read. In using it for this book I wanted to show how readable it is, but I still have certain reservations. However, it is preferable to all the romans. (In the particular choice of type for this book I was limited to what the printer held.)

The main reason why sans serif is so seldom used today for normal text setting is that in general there is not enough of it available. So for much printed matter and books like the present one, entirely set in sans serif, it will remain the exception. In such cases the text face will be a good roman, and sans serif will be reserved for emphasis.

Even more than the historic typefaces, the "artists'" typefaces are disturbing because of their strongly individual character, which is in direct opposition to the spirit of our age and makes them unsuitable for properly designed printing today. No period was so preoccupied with individualism as that from the beginning of the present century up to the outbreak of war. The "artists'" types of this period reached their lowest point. None are in any way better than their predecessor, which are preferable for their superior quality.

Nevertheless the classic faces like Walbaum, Didot, Bodoni, etc., cannot serve as bread-and-butter types today. In terms of their conception they possess romantic associations, they divert the reader's attention into certain emotional and intellectual spheres and clearly belong to a past with which we have no connection. A natural development—not a forced one—would hardly have brought them back again.

To my mind, looking at the modern romans, it is the unpretentious works of the anonymous type-designers that have best served the spirit of their age: Sorbonne, Nordische Antiqua, Französische Antiqua, and so on. These three typefaces and their derivatives are the best designs from the pre-war period.[2] They are easily legible; they are also above all in a technical sense useful and free from personal idiosyncrasies—in the best sense of the word, uninteresting. They can therefore be used everywhere, when a roman type has to be used because no appropriate sans serif is available.

On the Expressiveness of Type

Those who claim that sans serif is the typeface of our own age are often told that it does not express anything.

Do other typefaces express anything? Is it really a typeface's job to express spiritual matters?

Yes and no. The widely held belief that every typeface has some "spiritual" content is certainly not true of either gothic type (textura) or sans serif. The enormous number of typefaces available today, which express only an absence of creativity and are the result of the feebly eclectic nature of the pre-war period, may lead to the erroneous conclusion that gothic type expresses peace, solemnity, and religion, and italic, on the contrary, expresses cheerfulness and joy. However, all the innumerable things that can be expressed in writing, of *whatever kind,* at any time, are set down in one—or at most two—kinds of lettering or type. Yes, the character of gothic is religious and solemn, that of rococo (as far as the wealthy class is concerned) is light-hearted, but the typography of those times, even when expressing something contrary to the "zeitgeist," is always logical and stylistically consistent. In the Gothic period even profane texts were set in textura, and in the Rococo period an invitation to a funeral looks in no way different from any light-hearted printed matter of the same period.

All lettering, especially type, is first and foremost an expression of its own time, just as every man is a symbol of his time. What textura and also rococo type express is not religiosity, but the Gothic, not cheerfulness, but the Rococo; and what sans serif expresses is not lack of feeling but the twentieth century! There is no personal expression of the designer, nor was it ever his aim, except in the first years of our century. The different kinds of type get their character from the different ideas of form in every age. Every punch-cutter wished to create the best possible typeface. If Didot did something different from Fleischmann, it was because times had changed, not because he wanted to produce something "special," "personal," or "unique." The conception of what a good typeface should look like had simply changed.

The eclectic nature of the pre-war period led people to play with typefaces of every period, thus revealing their own artistic poverty. A book about the Thirty Years' War had to be set in a different face from Mörike's poems or an industrial catalogue. But St. Augustine was set in textura, not in uncial! All printed matter of whatever kind that is created today must bear the hallmark of our age, and should not imitate printed matter of the past. This applies not only to the typeface but of course to every element of the manufacture: the illustrations, the binding, etc. Earlier periods, unlike us, ever conscious of themselves, always denied the past, often very crudely; that can be seen in the building of cathedrals, in the general development of culture, and in typography. The punch-cutter Unger, creator of Unger-fraktur (c. 1800) and a famous typographer, declared that Schwabacher was an ugly type and introduced letterspacing for emphasis in fraktur (previously, Schwabacher had been used for emphasis in fraktur). He was absolutely right. His age, the Rococo, found that gothic, and its ways of expression, including Schwabacher, were out of harmony with their own times and hence ugly: Unger was merely its mouthpiece in our field of typography.

An art historian may prize the good qualities of an old Schwabacher type, and we too can see that it was an excellent face of its period, but we must not use it today, it is totally unsuitable for the twentieth century. So are all the other historical typefaces.

Like everyone else, we too must look for a typeface expressive of our own age. Our age is characterized by an all-out search for clarity and truth, for purity of appearance. So the problem of what typeface to use is necessarily different from what it was in previous times. We require from type plainness, clarity, the rejection of everything that is superfluous. That leads us to a geometric construction of form. In sans serif we find a type that comes very close to these requirements, so it must become the basis for all future work to create the typeface of our age. The character of an age cannot be expressed only in rich and ornamental forms. The simple geometric forms of sans serif express something too: clarity and concentration on essentials, and so the essence of our time. To express this is important. But it is not important to create special types for advertising perfume manufacturers and fashion shops, or for lyrical outpourings by poets. It was never the task of punch-cutters of the past to create a type for a single kind of expression. The best typefaces are those which can be used for all purposes, and the bad ones are those which can be used only for visiting-cards or hymn books.

A good letter is one that expresses itself, or rather "speaks," with the utmost distinctiveness and clarity. And a good typeface has no purpose beyond being of the highest clarity.

Sans serif, looked at in detail, is admittedly capable of improvement, but there is no doubt that it is the basic form from which the typeface of the future will grow.

Other individual expressive possibilities of type have nothing to do with typography. They are in contradiction to its very nature. They hinder direct and totally clear communication, which must always be the first purpose of typography.

Orthography As at Present or All in Lower Case

In roman type and its simpler form, sans serif, we possess faces that have been made out of not one but two alphabets. This combination took place in the fifteenth century. The one alphabet, the capitals, known as majuscules, was made by the old Romans as a form shaped by the chisel, at the beginning of our era. The other alphabet, the small or lower-case letters, called minuscules, dates from the time of the emperor Charlemagne, about A.D. 800; the so-called Carolingian minuscule, a written letter made with a pen, with ascenders and descenders. This script too was originally complete in itself. The concept of "capital letters" was foreign to it. It was during the Renaissance that these two forms of letter, the roman capitals and the Carolingian minuscules, were combined to make one alphabet, the "Antiqua" or "roman." This is the explanation of the dichotomy, especially noticeable in German, between the capitals and the smaller letters. It is much less notice-able in other languages, especially French and English, because they use capital letters much less often than in German. Settings in roman type in English always look better than in German because they employ fewer accents and in particular do not use capitals for the first letters of nouns.

For a long time now there have been efforts to abolish the use of capital initial letters for nouns and make German writing conform with the international style. This signaling of nouns with capitals started in the Baroque period and seems to us now no longer use-ful. The rules governing our use of capitals make teaching at school more difficult and also present problems in later life because of the many exceptions. Jakob Grimm, one of the founders of German studies, advocated its abolition already a hundred years ago, and referred to the Old and Middle High German literature in which capitals were used only for proper names and beginnings of sentences. Following him, capitals have been used by German scholars only in this way.

The aesthetic critic finds this mixture of two such differently designed faces unpleasing. For this reason many artists prefer to use capitals only, to avoid mixing them with lower case. In France recently there have been many examples of the independent use of lower case only—mainly in fashion publicity and the announcements in fashion-shop windows. Besides the exclusive use of lower case for text can be seen the use of capitals alone for headings—and vice-versa, capitals for text and lower case for headings. From this one can see that it is now recognized that the two alphabets of roman are really two different styles, and should be used in parallel, but not mixed.

The New Typography does not accept either of these alternatives to the previous sys-tem—adjustment to the international writing method, or division of roman type into capitals and lower case and regarding them as separate alphabets, even if this is against current opinion. It accepts neither the view of the Germanists nor that of the artists fol-lowing the eclectic French fashion. The New Typography demands *economy in type design.* To redesign our letters completely—as in shorthand and lettering for the blind—would be quite impractical and unacceptable. So we have to make do with the type we have, the capitals and the lower case. To decide which to choose is not difficult, because capitals in continuous text are too difficult to read. Lowercase letters are far easier to read, because of the ascenders and descenders which make complete words easier to recognize.

A completely one-type system, using lower case only, would be of great advantage to the national economy; it would entail savings and simplifications in many areas; and would also result in great savings of spiritual and intellectual energy at present wasted: we can mention here the teaching of writing and orthography, a great simplification in type-writers and typing technique, a relief for memory, type design, type-cutting, type-casting, and all composition methods—and so on.

At the same time as economic advantages, the use of minuscule would give us a stylisti-cally faultless letter, so scientific advantage would be combined with aesthetic.

So there cannot be any change in orthography if it means abandoning the concept of capitals and lower case. We can go on using the small letters, only the use of capitals is discontinued. (A subsequent continuance of capitals in some special kinds of writing could be considered.)

But whether roman and also modern sans serif lower case can continue to express the opinions and claims of the present is open to doubt. Their form has always too much of writing and too little of type, and the efforts of the future will be directed towards sup-pressing their written character and bringing them closer to true print form.

German orthography if it is to be truly contemporary must see changes, which will undoubtedly influence typeface design. Above all we must lose the burden of too much heavy philology in linguistics, and provide ourselves with self-explanatory signs for sch, ch, dg, drop the unnecessary letters (z, q, c) and aim at the rule "Write as you speak!" and its counterpart "Speak as you write!" On this basis a new and more practical orthography could be achieved, without which literature cannot succeed.

Of course such a revolution in orthography and type will not happen in a day, but its time will assuredly come. Whether consciously or unconsciously, cultural developments take place and men change with them. The typeface of the future will not come from a single person but from a group of people.

It is significant that one of the best new books on speech, type, and orthography has been written not by an architect or a philologist but by an engineer: *Sprache und Schrift* (Speech and Writing) by Dr. W. Porstmann. Anyone interested in these problems will find this essential reading.

At the same time, while the New Typography regards the removal of capitals as desir-able, it is not an absolute demand. But it lies, like a more logical design for our orthogra-phy, in our path: an unmistakable design for typography that is in harmony with the desires and demands of our time.

Mistakes Often Met

In the beginning, many saw a new formalism in the New Typography: that is, they adopt-ed some of its most obvious features—circles, triangles, rules—as geometrical features and used them as if they were the old kinds of ornament. The "elementary ornaments" (itself a contradiction in terms) brought out by some foundries under various names further helped to spread this misunderstanding. These basic geometric forms, which we like to use must however be functional: they must emphasize words or paragraphs or be justified by the formal harmony of the whole. But instead of this we still find truly childish, pseudo-constructive shapes, which are totally contradictory to the spirit of the New Typography.

The newspaper advertisement shown on the next page is a typical example of pseudo-contructivism, found all too commonly. Its form is not natural but comes from an idea before it was set. The advertisement is no longer typography but painting with letters, it turns good typography into borrowed, misunderstood, and thoughtless shapes.

Angenehme Selbständigkeit

mit aussergewöhnl. Einkommen bietet sich in Berlin, wie auch auswärts, organ. befähigten Kaufleuten als Repräcentanten eines erst-klassigen Reklame-Unternehmens. Branchenkenntnisse nicht erforderlich. Barkapital 6-8000 M. auch Referenzen müssen nachweisbar sein. Ausführliche Offerten erbeten unter J. H. 3967 an Rudolf Mosse, Berlin SW 19

An example of pseudomodern typography. The compositor has the idea of a prefabricated foreign shape and forces the words into it. But the typographic form must be organic, it must evolve from the nature of the text.

Wrong! It looks functional but when examined more closely we find it is superficial and does not express the text. In the middle, it is very difficult to find where to go on reading. Certain forms of abstract painting, understood only superficially, have been used in this piece, but typography is not abstract painting!

A similar example is in the business announcement above. Again, a previously conceived and meaningless shape is used, which has no connection with the text or its logical arrangement and in fact conflicts with it. Another serious fault is the lack of contrast in color, which emphasizes the bland and boring look of the whole.

The magazine cover on the facing page is an even worse example. It attempts to be "technical" but contradicts the whole nature of what actually is technical. Here we see the mixing-in of that "art" against which we are fighting—an artificiality which neglects truth and merely makes a "pretty shape" which fails to express the purpose of the design. Imagination must be used on the basis of actual purpose, if truth in design is to be achieved. (In painting it is different: no restrictions are laid down, because the work does not have a fixed purpose.)

One also often finds the use of historical typefaces (Schwabacher, gothic, fraktur) in the manner of contemporary typography. But it is wrong to use these historical forms in this

Wrong! The word "Revue" is hard to read because of the complicated type: and the abstract forms are used thoughtlessly, purely for decoration, including the crossed thick-thin rules. The white paper background plays no part in the design. The whole shows a complete misunderstanding of the aims of the New Typography—which does not arrange decorative forms, but designs—that is, it resolves the given text, which itself must show the simplest forms, into a harmonious whole.

way—they are foreign to our time and should be used only in a manner suitable to their own age. Can you imagine an airline pilot with a beard? The juxtaposition of positive and negative (reversed black to white) type, first introduced by commercial artists, can also be found in purely typographic work. There is no objection to this if it is based on logic (an important part of a word can be emphasized in this way)—but that is not often the case. A word is often broken for purely formal reasons. This is not a sign of the New Typography. Independent negative lines can of course be beautiful and are usually very effective.

Equally, setting in which blocks of text are arranged alternately on the left and right of an imaginary vertical line usually has a forced and unsatisfactory effect. The resulting uneven spacing and the violence of the block-shapes are merely unpleasing repetitions of old mistakes.

But no one will hold the New Typography responsible for all the mistakes made under its name. The value of the work of printers striving to create the typographical expression of our time cannot be lessened by failures always inherent in any new movement.

[1] There are movements in Russia, Turkey, and China today to do away with nationalistic typefaces and replace them with roman. In Germany, on the contrary, railway-station lettering in roman is being replaced by gothic—which for foreigners is virtually unreadable!

[2] In the postwar period, the typefoundries repeated their old mistakes in an even worse form; their daily "best sellers" have not the slightest importance for the future.

From *The New Typography: A Handbook for Modern Designers,* translated by Ruari McLean (Berkeley: University of California Press, 1995).

The Bauhaus Tradition and the New Typography

By L. Sandusky

I n September of last year the Association of Arts and Industries announced the establishment in Chicago of a "new" Bauhaus, with L. Moholy-Nagy as Director. The following month its doors opened to a group of American students, who began, a little uncertain, one would imagine, to grope their way toward a new philosophy of art and industry. It has now completed its first year. In the minds of many who had been interested in the Bauhaus as a cultural and historical phenomenon its reestablishment suggests far-reaching implications. Among other things, it brings to the fore again the problem of Continental modernism, which in printing and advertising design has made uneven progress in America.

The bodily presence of an American version of the internationally famous German school, which played so conspicuous a part in the development of the "New Typography," makes it timely and worthwhile to re-examine the set of circumstances which made it what it was. For the story of the Bauhaus is the story of how a considerable body of contemporary American printing and advertising came to be what it is.

The thing of first interest is that the Bauhaus stood resolutely for the "new" as against the "old." In the eternal battle (in all the arts and crafts through which men have sought in different ways and with differing practical aims to express themselves) between "tradition and individual talent"—between the authority of the past and the needs of today—it threw its weight persistently on the side of individual talent. It was the converging point of everything that was alive with burgeoning possibilities.

Established at Weimar, in 1919, by Walter Gropius, a young architect dissatisfied with the sterile imitation of outworn styles and irrelevant forms, the Bauhaus began with the avowed object, "not to propagate any style, system, dogma, formula, or vogue, but simply to exert a revitalizing influence on design." Denying the traditional distinction between the "fine" and the "applied" arts and conceiving of mass production as the greatest single reality of the day, it sought to come to terms with the "machine." It rejected at once the utopian "handicraft" idealism, which would save men's souls through the creative work of their hands, and the sterile aestheticism of "Art for Art's Sake," which would preserve art from the slightest taint of usefulness. It sought, in short, "to eliminate every drawback of the machine without sacrificing any one of its real advantages." This "machine aesthetic" it applied (though the first emphasis was on architecture) to almost every branch of design, including furniture, interior decoration, typography, and advertising design.

Such a working philosophy, with the sociological goal of averting "mankind's enslavement by the machine by giving its products a content of reality and significance," had much to do with making the Bauhaus, within the fourteen years of its existence, a worldwide influence. But the more important thing was that it offered, in a way unparalleled in history, the right conditions for the birth of the "new." It came at the right time, established itself in the right place, and attracted the right men.

2

The Bauhaus was born amid a welter of war and post-war "isms"—belligerent move-ments, many of them, with evangelical leaders and followers who armed themselves for the fray with elaborate theories and a set of manifestoes. It was a time of tumult and shouting. But it was, more than anything else, a time of general trading of ideas and men among the arts, of the attempt to give form in one art to ideas and impressions imported from another.

The Russian painter Vassily Kandinsky (among the first to join the Bauhaus staff) was thinking of his work in terms of music and putting on canvas mystical Debussy-like com-positions to which he gave the name "improvisations." Though they were (in his own words) painted "rather subconsciously in a state of strong inner tension," he was not unaware of the specific influences that played a part in determining them—the poetry of Maeterlinck and the music, not alone of Debussy, but as well of Wagner, Mussorgsky, Scriabine, and Schönberg. Of these men Scriabine had already composed music in terms of painting; and Debussy had, because of the obvious analogy of his work with the cur-rent school of French painting, earned the title "Impressionist."

Kandinsky belonged to a group known as the "Blaue Reiter," which included painters, poets, musicians, and dramatists. At the same time that he was discovering the *soul*—the *innerer Klang*—of nature and humanity as the goal of abstract painting, he was rediscover-ing music as the perennial methodological ideal of all the arts. His ideas were set forth in *The Art of Spiritual Harmony*, originally published, in 1912, as *Uber das Geistige in der Kunst*: "*They [the arts] are finding in Music the best teacher. With few exceptions music has been for some centuries the art which has devoted itself, not to the reproduction of natural phenomenon, but rather to the expression of the artist's soul, in musical sound.*

"*A painter, who finds no satisfaction in mere representation, however artistic, in his longing to express his inner life, cannot but envy the ease with which music, the most non-material of the arts today, achieves this end. He naturally seeks to apply the methods of music to his own art. And from this results that modern desire for rhythm in painting, for mathematical, abstract construction, for repeated notes of color, for setting color in motion.*"

While Kandinsky, preoccupied with music and painting, was unconsciously laying the "spiritual" foundation for many of the things being done today in advertising art (such, for instance, as the work of "Desha" for New York's Lord & Taylor); Alexander Archipenko (now a member of the staff of the new Bauhaus) was combining sculpture and painting as one art and experimenting with constructions in glass, wood, and metal, which were a kind of cross between sculpture and industrial design. In his emphasis on elements of form and rhythm he was, like Kandinsky, moving swiftly away from the tradi-tional conception of art as imitation of the surface characteristics of nature and life. In the same year that saw the publication of *Uber das Geistige in der Kunst* he produced his "Médrano" juggler—the first clear example of "machine age" sculpture—which gave impetus to "constructivist" tendencies in Germany, Russia, and Hungary and was the pro-totype for such contemporary American "constructivist" advertising art as that of L. L. Balcom and Warren G. Thomas.

What Kandinsky and Archipenko were doing others were doing. It was a time of breaking down the fences which tradition had so carefully built up about each art and craft and of the artificial distinction between what was useful and what was good-in-itself. It was a time of discovering "the interdependence of painting, sculpture, and the technique of modern industry" and of the underlying unity of all creative work.

For typography here was the beginning of what Paul Renner (designer of the typeface which acted in America as a kind of press agent for the New Typography) was later, with the perspective of time on his side, to regard as "a great cleansing process." It remained for the creator of Futura, in the same year that the Bauhaus closed, to summarize it as a creative phenomenon:

"We are always inclined to regard our own sphere of work as strictly fenced in on all sides against all other spheres; and the more thoroughly we farm our own field, the more do we incline to the intellectual attitude peculiar to the expert, to whom the past of his own particular craft is nearer and more familiar than the present aspect of any neighboring craft. We need not, therefore, be astonished to find that the renaissance of style which we have experienced in all regions of creative work . . . during the past decade should often have been imported into the several crafts by non-professionals from the outside."

It has, of course, always been true that new forms and new expressive idioms arise only as a result of influences from other fields than the one in which they obtain—for they are necessarily non-traditional. The point here is that the creative process which gives birth to the "new" was intensified during the period in which the Bauhaus took shape.

3

Because of their liberating force and because of their incidental suggestions for a new kind of typography, three influences of the period deserve special mention. They are a man, a movement, and a program for destruction.

The man was Guillaume Apollinaire (pseudonym of Wilhelm von Kostrowitzki), a poet with Montmarte proclivities and a penchant for adventure. He was, as one commentator has put it, the "Marco Polo of the new spirit." He reversed the time-honored platitude that "there is nothing new under the sun" by declaring that for the poet and the artist everything under the sun *must* be new. As self-appointed interpreter and aesthetician of the new movement in art and literature, he was always on the alert for the unusual and the startling. In Paris he struck up a close friendship with the men who were doing what was then a new and strange kind of painting—Matisse, Picasso, Braque, and Rousseau. He was among the first to champion the cause of Cubism, publishing, in 1912, a volume of appreciative essays entitled *Les Cubistes.* It was he who invented the word *Surrealism.*

In Caligrammes, a volume of poems about peace and war written between 1913 and 1916 and published a few months before his death in 1918, he ventured upon some experiments in typography, of which the poem *La Cravate et la Montre* is an example. In having it set in the actual form of a necktie and a watch he sought, not too seriously, an organic relation between the inside and the outside of the poem and something of that element of surprise which he regarded as a fundamental difference between the "new spirit" and all preceding artistic and literary movements. There was nothing very new or startling about this: yet, historically, it had a thrust in the direction of a new typography.

The movement was Futurism—a hot-headed revolt against the tyranny of the past in poetry, the drama, literature, music, painting, sculpture, architecture, and the graphic arts. Beyond that it had social and political ramifications. Its Italian founder, Flippo Tommaso Marinetti, was the champion manifesto-maker of the whole period of tumult and shouting. "We want to free our country (Italy) from the fetid gangrene of professors, archaeologists, guides, and antique shops," read the first *Futurist Manifesto*, published, in 1909, by a Paris newspaper. Among other things, the Futurists proposed that every artist should be banished at the age of forty from the art world, and his works along with him, so that with each generation a new cultural growth could spring from the root and not from the previous season's hardened wood.

The city of Venice was to them "a magnificent wound of the past." With 200,000 gaily-colored manifestoes they exhorted its inhabitants "to fill its small fetid canals with the ruins of its tumbling leprous palaces." They would abolish everywhere "the languishing curve of old architectures . . . and erect up to the sky the rigid geometry of large metallic bridges and factories." In painting they wanted to put the spectator in the midst of the picture. In sculpture they would destroy the "nobility of bronze and marble" by using every non-traditional material they could think of. Their poetry, for the most part, looked like a page from a book on symbolical logic. Their idea of the drama was that it should consist of things happening to the audience. And so it was on one occasion when Marinetti hurled back at the audience the missiles flung upon the stage in protest against the meaninglessness of a Futurist performance.

A good Futurist believed that "we must make a clean sweep of all hackneyed subjects and express henceforth the whirlwind life of our day, dominated by steel, egotism, feverish activity, and speed." His total aesthetic was nicely summed up in the feeling that a speeding automobile was more beautiful than the Victory of Samothrace. This aesthetic was carried into the sphere of printing under the head of *Typographical Revolution:*

"Our revolution is directed against the so-called typographical harmony of the page, which is opposed to the flux and reflux, the jerks and bursts of style that are represented in it. We shall use, therefore, on the same page three or four different colors of ink and, if necessary, even twenty different forms of type."

"Nouvelle conception de la page" Marinetti called it. The "SCRABrrRrraaNNG" composition from *Les Mots en liberté futuristes*, 1919, is a frequently reproduced example. However indiscreet and extravagant, here was an organic relation between the inside and the outside plus a kind of deliberate design for unrest.

The program for destruction was Dadaism. Some have preferred to think of it as an organized program for spoofing, others as war hysteria in the grand style. At all events, it was created in the war period, 1916, by a group of disillusioned writers and artists, who set about to confront one madness with another. The name of the "movement" was simply the first word that turned up in the dictionary on the insertion of a pen knife; it was launched from the Cabaret Voltaire, a literary night club in Zurich. The first official Dada publication was an indication of the network of influences that played upon it. Within its covers were brought together, among others, the names of Picasso, Apollinaire, Kandinsky, and Marinetti. Later publications, of which there were many, added such other names as Archipenko, Bergson, and Charlie Chaplin.

Though ostensibly bent on destroying all art tendencies by laughing them out of existence, the Dadaists could not escape the powerful influence of Picasso. They seized upon that part of his work which looked to them least like art—his *papiers collés*, paste-up, compositions using newspaper, imitation wood, and other materials for their texture values. Working half-seriously with anti-art materials and experimenting with accidental compositions, they developed a medium of expression which was to enter the New Typography first as "composite photography" and later as "photomontage."

Within the short lifetime of Dada (for it was soon to grow into Surrealism) there were demonstrations, performances, and exhibitions in Zurich, Berlin, Cologne, Hanover, and Paris. A journalist of the period describes one of them:

"With characteristic bad taste the Dadaists make their appeal this time to the human instinct of fear. The scene is a cellar with all lights in the shop extinguished. Moanings are heard through a trap door. Another wag, hidden behind a cupboard, insults the more important visitors. . . . The Dadaists, with no neckties and wearing white gloves, walk around the place. Breton crunches matches, G. Ribemont-Dessaignes keeps on remarking at the top of his voice, 'It's raining on a skull.' Aragon mews like a cat. Ph. Soupault plays hide and seek with Tzara; Benjamin Péret and Charchoune never stop shaking hands. On the threshold, Jacques Rigaut counts out loud the cars and the pearls of lady visitors."

It is not surprising that the announcements of such premeditated antics should take the form of the "Theatre Michel" handbill. These handbills, and other publications of the Dadaists, were, thinks Jan Tschichold, "the earliest documents of the New Typography."

4

It was a part of the Bauhaus philosophy that life was not rigidly departmentalized and that, since all branches of design were knit together by an underlying unity, each had something of value to give to the other. It was, therefore, psychologically prepared to be receptive to the rivulets of influence which crossed and re-crossed one another. It probably drew something from all the "isms" then current. But the more enduring elements in its typography derived primarily from two of them—Neo-Plasticism (or the de Stijl influence) in Holland and Constructivism (used here in a sense broad enough to include the allied movements of Suprematism and Non-Objectivism) in Russia and Hungary.

The activities of the de Stijl group—founded in 1917 by Theo van Doesburg, who has been described as a painter, sculptor, architect, typographer, poet, novelist, critic, lecturer, and theorist—covered almost as broad a field as the talents of its founder. The group made itself felt first through the abstract geometrical paintings of Van Doesburg and Mondrian. Seen through the prism of a "machine aesthetic" their simplicity in form and color—their "purified tonal and plane harmonies"—seemed right and appropriate for architecture, furniture, interior decoration, and typography which would be in consonance with the time. When Van Doesburg went to Germany in 1921, to divide his time between Berlin and the Bauhaus, the influence of the group had already been at work for two years.

The Constructivist influence on the Bauhaus followed close upon that of the de Stijl group. The movement—influenced, like every other tendency of the time, by Cubist art—had been initiated, in 1913, as Suprematism by Kasimir Malevich, who, in his effort "to free art from the ballast of the objective world" fled to the form of the square. To a startled public he exhibited as a work of art a plain black square against a white background. For him, it was a direct rendering of "the experience of non-objectivity." From this point onward he combined simple formal elements—the square, the circle, the parallelogram, the trapezoid, and others—achieving in some of his compositions, inspired by airplane views of cities, the first intimation of the diagonal axis and the internal tensions so prominent later in the New Typography.

The Suprematist Composition of 1914 is perhaps his nearest approach to practical design. Done in solid tones of black, white, blue, red, and yellow it gave the "new typographer" almost his whole range of color preferences. . . . It may seem an interesting commentary on the timidity of human nature that it took the audacity of a Malevich to suggest that there was plastic value in such simple geometrical elements as a square, a circle, and a line. Whatever may be the intrinsic value of his work as art, it had much the same kind of historical thrust in the direction of practical design as the work of the Cubists, the Futurists, and the Dadaists. It was a part of the cleansing process.

Malevich was followed by Alexander Rodchenko, who in 1922 deserted "art" for the more practical pursuits of theatre art, furniture design, photography, and typography, creating in a new field the design prototype of one of the most striking of the newer American magazines. The tendency toward utilitarian design was carried still further by El Lissitzky, for whom it was an easy step from his own abstract paintings, which he called "prouns," to a built-up architectural typography with plastic values.

The Hungarian wing of the Constructivist movement was represented by L. Moholy-Nagy, whose chief contributions to the New Typography were to be made as a member of the staff at the Bauhaus and as co-editor of the *Bauhausbücher* and the *Bauhaus* magazine.

Both de Stijl and Constructivist painting showed a marked architectural sense; but it was for Constructivism actually to invade the domain of architecture. It is significant that El Lissitzky regarded his "prouns" as a transition from painting to architecture and that Malevich had earlier done sculpture that looked very much like a building in the abstract. Modern architecture was recently defined by J. M. Richards, of the London *Architectural Review,* as Constructivist art applied to the science of building and Constructivist art, correspondingly, as architecture liberated from the dictatorship of function. As the best illustration of the close relationship he points to the London Zoo buildings, of which Moholy-Nagy, in 1936, made a film for the Museum of Modern Art and Harvard's Department of Architecture.

What Richards had in mind, though, was not painting, but a species of art, influenced by the "machine-age" sculpture of Archipenko, midway between painting and sculpture, on the one hand, and engineering mechanics and industrial design, on the other. It was an art in which "the school concepts of mechanics, dynamics, statics, kinetics, the problem of stability, of equilibrium were tested in plastic form." The quotation is from Moholy-Nagy's *The New Vision, from Material to Architecture,* in which he describes the basic training at the Bauhaus. By way of commenting on the exhibition of the Russian Constructivists in Moscow, 1921, he appraises the tendency:

"The constructivists reveled in industrial forms, so much so that a technical monomania governed them. As a transitional stage this interest was surely sound, for thereby the former dry musty conceptions of 'art' were given a new measuring rod from a different angle."

The whole Constructivist preoccupation with materials, abstract form, and mechanical stress-relations was put to work at the Bauhaus by Moholy-Nagy as an educational method; and it has ever since been in process of filtering into the industrial art schools throughout the world as a fundamental technique. Under his direction Bauhaus students experimented freely with old and new materials for textural contrasts, surface treatment, and massing effects. Their serious "play-activity"—for which they drew upon the collages of Picasso and the "rubbish pictures" of the Dadaists—included the materials of typography. The results that followed are observable today in a considerable body of printing, commercial photography, and advertising design, notably in some of the work of Lester Beall and the "montages" of Coutré Erman.

The force behind de Stijl and Constructivist art was that intangible "form-seeking" impulse which Sheldon Cheney, in *Expressionism in Art,* sees as the single unifying element in all the arts of the twentieth century. It is perfectly embodied in the deliberately abstract typographical compositions of Karel Teige, which we may take as representing in its purity the formal and abstract side of the New Typography. In the design and format of the *Bauhausbücher,* "the Futura" folder, the photographic poster by El Lissitzky, and the other pieces shown this abstract form is given content without destroying the plastic-architectural quality. In direct line of descent from these are the selected examples of recent American work, culminating in the 1937 announcement folder of the Society of Typographic Arts, the cover of *Cue* magazine, and the current work of Moholy-Nagy for the New Bauhaus.

Attracted by the more diffused movement of Expressionism, which the work of Kandinsky had largely initiated, the two streams of influence—one from Holland and one from Russia and Hungary—would probably have been consolidated in Germany had the Bauhaus not been there. The Bauhaus was in the right place at the right time to catch them, fuse them, and transmute them into "utilitarian functionalism," which in printing and advertising design was to become known variously as "Elementary," "Constructivist," "The New," and, in the Danish edition of Jan Tschichold's latest book, "Functional" Typography.

5

The New Typography was a philosophy and not a style. It was largely the failure to understand this which produced around 1928 what the late Frederic Ehrlich called the "Dark Cloud Era" and retarded in America an international movement which may be said to have begun in 1925 with the publication, in *Typographische Mitteilungen,* of Jan Tschichold's "Elementaire Typographic." In the decade preceding this event typography had been lifted out of the tradition of printing and placed squarely in the dual "tradition" of abstract art and the New Architecture.

The basic element in its ideology is probably as old as man. It was a determining force in the mind of an American architect a half century ago. It was Louis Sullivan's dictum: "Form must follow function." It was the quite simple and altogether reasonable idea that there should be an organic relation between the inside and the outside of a building—between the materials out of which it was made, the purpose which it was to serve, and the outward visible form which it took. Though Sullivan himself prospered as an architect, America was not wholly hospitable to the idea. In Holland and Germany it found better soil in which to grow. It took root at the Bauhaus and was importantly illustrated in the Bauhaus building at Dessau, designed by Walter Gropius.

Just as architecture became a "machine for living" (or for doing business in or for learning things in), so typography became a machine for communication. In design for publicity the intention was to project a persuasive message into the reader's psyche with the highest immediacy of meaning and with the greatest possible psychological impact. The ammunition for this purpose often included asymmetrical relationships of masses, lines (conceived of as points or masses in motion), arrows, bullets of color, oblique and vertical direction contrast. The cue for using these devices and the ordering principle for handling them, apart from the intention to be architecturally simple and direct, was derived mainly from abstract painting. Jan Tschichold has developed the implied analogy:

"All abstract pictures, particularly the quite simple ones, show elements of painting or graphic art which are at once clearly defined in form and in plain relation to one another. From this to typography is no great step. The works of abstract painters are symbols of the subtle arrangement of simple yet strongly contrasting elements. Since the new typography sets itself no other task than the creation of just such arrangements, it is possible for many works of abstract painters and sculptors to act as inspirational models."

But there was more to the New Typography than merely organizing the visual material into an over-all form that would be organically related to its content and purpose. For there were always alternatives, and neither architecture nor painting had much to say about the use of typefaces. Beyond the functional requirements of a particular job there was a margin of creative freedom, within which the designer expressed his own peculiar sensibilities and sought, frequently if not always, to tie his work in with the Zeitgeist—the "form-seeking" impulse of the time.

It was in the effort to catch the "feel" of the machine age, and at the same time to create designs that would be economical of the mental and visual energies of the reader, that the New Typography developed an affinity for "constructed" typefaces. The first preference was for a block letter similar to the Venus-Grotesk used in the Bauer booklet *Futura Schmuck* and in the folder announcing the Bauhausbücher. The first book on the New Typography was set in a light sans serif midway between Venus and Futura. During the period 1925 to 1930 Herbert Bayer, Jan Tschichold, Karel Teige, and others experimented with reform alphabets, all working more or less on principles stated by Bayer:

"Geometric foundation of each letter, resulting in a synthetic construction out of a few basic elements. Avoidance of all suggestion of a hand-written character. Even thickness of all parts of the letter, and renumeration of all suggestions of up and down strokes. Simplification of form for the sake of legibility (the simpler the optical appearance the easier the comprehension)."

The immediate outcome was Bayer's Universal type, after which the letters in the name "The New Bauhaus" were modeled by Moholy-Nagy. Close by in spirit was Paul Renner's first Futura, more rigidly abstract than the version which reached America. Tschichold produced a design based on a phonetic alphabet, as radical, though in a different direction, as A.M. Cassandre's current Peignot, which we may perhaps take as the final expression and modification of the geometric urge.

There was, however, never any absolute insistence on a typeface whose design, like these, was based on the square-circle-line motif. Bayer Type is a case in point. Tschichold's *Typographische Gestaltung,* published in 1935, is set in Bodini. On its title page a "bank" script is mixed with Georg Trump's City, to which the author elsewhere accords the highest place among egyptian faces. Not even the Cheltenham-like face used in the Danish edition, 1937, of the same book, though it forsakes the geometric ideal entirely, is inconsistent with the philosophy behind the New Typography. For it was recognized that type designs, as carriers of verbal meaning, could never depart too far from what people were used to reading—however great might be the need for differentness or for falling in with the *Zeitgeist.* In the total design, using elements that had an immediate visual, rather than verbal meaning, the typographer could make up for the lack of freedom which the necessity of using type imposed on him.

If he chose a traditional typeface, as he frequently did, it was because he thought he could do a better total job with it than without it. He still had no predetermined over-all form into which he could pour his persuasive message, like water into a jug. Having traded tradition for a philosophy, his problem was one of analysis and experiment within the discipline of an ideology. His solution of the problem was not always clear. Looking at the final results from the outside, without his ideology, it was often impossible to rationalize many of the things which the analogy of typography to abstract painting and the New Architecture determined in his work. Surface characteristics were, therefore, widely imitated. In America the New Typography tended to become what it preeminently was not—a predetermined style.

The New Painting and the New Architecture constituted a sharp break with the past. The gap between the "old" and the "new" was, as history goes, an enormous one. So also was the gap between the old typography and the new. Yet, in a sense, none of them was new. They were all in theory a return to a kind of original sanity—to a pristine unity of life.

6

The preliminary development of the New Typography at the Bauhaus was largely in the hands of three men—Walter Gropius, Laszlo Moholy-Nagy, and Herbert Bayer. They were the right men because they were prepared by training, inclination, and experience to view with an open mind the experimental typography then being done in Holland, Russia, Germany, Italy, Hungary, Czechoslovakia, France, and Switzerland.

Walter Gropius was first and last an architect. Though he did not himself venture into typography, he was, as director of the school, interested in it as one of many coordinated activities. Herbert Bayer, who had earlier been a student at the Bauhaus, was a self-taught painter with Surrealist tendencies before he joined the staff in 1925 to teach advertising design and typography. Moholy-Nagy had turned from the study of law to become a painter, photographer, typographer, and designer for the theatre and film—in all of which fields he has made significant contributions. His pioneer work in developing the photogram, photomantage, and "negative" printing is only now beginning to take effect. Last year his "rhodoid" technique, illustrated in the jacket of the Gropius book, was in evidence at the Art Directors' Show in New York. His time at the Bauhaus was during the important formative period, 1923 to 1928, which produced, among other things, the *Bauhausbücher,* now to be continued in America under the same editorship.

It would not be quite true to say that this triumvirate created either the Bauhaus Tradition of the New Typography; but the work of Moholy-Nagy and Bayer was quickly noted throughout Central Europe. Among the first to feel its underlying sanity (though they may have rejected some of the surface characteristics) were Jan Tschichold and Karel Teige, to the latter of whom we owe the initial formulation of its ideology. Briefly it involved: (1) Freedom from tradition. (2) Geometric simplicity. (3) Contrast of typographical material. (4) The exclusion of any ornament that was not "functionally" necessary. (5) A preference for photography, machine composition, and combinations of the simpler primary colors. (6) A recognition and acceptance of the "machine age" and of the utilitarian purpose of typography.

Of this credo Jan Tschichold has from the outset been the chief protagonist, though little of his work has been translated from the original German. In the summer of 1936 *Industrial Arts* published a small portion in English of *Typographische Gestaltung* under the title "Abstract Painting and the New Typography." The following summer he discussed "Type Mixtures" in the new English quarterly *Typography.* His most recent writing in

English is included in *Circle,* and "International Survey of Constructive Art," published last year in England.

Though the Bauhaus closed its doors in 1933, its philosophy persisted through the work of individual men on the Continent, in England, and in America. In February of last year Walter Gropius was brought over to America to become a Professor of Architecture at Harvard University, from which point he now acts as advisor to the staff of the New Bauhaus. Josef Albers, who continued the work of Moholy-Nagy at Dessau following 1928, and Xanti Schawinski have for some time been teaching at Black Mountain College in North Carolina.

The three men most influential in carry on the Bauhaus tradition in typography have not been inactive. Bayer, as Director of the Berlin Dorland Studios, has wielded a continuous influence on the Continent. Tschichold continues to write from Switzerland. Moholy-Nagy now heads a New Bauhaus. Within the last two years all three of these men have exhibited their work at London galleries. All three of them have been featured recently in English periodicals. In the light of these facts one is tempted to agree with Paul Renner in thinking that "the wish is father to the thought" among those who still predict an end for the New Typography or who perhaps like to think of it complacently as decadent.

7

The New Bauhaus is the final result of efforts on the part of the Association of Arts and Industries, extending over a period of years, to create a school which would train young people to work realistically and significantly in that middle field between art and industry. This year only the basic training courses have been given. Next year the program will included typography and advertising design. Spiritually and philosophically the new school is carrying on from the point at which the old Bauhaus left off.

In *Art and the Machine,* which pays generous tribute to the pioneer work of the old Bauhaus, Sheldon and Martha Cheney venture the belief that "today, for the first time since the Middle Ages, we are at a new major beginning, with new dimensions, new proportions, new possibilities, new freedom. . . . " If this be true it may not be too much to expect the new school to play in America a role comparable to the role played by its famous predecessor.

It may be that the New Bauhaus will find in America the right time, the right place, and the right men. Of the right men it already has one in L. Moholy-Nagy, whom Herbert Read believes to be one of the outstanding creative intelligences of our time.

From *PM,* (June/July 1938).

The Consistency of Jan Tschichold

By Jerry Kelly

an Tschichold burst onto the typographic scene as a leading proponent (if not the leading proponent) of the modern asymmetric style with the publication of "Elementare Typographie" in 1925. This was followed by *Die neue Typographie,* the gospel of the movement, in 1928; and *Typographische Gestaltung* (later translated into English with the title *Asymmetric Typography*) in 1935. In the late 1930s, after more than a decade as one of the most influential exponents of the New Typography, Tschichold made an apparent about-face and abruptly evolved a rigidly classic, symmetrical style.

Much has been written and said about Tschichold's well-known conversion from a pioneer of the modern typographic movement to his strict adherence to a traditional symmetric style. Max Bill asserted in *Schweizer Graphische Mitteilungen* that Tschichold was a renegade from his own teaching. As Ruari McLean noted, "Tschichold has been criticized because he preached a revolutionary gospel, then changed his mind and returned to convention." An article in *Modern Graphic Design* accused Tschichold of turning "his back on the philosophy and work which brought him admiration and acclaim."

So what should we make of this enigmatic typographer and his about-face, which was to become the most notorious typographic catharsis? Many from Tschichold's own camp, like Bill, were to feel betrayed by one of their leaders, while the conservative typographic elite, such as Morison, Updike, et al., were cautious in welcoming him as a convert to their aesthetic.

Tschichold's own explanation of the immediate reason for his change of style comes from an unexpected quarter. He likens *Die neue Typographie* to National Socialism and Fascism, seeing "obvious similarities . . . in the ruthless restrictions of typefaces, a parallel to Goebbels's infamous political alignment, and the more or less military arrangement of lines." Tschichold did not want to be "guilty of spreading the very ideas which caused him to leave Germany."

It is obvious that Tschichold was deeply upset by his harsh treatment at the hands of the Nazis. In 1933, after establishing himself as a leader in his field and teaching at respected institutions in Germany for twelve years (his entire adult life until then), he and his wife Edith were arrested. He soon left Germany for Basel, Switzerland, where he was to live for most of his remaining days (with the notable exception of a few years in England, where he reformed the typography of Penguin books after the war). The blow to his self-esteem, let alone his career and position as a noted authority, must have been tremendous to such a proud and vocal man as Tschichold. One can see how someone as dogmatic as he would react strongly against all he once held as true—among which was a belief in German typographic eminence and the New Typography.

Tschichold has written "so many things in [*Die neue Typographie*] are erroneous because my experience was so small" and "today I do not entirely agree with the statements [I made in *Asymmetric Typography*], no matter how effective they have been as a basis for the creation of a new style. The harsh rejection of the previous style, however, is the condition for the creation of a different one." Perhaps one can detect in these statements some reaction to Tschichold's treatment by the Nazis, or even a slight rationalizing of the polar extremes his typographic philosophy was to espouse.

However, astute observers have noticed that any dichotomy in Tschichold's work may not be as good as it appears on the surface. Noel Martin has written that "those who find his later work antiquated have looked only superficially," and Hans Peter Willberg wrote, "it seems to me that in fact the early and later Tschichold are not so far apart: both had the same aims: it was just how they achieved them that was different. The aims were clarity, order, transparency of meaning, simplicity in design." This was, indeed, the case. A comparison of Tschichold's early writings, when he was an outspoken proponent of the New Typography, and his later articles, elucidating his views on the beauty of classical typography, reveal many similarities popping up amongst the oft-noted differences. For example, no one would be surprised that Tschichold wrote in one of his later publications "capitals should always be letterspaced. Their letterspaces should be carefully well-balanced by the use of several different sorts in accordance with their optical value." Yet in a much earlier book, *Asymmetric Typography,* Tschichold wrote "faultless letterspacing [of capitals] to achieve an even rhythm is absolutely necessary."

Tschichold grew to regret his early belief that sans serif types were the proper vehicle for modern writing. *Die neue Typographie* was set in sans serif, but surprisingly *Typographische Gestaltung* is set in a serif type, Bodoni, with an egyptian, City, being employed for the headlines. All of Tschichold's later books were, of course, set in traditional serif types. It is consistent for him to have said late in his career that "the classical typefaces such as Garamond, Janson, Baskerville, and Bell are undoubtedly the most legible." He wrote, "it was a juvenile opinion to consider the sans serif as the most suitable or even the most contemporary typeface. A typeface has first to be legible, or rather readable; and a sans serif is certainly not the most legible type when set in quantity, let alone readable." What is odd, however, is that as early as 1935 in *Typographische Gestaltung,* he said "for body matter, nearly all the classical romans are suitable. Caslon is one of the most beautiful." This shows more consistency in Tschichold's typographic dogma than is generally thought. Even more traditional are the following ideas on placement from the same 1935 publication: "the type area of a novel and its placing on the page are also hard to improve," referring to the norms of classical book typography.

Tschichold's style before and after his so-called 'conversion' of the late-1930s look radically different on the surface. Surely one sees more classical types, centered layouts, and generally traditional typographic design after this change. But a more comprehensive study would reveal similarities between Tschichold's asymmetric and symmetric work. I would summarize these consistent elements as follows:

1) The choice of clear, well-proportioned typefaces (whether they be serif or sans serif types). In his later typography Garamond, Baskerville, Bembo, Bell and other classic roman types dominate; but even in his early period, where there is a wide selection of sans serifs, egyptians, scripts, etc., the typefaces used are always scrupulously selected as among the finest of their kind. Mediocre types of any variety are avoided.

2) Meticulous letterspacing of words set in capital letters. Tschichold was notorious as an uncompromising perfectionist regarding the letterspacing of all-cap words. Whether in his title pages for Penguin books or in his early film posters, words in all-caps are carefully letterspaced. In this regard there is more consistency between his early and late work than between his classical title pages and, say, D. B. Updike or Bruce Rogers, who occasionally set words in all-caps with little or no letterspacing to achieve a specific effect.

3) Exceptional care with the placement of various items on the page. Whether in his traditional or modern designs, Tschichold carefully balanced all the elements he had to work with. All the weights, tensions, white spaces, etc., were thoroughly considered in achieving a successful composition, whether it be symmetrically or asymmetrically arranged.

4) Thoughtful consideration of materials. Unlike other important typographers of this century, Tschichold worked mostly on inexpensive publications. It is rare that he had the opportunity to work with handmade papers or specially manufactured typefaces, yet whatever the limitations placed on him, he always showed sensitivity to selection of the most appropriate materials. Paper should be chosen based on its tone, weight, grain, texture, and suitability to printing process, which in turn was chosen for its ability to handle the task at hand, whether it be color reproduction, letterpress or gravure halftone. Typefaces were also carefully selected for their appropriateness to the job, often resulting in the use of some uncommon fonts or even Tschichold's own accomplished hand-lettering.

5) The use of a fairly limited palette of typefaces and elements on the page. There is a well-known Tschichold axiom that three sizes of type are almost always sufficient. This is in keeping with the overall impression of Tschichold's late work, but as early as 1935 he wrote, "too many sizes in one job are impractical and I seldom give good results."

In these key areas there is a strong consistent streak in Tschichold's work, whether it be from 1930 or 1960. Looking beyond the surface of Tschichold's typography, we see more similarity between early Tschichold and late Tschichold than between Tschichold's work and that of his contemporaries. Based on the above principles there is more in common between Tschichold's title page for *Die neue Typographie* and his *Utopia,* than between his *Utopia* and Bruce Rogers's design for the same title.

Tschichold's attention to these often overlooked fine points of printing set him apart from most of his peers, whether they be Bauhaus designers or traditional typographers. There is a care in spacing, balance, and placement, and an unusual selection of typefaces in Tschichold's work that makes it readily identifiable as his own.

Hans Peter Willberg has noted that "Tschichold's supposed change of opinion is still today, after forty years, a subject for discussion and argument." The discussion has scarcely subsided. Today it appears that students of typography all too often choose to disregard Tschichold's later work. The subtle principles which form the common thread between his early, asymmetric typography and his mature classical work are little noticed among today's fashion-conscious designers. Who today pays attention to paper grain or careful hand letterspacing of capital letters? Instead, the focus is on the apparent dichotomy in Tschichold's typography.

As Kurt Weidmann wrote, "Tschichold fought his battles as an extremist. The passing of time has left one thing clear: the quality of his work. In everything he did, that remains." With his gift for clarity, Tschichold himself gets straight to the point: "the truth is both symmetry and asymmetry are useful principles, dependable tools for the designer."

Whichever mode Tschichold worked in, he created beautiful typography. The effort he put into the finer points of typography will yield the most to the student of his work. The difference between classical and asymmetric typography is less important. It is the consistent elements of Jan Tschichold's work which set him apart from his peers.

From *Jan Tschichold: Reflections and Reappraisals,* edited by Paul Barnes (New York: Typoscope, 1995).

The Cult of Lower Case

By Douglas C. McMurtrie

 novel feature which characterizes the work of some modern typographers is the exclusive use of lowercase letters, entirely rejecting capitals, even as initials in words that begin sentences. Particularly in headings and in proper names, the lowercase initial presents a really startling innovation to eyes accustomed to the well-established convention of capitalization.

The practice of using only lower case seems to have made its first appearance in the United States in the work of some of our "minor poets," notably (if only because more widely published) Don Herold—or don herold, as he causes his name to be printed. It also appeared in the witty contribution signed "archy the cockroach" in the newspaper column conducted by Don Marquis. Archy, according to Mr. Marquis, came out at night and wrote upon the editorial typewriter, by jumping on the keys. As he could not overcome the mechanical difficulty of holding down the shift key and at the same time jumping on another, he was necessarily limited to the use of the lowercase alphabet. Archy quickly became deservedly famous, and as his peculiar manner of writing spread among literary innovators, his name was conferred upon the new style, which is now often referred to, in a not too dignified manner, as "cockroach typography."

Is this so-called "cockroach typography" merely a freak of the moment, without sound foundation? If so, it is indefensible. Or has it, on the other hand, perhaps without conscious intention, touched upon some fundamental principle of letter use which justifies the exclusion of capitals as a contribution to legibility or other typographic advantage? If the latter, the innovation deserves serious consideration.

At first glance, the omission of capitals looks very much like pure freakishness, the result of an effort to be different at any cost, or (as in the case of Herold and Marquis) of an effort at typographic humor. But the practice is now followed by some earnest and thoughtful European typographers, whose work cannot be dismissed from our attention with a mere wave of the hand. In Germany particularly, this "kleinschreibung," as it is there called, has become a really serious matter, involving the attention not only of printers, but of scholars and even of governmental authorities. The champions of the new style exclaim, "You do not use capitals in speaking, so why write with them?" They also emphasize the economic advantages of printing with the small letters only—saving of space in cases and in type storage, savings in the cost of type equipment, saving of the time of compositors, and so on.

On the other hand, the champions of the capitals maintain that the phenomena of language—words and their visible representation in letters—must not be dragged into a change in art forms. The new typography must not interfere with the evolution of speech, spoken and written—it must take the language as it is and confine its innovation to matters purely typographical.

In Germany the controversy over capitals rages more fiercely than in other countries because in German orthography the use of capitals is extended to every noun or word used as a noun, and the capital letter is therefore much more common in German printing than elsewhere. But even with our much more restricted use of capitals, the change to no capitals at all gives to printed matter a very strange appearance. However, modern typography is not troubled about strangeness as such; it asks only for the most direct and simple method of expressing the function of type. From this point of view, the abolition of capitals has theoretically much in its favor.

I say "theoretically" because there are a number of other changes in current practice which are theoretically of unquestioned wisdom and advantage but which have not been brought generally into practical application. Among such proposals may be mentioned the metric system of mensuration, simplified spelling, a universal language, the thirteen-month calendar. Some of these involve practical difficulties, it is true, but the immense inertia of established custom is the main reason why some if not all of these and similar proposals have not already been adopted.

The proposition that the lowercase alphabet be used exclusively in our printing stands, in my opinion, in the same class with other proposals mentioned. Theoretically it may be advisable, but it would take a wiser man than I am to predict whether or not it will make headway against the forces that tend to maintain "things as they are." Meanwhile, it will be interesting to watch developments, and wise to keep an attitude of open-mindedness.

As the struggle for and against the continued use of capitals promises to be a feature of considerable interest in the development of modern typography, it may be well to review here the actual status, typographically, of our capital letters. How did we come to use them in the first place? And do they, or do they not, contribute to our ease of reading and of comprehending what we read?

Historically, capitals are a survival of a form of writing long, long since abandoned. In the history of writing, the forms of the so-called "roman" letters were originally those of our present capitals. In the course of time, efforts to write these somewhat angular characters with more ease and grace, influenced perhaps by the letterforms current in the cursive handwriting of the time, resulted in the development of the so-called "minuscule" letters, out of which grew our present lowercase alphabets. The original forms of the letters then became archaic. They were retained, however, by the scribes for headings (in Latin, *capita*) and for lending distinction or emphasis to certain words in the text, particularly to the names of the great and powerful. It also became the style to open each sentence with a capital. The earliest printers meticulously followed the usage of manuscript scribes, and thus fixed the use of capitals in typographic practice.

There is nothing intrinsically necessary about the letterform that we call capitals. Other systems of writing and printing function adequately without any similar differentiation of letterforms. I have not yet seen this point adduced in the argument in favor of "kleinschreibung," but its advocates are welcome to the suggestion that Arabic and Hebrew are written and printed with no letters of distinct form for initials and the like. The same is true of the vernaculars of India, Burma, Siam, and many other lands that have their own national alphabets. It is only the "white" races, the peoples of European residence or origin, that have this peculiar institution of two different forms of letters.

It would seem that the capital letters in our alphabets hold their jobs only through the influence of tradition. But these are indeed trying days for traditions. About all manner of things, people are asking "Why?" And that most explosive little question is dynamiting away traditions much dearer to the human heart than the use of capitals. These ancient and honorable majuscules have served for centuries at the doorways of our sentences, occasionally announcing names or parading in headlines or on title pages. And now some typographers are beginning to question whether they are useful as well as traditional. Do they, or do they not, contribute to our ease of reading and of comprehending what we read?

The moment we ask the question, there comes to mind the name of Benjamin Sherbow—the lamented "apostle of lower case." There was a time when almost all headings and display lines were set in capitals throughout. To his leadership in pointing out the much greater legibility of lines in lower case is due in large degree to the marked change in the style of advertising typography. I well remember a diminutive booklet (a copy of which I am not now able to locate) which was entitled 'easy to read.' In this and in his other writings, he preached in season and out of season the virtues of lower case for copy which the typographer desired to get read, pointing out the fact that with ascenders and descenders the small letters have more numerous points of differentiation in their form than do capital letters.

The difficulty of answering this question scientifically is the difficulty of measuring the ease of reading, and still more, of measuring ease of comprehension. However, some attempts have been made at this measurement; but they have succeeded only in showing that connected text printed all in capitals takes more time to read and understand than when printed in the usual way. The experiments of Tinker and Patterson in 1928 are quite conclusive as to the relative readibility of all-capitals and of lower case in continuous text, but give no light on the question of whether a text with no capitals at all is, or is not, more difficult to read than one with capitals and lower case combined in the usual manner. But this matter of reading is to a very great extent a matter of eye training and eye habits. Ease of reading depends almost entirely on eye habits. We have learned to depend on the following initial capital as well as on the concluding period to mark our sentence breaks. In the case of familiar proper names, we depend in part upon the initial capital for the familiar "total word form" by which we perceive and recognize the word as a whole; to our eyes, in the present state of our habits, Anthony is more immediately intelligible than anthony.

In other words, capital letters are necessary to our reading comfort only because we are used to them. If they are kept to their traditional duties as openers of sentences and announcers of names, perhaps they help a little; certainly they do not hinder enough to be harmful. In mass formation (except for certain more or less habitual little groups) they are a nuisance and a bother. But we of the present generation would miss them and be a little disconcerted in our reading if they were suddenly to be everywhere abolished. A later generation, however, brought up on nothing but lowercase letters, would be much more disconcerted if the capitals were as suddenly to reappear.

From *Modern Typography & Layout* (Chicago: Eyncourt, 1929).

The Philosophy of Modernism in Typography

By Douglas C. McMurtrie

ypography has become a medium of communication for the people as a whole and not solely for some select group. Therefore, not until the new spirit of modernism has quite deeply penetrated the popular consciousness, does printing begin to reflect it. Hence the modern movement has been slow in making its impress on the art of typography. But once the new influences were felt in the printing world, the first rumbles rapidly grew into a roar. Typography, like the other applied arts, has been shaken from its old foundations and is being reconstructed along modern lines. Let us consider, then, what the reconstruction is bringing forth, bearing in mind that the underlying principle of the new design is the dictum "Form follows function."

The primary function of typography is to convey a message to the comprehension of the readers to whom it is addressed. Some of these readers may not be particularly interested in the message; hence it is necessary to set it out in type in such a manner that it may be read with the greatest possible ease and speed. Clarity is the essential feature of modern typography. Any form which does not first express the function of legibility is not in the true spirit of modern typography, no matter how striking or "modernistic" it may otherwise be.

In former days there was little reading matter, but there was much time available for reading. Today there is a plethora of printed matter clamoring for the attention of people who live at a tempo that leaves them relatively little time to read. To stand any chance of getting read and understood, therefore, the modern message in type must tell its story just as directly and vividly as possible. The outward form of modern typography is of little importance in itself; the expression of the sense of the copy is vital. Easy comprehension of the message, which in typography represents function, is therefore the determinant of form.

According to the principles of the modern typographers, there is permitted no formalism of arrangement. It would represent but slight advance, they argue, to free ourselves from one formalism only to yield in subjection to another, even though represented in newer and sounder rules. We must be guided solely by interpretation of the copy.

The arrangement must therefore be held fluid, so as to permit indication of the comparative importance of portions of the copy by variations in type size or weight, and the accentuation of individual words or sentences by any sound methods of display.

As all art of any vitality is a reflection of life, the typography which is truly representative of its period is expressive of the life of that period. Perhaps the most typical characteristic of present-day living is the quick tempo at which it moves. The tempo of our typography should be in keeping. It should be dynamic rather than static. Its balance should be that of motion rather than that of rest. The balanced compositions suited to the leisurely contemplation of an earlier generation must give place to arrangements in which the sense of movement is inescapable. For we of the present age must, so to speak, read as we run.

The modern typographer contends that symmetrical layout is an outworn form. If all lines are centered on a median axis, this arrangement argues for a special emphasis or significance in the centers of the lines which, of course, they do not have. Or it brings the eye repeatedly to a point of rest, which impedes the movement of the message. If there is any special emphasis or accent point in lines of open display composition, it is at the beginning—in musical parlance, at the point of "attack."

If we grant this contention, we find that the most rational positioning of display lines is to make them flush at the left of the page or of the advertisement, the point to which the eye automatically returns after reading the preceding line. One advantage of this arrangement is that lines of unequal length will fall more easily into a form which does not offend our sense of fitness, than would the same lines if centered.

In left-hand flush arrangements it seems possible to have lines succeed one another with little thought of their relative lengths or sequence, and still obtain an attractive and readable layout. This is clearly shown by the arrangement of the chapter heads in this volume.

"Pretty" layouts on the one hand, and exceedingly bizarre arrangements on the other, are to be frowned upon as diverting attention from the message itself to the physical form of its typography, which is always to be considered not as an end in itself, but only as a means to the end that the message be read.

For like reasons, ornamentation in the usual sense is excluded from the modern typography. The only purpose of ornament is to make of the layout an attractive picture, which is not a proper aim, as the sole object should be to get the printed story comprehended by the reader. Anything standing in the way of this objective must be sacrificed.

There is one exception to this general rule. Ornament which is "organic" to the copy—that is, ornament which promotes comprehension of the copy—is permitted if of extremely simple character, so that it does not become an object of interest in itself.

As to types, the tools of the typographer, the idea is to keep them as elementary as possible in form and design, without eccentricities which will attract attention to themselves, and correspondingly detract from the acuity of attention given to the sense of the copy. The more advanced of the modern typographers would even wish to standardize all types in one simple form, so that all attention to printing would be directed, without distraction of any kind, to the story being told in type.

Finally, in modern typography we are to depend on ourselves alone for the working out of any typographic problem, and not depend on the solutions or practices of another age. We are to do our creative work in the spirit of the present and to let it be truly expressive of our own interpretation of the message we are transmitting to readers through the medium of type.

Such, stated in briefest form, is the underlying philosophy of modern typography. I have stated it theoretically because, in essence, its tenets are sound and will commend themselves to the judgement of open-minded typographers. The following chapters of this book will be concerned largely with the practical application of these principles in the working out of everyday problems, and most of these applications will be discussed in detail.

But before passing to the consideration of modern typography in practice, it may be well to remind ourselves that the movement is still in its beginning stages and that a great deal of the current work is patently immature. Even the best of the modern typographers have not as yet found themselves in their new milieu. To express it differently, they are not yet fluent in the new idiom of typographic speech. They have taken a great step forward in achieving real emancipation from the rules and regulations of a codified typography. They have worked out a philosophy they consider sound. But the actual examples of their work fall far short, we must admit, of the idealistic expectations we might conceive from a reading of the manifesto of a modernist typographer.

We have, if you will, so far as execution is concerned, the uncertain steps of an infant Gargantua who, even in his babyhood, has shaken the world of type to its very foundations. Added strength, an increased sureness of step, and a greater degree of wisdom, we may expect with the maturity to which he is approaching nearer day by day.

From *Modern Typography & Layout* (Chicago: Eyncourt, 1929).

Why Go Modern

By Frederic W. Goudy

his is the first time I've had the pleasure of addressing the Advertising Typographers Association of America, Inc., although I have known many of its members for years. I recognize here this morning the faces of a number who have heard me speak before other organizations. It seems to me that it is quite fitting that a designer of types should be asked to address an organization whose business is so largely concerned with the interesting use of printers' types, some of them furnished by the typefoundry, others from the composing machine makers, and now and then some of my own designs.

I have heard it said of me that I have no great interest in typefaces primarily made for advertising purposes. This is not true. Of course I am not interested in badly designed types for any purpose, whether for book or advertising display doesn't matter. I once told the advertising manager for Marshall Field & Company, of Chicago, who had asked me to make a commercial design for him and who feared I might regard his request as an invitation to do something I might think not quite dignified, that as long as he didn't wish me to lower what I regarded my standard of excellence, or to do something I felt was contrary to the principles of good design, the mere fact that it was for advertising purposes would not have any bearing on the matter. And I feel much the same even now about types that are to be used for publicity. I prefer to design type for books; but is it not a fact that a great portion of many advertisements are set in one or more of purely book types with the display lines or lines for emphasis or contrast in a face that obviously would be incongruous for the text of a book? Knowing that my book types are likely to be so used I keep the fact in mind as I design a type primarily for book use.

I am not an advertising man, nor an advertising typographer, but the fact that I have had much to do with the fraternity gives me the right to address you as one whose perspective is possibly better than that of some of you who are too near your work to get the general effect of it as a whole. I maintain that the end of all advertising is to sell merchandise; therefore it is necessary to touch the susceptibilities of potential buyers of merchandise. Advertising psychology deals primarily with the public consciousness; our advertisement is then either artistic, literary, humorous, or severely commercial according to the particular public it is desired to interest. The advertisement is then your business solicitor, and like your salesman, it should be dressed well for the occasion, that is, in types suitable for the purpose. I can see no reason why more beautiful display types with simple, legible book letters, well arranged, should not attract just as many buyers and just as surely as the use of freakish, bizarre, or ornate types can do so.

I do feel that printing for commerce should avoid any effort toward pseudo-estheticism and should present rather its own proper goodness; it should be studiously plain and starkly efficient. This sort of typography requires types free from studied exuberance and fancy. Sometimes types, good enough in themselves, are employed to make the work in which they are used appear to be better than it really is, that is, they attempt to give a manner or treatment suitable for a fine book to a piece of advertising. To me the effect is nauseating, not because it is advertising, but because of the wrong viewpoint and the wrong use of the material employed. When printing for industry becomes too elaborate and too fanciful its vulgarity of display becomes impertinent indecency which I resent.

Now there is one phase of advertising display that is seldom touched on and it is a phase which I regard as one of the fundamental items all of good work as well as one which should vitally interest the advertising typographer who cares anything for the ideals of his craft. Too many advertisers devote their thoughts toward the technical or mechanical details of their work to the exclusion of the esthetic side, without which their work is mere drudgery and commonplace commercialism. There are many technicians, too few idealists, and mere handicraft by itself, no matter how skillfully performed, is not all that is necessary to redeem art. I refer to the matter of *taste* in advertising typography. With your permission I shall quote liberally from an article I contributed last year to *The Advertiser* and I trust my good friend Manuel Rosenberg, the editor, will not object to my use of it here.

We frequently hear the expression, "After all, it's a matter of personal taste" as though the statement excused or explained away any and all departures from well-founded methods that conform to accepted standards of "taste." How often is the expression, "I know what I like" proposed as the final test by which a thing is to stand or fall, and to question the statement as incontrovertible is likely to be taken as an insult. What *he* may like, is the shrine at which is offered up the incense of his admiration; whether it meets the admiration of other devout worshipers or not doesn't matter.

To like a thing is not necessarily to exercise good taste, since, in respect to one's liking, every one is a law unto himself. One may even thoroughly dislike a thing and yet admit that it is good. To be able to recognize merit apart from one's likes or dislikes is a faculty closely akin to taste. To express a liking for a bad thing is not an expression of taste; it is a mere opinion or preference.

Taste, like our consciences, may not always be right; we may be conscientiously in error. A sound theory may apply equally to a bad piece of work as well as to one finer; but good taste can apply only to a thing essentially good. Taste is, then, our authority. But what is taste? To me it is the ladder by which we climb toward a greater perception of beauty by exchanging progressively something we recognize instinctively as not good, for something less gross, until finally one's taste becomes a discriminating faculty one exercises almost intuitively.

No one wishes to be thought wanting in taste, yet one often freely admits a lack of knowledge of certain things without chagrin; he will not as a rule argue with his physicians or his attorney, admitting of course their greater specialized knowledge; but as to a question of art or artistic craft, he reserves the right to assume that what he likes constitutes the last word in taste. A confession of a lack of taste on his part may seem to mean a confession of poor breeding—that is what he fears.

Frequently we come across one, otherwise cultured, but with neither experience nor training in craft, who attempts to speak of the qualities of workmanship. His judgement expresses only his personal opinion. How can he detect the restraint displayed by the craftsman in his work? How can he judge of its subtleties of handling, never having experienced the joy of accomplishment? He is a mere looker-on; his theories are second hand; his judgement is immature.

The quality of taste revealed in the art of bygone days was the outcome, usually, of simplicity in work—our times have fallen out of tune with simplicity; modern taste will then have to depend on increased knowledge of good work and find its roots in greater culture.

A man's work betrays always something of the man himself. The cloak it wears does not disguise the individual, and what lies under it is what determines the degree of his cultivation, his knowledge, his experience, the things he doesn't consciously put into his work, but which he cannot leave out, are the things that constitute the quality in his work which we distinguish as the measure of his taste.

An ignorant printer, or indeed any ignorant workman, is seldom aware of the depth of his ignorance, and frequently is incapable of learning because he will not trouble to learn nor follow the rules based on the experience of others. He arrogates to himself a knowledge and degree of taste that deceives only others equally ignorant. I do not address my remarks to him, although like the poor, he is always with us.

But what has all this to do with advertising typography? Taste in printing determines the form it is to take, the selection of a congruous type suited to the purpose for which the work is intended, the quality of the paper selected, the care and labor and cost that can be devoted to it in direct ratio to its ultimate value. Taste determines, too, whether there shall be decoration or not, how much of it, where it is to be introduced—in short, what is admissible and what is becoming. Quaintness in an old piece of printing may be admired because of its sincerity; to revive it in a piece of modern work is distasteful—hateful, even, because of its affectation.

Workmanship divorced from design cannot live: Printing without design cannot be good. Ornament divorced from craftsmanship is affectation, since decoration is not entirely a matter for the eye alone, but is largely an evidence of exuberance of fine craftsmanship and of one's joy in performance.

The esthetic appeal is universal. Once largely the result of blind instinct, it is now recognized to be far-reaching even for business uses.

As to the newer types, offered for the advertiser's use: How many or how few printers or printers' advisers are competent to decide whether a typeface is really good, or whether it is merely a revival of an older face suited to the earlier conditions and environments when it was designed, or whether it is the product of an ignorant designer with facility of hand only, but without knowledge or taste? They "know what they like!"

And there's another thing that seems to me to be too often honored in the breach—the lack of *style* in advertising typography. What do I mean by style? Style is a subtle quality inseparable from the tools and materials employed and is not attained by a preconceived attempt to include it. Nor is it a dress of thought or form, a robe to be put on or off at will. It is instead the living expression controlling both the form and vital structure of the means for communicating an idea—an intimate and recognizable quality in the work of a craftsman wholly unconscious of style or of any definite aim toward beauty. It is the subtle attribute in his work which relates it to his own times and is influenced by his environment and the stress of necessity.

If one's work shows style it is quite likely the other items of simplicity, dignity, legibility, and beauty will also be found in company with it. No art, no great printing even, ever developed by the rejection of the canons a good design found always in the work of preceding generations. Style in printing or in type, always has grown out of a preceding style; a new style is not created out of nothing merely by taking thought, it is developed by gradual modifications of older work and follows inevitable but slow developments repugnant to one impatient to produce something novel. In the search for novelty, the demands for beauty, balance, charm, are outmoded. I find that many of the types in common use today simply plagiarize the work of the dead; they lack entirely the precious quality of personality. Too often their creators accept perverse and deliberate ugliness often for the sake of alleged newness or originality.

As I have said many times: Type, to be good, must be legible—not only legible but pleasantly and easily readable, decorative in form, but not ornate; beautiful in itself and in company with its kinsman in the font; austere and formal, but with no stale or uninteresting regularity in its dissimilar characters; simple in design, but not the bastard simplicity that is mere crudity of outline; elegant, that is, gracious in line and fluid in form, but not archaic; and above all it must possess unmistakably the quality called "art" which is the spirit the designer puts into the body of his work, the product of his study and of his taste.

How many types now demanded by the advertiser or his typographic advisers will submit to an analysis of this sort?

And this lengthy preamble brings me somewhat tardily to the nub of my rambling remarks. I told Mr. Abrahams he might announce my subject as "Why Go Modern?" I was sure someone would bring up the question as to what I think of the modern movement in types and type arrangements and I wanted to anticipate the request. As I said earlier in this paper, "I am not an advertising man," although much of my work is used by advertisers. A great deal of modern advertising displeases me; I fear I may be coming old-fashioned in my second childhood. When I could not side-step the inquiry as to what I think of modernism and was pressed for an answer I found often that the inquirer doesn't know much about the matter either, so I could approach the matter safely. Quite frequently I found he wanted to do some bizarre arrangement of his own that he thought or hoped might be in the modern spirit, and wished merely to be bolstered up in his presentation of it, or be reassured by my favorable opinion.

This happened so often that I decided to attempt to analyze, as far as I can (and largely for my own satisfaction), just what constitutes modernism in the present day use of the term, and I beg to quote a portion of some remarks I made a few months ago at the Advertising Club Alumni: "The fight really is between formalism and modernism. Each has the same objective, that is, the presentation of a message in type, each has the same materials. Here we start even, but soon we become aware of a definite departure in aims, or rather in the methods of attaining the aims, that whereas the traditionalist prefers, as a rule, the simpler forms of roman letters and simple, straightforward arrangements of them, the modernist prefers sans serifs—bolder, blacker, and more erratic forms—hoping thereby to attract attention by reason of a lively distinction, a vivacity, and usually the whole arranged with a studied disregard for charm or beauty. The decorative elements, as used by the traditionalist, are very definitely related in period and character with the types employed and are esthetic and traditional in their forms. The modernist, on the other hand, uses mere type spots of abstract design entirely unrelated to the text; his types contain nothing of romance or sentiment, and his arrangements follow no known law of order or beauty. His whole idea is that of a complete revolution of all the principles that have governed good typography since its invention by Johann Gutenberg, five hundred years ago. He attempts to create an effect that will startle, intrigue, catch the eye, and is content to let balance, rhythm, harmony, beauty, fall like chips, where they may.

The traditionalist attempts to interpret his copy, to make every effort to emphasize the presentation of the message itself, but without calling undue attention to the means of its presentation for its own sake. To me a thing may be useful and at the same time be ugly, yet most people resent mere ugliness. The modernist gets attention value possibly by his bizarre types and arrangements, but not always favorably. Type is not more legible because ugly, nor less legible if it presents a measure of beauty, and beauty is still compatible with utility. Beauty in advertising after all is little more than a pleasing arrangement of lines of lettering that break the surface pleasantly, and at the same time tell the story clearly and simply.

To my eye, the modernist's sole aim seems to be to express himself or his own skill in his arrangements, instead of attempting to present the thing he is paid to exploit—the thing the customer or the advertiser wishes to advertise. You may imagine from the foregoing that I am a traditionalist.

Once, while making a talk that I hadn't taken the precaution to put into written form, as I have these few remarks, and my talk probably was rather rambling, one of my audience went out into the lobby. There he met a man just coming in who asked him if Goudy had finished yet. He replied, "Yes, he finished some time ago, but he won't stop." Before anyone here can make such a comment, after reiterating my pleasure at being here, I am going to *stop* right now.

153

From an address to the Advertising Typographers Association of America, Virginia Beach, Virginia, 1938.

The Good Old Neue Typografie[1]

By Paul Rand

In the folder titled "Typography U.S.A.," the Type Directors Club announces: "At last a new form . . . an entirely new concept in typography has been realized, a typography that is purely American. This new typography, the product of contemporary science, industry, art, and technology, has become recognized internationally as the 'New American Typography'."

In the light of what has happened and what is happening in this field in America, it is very difficult for me to understand this claim. This is not to say that the statement is deliberately misleading, but, merely that I, personally, am unaware that anything of the sort is occurring.

The folder goes on to ask: "What is this new form?" I can only answer that I don't know. And to the next question: "What does it look like?," I can only say that the best of it looks like typography that could have come from Germany, Switzerland, England, Holland, France, etc. Briefly, it is an offspring of the "international style," which means, as I am sure we all understand, a blending not only of the ideas of different peoples but an interaction of the different arts—painting, architecture, and literature, as well as the so-called applied arts, as exemplarized in the ideograms of Apollinaire, the montages of Picasso, Schwitters, and Lissitzky, the paintings of Doesburg and Leger, the architecture of Oud and LeCorbusier, as well as countless others.

To deny the fact that American Typography is basically a continuation of, sometimes a retrogradation from, and, sometimes, an improvement upon the "new typography" which was fathered on the continent of Europe, would be to ignore the revolutionary impact on all the arts of Cubism, Dadaism, and all the other "isms" and to overlook the influence of movements such as de Stijl and the Bauhaus, as well as of individual pioneers who actually changed the face of traditional typography.

If one compares American typographic contributions with those of American illustration or even American motor car or refrigerator design, there is little question that there is such a thing as "American" illustration, "American" motor car design, or "American" refrigerators. In none of these cases am I discussing relative merits, I am merely pointing out that they are American and not Americanized. On the other hand, I believe the "New American Typography" can more accurately be called the New Americanized European Typography since there can be little doubt as to its origin.

This is not to say that there are not individual American designers who have made valuable contributions to typographic design, particularly in the graphic arrangement of the printed page, but, these contributions have been mainly in the nature of variations of basic European principles; nor is it to belittle the fact that an American designer, such as Morris Benton, in redesigning such typefaces as Garamond and Bodoni, has done significant work. In this connection, however, it is my understanding that in this symposium we are primarily concerned with formal typographic arrangement, and that while the redesign of typefaces or the creation of new typefaces its vitally important, the typeface is but an ingredient in the overall design complex. Furthermore, it is somewhat ironic to note the very generous use of European typefaces in the "The New American Typography." How many printed pieces use, for example, such faces as Venus, Standard, or Didot, not to mention the classical designs—Garamond, Caslon, Baskerville, Bodoni, Bembo, etc., etc.—all of European origin? As to the question what effect certain indigenous factors such as the difference in language have on typographic usage, I would say that I believe this to be a rather superficial conditioning factor.

As I write this paper, it is difficult for me to think of any single book on American modern typography, which would, for example, equal the Swiss publication, *Satztechnik und Gestaltung,* let alone such classics as Tschichold's *Die Neue Typografie, Typographishe Gestaltung,* or even his later, more conventional book, *Designing Books.* In 1929 Douglas C. McMurtrie wrote *Modern Typography and Layout,* a book which contained some good illustrative material as well as some revealing text. The makeup of this book, however, was not only in the modernistic style, but a monstrous example of American typography.

I would, nevertheless, like to emphasize once again that no fair-minded person, American or otherwise, can deny the influence of such American designers as Goudy, DeVinne, Bruce Rogers, and Dwiggins, not only on American but on European typography as well. However, when we compare the enormous impact on modern typography of just one European designer, such as Jan Tschichold, there is little doubt that the influence of the aforementioned designers has been far more limited.

It would seem to me that before we are able to evaluate the "New American Typography," we must necessarily place it in its historical, political, and linguistic context—a rather complex undertaking for designers, people actually engaged in doing rather than philosophizing, to cope with. Furthermore, in all humility, I believe that at the present time we are too close to the trees, so to speak, to evaluate the situation. No doubt, in time we can hope to produce a more indigenous kind of typography, one which satisfies our basic needs through original formal solutions, rather than one which is self-consciously obsessed with style. I am afraid that at the present time, at least for me, it is, therefore, impossible to answer the question— "What is this new form?"

I would like to conclude by saying that good typography, American or otherwise, is not a question of nationality, but of practicality; namely, it is that of resolving the specific problem in adequate formal terms. In the early twenties, when Tschichold wrote his revolutionary book on modern typography he did not call it German or Swiss or French, he called it simply—"Die Neue Typografie."

---

[1]Although the *f* appears in Paul Rand's original publication of this article in 1960, only two years ago was this letter generally accepted as an alternative to the *ph* in the German word "typographie."

From an address to the Type Directors Club, New York (18 April 1959), published in the papers of the "What Is New in Typography" conference, 1960.

Typographical Warfare

By Otl Aicher

ome wars end in exhaustion. Heads down in the trenches, nothing stirs.

The twentieth century kicked off with a typographical declaration of war. First, Art Nouveau took it upon itself to alter letter styles at random, usually those used for book covers, in line with the philosophy the arts and crafts movement. But that was in itself a critique of historicism, the conventional roman type, from within, as it were. The historical rudiments were merely filtered through the informality of the arts and crafts.

Anyone could design their own *A,* which didn't need to be part of a legible script but was merely a feature in the aesthetic embellishment of book covers. Letters acquired an aura of culture that was supposed to permeate everyday objects in terms of formal principle, style, and aesthetic structure. They "dressed" fashionably.

Graphic art was in its element. It was difficult to decide whether Gustav Klimt was a painter or a graphic artist. Mackintosh created architecture as if he were a graphic artist, and his items of furniture were primarily symbols, symbolic artifacts, and symbolic structures, and only then objects with a function. Archetypal graphic forms such as interlacing foliage, lines, undulations, checkered patterns, and of course the circle, triangle, and square figured prominently, the latter well in advance of the Bauhaus. Friedrich Schuhmann's book on the square appeared at the turn of the century.

The circle, triangle, and square also turned up in a rather different context, namely in industry, where they figured not in graphics but in technical production.

A bench plane produces flat surfaces, a lathe cylindrical forms. Transposition and rotation were the basic techniques of industrial production. The identification of primary geometric forms with social movement and production technology freed them from the psychologism of Art Nouveau.

The square, circle, and triangle were the symbols of a new era, a new culture, a total renunciation of historical values. Klimt's circles and squares had basically been elegant decoration. Now, the fundamental elements of being and the world came to symbolize technological production, the industrial society, proletarian solidarity, internationalism. They became aesthetic standard-bearers in the fight against redundancy and irrelevance.

Paul Renner conceived the first scripts based on the circle, triangle, and square that went beyond the formal fripperies of Art Nouveau to become substantive design. In England there was Edward Johnston.

Of course unadorned sans serif scripts, known as "grotesque" type, had been in use virtually throughout the nineteenth century. Since they were written not with a pen but lithographically, i.e., on stone, they were also referred to as "stone scripts." The most famous was the later much-feted jobbing sans serif, also the progenitor of Helvetica. At a certain distance from the bourgeois cultural debate surrounding Art Nouveau, ingenious typographers from the newspaper sector had devised typefaces that owed nothing to historicism or the formal registers of the cultural elite. The same happened in architecture, too.

In 1911, Gropius built the Alfeld boot-tree factory, generally recognized as the first example of modern architecture. In actual fact, the era of industrial architecture had been ushered in in 1851 with Paxton's Crystal Palace. The founding fathers of the new architecture were Franuois Hennebique, Ernest L. Ranson, Louis J. Kahn, and Robert Maillart, not Peter Behrens or Walter Gropius.

Modern typography had been practiced long before Paul Renner and Jan Tschichold proclaimed the new typographical century. War only broke out when typography was turned into a cultural doctrine or ideology in the wake of the first abstract art.

The enemy was historicism, classicism, the typography of such as Garamond, Bodoni, Didot, or Caslon, the typography of the classical roman type. In the cultural arena there were those who were again writing whole books by hand, using convoluted medieval Gothic scripts, but the age of such scripts was nevertheless past. But classicism continued to function as the showcase language of State and Church, of domination and power, of education and culture.

And this war between the classicist typography of roman type and the modern sans serif typeface is still to all intents and purposes being waged today. The entire century has borne its mark. But the factions are weary. Justifiably so. As in all wars, the grievance is ideological rather than practical.

Those advocating Bauhaus, Le Corbusier, Mondrian or Hugo Ball also side with sans serif, compasses and ruler, industry and technology. Those favoring eternal values and Western tradition, and at the same time the virtues of the absolutist state, take up arms for roman type. And, as ever when ideology determines the proceedings, it has become a very grim affair.

The future began with a new script called Futura that was not written but drafted with compasses and ruler. The A was based on a triangle, the H on a square, and the O on a circle.

It was through discussions with Paul Renner that I got into typography. Previously, I had written in the vein of Rudolf Koch or Charles Morris.

A key figure was Jan Tschichold, who like Renner was employed at the Munich Gewerbeschule. He even liberated the Bauhaus from its Expressionist framework, and was able to cite reasonable grounds for whatever he did: Functionalist typography had arrived. Typography had passed from being an ideological issue to being a thought process.

But Jan Tschichold sold out, as one might say. Coextensively with the Third Reich and the resurrection of roman type—which after initially being branded as "non-Aryan" even served as a vehicle of State projection—he too returned to the graphic tradition of the humanists, to the roman capitals and to centered text, the arrangement of type around a central axis.

But had Tschichold really sold out? I don't think so. He simply felt that, though sans serif typefaces are fine for advertising purposes, they're not good for books or lengthy pieces of text. That triggered a controversy that even found its way into the press. War had reached new depths.

Personally, I never fully accepted the arguments of either faction, even in discussions with Paul Renner. It's quite true that a novel set in sans serif is unpalatable. But it can be argued just as convincingly that roman type with its serifs is over-elaborate. As early as 1947 I therefore set about creating letters without serifs but with an expanded downstroke, a sort of roman-sans serif mongrel.

My interest in this question has been an abiding one. Is a graphic style combining the advantages of roman type with those of sans serif feasible?

By 1958, my answer was ready. Drafts were hanging all around my office. I drafted innumerable variants of a script that had to be as legible as roman and as uncluttered as sans serif. A typographer who has since made a name for himself paid me a visit. A year later my design appeared, with slight modifications, in his name.

I was so staggered I didn't attempt to design letters again for years. I now saw typographers as a treacherous bunch and took no further part in their discussions. In any case, these mostly involved aesthetic nit-picking and tended to become more and more heated as they declined in substance.

I regained my composure when I became acquainted with the Univers face that Adrian Frutiger had brought out in 1957, a major typographical landmark.

Univers as not a dyed-in-the wool sans serif. The range of strokes was greater, though remaining within the overall sans serif format. Univers walked tall alongside jobbing sans serif and Helvetica, and outmaneuvered them simply because of its concessions to roman type.

I began again from scratch, this time with an unshakeable inner conviction and a well-defined program. I wanted to end the feuding between roman and sans serif. Not simply for the sake of peace but because the differences were ideological contrivances. My program was addressed less to aesthetics than to legibility. The question that haunted me was why there are different degrees of legibility, how these are manifested, and how they come about. In a sense, this approach put me at odds with both factions. Seen another way, though, I was also able to glean something from them both.

It is my conviction that our graphic culture still has a long way to go. And we should be doing our bit towards an accessible style of script.

That doesn't mean I'm in favor of devising new scripts willy-nilly, quite the reverse. It's simply a matter of designing better scripts. In the process of assessing advantages and drawbacks, it is quite conceivable that someone, somewhere will bark up the wrong tree from time to time. But it's the aim of optimization and that's what is important. The proceedings need to be revitalized. One can approach the old factions from new conceptual angles and challenge that force them to re-examine their own positions.

Of course, most typographers concern themselves with the undemanding and uncontroversial questions of style and taste. But suddenly the Times typeface produced by Morison in 1932 is making people everywhere sit up. I have followed this typeface attentively through the years and, as with Univers, assessed its performance in every conceivable context, gaining invaluable insights in the process.

The question that has occupied my mind for as long as I can remember has now once again become a burning issue of contention: Are there just two separate graphic cultures or are we making deep inroads into new dimensions? Concretely, which script would be as legible as roman and as straightforward as sans serif? When we have such a script—and of this I'm certain—we can put the war behind us.

From *Typographie* (Lüdenscheid: Ernst and Sohn Verlag, 1988).

Zombie Modernism

By Mr. Keedy

his is a very scary essay. It's about death and denial. But you don't have to be afraid to read it, because it's just language, and meaning is arbitrary. At least that is what those nasty postmodernists and deconstructivists want you to believe. But we know better. There is a right way and a wrong way to do everything. A good way and a bad way, a rational way and a crazy way, a clear way and a chaotic way, the modern way and the modern way. In graphic design, there is no alternative to modernism. To predate modernism is to be a commercial artist, printer or scribe, not a designer, because the designer was born out of modernism. To postdate modernism is equally incomprehensible for most designers, because it exists outside their realm of comprehension.

In most areas of cultural production such as art, architecture, music, and literature, modernism was just one more event in a continuing life cycle. Graphic design, on the other hand, did not have sufficient time to develop a mature sense of self—the umbilical cord had not been severed yet. So when modernism died, many designers' ideology died with it. However, they did not go peacefully into that dark night. They refused to acknowledge their own ideological demise, and they continue to haunt the living, moaning and groaning because they no longer belong to this world. That is the fate of the Zombie Modernist, the living dead who design among us.

In the beginning, when modernism was young, it was a radical idea that positioned itself in opposition to a more conservative traditionalism. As time went on, the modernist ideology spread into all areas of cultural production, eventually becoming the dominant esthetic ideology. Design was an extremely effective tool in converting the masses to modernity; it spread modernism from a few liberal thinkers to a conservative majority. Consequently, designers defined design as a modernist practice, and design's history and theory exist almost exclusively within the modernist paradigm.

Unfortunately, design's modernism is an ill-considered version of art modernism, one that is based on an Enlightenment faith in progress and singular answers, reinforced by a rationalist universalism. Modernist design theory has developed little beyond the reiteration of modernist platitudes that are endlessly repeated but that are not expanded, questioned, or adjusted to meet the needs of design theory and practice.

Only in the past few years has there emerged a sufficient amount of work and writing to challenge the hegemony of design modernism. This has prompted some modernist designers to re-evaluate and re-define modernism. They want to appear relevant, without giving up the privileged position that a universalist dogma constructs. These last ditch efforts superficially pay lip service to, and subsequently disavow, the importance, complexity, and diversity of contemporary culture.

Design modernism's hegemony reveals itself in its countless annual shows and publications that primarily function to establish a universal standard of "excellence" by a contrast canonizing of "modernist masters" in design,[1] the absolutist, rationalist, obsession with, "problem solving," "clarity," and "legibility," and the paranoid attacks against anything that is pluralistic, de-centered, or new.

The core philosophy of modernist design is in instrumentalist, or pragmatic thought. "Pragmatism is America's only native philosophy."[2] It is goal oriented, practical, and distrustful of all things metaphysical. Paul Rand frequently quotes John Dewey: "In Deweyan pragmatism there is no ecstasy, no Dionysian muse, no charismatic illumination."[3] It is this pragmatism that is at the root of America's "down to earth" but decidedly "cranky" tone in criticism (this essay not excluded).

In Europe we find, not surprisingly, that design critic Robin Kinross's philosophical hero is the neo-pragmatist, Jürgen Habermas, the German hyperrationalist whose faith is that "language, however distorted and manipulative, always has consensus or understanding as its inner *telos*,"[4] and that "the truth of statements is linked in the last analysis to the interpretation of the good and the true life."[5]

Habermas's and Dewey's pragmatism is not an unlikely source of interest for designers, particularly die-hard modernists. I wonder how our pragmatist critics overlooked Richard Rorty, America's best known (neo-pragmatist) philosopher, who makes use of the ideas of Dewey and Derrida. Many designers are disturbed by the Marxist and leftist politics of postmodern theorists, but absolutely nothing has been said of the right-wing conservatism of the modernist theorist. Is that simply because design consists of a silent conservative majority? Following the historical model of early, classical, and late periods, I would categorize modernist ideology in graphic design as: starting with the (early) pragmatic, art historical dogma of Paul Rand, ossifying into the (classical) traditionalist, hyperrationalism of Robin Kinross, only to dissipate into the (late or rococo) decorative, modernism of Dan Friedman.[6]

Although the work of these modernists differs greatly, the message is the same: "I am the voice of clarity and reason," "I am the voice of authority and progress," and "I am in charge of this family's values." From the Bauhaus to our house, this "father-knows-best" baloney has always passed for design theory. Graphic design's alleged birth place, the Bauhaus, has, from the start, been idealized and mythologized by designers. "The pathos of such idealism has been revealed by subsequent events. The fact that the school was destroyed by Fascism may have enhanced its credibility in post-war Europe and the United States, but its ideal of universality was a myth and mirage, shattered by the war, politics and the demands of consumer society."[7]

Creation myths die hard, if at all. The Zombie Modernist refuses to let go of modernism at any cost.

For the Zombie Modernist, everything outside of modernism is chaos, superficial, trendy, of poor quality, and just an empty formal style. It became increasingly difficult for designers to keep the myth alive. Gropius himself, in an effort to recuperate modernism in design said in 1968: "The complexity and psychological implications, as we developed them at the Bauhaus, were forgotten and it [modernism] was described as a simple-minded, purely utilitarian approach to design."[8] The fact is, for the most part, it was a simple-minded, purely utilitarian approach that continues to be taught the same way today. Likewise, the Granddaddy of all Zombie Modernists, Paul Rand, complains in his latest book that "The Bauhaus, into whose history is woven the very fabric of modernism, is seen as a style rather than as an idea."[9]

Echoing that sentiment, the radical Zombie Mod Dan Friedman says in his latest book, "Many in design think of modernism as a style that began in the Bauhaus in the 1920s and feel into disrepute in the 1960s. But modernism means different things and is traced to different origins by different people. Philosophers, for example, trace it to the seventeenth century and the dual influences of rationalism and humanism."[10] I am not sure exactly what the point is, but I'm sure there is one. The important thing is that modernism is not a style.

That's right, modernism is no longer a style, it's an ideology, and that ideology is conservatism. Modernism, unarguably design's greatest asset, has become its greatest liability because it is inextricably bound to conservative dogma. As such, design has become primarily an ideologically conservative practice. In *Design, Form, and Chaos,* Paul Rand quotes A. N. Whitehead: "*Mere change without conservation is a passage from nothing to nothing.* Mere conservation without change cannot conserve." (The emphasis on the first sentence is Mr. Rand's.) This quote is instructive not only as an illustration of Mr. Rand's usual harping against change, but also for its assumed goal to "conserve." Modernist designers believe the function of design is to "conserve" universal values in designed objects. I suspect most designers are comfortable with that idea, even though few of them will admit it publicly. Most designers claim to be very liberal, or even radical, like their early modern art heroes. But this is 1995, not 1925, and we are formulating design practice, not art history. Recently I interviewed design critic Rick Poynor, and I asked him if he was a modernist or a postmodernist. He said, "The problem I have with postmodernism is the relativism and nihilism that follows it."[11] Understandably, many design critics are reluctant to give up the absolute values of modernism because that is what makes design criticism an easier, right or wrong proposition.

By contrast, the contextual postmodern approach is "relative," because the discourse is relative to the subject at hand. This greater demand for specificity and complexity is often dismissed as "nihilism" or "chaos." Mr. Poynor went on to say, "So I recognize what you say; that there is, at times, in the way I write and in the areas that interest me, a split between those two areas of thinking (modernism and postmodernism)—an acknowledgment of one, and maybe a hankering after the other."[12] It is precisely this fearful and nostalgic "hankering" for modernism that has retarded the intellectual growth of design theory and criticism, and has hidden a deep seated conservatism.

My aim in this essay is to examine modernism in design, not make a case for postmodernism. If you would have told me ten years ago that I would still be making a case for postmodernism in design in 1995, I probably wouldn't have believed it because the political imperative that drives modernism-at-all-cost in design was not as evident to me then, and I assumed design would move along with other cultural practices.

How, then, should postmodernism in general be evaluated? My preliminary assessment would be this: That in its concern for difference, for the difficulties of communication, for the complexity and nuances of interests, cultures, places, and the like, it exercises a positive influence. The metalanguages, metatheories, and metanarratives of modernism (particularly in its later manifestations) did tend to gloss over important differences, and failed to pay attention to important disjunctions and details. Postmodernism has been particularly important in acknowledging "the multiple forms of otherness as they emerge from differences in subjectivity, gender, and sexuality, race and class, temporal (configurations of sensibility) and spatial geographic locations and dislocations."[13]

Zombie Modernists survive by eating the living flesh of postmodernism

The Zombie Modernist's biggest enemies are postmodernism and deconstruction because they reveal that the simplistic, rationalist/universalist modernism of design is long dead and starting to stink.

"We know the world only through the medium of language. Meaning is arbitrary. Meaning is unstable and has to be made by the reader. Each reader will read differently. To impose a single text on the readers is authoritarian and oppressive. Designers should make text visually ambiguous and difficult to fathom, as a way to respect the rights of the readers."[14]

This is the "straw man of postmodernism that Robin Kinross props up so he can knock it down with his universalist, rationalist, truth-seeking, neo-con rant titled *Fellow Readers.*

That we understand the world through language, that meaning is unstable, and that people tend to interpret things differently are hardly radical or wacky ideas. What is wacky is Kinross's hilarious interpretations of how postmodernist designers react to this condition. It does strike me as a bit "authoritarian" and "oppressive" to "impose" a single *anything* on any one. I like choices. People who believe in democracy are nutty that way. However, *assuming* a single reading from a text is just plain stupid (even Mr. Habermas has failed to make a convincing argument). Given that multiple readings are inherent in most texts (too relativist an idea for Kinross because "truth" loses its absolutism), it doesn't make any sense to make the text even more "difficult to fathom" unless you absolutely hate the reader.

But Mr. Kinross already knows that the whole point of his ridiculous characterization of poststructuralist theory is to insist that without modernism all its chaos, obscurantism, lies, and nonsense meant to draw attention to megalomaniac designers **(like me, me, me)**.

Robin Kinross is an Enlightenment Era throwback who has taken it on himself to be the quality control officer of our "common society." He goes about this task with a decidedly "un-common" set of ideological and formal values that never seem to make their way beyond the posh and precious world of limited edition, fine, collectable books. As one of society's "common folk," let me be the first to say, "Gee, thanks, Robin!"

I have included Mr. Kinross as the European representative of fundamentalist, modernist thinking. There are others, but he presents the most compelling argument, such as it is. As with most cultural concerns, the "European version" is "classier" than the "American version," but the political strategy is the same. The usual party line of the far right is: We are being led astray by "bad people" (academics, pinkos, perverts), and they are steering us away from the "truth" (family values, Jesus, order, clarity) for their own "selfish gain" (wealth, fame, power). We must get back on the "right track" (throw the bums out, vote for me, buy my vision).

Modernism in design went from a radical idea to a liberal ideal only to stagnate as conservative dogma. Because the Zombie Modernist doesn't want to come to terms with the fact that their ideology is dead, they are always trying to *rationalize* away (they think they own exclusive rights to everything that is rational) the postmodern condition the rest of us know as reality. That is why postmodernism must be discredited and exposed as empty formalism (a style), and one should never "attempt to go beyond Modernism." Typically, it goes something like this: "It (postmodern design) concentrates on visual techniques and individual solutions rather than on cultural context. Much of this 'Postmodern' design uses a visual vocabulary pioneered by the 1920's avant-garde, yet without the critique of cultural institutions that informed the found-object collages of Kurt Schwitters, the typographic havoc of the Futurists, or the socially engaged design of the Constructivists. Our attempts to go beyond Modernism are often realized by referring to visual techniques that we have been taught represent radicality: avant-garde design of the 1910s and 1920s."[15]

Like the smooth "double talk" of Ronald Reagan, this makes sense if you don't think about it in any detail or any *actual* context. But the idea only makes sense in a contextless void, where there is no distinction between art and design or past and present—in the "metacontext" of design modernism. Even if we accept the dubious claim that art movements like dada and constructivism were effective as critical social discourse (as if Lissitzky's prouns and Schwitters' collages really enlightened the mostly illiterate masses who somehow had the luxury of visiting art galleries and museums from 1910 through the 1920s), whoever said it was design's ambition to "critique its cultural institutions, or its clients"? The strategy of subversion is an art world pretension that has little relevance to design practice. To criticize design for its lack of "cultural critique" makes about as much sense as criticizing art for its inability to "solve problems." Art exits outside (above) society and is expected to be critical of it. Design exists inside (below) society and is expected to serve it. Many young designers today refuse to accept that simple distinction, or any distinction between art and design, because they think art is somehow "better" than design (I think it has something to do with the fact that design is taught in ART schools). Actually, most postmodern design was and is engaged in a critique of a cultural institution. Obviously, postmodern design is very critical of modern design—design's cultural institution. The effectiveness of its criticism is evident in how afraid the modernist designers today are of postmodernism.

The other half-baked idea, expressed in the quote above, is how those postmodern designers stole their forms from early modernist artists and are therefore less original (Never mind that the modernist designers also stole their forms from modern art). The modern art paradigm of originality or—Who Did it First?—assumes to be the most important factor in evaluating design (even though the art world itself has discredited that as a primary criteria years ago). Obviously the art world did it first because, at the time, graphic design as a discipline didn't even exist. So if we judge design by modern art standards (as most of our so-called design critics do) then the design can't possibly go beyond (art) modernism. It can only catch-up, at best. Using art world paradigms for graphic design criticism not only renders postmodern design useless, but the validity of design practice itself is always in question.

If the Zombie Modernists can't discredit postmodernism, then they try to co-opt it. Whatever threatens to be new, or different, must immediately be subjugated to modernism. In an essay about Neville Brody's new project, *Fuse,* Michael Rock writes: "While the forms assume the variegated surface of post-modernism, the underlying issues indicate that projects such as *Fuse* are deeply rooted in Modernist goals of avant-garde experimentation and artistic originality."[16] Sounds familiar? Michael Rock points out that

Fuse is just continuing in the modernist tradition (art tradition, that is. Never mind that *Fuse* exists in the design context). He then goes on and uses (Art critic) Rosalind Krauss's postmodern critique (of modern art) to lambaste the whole project. Is he advocating postmodernism? Art criticism? Of course not. The main point he feels compelled to make is that *Fuse,* like everything else in design, is still just "gold ol' modernism."

Mr. Rock continues: "The stranglehold of a single, homogeneous Modernist theory is a designer's fantasy." As proof of the fact, he offers that "Even a cursory glance through a type house manual or popular magazine from the last thirty years should dash the idea that the world ever tottered on the brink of Global Helvetican domination."[17] But is that proof an alternative *theory* to modernism?

I know I will be accused of portraying modernism in design too narrowly and simplistically, particularly now that we have entered the revisionist-modernist era, when issues raised by postmodernism are routinely claimed as modernist by dredging up obscure precedents in modern art practice. It is no fantasy that there have been very few voices reaching the entire design community. The ones that have, however, are modernist ones ("Oh, but the times, they are a-changin'!").

If the hegemony of modernist design theory is a fantasy, where are all the essays and books on postmodern design theory? Where should we look for them? Certainly not in *I.D.* magazine, where Ralph Caplan has been dispensing his "good-old-boy," "commonsense," modernist pap for years, only to be replaced by Mr. Rock's own, "pedantically correct," "middle-of-the-road," modernism. Sounding a lot like *previous* Yale professor Paul Rand, Michael Rock writes in the *AIGA Journal:* "Perhaps the most socially *irresponsible* work is the overdesigned, overproduced, typographic stunts that serve no real function, speak only to other designers and the cultural elite, and through opulence and uselessness revel in a level of consumption that glorifies financial excess."[18]

I doubt if Mr. Rock would complain about architects, doctors, engineers, and scientists speaking only to themselves. Of course they talk to themselves; they are experts, specialists, and professionals. Because design is not a profession,[19] designers do not understand that professionals have a responsibility to each other to keep practicing at the highest level. That is how they protect the credibility and the value of their profession.

Designers, however, have the trade mentality that the more accessible their work is, and the greater the number they can service (over one billion served daily!), the more secure their jobs will be. This trade mentality is ironic coming from someone like Michael Rock who is not a professional as a designer, but as an educator, a degreed, accredited, professional.

One can only guess who this "champion of the people" and current Yale professor considers the "cultural elite,"[20] but the fact that design critics pick up the rhetoric of the far right should come as no surprise. Whether it is politics, economics, aesthetics, or design, conservatism is still conservatism.

Most of the current debate in graphic design is characterized as a generational split between the older modernist and the younger postmodernist. As I have pointed out in this essay, there are more than a few vocal young modernists, as well as a few older postmodernists (Ed Fella, for example). It would be more accurate to characterize our current situation as the backlash of an entrenched conservatism against a real, or perhaps only imagined threat, of a relativist/liberal agenda. Design is certainly big enough to hold designers with conservative and liberal agendas, but I guess it's just a bad time for liberals everywhere now.

Ask yourself this question: If Newt Gingrich and Rush Limbaugh were graphic designers, would they be:

(A) Complaining about the "visual pollution," "typographic stunts," and the many shortcomings of deconstruction and postmodernist design in centrist publications like *ID, Print, CA,* and the *AIGA Journal?*

Or would they be:

(B) Writing about new ideas and work in smaller circulation publications like *Émigré,* and academic publications like *Visible Language, Design Issues,* or ACD's *Statements?*

Hmmm?

As it became embarrassingly obvious that there were fundamental flaws in modernism as it traditionally functioned in design, some designers started to redefine modernism as a one-ideology-fits-all metaphilosophy.

"I view modernism in design as a broad, potentially open-minded, and inexhaustible way of thinking that began in the mid-nineteenth century and continues today among the majority of us who believe that we should use all existing means to understand, improve, change, and refresh our condition in the world."[21] Sounding suspiciously similar to the ingratiating speeches made by beauty pageant contestants, as in ". . . and I wish for world peace," modernist designers try to prove that their ideology is still *universally* relevant through a new (trendy?) commitment to good citizenship.

"Modernism ran out of steam over a decade ago. But at its core is an ethic—the responsibility that a designer has to actively contribute to, indeed enhance, the social, political, and cultural framework—that continues to inform even the most diehard Postmodernist."[22] Wow, I had no idea that the whole concept of being a productive, responsible citizen was invented by modernism! I thought it was just something modernists used to justify their aesthetic self-indulgence (I guess that's just the nihilistic, postmodern cynic in me).

"Although the rhetoric proclaimed better goods or living conditions, the intended consumers, the public, had little chance to influence or shape Bauhaus ideology. The public became a misunderstood and mostly unwilling participant, blamed for its lack of worldly perspective and aesthetic-value discrimination."[23] Maybe the Bauhaus doesn't represent the "ethical core" of modernism. But then, what does? That's the great thing about modernism: you can pretty much take your pick from the past six decades.

In an effort to avoid change, contemporary modernist designers indulge themselves in a pathetic, kinder, gentler, morphing ideology that is virtually meaningless. The only connection that the current modernism has to what was once understood as modernism is that it is now *rationally* and *universally* useless. This "new" or "late" modernism is an exhausted modernism that the designers prefer to a vibrant but uncertain postmodern future.

The myth of universal modernist values is so pervasive in design, that it swallows up even the possibility of an alternate ideology. "The fact is, it's foolish to deny that anyone who seriously explores the outer limits and inner soul of visual communication is not in some way a Modernist. Or as Pogo's Walt Kelley said: "We have met the enemy and it is us."[24] I believe it would be more accurate to say "We have *reinvented* the enemy and it is us." By co-opting all change and difference into a simplistic modernist paradigm, we prohibit design from ever growing up and leaving its conservative modernist home.

Imprisoned in a dilapidated old house built by modern art, design is unable to strike out on its own and make a place for itself in the world. Thus design's "outer limits and inner soul" is immobile, caught between heaven and earth, in a no-place, we call purgatory—the zombies' fate.

"Today no designer or design organization could or would contemplate universal solutions to the problems of design for the real world. We are still in search of a theory, social commitment is still elusive, so we indulge in our fantasies, ironies and pastiche, which are more comforting (and more profitable) than that respect for 'stern realities' that Gropius demanded from architecture and design."[25]

Designers should stop "hankering" after a mythical modernist ideal, or pretending that art theory is a viable theoretical model for design. We don't need to "conserve" our past and resist change. We need to construct our future theoretical discourse, carefully, around the particular and exciting context of design. We must allow ourselves to look at design in new and challenging ways, we must look for—ourselves.

---

[1]Books on design can be divided into two types, "serious" monographs on famous modernist masters (the canon), and "fun" collections of vernacular ephemera (the "other").

[2]John Patrick Diggins, *The Promise of Pragmatism: Modernism and the Crisis of Knowledge and Authority* (Chicago: University of Chicago Press, 1995).

[3]Ibid.

[4]Terry Eagleton, *The Ideology of the Aesthetic,* Basil Blackwell, 1990.

[5]Quoted in Thomas McCarthy, *The Critical Theory of Jürgen Habermas* (London, 1978), p. 273.

[6]Dan Friedman is not a designer. "I have chosen to define my position as that of an artist whose subject—design and culture—affects all aspects of life." However his new book, *Dan Friedman: Radical Modernism,* has been reviewed and received as a design book (I found it in the design section of my local bookstore), and he continues to be a design educator, so I am treating him here as a designer. His impact on design was substantial; his impact on the art world has yet to be seen.

[7]Gillian Naylor, *The Bauhaus Reassessed* (E. P. Dutton, 1985), p. 180.

[8]Ibid.

[9]Paul Rand, *Design, Form, and Chaos* (New Haven and London: Yale University Press, 1993), p. 212.

[10]Dan Friedman, *Dan Friedman: Radical Modernism* (New Haven and London: Yale University Press, 1994), p. 114.

[11]Rick Poynor, "An Interview with Rick Poynor," by Mr. Keedy, *Émigré,* no. 33 (Winter, 1995), p. 35.

[12]Ibid.

[13]David Harvey, *The Condition of Postmodernity* (Blackwell, 1990), p. 113.

[14]Robin Kinross, *Fellow Readers: Notes on Multiplied Language* (London: Hyphen Press, 1994), pg. 5.

[15]Mike Mills, "The (layered) Vision Thing," *Eye,* no. 8, vol. 2, (1992). The title is a reference to George Bush. Ironic, Huh?

[16]Michael Rock, "Beyond Typography," *Eye,* no. 15, vol. 4 (Winter 1994), p. 31.

[17]Ibid., p. 27.

[18]Michael Rock, "Responsibility: Buzzword of the Nineties," *AIGA Journal,* vol. 10, no. 1 (1992).

[19]A professional is someone who has a specialized knowledge, skill, and training that is regulated by their peers. Professionals establish standards of employment and advancement, practice, research,

development, and education, to further that practice. Although most practicing designers today receive degrees from accredited universities, there is absolutely no necessity to have a degree to practice, and there are no regulated standards for practice or teaching. Design educators are, however, the only professionals in design, because they are professional educators.

[20]"Newt Gingrich, the new Speaker of the House, promises to furnish many ingenious demonstrations of ways to dress authority in the rhetoric of anti-elitism. So far, his handling of his status as a former professor has proved the most instructive. When he first made his ill-fated appointment of a new House historian, Gingrich explained in a public appearance that he was, in fact, a pro. 'As a Ph.D. in history,' he said, 'I think I have the right to select an academic who has legitimate credentials . . . I think I may be peculiarly, of all the people who have been Speaker, in a legitimate position to make a selection that I think will be helpful in re-establishing the legitimacy of history.'

"But when at the same appearance he was asked about his qualifications for teaching his course on American history at Reinhardt College, he was quick to put his anti-professionalism on display. 'I teach a course which is an outline of my thoughts at fifty-one years of age, based on everything I've experienced, which is, frankly, rather more than most tenured faculty,' he noted. 'I haven't written twenty-two books that are meaningless.' He's not a professional academic after all. He's a citizen professor. We're going to see more of them."

Louis Menand, "The Trashing of Professionalism," *New York Times Magazine* (March 5, 1995), p. 43.

[21]Dan Friedman, *Dan Friedman: Radical Modernism* (Yale University Press, 1994), p. 114. I consider the consistently favorable reviews of *Radical Modernism* as emblematic of the myopic, New-York–biased design press, and the general dumbing-down of America.

[22]Steven Heller, "Design (Or Is It War?) Is Hell," *Émigré*, no. 33 (Winter 1995), p. 48.

[23]Dietmar R. Winkler, "Morality and Myth: The Bauhaus Reassessed," *AIGA Journal*, vol. 7, no. 4 (1990).

[24]Steven Heller, "Design (Or Is It War?) Is Hell," *Émigré*, no. 33 (Winter 1995), p. 48.

[25]Gillian Naylor, *The Bauhaus Reassessed* (E. P. Dutton, 1985), p. 180.

From *Emigre*, no. 34 (Spring 1995).

Practice: How Type Works

First Principles of Typography

By Stanley Morison

ypography may be defined as the craft of rightly disposing printing material in accordance with specific purpose; of so arranging the letters, distributing the space, and controlling the type as to aid to the maximum the reader's comprehension of the text. Typography is the efficient means to an essentially utilitarian and only accidentally aesthetic end, for enjoyment of patterns is rarely the reader's chief aim. Therefore, any disposition of printing material which, whatever the intention, has the effect of coming between author and reader is wrong. It follows that in the printing of books meant to be read there is little room for "bright" typography. Even dullness and monotony in the typesetting are far less vicious to a reader than typographical eccentricity or pleasantry. Cunning of this sort is desirable, even essential in the typography of propaganda, whether for commerce, politics, or religion, because in such printing only the freshest survives inattention. But the typography of books, apart from the category of narrowly limited editions, requires an obedience to convention which is almost absolute—and with reason.

Since printing is essentially a means of multiplying, it must not only be good in itself —but good for a common purpose. The wider that purpose, the stricter are the limitations imposed upon the printer. He may try an experiment in a tract printed in an edition of fifty copies, but he shows little common sense if he experiments to the same degree in a tract having a run of fifty thousand. Again, a novelty, fitly introduced into a sixteen-page pamphlet, will be highly undesirable in the 160-page book. It is of the essence of typography and of the nature of the printed book *qua* book, that it perform a public service.

For single or individual purpose there remains the manuscript, the codex; so there's something ridiculous in the unique copy of a printed book, though the number of copies printed may justifiably be limited when a book is the medium of typographical experiment. It is always desirable that experiments be made, and it is a pity that such laboratory pieces are so limited in number and in courage. Typography today does not so much need inspiration or revival as investigation. In this paper it is proposed to formulate some of the principles already known to book printers, which investigation confirms and which non-printers may like to consider for themselves.

The laws governing the typography of books intended for general circulation are based first upon the essential nature of alphabetical writing, and secondly upon the traditions, explicit or implicit, prevailing in the society for which the printer is working. While a universal character or typography applicable to all books produced in a given national area is practicable, to impose a universal detailed formula upon all books printed in roman types is not. National tradition expresses itself in the varying separation of the book into prelims, chapters, no less than in the design of the type. But at least there are physical rules of linear composition which are obeyed by all printers, Anglo-Saxon or European, who know their job. Let us see what these rules mean.

Now normal roman letter (in simple form without special sorts, etc.) consists of

A B C D E F G H I J K L M N O P Q R S T U V W X Y Z
A B C D E F G H I J K L M N O P Q R S T U V W X Y Z
a b c d e f g h i j k l m n o p q r s t u v w x y z
A B C D E F G H I J K L M N O P Q R S T U V W X Y Z
a b c d e f g h i j k l m n o p q r s t u v w x y z

The printer needs to be very careful in choosing his type, realizing that the more often he is going to use it, the more closely its design must approximate to the general idea held in the mind of the reader who is accustomed to the normal magazine, newspaper, and book. It does no harm to print a Christmas card in blackletter, but who nowadays would set a book in that type? I may believe, as I do, that blackletter is in design more homogenous, more picturesque, more dramatic, and more lively a type than the gray round roman we use, but I do not now expect people to read a book in it. Jenson and Caslon are both relatively feeble types, but they represent the forms accepted by the community; and the printer, as a servant of the community, must use them, or one of their variants. No printer should say, "I am an artist, therefore I am not to be dictated to. I will create my own letterforms," for, in this humble job, individualism is not very helpful. It is no longer possible, as it was in the infancy of the craft, to persuade society into the acceptance of strongly marked and highly individualistic types—because literate society is so much greater in mass and correspondingly slower in movement. The good type designer knows that, for a new font to be successful, it has to be so good that only very few recognize its novelty. If readers do not notice the consummate reticence and rare discipline of a new type it is probably a good letter. But if my friends think that the tail of my lowercase *r* or the lip of my lowercase *e* is rather jolly, you may know that the font would have been better had neither been made. A type which is to have anything like a present, let alone a future, will neither be very "different" nor very "jolly."

So much for type. The printer possesses also spaces and leads as a normal part of his typographical material, straight lines of metal known as rules, braces, and finally a more or less indiscriminate collection of ornaments—head and tailpieces, flowers, decorated initial letters, vignettes, and flourishes. Another decorative medium at his option lies in his command of color; red is, with sound instinct, the most frequently used color. For emphasis, heavy faces are used. White space is an important "item" of composing room equipment—margins, blanks, etc., being filled in with what are known as "quotations."

Composition is the intelligent selecting and arranging of these elements. Imposition is the placing of the composition upon the sheet. Printing includes impressing in due order, perfecting the register (backing up), regulating the inking, and achieving a crisp typepage. Finally the tone, weight, and texture of the paper are important factors entering into the completed result.

Typography, therefore, controls the composition, imposition, impression, and paper. Of paper, it is at least necessary to demand that it be capable of expressing the value of the composition; of imposition, that the margins be proportionate to the area of the text, affording decent space for thumbs and fingers at the side and bottom of the page. The old-style margins are handsome in themselves and agreeable to the purpose of a certain kind of book, but are obviously not convenient in books where the page dimension is unavoidably small or narrow, or the purpose of the book is to be carried in the pocket. For these and other kinds of book, the type may be centered on the measure of the page, and raised above ocular center.

Imposition is the most important element in typography—for no page, however well composed in detail, can be admired if the *mise-en-page* is careless or ill-considered. In practical printing today, these details of imposition are on the whole adequately cared for; so that it is possible to report of English books that the mass presents a tolerable appearance. Even a badly composed work may give a good appearance if it is well imposed— good imposition redeeming bad composition, while a good composition would be effectively ruined by bad imposition.

The printer, therefore, first determines his imposition and then tackles the details of composition. The first principles of composition do not require much discussion since they necessarily follow from the conventions of the alphabetical printing in the roman letter accepted by those for whom we are printing. The matter is relatively simple. First, it is certain that the eye cannot read with ease any considerable number of words composed of letters embodying sharply contrasted thicks and thins; secondly, it is nonetheless certain that the eye cannot agreeably read a mass of words composed even in a rightly constructed letter, if the line is beyond a certain length. The most expert reader's eye cannot seize more than a certain number of words in a given size except in a proportionate length of line. Thirdly, practice proves that the size of the letter must be related to the length to the line. Respect for these principles will generally protect the reader from the risk of "doubling" (reading the same line twice). The average line of words which the reader's eye can conveniently seize is between ten and twelve. Nevertheless, the typography, while exerting himself to the utmost to respect this ocular truth, is daily confronted with the fact that unavoidable conditions make it impossible for him to secure a type of the duly related size, and that he is driven to use a relatively small type. To obviate here the risk of "doubling," he consistently inserts proportionate leads through the matter, so opening the lines that the eye comfortably travels the returns from beginning to end and end to beginning. The practice of leading, denounced in certain quarters as essentially evil, is an inevitable necessity; and the skilled typographer, making the best use of his material, makes, in turn, wise use of leads. The orthodox high-brow view that leads, in every instance, produce an unhappy weak-looking effect does not survive a wide experience. On the contrary, it will be found that their absence may effectively ruin even a composition in large type, so that it is true to say that the intelligent use of leading distinguishes the expert from the inexpert printer. A slight differentiation of typeface may make the practice advisable. Clearly, while a 12-point letter, with very long ascenders and descenders, would not require leading unless set to a measure of more than three-and-three-quarter inches, there exist letters with short descenders designed to sustain leading by rule rather than by exception. Baskerville is a type to which leading is invariably an advantage. The problem of determining the amount to be given is not to be settled by considering only the ascenders or the body of the type, because breadth of letter is also a factor to be reckoned with—some letters are narrow in respect their to height, while others are wide. A composition in a round, open, wide letter, chosen because it is rather loose (that is to say, the space between letters is greater, or appears greater, by reason of the curves of the *c,o,e,g*) gains in consistency when there is a satisfactory lead between the lines. It may be argued that loose setting is not admirable in itself; to which it may be replied that the printer is generally bound to carry out the instructions of his customer; often to respect the wishes of an artist who may be illustrating the work; and, not seldom, committed by the publisher to a paper-size dictated by irrelevant considerations.

Further, it is obvious that the space between words composed in a condensed letter may be less than that between words in a round, wide form of letter. Where there is no leading between the lines, and a composition is, for extrinsic reasons, necessarily tight, it may be an advantage to set leads between the paragraphs, though this may result in pages with uneven tails. In paragraphing, it is important to realize that the opening sentence of a work should automatically manifest itself as such. This may be secured by the use of the large initial letter; the printing of the first word in capitals, or small capital; capitals *and* small capitals; or by setting the first word into the margin. On no account should the opening of a chapter be indented, since indention should mark (and always mark), the subsequent sections, i.e., the paragraphs, of the text. The abolition of paragraph-indentions is plainly an undesirable practice; nor is setting the first word in capitals or small capitals an agreeable substitute for the indention. The space of the indention should be sufficient to be noticeable.

As both measures must be related, displaying a proportion pleasing to the eye, the depth of the page follows from its width. It seems that the symmetry of the rectangle or oblong is more pleasing than that of the square; and as an oblong drives out the line to an impossible length, and a two-column arrangement is tedious, the rectangle has become the normal page.

These are the elements of typography; and a volume built up of type-pages composed in accordance with them will be generally satisfactory. There only remain the page headings and the folio. By ranging the headings inside towards the gutter, to the left and right respectively, two pages are fixed as a unity; but they can also be ranged outside to the right and left, or they may be centered. The folio may be centered at the foot, or range either way at the top or bottom, but it cannot be centered at the top without canceling the running page headline—only to be done by exception. The running headlines may be set in capitals of the text, in upper- and lowercase of the text, or in a combination of capitals. Full-sized capitals overemphasize what is, after all, a repetitive page-feature inserted chiefly for the convenience of librarians interested in the identification of leaves which have worked loose.

If set in upper- and lowercase, the headline loses in levelness, so that it seems well to employ small capitals; these are best separated by hair spaces, since the unrelieved rectangular structure and perpendicularity of capitals tend to defeat instantaneous registration. Full-sized capitals may well be used for chapter headings, with the number of the chapter in smalls; both indications being hair-spaced.

The reader, traveling from the generally invariable blank at the end of a chapter to the beginning of the next, finds a dropped chapter head an agreeably consistent feature, which saves him from feeling suffocated or overpowered by the text.

The foregoing directions, elementary to most readers, affect the main part of the book, its body. There remains a section which goes before the text, known as the "preliminaries," often highly complicated both in respect to arrangement and craftsmanship. Before considering these, it may be well to summarize our present findings—to concentrate them into a formula. According to our doctrine, a well-built book is made up from rectangular pages arranged in paragraphs having an average line of ten to twelve consistently spaced upper- and lowercase words, set in a font of comfortable size and familiar design; the lines sufficiently separated to prevent doubling and a composition being headed by a running title. This rectangle is so imposed upon the page as to provide center, head, foredge, and tail margins of dimensions suitably proportioned to the length of line and to the disposition of space at those points where the text is cut into chapters, and where the body joins the prefatory and other pages known as "preliminaries."

Now these first pages, being intended rather for reference than for reading and re-reading, are less strictly governed by convention than the text pages. They consequently offer the maximum opportunity for typographic design. The history of printing is in large measure the history of the title page. When fully developed, the title occupied a recto page, either partially or wholly; and the title-phrase, or a catchword of it, has generally been set in a conspicuous size of type. Sixteenth-century Italian printers generally use large capitals copied from inscriptions, or by exception, from caroline manuscripts; while English use emulated the French in employing a canon line of upper- and lowercase, followed by a few lines of pica capitals. Next came the printer's device, and at the foot of the page, his name and address. These large sizes of upper- and lowercase, being an inheritance from printers who were accustomed to blackletter (which cannot be set in solid capitals), have gone. The device has also vanished (except in the books of the University Presses), and thus the contemporary title page is a bleak affair, exhibiting in nine out of ten cases a space between the title and the imprint of the printer-publisher, so that this blank tends to be the strongest feature on the page. When the device was first abandoned, the author, printer, or publisher, took advantage of the leisure of the reader and the blank at their disposal, to draft a tediously long title, subtitle, and list of the author's qualifications, designed to fill the entire page. The present-day publisher goes to the other extreme, reducing the title to as few short words as possible, followed with "by" and the author's name. A professional writer may insert, e.g., "Author of *The Deluge*" under his name, or there may be incorporated a motto; but apart from such exceptions, three and sometimes four inches of space separate the author's name from the first line of the imprint. The result is that unless the title is set in a size of type out of all relation to that of the remainder of the book, this space is more conspicuous than the chief line. Yet, it is clear that a volume in 12-point does not require a 30-point title unless it be a folio in double-column. There is no reason, other than a desire to be "different," for a title page to bear any line of type larger than twice the size of the text letter. If the book be set in 12-point, the title need be no larger than 24-point—and may decently enough be smaller. As lowercase is a necessary evil, which we should do well to subordinate since we cannot suppress, it should be avoided when it is at its least attractive—in large sizes. The main line of a title should be set in capitals and, like all capitals, should be spaced. Whatever may happen to the rest of the composition, the author's name, like all displayed proper names, should be in capitals.

Here we may pause as to counter an objection. It will be contended that whatever the value of our preceding conclusions, their adoption must mean increased standardization— all very well for those who have an economic objective but very monotonous and dull for those whose aim is that books shall possess more "life." This means that the objectors want more variety, more "differentness," more decoration. The craving to decorate is natural, and only if it is allowed the freedom of the text pages shall we look upon it as a passion to be resisted. The decoration of title pages is one thing,—that of a font to be employed in books is another. Our contention, in this respect, is that the necessities of a mass-production book and the limited edition differ neither in kind nor in degree, since all printing is essentially a means of the multiplication of the text set in an alphabetical code of conventional symbols. To disallow "variety" in the vital details of the composition is not to insist upon uniformity in display. As already pointed out the preliminary pages offer scope for the utmost typographical ingenuity. Yet even here, a word of caution may be in place, so soon do we forget, in arranging any piece of display (above all, a title page), the supreme importance of sense. Every character, every word, every line should register with maximum clearness. Words should not be broken except unavoidably, and in title pages and other compositions of centered matter, lines should never begin with such feeble parts of speech as prepositions and conjunctions. It is more reasonable, as assisting the reader's immediacy of comprehension, to keep these to the ends of lines or to center them in smaller type and so bring out the salient lines in a relatively conspicuous size.

No printer, in safeguarding himself from the charge of monotony in his composition, should admit, against his better judgment, any typographical distraction doing violence to logic and lucidity in the supposed interests of decoration. To twist his text into a triangle, squeeze it into a box, torture it into the shape of an hour-glass or diamond is an offense requiring greater justification than either the existence of Italian and French precedents of the fifteenth and sixteenth centuries, or of an ambition to do something new in the twentieth. In truth, these are the easiest tricks of all, and we have seen so much of them during the late "revival of printing" that we now need rather a revival of restraint. In all permanent forms of typography, whether publicly or privately printed, the typographer's only purpose is to express, not himself, but his author. There are, admittedly, other purposes which enter into the composition of advertisement, publicity, and sales matter; and there is, of course, a very great deal common to both book and advertisement composition. But it is not allowable to the printer to relax his zeal for the reader's comfort in order to satisfy an ambition to decorate or to illustrate. Rather than run this risk the printer should strive to express himself by the use of this or that small decorative unit, either of common design supplied by the typefounders or drawn for his office by an artist. It is quite true that to an inventive printer decoration is not often necessary. In commercial printing, however, it seems to be a necessity, because the complexity of our civilization demands an infinite number of styles and characters. Publishers and other buyers of printing, by insisting upon a setting which shall express *their* business, *their* goods *their* books, and nobody else's goods or business or books, demand an individuality which pure typography can never hope to supply. But book printers, concerned with the permanently convenient rather than with the sensational or the fashionable in printing, should be on their guard against title page borders, vignettes, and devices invented to ease their difficulties. There is no easy way with most title pages; and printer's task is rendered more difficult by the average publisher's and author's incompetence to draft a title or to organize the preliminaries in reasonable sequence.

Those who would like to lessen or vary the tendency toward standardization in day-to-day book production have a field for their activity in the last-mentioned pages. Their position on their respective pages and their relation to each other are not essentially invariable. Nevertheless, as it is well for printers and publishers to have rules, and the same rules, it may be suggested that the headings to preface, table of contents, introduction, etc., should be in the size and font of the chapter heads; and should be dropped if they are dropped. The order of the preliminaries remains to be settled. With one exception, all should begin on a recto page. The logical order of the preliminary pages is half-title or dedication (I see no reason for including both), title, contents, practice, introduction. The certification of "limitation," in the case of books of that class, may face the title where there is no frontispiece, be incorporated with the half-title, or be taken to the end of the volume. Copyright notices can be printed on the verso of the title page. This order is applicable to most categories of books. Novels need neither table of contents nor list of chapters, the one or the other is generally printed. If it is decided to retain either, it would be reasonable to print it on the back of the half-title and facing the title page, so that the structure, scope, and nature of the book will be almost completely indicated to the reader at a single opening. Where the volume is made up of a few short stories, their titles can be listed in the otherwise blank center of the title page.

Besides fiction, belles-lettres and educational books are habitually published in portable, if not in pocketable formats, crown octavo ($7\frac{1}{2}'' \times 5''$) being the invariable rule for English novels published as such. The novel in the form of biography will be published as a biography, demi octavo ($6'' \times 8\frac{1}{2}''$), the size also for history, political study, archeology, science, arts and almost everything but fiction. Novels are only promoted to this format when they have become famous and "standard." *Size,* therefore, is the most manifest difference between the categories of books.

Another obvious difference is *bulk,* calculated in accordance with the publisher's notion, first, of the general sense of trade expectation and, secondly, of the purchasing psychology of a public habituated to certain selling prices vaguely related to number of pages and thickness of volume (inconsistently enough, weight does not enter into these expectations). These habits of mind have consequences in the typography; they affect the choice of font and size of type, and may necessitate the adoption of devices for "driving out," i.e., making the setting take up as much room as possible. By putting the running headline between rules or rows of ornaments; introducing unnecessary blanks between chapters; contracting the measure; exaggerating the spaces between words and the lines; excessively indenting paragraphs; isolating quoted matter with picas of white space; inserting wholly unnecessary sectional titles in the text and surrounding them with space; contriving to drive a chapter ending to the top of a recto page so that the rest of it and its verso may be blank; using thick paper; increasing the depth of chapter beginnings and inserting very large versals thereto—and so on, the volume can be inflated to an extra sixteen pages and sometimes more—which is a feat the able typographer is expected to accomplish without showing his hand.

Limited editions of standard authors, or of authors whose publishers desire them to rank as such, are commonly given a rubricated title. A dreadful example of overdone rubrication is to be found in a recent edition of Thomas Hardy's verse, in which the running heads throughout the book are in red—the production of a firm which desired to make an impression on the purchaser in view of the price asked for the edition. This could be better done by reserving color for the initial letters. Handmade paper is generally used for *éditions de luxe,* and none but the brave will disregard the superstitious love of the book-buying classes for its untrimmed, ugly, and dirt-gathering edges—for consumer-demand is finally responsible for the issue of books which are not books printed by presses which are not presses.

It is hoped that our setting out of the first principles of typography, as above, may give the amateur some sort of "yardstick" which he can apply, not only to the entries comprised under the booksellers description "press-books," but to the, as a rule, more interesting output of the industrial printing-houses responsible for the printing of books which need printing.

From the *Fleuron: A Journal of Typography* (Cambridge: Cambridge University Press, 1930).

Is the Abolishment of Justification Desirable?
Comment on "A Proposed Reformation in Manual
Type-Composing, Demonstrated."

By Anonymous

owever advantageous it may be from an economic standpoint to dispense with justifying the lines in a page or column of types, so as to square up the printed surface and give it the geometrical proportions to lock up tightly in the forms, there are certain other considerations to be dealt with in an innovation looking to that end. In the last number of *Paper and Press* appeared an article (with caption quoted in the foregoing subtitle), extracted from the editorial columns of the *Home Journal,* New York, a brief summary of which is not out of place in this connection. Taking as its text the interesting abolition of justification, which the publishers of *Liberty,* and also those of the *Lark,* San Francisco, have adopted, the benefits of the new method are thus set forth: "that there is a gain esthetically in the increased beauty of the page, due to the abolition of unequal spacing, the relief that the eye finds in lines of unequal length, and the greater ease with which it passes from one line to another; and that there is a vast gain economically in the saving of time and labor effected, both in the setting and the distribution of the type; in the consequent cheapening of newspapers, periodicals, and books; in the competition which it offers to the type-setting machines, forcing their proprietors to rent them on more reasonable terms; in opening avenues of employment for printers whom the machines displace; and in the liberation of skilled labor for employment in higher capacities by so simplifying the work of ordinary typesetting that unskilled or less skilled labor can easily perform it."

Dividing the subject into its legitimate phases, and disregarding, for the present, the industrial and economic phase, let us seek to ascertain its artistic advantage, which is not the least of those attributes. The newspaper-publisher lays little or no stress upon the chiseled nicety of his letterpress, and the esthetic factor has, in consequence, no claim upon his favor; but the book-publisher, who is primarily to be catered to in typographic reforms purporting to be esthetic, is differently situated, has quite another constituency to please, and, in the degree of his rank as an art-publisher, must be careful that he does nothing to jeopardize the beauty of his productions by reforms hastily inaugurated. It is hence necessary to inquire in what the real beauty of a printed page resides. Esthetically, and entirely disregarding other considerations, the page should be a unit; it is indifferent how many factors may combine to produce the ultimate appeal, as long as that appeal is congruous, unified, and perfectly balanced. The nature of the elements which combine to produce this effect are, of course, pre-eminent. No one of them must intrude by its separateness from the others, and at no one point must the impression made on the eye by proportions, whether of letters, margins, white and black of types and surface, detract from the appearance of simplicity. In reality, simplicity is the very last thing which enters into the make-up of an artistic page; the aim is to get the effect of simplicity, and when that is achieved at no sacrifice of perfect unity, the book-page is styled "a work of art." In order to test the practicability of the theory of "no justification," I have had this article set throughout on the principle advocated, and have introduced the illustrations as better displaying the needs of modern periodicals and books. It is quite certain that no artistic gain has resulted from the absence of justification, if any standards exist by which artistic gain can be adjudged. The effect is exactly what the editors of our esteemed contemporary used as arguments against justifying the lines, viz: the unequal spacing with which the eye was offended; the only difference here is that this inequality is all removed to the end of the lines, and that, instead of meeting the effects of bad spacing in the units of the line, the eye meets them in the units of the page—which is just as bad, at least from the esthetic standpoint. To say that there is an increased beauty imparted to the page by abolishing unequal spacing where it affects the words in a line, yet retaining it at the end of the lines in the page, is to detract from the congruity of the page itself, especially when more than one column is used—the case with most periodicals. It is a sop thrown to the slovenly compositor, which the skilled workman neither needs nor wants. There should be no gaps between words in a justified page of types, and there should be no gaps between columns in a page where two or more columns are run. The eye travels across the line, brings up at the termination thereof in a purely automatic manner when there are no gaps in the spacing, and passes on to the following line with little or no difficulty. To infer that the eye finds relief in lines of unequal length, and thereby passes with more ease to the succeeding line, is a matter of opinion in which we differ with the valued source mentioned. In a book page the same thing can be said. The pleasure afforded one in looking at a page with its straight, vertical lines, conforming with the lining of the letters themselves, resides in the very thing which the abolition of justification likewise abolishes, i.e., its regularity of body. For this reason it is not permissible in good offices, as the author of the article himself affirms, to terminate two successive lines with a hyphen, because the eye will be offended by the gaps created in the right descending line of the page. Just "as the artistic printer avoids division as far as possible," so will he avoid translating his overplus of space to a location where it will intrude itself constantly upon the reader's vision. It seems better, as long as spacing is requisite in order to make a page square up solidly for the chase, to divide the spaces and hide them, if at all possible, in the line itself, rather than to accentuate them in the page. The page of blank verse, or that of rapidly moving dialogue, is not the most eloquent example of esthetic typography; while to point to "an attractive Gothic appearance," as acquired by the uneven edge, is to forget the beautiful effects gotten by those masters of Italo-Gothic, Ratdolt, and Pictor, with others, who designed square borders within which to place their titles and to begin their books. It is to pass by that which helps to make the books of William Morris so precious to the book-lover, and the choice decorated book-pages of Walter Crane of so much artistic value. Take the books of the Quattrocento, that era of Italian excellence, and note how the border environs the illustration in almost every instance; then make the comparison with the vignetted illustration of some modern books, and perceive how weak and lacking in organic beauty the one is, and how strong and vigorous the other is in its impression of growth. It is for similar reasons that we advocate the geometrical page, meaning thereby the page whose superficies is a quadrangle. It is in better taste whenever initial letters are used, better whenever illustrations are overrun in the text, and better in itself from an artistic standpoint. Such, at least, represents our own opinion. The custom dates from illuminated manuscripts, is a relic of a period when art was sought for itself alone, and economic considerations seem to be the sole reasons for abrogating its claims to still exist. The problem is to be solved, but it will be solved in other ways; so indications now seem to warrant us in asserting.

The immediate economies of dispensing with justification are apparent; but we are seriously skeptical of the gain which is assumed to accrue to the printers thereby. What advantages there might be would fall into the consumer's lap. It is said there would be a "daily addition to the world's productive power of the labor of 200,000 people"—possibly not an exaggerated estimate of what the innovation would accomplish; but is it not also true that the argument is more theoretical than practical, granting the importance of machine composition? Even though the machine is omitted from the calculation, are not the benefits rather visionary to the present compositors, who have grown up in the business, and who, by doing away with the very thing it has taken them years to learn, are thus thrown out of employment? We fancy the present generation of compositors would make rather poor producers if compelled to engage in other fields, unless they were young men with life all before them. Machine composition, however, must be considered. Nor would the abolition of justification enable the compositor to compete any better with these displacers of hand labor. It would place him even in a worse position than before, for when the machines do not have to justify, their construction will be simplified, their cost reduced, their output increased, and the gain to the compositor vanish into thin air. Will the employing printer or publisher be benefited by the change? At the outset yes; ultimately, no! Admitting that the new system will increase the capacity of a good compositor, on careful work, from five-thousand ems to seven-thousand ems per day, the gain to the employer will be the price of two-thousand ems; but soon his competitors inaugurate the method, machine competition takes it up, the voracity of competition adapts itself to the new conditions, and prices go down in exact proportion to the increased output.

In citing the advantages of an innovation, which seems to be successful because not without a precedent, there is no little danger of magnifying them at the expense of other and less apparent factors. Such seems to have been the pitfall into which the capable editor of the *Home Journal* has fallen. To the present writer, the question of justification or no justification appears to present mighty advantages, but they are all on the economic side, and entirely benefit the consumer. It also appears to be true that the employer will gain nothing by the change, while the employed will lose what the public get. If "the introduction of machines into newspaper offices is throwing hundreds of printers out of employment, and the discharged men are flocking to the book-offices in search of work," will that work be found there for them if the new method is adopted? Scarcely; for the machines will enter at once when this problem is settled. The displacement would be even greater.

It must not be inferred from the foregoing that we are taking issue with any proposal to deal intelligently with the vexed question of justification. We, too, believe that there is far greater waste of time and labor in the adjustment of spaces in a line of types than is necessary. The way of rectifying it, however, will abide with the machine, and it is the function of the machine of the future to so equalize the spacing that no difference will exist in that between any two words in a given line of types. Until then, it is almost certain that the art of the book compositor will continue to exist under conditions which require the exercise of intelligence and skill, rather than under conditions where manual labor is purely mechanical.

The problem of self-justification, so far as the types themselves are concerned, has not been left without attempts at solution. In his humorous little pamphlet, a copy of which was no doubt sent to the majority of employing printers in this country when it was issued from the press, Herbert L. Baker alludes to the adoption of an even part of a pica as a unit, and casting every character in the font to some multiple thereof. Thus, the *i, j, l* points, and all other thin characters, stand for two units; the *e, r, s, t* figures, and kindred medium letters, represent three units; the *a, d, n, u, y,* and those of similar size, are considered as made up of four units; while the *w, œ,* etc., denote five units; and the *m, W, M,* and largest characters, represent six units. "Since," says he, "the unit is an even part of pica, it stands to reason that any regular pica measure would contain an even number of units. If the unit were one-twelfth pica, a measure of two picas would contain twenty-four units—no matter whether caps, lowercase, or figures were used, when each letter represents a certain numbers of these units. According to the above plan, the word 'was' would fill exactly twelve units, or one pica—*w*(5)*a*(4)*s*(3)—without any spacing whatever. Now we will stretch this measure to say thirteen ems pica, and isn't it plain that even units would exactly fill the line without any odd-size spaces?" Mr. Baker points out that only two spaces are needed in such a system, one unit (or thin space) and two unit (thick space), with three unit for an en-quad, and four unit for an em-quad, etc. The line is thus spaced tight or loose, the purely empirical factor being eliminated. This system, in a word, is that of Mr. Benton, whose self-spacing type is too well known to require further explanation.

Artistically, the book-page is an entity, to the beautifying of which much thought is now being given; in its symmetrical proportions resides its greatest charm. This we conceive to be the principal reason for retaining justification; for, as the eye would be repelled by gazing at the jagged outlines of a building which did not stand forth with unbroken walls, so it would be offended by the incongruity and non-solidity of a page with ragged edges standing out against the white.

From *Paper and Press* 21, no. 5 (1895).

Typographic Heresies: Some Notes on Experimenting With Type

By Eugene M. Ettenberg

n its modern sense, typographic experimentation started with the "Dada" and "Surrealist" movements. The Dada painter-designers employed type in posters, manifestos, and in publications with the same vicious, mock-humorous touch that characterized their pictures, sculpture, poetry, and music. Their very type selection and the way letters were scattered on the page, intermingled with ink blots and other such devices, was a protest against the mediocre, static, devitalized typography of the 1916 to 1922 period.

The Surrealists, such as Max Ernst, Hans Arp, and Man Ray, fed more fuel to the fire started by Dadaists by picturing incongruities, dreamlike fantasies, and by using such devices as distorted perspective, the double image, or collages, to give composite images. Snips of newspapers, railway tickets, photographs, and trash from the streets went into the composition of these collages. In addition, Kurt Schwitters and Raoul Hausmann, to name but two, made frequent use of typographic fragments.

The teachings of the Bauhaus from 1919 to 1928, particularly those of Moholy-Nagy, Herbert Bayer, and Josef Albers, carried typographic experimentation still further. Moholy-Nagy insisted that "a new typographic language must be created, combining elasticity, variety, and a fresh approach to the materials of printing, a language whose logic depends on the appropriate application of the process of printing." The school had much to do with furthering the then new sans serif types such as Futura and with the insistence on sharp contrast between bold and extra bold faces types combined with text—to replace the over-all polite gray pages of the Twenties. Jan Tschichold's *Die Neue Typographie,* published in 1928, advanced type thinking right up to the present time, with his advocacy of asymmetric design, radical use of white space, bold silhouetting of photographs and substitution of color bands and rules for useless ornament.

As we examine the work of these schools today, some look dated and weary. They were experiments that served their purpose—as stepping stones; pyrotechnics that lit the sky for one brief moment and then burned out. Others look wild and untamed—unharnessed thoughts that left nothing but froth with even their most sympathetic viewers. Finally, there are some that indicate a new direction—not always clearly—but signpost they are to tomorrow's typography.

From *American Artist* (February 1954).

Typographical Topography

By Stefan Themerson

What's the matter with you? What's happened?" Brutus asked.

"Nothing," I said.

"How do you mean: nothing! You open the book, you glance at the page, then you slam the poor thing as if it were a door to I don't know what, and you call it 'nothing.' Without having read a word. . . ."

"You are wrong. I have read a whole sentence. I can quote it: 'Today we are in the throes of another technical revolution in printing.'"

"Well?" he asked. "There's nothing wrong in it, or is there?"

"No, there isn't."

"Why be so angry then?"

"Because it is prose."

"And you expected it to be what? Poetry?"

"Yes."

"Why?"

"Because of its layout. A silly new fashion: unjustified setting. I wonder who could justify it."

"Surely, this isn't of such great importance. . . ." he began.

"It isn't," I agreed. "All the same, I'm used to it that, when I open a book, I can tell at once, without reading a word—"O, this is a novel; and that one is a play. Here is pure mathematics and there is a musical score. This is a dictionary, that is a telephone book, and that other one is a volume of poetry." Now, because of that unjustified setting all that is no more possible, something essential has been destroyed. Now, when I looked a moment ago at a page of that book, I knew it was not a collection of sonnets, nor was it a Swinburne or Mayakowsky. But it could have been a T.S. Eliot, or C. Day Lewis. Typographically speaking. The only thing I didn't expect was that it would be prose."

"Well, suppose Monsieur Jourdain had told you it was prose?"

"Very, very clever!" I said. "But I still wouldn't be able to see what sort of prose. A page of a book is like a human face. Look at a page by Hemingway and compare it with Sterne and Marcel Proust. They are different typographical beings. But force upon them those ragged edges, and the influence of the author's style on the physical aspect of the page, their typographical physiognomy will disappear. No, unjustified setting is a sort of '*gleichschaltung* through diversity,' a very phoney diversity. Produced methodically by chance. For the comfort of the keyboard, and not for the comfort of the eye. The eye tolerates quite well thin spaces, and middle spaces, and thick spaces. There is absolutely no reason why we should be more puritan than our eye is and affect extreme strictness by using middle spaces only. On the contrary, by using them all, but intelligently (plus an occasional hair or a nut), one should be able to justify any line to a fixed length so that the reading eye will proceed quietly to the right, even if it meets on its way an odd nut or a mutton. It is the end of the line that halts it and sends it back to the left. With justified setting this scanning business is painless, and the eye doesn't take more notice of it than the foot does when you stroll along a promenade thinking of things that have nothing to do with walking. But when you force upon the eye that haphazard rhythm created by those paths of uneven length the process of reading becomes something self-conscious, like walking on a sort of crazy pavement where your foot doesn't know how long the next step will have to be. Poets are well aware of it all. That's why the break-line is one of the main weapons in their arsenal. They know that at the end of a line, the eye halts, the lungs fill with air, mind is in suspense, the ear muffles the echo of the sound of the last syllable and prepares to receive the new string of rhythmical noises, the heart . . ."

"Good gracious," Brutus interrupted me, and I stopped.

"Well, all right," I said after a while, melancholically. "Anyway, you will agree that something extreme does happen at the end of a line. If I had to, I would rather leave the left-hand edge unjustified."

"Ha,ha," said Brutus.

"What are you laughing at?" I asked.

"Nothing,", he said. And continued to giggle.

"Come out with it," I said sternly.

184

"It's nothing," he repeated. "It's only that when you were talking about justifying setting to the left-hand edge of the type area or to the right-hand edge, a thought came to me—Why not justify at the centre?"

"Brutus," I exclaimed. "You have made a great discovery! You have just discovered something I did twenty years ago."

"I'm very proud of it," he said.

"So you should be," I said.

"Well, what did you do twenty years ago?" he asked. "Concrete poetry? Or was it dada?"

"Brutus," I reproached him, "don't be sarcastic. It had absolutely nothing to do with either dada or concrete poems. It was semantic poetry."

"O, was it?" he sort of gasped.

"Yes, it was," I said quietly.

"Well, what has it to do with the problem of unjustified setting?"

"Plenty," I said. "Twenty years ago I met a man who had three legs and wanted me to translate some poems not from one tongue into another but from a language composed of words so poetic that they had lost all their impact, into something that would give them a new meaning and flavor. I decided to do it by replacing some of the key-words of those poems by their definitions. For instance: instead of the word war, I put: 'The open conflict between nations, or active international hostility carried on by force of arms.' Instead of the word snow, I wrote: 'multishaped crystals, belonging to hexagonal system, formed by slow freezing of water-vapour.' This, of course, created a typographical problem. How to print five, ten, fifteen words in place of one, and so that they would hold together as one entity. Well, I said to myself, you may read a musical score horizontally, following the melodic line, and you may read it vertically, following the structure and arrangement. Why shouldn't it be the same with poetry? Typographical topography of a printed page is two-dimensional, is it not? If I have a number of words that form one entity, I told myself, why shouldn't I write them as I would write the notes of a chord: one under another, instead of one after another? Internal vertical justification is the answer to my problem. I.V.J."

"Well," Brutus said, "that was a very particular and specific case. You couldn't apply your I.V.J. method to other cases."

"Why not?" I asked.

"I don't know, but. . . ."

"But! But!" I exclaimed. "You could certainly apply it to Churchill's speeches, and it would make many scientific books read more clearly. It would . . . well, do you see that little booklet in white covers? It contains no verses. It contains prose. It is a paper read to members of the Double Crown Club by Herbert Spencer. I propose to apply my I.V.J. treatment to it."

"Good," Brutus said. "But before you start, may I go for a walk?"

"Alone?"

"Yes."

"All right. But do remember: don't go off the pavement; don't stand too long under the lamp-post, and, for heaven's sake, don't talk to people. They may have a heart attack if they see a talking dog."

I opened the door for him then came back to my typewriter and started to type, according to my I.V.J. rules, as follows:

```
It is a well-worn platitude that the purpose of the printed word is to be read.
                      This is a gross understatement.
The purpose of all printing, whether of words
                             or of pictures,
     is to communicate - ideas,
                          information,
                          instructions
                     or emotions.
The printed message should be not merely read
                             but understood;
     its purpose is to spark off ideas
                          or activities.


Society will, in
             the
             long
             run,
        use printing only for those tasks
                        which printing can fulfil more effectively,
                                                      reliably
                                             & economically
                               than other competing mediums
                                                           of
                                                           communi-
                                                           cation.
```

The present decade is a fascinating
                    & exciting period in printing
                            & publishing.

A wide range of technical developments
    is waiting to be exploited by imaginative printers,
                            designers
                            & authors
                    & bold publishers willing to adopt
                                    energetic
                                    (and not necessarily conventional)
                                    methods of selling
                                            & distributing their
                                                    products.

In a century so packed with important developments in science
                                    & technology
                                    & man's political ideas
                                        & social outlook,
    the book as a tool of civilization has an invaluable function to perform.

If all the achievements of scientists,
                        scholars
                        & technologists in this century
            are not suddenly to collapse like a house of cards,
specialists in one field must
                    somehow
                    keep in touch with the thoughts
                                & aims
                                & achievements of other men
                                            working in others.

Television,
    films,
    radio all have an important part to play in answering this challenge.

But
186   the book still has unique advantages: it is passive;
                                                 it is permanent;
                                                 it is portable.

            In the end,
    the word was rescued from all this gimcrackery
            by painters,
            writers,
            architects
            & others   who came to printing from outside the industry
                    & who,
                        during the first half of this century,
                    gradually eliminated vulgar affectation
                        & restored to printing both logic
                                            & discipline.

Today we are in the throes of another
                        technical
                        revolution in printing.   Metal
                                                    is
                                                gradually
                                            being eliminated
                                                from
                                            composition.

                                        Released
                                        from
                                        its
                                        discipline,
    the designer is free to place his lines of type at a$_n$gles,
        & he can c$_u$r$_v$e,
                cut. $_p$l^a^{y} l i n e s
                or split dis
                    & juxtapose one line of type closely
                                            against
                                            another,

        or he can,   u
        if he wishes, superimpose one w$_o$rd
                                        another.

This freedom from mechanical restriction
        provides the designer
with wonderful opportunities for producing imaginative
                                    & sympathetic
                                      visual
                                      solutions
                        & of conveying the author's message
                                with
                                great
                                precision.

    But equally the designer can, if
                                he
                                chooses,
                        use this new opportunity
                        - as the late nineteenth-century compositors used theirs -
                        not for better communication
                        but
                    merely for superficial pattern making.

The future   will depend ultimately upon how responsibly designers face up to their task.
   of
the printing
    industry

While printing serves society as an efficient means of communication
        it will survive.
    If it ceases to fulfil this function more effectively
                                    than other mediums of communication
        then it will wither.

Because it had no adequate alternative
                        means
                        of
                        communication,
        late-nineteenth century was
                        I think
                        more tolerant of its printers frivolity   187
                        than
        late-twentieth century society
                        is
                        likely
                        to be.

But far too many art
                &
                design schools
    have been content simply to turn out skilful
                                performers in an accepted idiom
                        rather than men able to think
                                    out solutions in a logical
                                            & creative way.

Unfortunately, there are
                I believe
                close
                & uncomfortable parallels between late nineteenth-century typography
                                                &
                                                the situation in graphic design today.

                        Until the middle of the nineteenth century
typographical experiments were largely confined to variations of the type design,
                        but the invention of the platen machine
                        led,
                        about 1870,
                        to a new kind of printing known as 'Artistic
                                                            Printing'.

This style made considerable use of coloured inks
                        & of elaborate ornament
                                & decoration
                        (often quite unrelated to the subject matter of the
                                                                    text),
        and
    incidentally
            brought about the first real departure from the centred of the book printer.
                                                            layout

Artistic
Printing,   at its best, encouraged high standards of craftsmanship
                              & considerable technical ingenuity.

        But,
        especially in the diluted form of its commercial application,

        it was skill misapplied so far as the true purpose of printing is concerned.

        It was not long before most printers had utterly lost all notion of true
                                                           printing
                                                           tradition.

        They had squandered their creative inheritance
            & were either imprisoned in a web of sterile convention
                        or involved in an orgy of technical gimmicry
                        without any discernible regard for the printed word
                                                    as a means of
                                                    communication.

        Not surprisingly
        quite soon
        they lost the respect of both the public in general
                                    & their customers in particular.

        Aesthetically bankrupt
                & confused,
        the printing industry was quite incapable of picking up,
                                    or even of recognising,
                                        the frayed ends
                                        of its severed traditions.

        It was ready to relinquish
                    (though not without resentment)
                    control of design to 'amateurs'
                                such as William Morris
                                    & those who followed in his wake.

The flippant
  & irresponsible use of important technical
                              inventions
                    debased late nineteenth-century printing.

The printing industry lost sight of its true function
                    & allowed its compositors to manipulate words
                                for their own
                                    & their colleagues' amusement
                    without regard to the value of the results as communication.

        They will concentrate on standards of press work
                                    & reproduction
                                    & service
but they will not be in any way responsible for the layout
                                        or initial preparation of what they print.

But the effect of this movement away from the traditional pattern of the industry
            will be,
            I think,
            to confirm the position
                    & the structure of the relatively small number of firms,
                                                    of medium size,
                                                    who
                                                    successfully
                                                    provide
                                            an integrated design
                                            & printing service.
In short I think the future
                    pattern is likely to be this:

Most printing design will be planned by professional designers in private practice.

Most printers will print
                    but
                not design
                or
                    take any part in the initial preparation of what they print.

But a limited
        number of firms
                in which design
                        & production have been properly co-ordinated
        will continue to offer clients a 'package
                                          deal'.

These
firms will inevitably specialise,
                        in the type of work they produce,
                        to a far greater extent
                                than is usual at present.

In those printing firms in the future the designer will play a vital role in the shaping
In which offer such a service   of policy

It is therefore, I suggest, quite clear that in future,
whether he acts in private practice
                or
                        as a principal of a printing office,
        the designer is going to be faced not only with opportunities
                                but also with considerable responsibilities.

But is the design   in fact equipped to meet these responsibilities ?
            profession

And,
especially,
        is design   in this country geared to the probable future demands of society
            education   & industry ?

Increasingly
during the past twenty years,
        graphic
        & industrial design   189
        & typography have passed into hands that have been
                                formally trained to serve the requirements
                                                of the profession
                                        & to produce work of a high standard
                                                of technical
                                                competence.

I have said that the purpose of all printing is to communicate.

Printing does this most effectively when it is consciously planned
                                                & arranged
                                by
                                someone
                                qualified by his training
                                                & experience
                                to attempt
                                        to equate the demands of author,
                                                        reader
                                                        & producer.

This, today, is the function of the professional
                                    designer.

        The properly trained professional has a clear understanding
                                designer   of the techniques
                                                        of modern printing.

His task is to lay out
                & arrange a piece
                        of
                        printing so
                                that it will serve its purpose effectively
                                        & with reasonable economy.

His specifications
        & instructions must be clear
                        & precise. And it is his responsibility
                                        to ensure
                                        that he retains adequate control over his work
                                                during the course of production.

It is sometimes suggested that the designer
                         should not
                         concern himself with the process
                                              of
                                              production.
                    This
                    I believe
                    is
                    rank nonsense.

Are building   and construction   no concern of architects ?
    materials   techniques

                                                                        p
                                                                        a
The competent graphic   today is not just a man who decorates the surface of a sheet of p.
              designer   e
                                                                        r
The paper,
the printing technique,
the method of binding   -   these are all things that vitally affect the function,
                                                        the appearance
                                                        & the cost of any piece
                                                                        of
                                                                        print
                    & as such
                        they are all part of the designer's responsibility.

The growth of offset litho
             & gravure,
         of photocomposition
             & other ways of producing text matter in an acceptable form for photographing
                                                        on to the plates,
         will, I believe,
         lead   during the next twenty years
         to great changes in the organisation of the printing industry in this country.

190
         For reasons both of economy
                          & expediency,
         the great majority of printing firms
             will gradually relinquish all control over the preparation of the printing forme
                                                        or artwork.

There is, of course, no such thing as 'undesigned'
                                       printing.

No matter how brief the message
         (or how bad the end result)
all printing is designed by somebody - the client,
                                       the printer's representative,
                                       the order clerk,
                                       the works manager,
                                       the composing room overseer,
                                       the keyboard operator,
                                       the compositor at the case.

Indeed, quite often they all take a hand in shaping the final result.

Somebody has to decide the format,
                        the width of margins,
                        what typeface to set the words in,
                        the size
                            &
                        position of illustrations,
                        the colour of ink
                            & kind of paper,
                        the method of binding.

   Consciously considerations of taste,
 or
 unconsciously   fashion,
                                     tradition,
                                     convention,
                                     convenience,
                                     efficiency
                             & expediency   determine the final result.

When printing was a far less complex activity than it is today,
        printing offices were small
                            & compact
    & all these decisions were made by the master who personally discussed each job
                                             printer   with his customer
                                                    & personally instructed
                                                            the members of his 'team'
                                                            (and often
                                                            carried out
                                                            part of the work himself)

The master   standards were higher
    craftsman's &,
                    generally,
            his personal
                    skills were greater than those of his employees.

Today most high-quality is produced in relatively large printing
           printing   offices.

At his most effective,

today's master is a business man
        printer   with a shrewd understanding of economic trends,
                        able to weather takeover bids
                                    & all the demands
                                        & machinations of twentieth-century
                                                          commerce
                        & to negotiate with staff
                                    & trade unions.

        He creates opportunities for good work
                                    & printed results
                            in which he
                                    & his staff can take pride.

                                                                        191

The owner of a book can take what it has to offer
                        wherever
                    & whenever he wishes –
                            & at his own pace.

He can consult several books on the same subject
                        at the same time, and so try to arrive at a balanced
                                                                    personal
                                                                    judgment.

No other method of communication offers all these advantages.

And what is true of the book
            is equally true of many other kinds of printing.

But while it is true that
                for many purposes
                the printed word has advantages over other existing techniques
                                                                        of
                                                                        communication,
            it does not automatically follow that the printing industry,
                                            as it is at present organised,
                                            can rely upon a rosy
                                                    & assured future.

Many important developments in the past 10   'office
                            or 20 years have been in the field of   printing'.

    Like the scribes of the xvth century,

many of today's professional take a rather lofty view of such developments.
                printers

But some of the techniques of office   offer considerable advantages of speed,
                            printing   convenience,
                                                                        & cost
                                                    over conventional
                                                    printing
                                                    methods.

The end product may not be of the same quality as 'proper printing',

   but then conventional printing is itself a poor substitute for calligraphy.

And just as conventional printing gradually evolved its own aesthetic standards

   so too will the newer techniques
                  of
                  reproduction.

There are therefore today several alternatives to conventional printing as a means
                                                        of
                                                        communication.

Printing, if it is to be effective
            & is to compete with other media,
has to be good.

And good
   in this sense
   means not just technically well-printed
                  but well-designed.

And well-designed means properly planned to do its job -
                  clearly laid out, certainly,
                              but also
                  printed on the materials
                     & by the process
                     & to the standard appropriate to its particular purpose
                                                              & function.

Extravagantly produced ephemera may,
                        technically,
                        be good printing
               but it is not good design.

From *Penrose* (1965).

On the Choice of Typeface

By Beatrice Warde

he legibility of a typeface has an exact parallel in the audibility of a human voice. A lecturer must make every word audible and distinct; yet within the limits of audibility lie the whole range of speaking tones from a metallic monotonous drawl to the infinitely flexible and persuasive tones of the good speaker.

Type, the voice of the printed page, can be legible and dull, or legible and fascinating, according to its design and treatment. In other words, what the book-lover calls readability is not a synonym for what the optician calls legibility.

In choosing a type design for book printing the problem of ocular legibility has in most cases been solved in advance; that is, it is very unlikely that a typefounder or composing-machine manufacturer would produce and offer to good printers a face of which any two characters had confusing similarity, or in which any one letter ignored the "code" which governs its design in roman or italic. The size must be chosen in view of whether the work is one of reference, that is, to be read in short sections by people who are concentrating, or a novel to be read uninterruptedly by people who are enjoying themselves, or an educational book for young and reluctant eyes. Here again the makers are not likely to cut a small size so small as to be "illegible"; though any size may be called "unreadable" when it is too small or even too large for a given purpose—a reader's, not an oculist's purpose.

The moment the question shifts to *readability,* however, these elementary precautions give way to endless and delightfully varied experiments no less effective in each minute difference than is a change of timbre in a speaking voice. Set a page in Fournier against another in Caslon and another in Plantin, and it is as if you heard three different people delivering the same discourse—each with impeccable pronunciation and clarity, yet each through the medium of a different personality. Perhaps the layman would not be able to tell one old-style setting from two others of the same group; yet he could not read the three pages in turn without at least a subconscious discrimination. The smallest variation in serif-construction is enormous compared to the extent to which a disc of metal, in a telephone receiver, vibrates to electric shocks produced by one voice and another; yet we find it easy to deduce from one such set of vibrations that an old friend is asking us to "guess who this is!"

Physical Considerations

The beginner in book typography is prone to import aesthetic sentimentality into what is first of all a matter of convenience. Baskerville and Fournier were both designed during the eighteenth century, and some people think that they represent in miniature, and in terms of their respective national cultures, the clarity and good manners of that age. But should you label an old or modern author *"dix-huitième"* and start matching his words to what you consider a type of the era, it would be better first to remember that Baskerville, being relatively generous in set-width, will "drive out" the book; whilst Fournier, a neatly condensed face, will be more frugal of space. Thus *Pride and Prejudice* by Jane Austen, produced by Peter Davies Ltd., had a large amount of text to begin with, and not too many pages were to separate one illustration from the next: Fournier, in a beautifully legible small size, solved the problem. Baskerville, conversely, printed on bulky paper, has saved many a fine book from seeming to offer less than the money's worth. The typographer, whether he be connected with the printing or publishing office, should be able at a few minutes' notice to calculate ("cast off") how many pages the copy will come to in a given face, taking into account the point size, set-width, number of lines, and leading between the lines.

The word "set," which appears in our type specimen books, means that an actual type of the widest letter in the font (such as cap. *M*) will be as many points wide as the number given, and that the narrower letters will be proportionate to that width, if the type is cast on that indicated "set." Thus a font like Baskerville, of which the 12-pt. is "12 set," is going to occupy more space, word for word, than Bodoni 135, 12-pt., which is 11¾ set; Centaur and Garamond 12-pt., which are 11¼ set, will take less space; and Fournier, which in 12 pt. is 10¼ set, will vary from the width of Baskerville by the proportion of 10¼ set to 12 set.

Some typefaces are more successful in the sizes above 11-pt. than in those below it. The fine cut of Bodoni demands in justice exquisite printing for 6- and 8-pt.; Caslon and Garamond seem to many to improve as the sizes increase. Aldine Bembo 270, used on these pages, is one of the new Old Faces that preserves all its freshness and charm in the smallest sizes. Fournier and Monotype Plantin, for different reasons, are highly successful in the smallest settings as well as in and over the normal sizes. Centaur is a fine type in any size, but certain subtleties of cutting cannot be appreciated below 24-pt., and these details go to make it as successful an upper and lower case for poster work as has ever been designed.

If the quality of paper is known in advance—as it must be in most cases, and especially where illustrations are used—this will influence the choice of a typeface. Old Face was not designed for calendered paper, which did not exist until Baskerville's experiments; the difficulty arises in the fact that a smooth-finished surface of paper takes the inked copy with such ease that little or no impression *into* the fabric of the paper is necessary, and, therefore, the only ink which comes off the type is that on the actual printing surface. In general, calendered or shiny surface ("art") paper needs such a face as Monotype Plantin, which is not noticeably thinned down by such treatment.

In the old days a printer had no reason such as these for stocking different typefaces. He worked on one kind of paper: handmade pure rag, with the corrugated surface left by the wires of the paper-mould—a surface now known as antique laid. He had only one process by which pictures and type could be printed simultaneously. Nowadays he also has to be the master of a process as different from the old type-printing as the "kiss" impression of thousands of shallow dots of metal on smooth paper is different from the pressure of a deep-cut type and wood-blocks into damped paper. The modern printer is versatile, as his ancestors never dreamed of being; he prints from a rotary as well as a flat surface, and often from rubber or copper cylinders. He has long recognized the necessity of using a special kind of paper for each process. Nowadays, if only to prevent set-off, he has learned to stock special inks for special papers. But some survival of craft tradition prevents many printers from realizing that a face, like an ink or a paper, can be suitable or unsuitable for a given process. There is still a widespread feeling amongst them that the typographers ought to settle on one perfect type, and thus eliminate the expense of stocking, not that one font of 12-pt. which the old printer would call simply "our pica," but at least three or four different sets of 12-pt. composition matrices—chosen, be it noted, not for aesthetic reasons, as all can be "good" designs, but for as practical reasons as hold good in the paper-stores. Quite apart from the survival of the "One face" tradition, there is the fact that a composition series costs money. It is therefore necessary for laymen, buyers of printing, to discipline their enthusiasm for new faces.

If a Monotype user has four body composition faces, and each is well-designed and adapted to a particular printing process, and if the four designs are sufficiently different to convey four different "tones of voice" it would be inordinate to expect that man to increase his type repertory without very good reason. A customer can confer a great benefit upon a hitherto undistinguished printing office by clamoring for one fine composition face where there was none before; but on the other hand to wave aside Bembo and insist on Centaur or vice versa, is an ungrateful act. Besides, if there is a really defensible necessity for Bembo in that particular job, why not reward the master printer who, independently and of his own judgment, invested in that type without being prompted? In short, the man who wants a choice of good typefaces must go where they are or else accept what he is offered—unless he is willing, in token of his sincerity, to go shares with his printer and help purchase that font.

Let us leave this matter with the admonition that most old faces look anemic on coated paper, that a few types like Plantin Light 113, Ehrhardt, Bembo, Imprint, and Bell, are adaptable to varying processes, and that no printer ought to put in a composition face except that a *number* of customers over a *number* of years may be advantageously served by it.

One other mechanical point in the choice of typefaces has to do with combinations of different alphabets. Nowadays italic is thought of as a part of the whole font loosely called "roman," but the appearance in a page, or even a long sentence, in italic would show why this form of letter, at least until the middle of the sixteenth century, was considered as an entirely separate alphabet. When italic was thought of as separate cursive a certain latitude and individuality was allowed to it. Garamond italic, for all its whimsical and charming irregularity of slope which lends piquancy to certain italicized words, does not invite the effort of reading in entire poems or paragraphs as well as the disciplined Baskerville or Bell italics. The kind of cursive called Chancery, to which family Blado, Bembo, Arrighi, and Lutetia italics belong, has such beauty in its own right as to justify its use in long passages or even whole books; and as far as combination is concerned, there seems to be a closer correlation between the Chancery letter and the essential form of Roman Old Face than can otherwise be found before the eighteenth century. Another question in regard to combinations; Is an exotic font to be used anywhere in the text? If so, neither it nor the body roman must be too discrepant in weight, serif treatment, and general appearance. Perpetua is one of the few types which may be said to have "a greek" in the sense that most romans have "an italic"; in general one must be one's best to see that a warm Renaissance letter like Poliphilus is mated either with New Hellenic (for color) or the Aldine Greek, Series No. 283, rather than with a Greek cursive of the brilliance of Didot's. Even the extent to which capitals are used has some bearing on the choice of typefaces. The almost superstitious regard for Caslon Old Face has been such that only a typographer of our own time has dared to point out that its capitals, especially the capital *M,* are so heavy in contrast to the lowercase that very frequent use of them on a page creates a spotty effect.

And still we have not reached the really interesting part of choosing a typeface. All this preliminary matter has consisted of a recognition of certain physical facts—which, if the craft is to maintain its touch with the real world, must always be considered first and foremost. But beyond all the questions of relative width, color, suitability for certain processes, and optical legibility, lies the whole fascinating field in which the skilled typographer is at home. We must perforce leave him at this point. Looking at a number of books, he will improvise his own dogma as to the very delicate matter of suitability—a matter in which practically every canon of good taste and every detail of a cultural background and literary training are involved. We can offer only two generalizations to accompany him on his journey.

The first is that before any question of physical or literary suitability, must come the question of whether the face itself is tolerable or intolerable as a version of the roman alphabet. If a single letter is warped, emphasized above its fellows, made grotesque (as in this ugly *g*) or snub (as in any non-kerning *f*); if the letters, however pretty in themselves, do not combine automatically into words; if the fourth consecutive page begins to dazzle and irk the eye, and in general if the pages cannot be read with subconscious but very genuine pleasure, that type is intolerable and that is all there is about it. It must be wiped out of the discussion. There are bad types and good types, and the whole science and art of typography begins after the first category has been set aside.

The second generalization is, briefly, that the thing is worth doing. It does genuinely matter that a designer should take trouble and take delight in his choice of typefaces. The trouble and delight are taken not merely "for art's sake" but for the sake of something so subtly and intimately connected with all that is human that it can be described by no other phrase than "the humanities." If "the tone of voice" of a typeface does not count, then nothing counts that distinguishes man from the other animals. The twinkle that softens a rebuke; the scorn that can lurk under civility; the martyr's super-logic and the child's intuition; the fact that a fragment of moss can pull back into the memory a whole forest; these are proofs that there is reality in the imponderable, and that not only notation but connotations is part of the proper study of mankind. The best part of typographic wisdom lies in this study of connotation, the suitability of form to content. People who love ideas must have a love of words, and that means, given a chance, they will take a vivid interest in the clothes which words wear. The more they like to think, the more they will be shocked by any discrepancy between a lucid idea and a murky typesetting. They will become ritualists and dialecticians. They will use such technically indefensible words as "romantic," "chill," "jaunty" to describe different typefaces. If they are wise, they will always admit that they are dealing with processes of the subconscious mind, mere deft servants of the goddess Literature. But just as the poet prefers that the wireless announcer at the reciting of his verse over the wireless should choose neither a harsh nor a maudlin tone, but a sympathetic one, so will any author cock an anxious ear before the printing type that carries his words, and ask in his pride neither for officious flattery nor harsh mistreatment, but for justice tempered with mercy.

From *The Crystal Goblet: Sixteen Essays on Typography,* edited by Henry Jacob (Cleveland and New York: The World Publishing Company, 1956).

Grid and Design Philosophy

By Josef Müller-Brockmann

he use of the grid as an ordering system is the expression of a certain mental attitude inasmuch as it shows that the designer conceives his work in terms that are constructive and oriented to the future.

This is the expression of a professional ethos: the designer's work should have the clearly intelligible, objective, functional, and aesthetic quality of mathematical thinking.

His work should thus be a contribution to general culture and itself form part of it.

Constructive design which is capable of analysis and reproduction can influence and enhance the taste of a society and the way it conceives forms and colors. Design which is objective, committed to the common weal, well composed, and refined constitutes the basis of democratic behavior. Constructivist design means the conversion of design laws into practical solutions. Work done systematically and in accordance with strict formal principles makes those demands for directness, intelligibility, and the integration of all factors which are also vital in sociopolitical life.

Work with the grid system means submitting to laws of universal validity.

The use of the grid system implies

the will to systematize, to clarify

the will to penetrate to the essentials, to concentrate

the will to cultivate objectivity instead of subjectivity

the will to rationalize the creative and technical production processes

the will to integrate elements of color, form, and material

the will to achieve architectural dominion over surface and space

the will to adopt a positive, forward-looking attitude

the recognition of the importance of education and the effect of work devised in a constructive and creative spirit.

Every visual creative work is a manifestation of the character of the designer. It is a reflection of his knowledge, his ability, and his mentality.

What Is the Purpose of the Grid?

The grid is used by the typographer, graphic designer, photographer, and exhibition designer for solving visual problems in two and three dimensions. The graphic designer and typographer use it for designing press advertisements, brochures, catalogs, books, periodicals, etc., and the exhibition designer for conceiving his plan for exhibitions and show-window displays.

By arranging the surfaces and spaces in the form of a grid the designer is favorably placed to dispose his texts, photographs, and diagrams in conformity with objective and functional criteria. The pictorial elements are reduced to a few formats of the same size. The size of the pictures is determined according to their importance for the subject.

The reduction of the number of visual elements used and their incorporation in a grid system creates a sense of compact planning, intelligibility, and clarity, and suggests orderliness of design. This orderliness lends added credibility to the information and induces confidence.

Information presented with clear and logically set out titles, subtitles, texts, illustrations, and captions will not only be read more quickly and easily but the information will also be better understood and retained in the memory. This is a scientifically proved fact and the designer should bear in constantly in mind.

The grid can be successfully used for the corporate identities of firms. This includes all visual media of information from the visiting card to the exhibition stand: all printed forms for internal and external use, advertising matter, vehicles for goods and passenger transport, name-plates and lettering on buildings, etc.

The Typographic Grid

The grid divides a two-dimensional plane into smaller fields or a three-dimensional space into smaller compartments. The fields or compartments may be the same or different in size. The fields correspond in depth to a specific number of lines of text and the width of the fields is identical with the width of the columns. The depths and the widths are indicated in typographic measures, in points and ciceros.

The fields are separated by an intermediate space so that on the one hand pictures do not touch each other and legibility is thus preserved and on the other that captions can be placed below the illustrations.

The vertical distance between the fields, is one, two, or more lines of text, the horizontal space depending on the size of the type character and of the illustrations. By means of this division into grid fields the elements of design, viz. typography, photography, illustration, and color, can be disposed in a better way. These elements are adjusted to the size of the grid fields and fitted precisely into the size of the fields. The smallest illustration corresponds to the smallest grid field.

The grid for a 1/1 page comprises a smaller or larger number of such grid fields. All illustrations, photographs, statistics, etc., have the size of one, two, three, or four grid fields. In this way a certain uniformity is attained in the presentation of visual information.

The grid determines the constant dimensions of space. There is virtually no limit to the number of grid divisions. It may be said in general that every piece of work must be studied very carefully so as to arrive at the specific grid network corresponding to its requirements.

The rule: The fewer the differences in the size of the illustrations, the quieter the impression created by the design. As a controlling system the grid makes it easier to give the surface or space a rational organization.

Such a system of arrangement compels the designer to be honest in his use of design resources. It requires him to come to terms with the problem in hand and to analyze it. It fosters analytical thinking and gives the solution of the problem a logical and material basis. If the text and pictures are arranged systematically, the priorities stand out more clearly.

A suitable grid in visual design makes it easier

a

to construct the argument objectively with the means of visual communication

b

to construct the text and illustrative material systematically and logically

c

to organize the text and illustrations in a compact arrangement with its own rhythm

d

to put together the visual material so that it is readily intelligible and structured with a high degree of tension.

There are various reasons for using the grid as an aid to the organization of text and illustration:

economic reasons: a problem can be solved in less time and at lower cost.

rational reasons: both simple and complex problems can be solved in a uniform and characteristic style.

mental attitude: the systematic presentation of facts, of sequences of events, and of solutions to problems should, for social and educational reasons, be a constructive contribution to the cultural state of society and an expression of our sense of responsibility.

Systems of Order in Ancient and Modern Times[1]

Just as in nature systems of order govern the growth and structure of animate and inanimate matter, so human activity itself has, since the earliest times, been distinguished by the quest for order. Even the most ancient peoples created ornaments with mathematical forms of great beauty.

The desire to bring order to the bewildering confusion of appearances reflects a deep human need.

Pythagoras (580–500 BC) taught that simple numbers and their relations to each other, and also simple geometrical figures constructed to such measures, are an image of the innermost secret of nature. He discovered that the harmony of musical intervals depends on the simple numerical relations of spatial distances on the harp string and in the flute.

The Greeks also discovered the proportions of the Golden Section and showed that it is present in the proportions of the human figure. It was on these that architects, painters, and sculptors based their work.

The artists of the Renaissance found the basis for their compositions in measure and proportion. Dürer spent his time in Italy studying the mathematically conceived works of contemporary artists and returned to Germany with the knowledge he had acquired.

Philosophers, architects, and artists, from Pythagoras, Vitruvius, Villard de Honnecourt, Dürer, and others down to Le Corbusier have left behind doctrines of proportion which give us a fascinating insight into the mathematical thought of their time.

---

[1] "Order Is the Actual Key of Life" by Le Corbusier, *Modulor I,* p. 77.

From *Grid Systems in Graphic Design* (Niederteufen: Verlag Arthur Niggli, 1981).

On Classifying Type

By Jonathan Hoefler

f there is a Holy Grail of typography it is surely the Omniscient Typeface Classification System, which will organize and index the complete typographical output of mankind. Countless individuals have set to the task of developing such a thing: printer-scholar Theodore Low deVinne, historian A. F. Johnson, critic Beatrice Warde, educator Alexander Lawson, writer Robert Bringhurst, and scores of professional organizations. I suspect that every typophile who has ever spent more than ten minutes trying to locate an obscure typeface in a poorly organized specimen book secretly dreams of devising the ultimate system by which typefaces are classified.

I must confess that I don't share my colleagues' fascination with this challenge. Whether something is a humanist sans serif or a neo-grotesque seems largely irrelevant in light of current typography, where the motivation to create new typefaces has been transcended by the drive to invent new kinds of typefaces. Whether this is an artistic endeavor or an imperative of the marketplace is debatable, but it has remained a consistent theme in typography for nearly two centuries. Editors of type specimen books who don't know where to file Remedy or Hard Times should take heart: a freakish design of 1815 was so vexing to compositors that they ultimately resorted to giving it its own designation. What subsequent generations referred to alternately as the egyptian, doric, ionic, or antique, history now remembers as the first sans serif.

This is not to suggest that the development of a classification system is futile but rather, that it is an infinitely complex task that requires the sensitivity of numerous disciplines—typography being only one among them. Attempts at typographic scholarship have long been impeded by the difficulties of describing typefaces, let alone organizing them. Where biologists have the benefit of the Linnaean system for comparing *homo sapiens* to *homo erectus,* and librarians can be certain that even as-yet unimagined volumes on architectural technique will be found under Dewey 692 (i.e., building construction practices), typographers have only the vaguest standardized terms for describing how Caslon differs from Janson. A taxonomy for type, if it were comprehensive, adaptable, correctable, expandable, generally accessible yet infinitely refined, would be of immense use to anyone connected with letters. If it chronicled the cultural, aesthetic, technological, and literary factors that have influenced type design—instead of postulating a neat progression of styles, implying an uncomplicated evolution—it might approach a more faithful record of the rich and complex history of typography. But the timeworn attempt to find a single best way to organize typefaces remains a hopeless pursuit: like asking, "What's the best way to drive across the United States?" it anticipates a simple response to a complex issue.

The Central Lettering Record

A research team at the Central Saint Martins College of Art & Design in London has recently taken up the challenge to build a better system, as part of an ambitious project to extend the resources of the *Central Lettering Record*. The Record, as its name suggests, is an archive of lettering of all varieties: as distinguished from typography, which refers exclusively to the study of printing types, lettering subsumes a host of related disciplines, each of which brings its own visual vocabulary to bear upon the shape of letters. The Record includes Studies of epigraphy (stonecutting), paleography and calligraphy (handwriting, in varying degrees of formality), architectural lettering, and modern commercial signage in a number of materials. There are letters in neon, plywood, vinyl, and vacuform plastic—media that have yet to engender their own fields of formal study.

The interest in lettering inspired by Edward Johnston early this century began to wane by the 1950s, when British design educators started to take an increasing interest in modernism. To counter the declining interest in non-typographic lettering and to provide an archive for their students at the Central School of Arts and Crafts (later partnered with Saint Martins to become the Central Saint Martins College), Nicolete Gray and Nicholas Biddulph began to amass a collection of alphabetic artifacts and photographs which now forms the core of the Central Lettering Record. After a period of some disuse, a renewed interest in the Record has prompted both its reorganization and its expansion to include typographic developments of the pass decade. In connection with this ambitious project, a research group within the college is working to develop a CD-ROM on the history of typography, which will present both new and old typefaces in the context of the Record's well-developed collection of typographic artifacts.

At last year's meeting of the Association Typographique Internationale in The Hague, Ed McDonald, Eric Kindel, and Catherine Dixon of Central Saint Martins presented a preliminary version of the CD-ROM. While the project has undergone considerable changes in the past six months—including a seismic overhaul of the classification system that had been introduced in the winter 1995 issue of *Eye*—both the architecture of the system and its user interface represent a unique and refreshing approach to the documentation of type history. Perhaps more impressive than the work as it stands today, is its potential for future scholarship, which suggests that when complete, the CD will serve as a comprehensive review of more than five centuries of typography. While the CD itself remains a work in progress, the process by which this vast collection has been edited and organized already serves as an interesting study of the challenges facing the typographic archivist.

Where History Begins

The history of typography as conventionally told begins with Johannes Gutenberg and his celebrated 42-line Bible, printed circa 1455. However, current scholarship reminds us that Gutenberg is preceded by at least eight centuries of printing in the Far East demanding that this discussion be framed as the history of typography in the West, or more precisely, the history of European typefaces manufactured in the manner of Gutenberg. Ignoring for a moment the blackletter script after which Gutenberg patterned his types (because our discussion is about type, not calligraphy), we might proceed safely to the topic of major innovations in type, as they appear in the timeline, for almost ten years. The traditional next stop after Gutenberg is the work of the Italian humanists in the late 1460s, which culminated in Nicolas Jenson's roman of 1470 (which we know through countless revivals, including Centaur and Adobe Jenson). The types of this period show the sudden influence of the humanist miniscule, a style of handwriting which took hold as part of the broader influence of secular humanism in the late fifteenth century. This form of letter might be thought of as the last evolutionary stage of the Carolingian miniscule, a style advanced by Charlemagne in the eighth century, representing an attempt to consolidate the many kinds of regional handwriting used throughout the Holy Roman Empire—resisting this excursion into a discussion of politics and script, let's continue with Jenson's type and its many merits.

Aside from being attractive, Jenson's type is unique in its approach to lettering, which involved reconciling the two alphabets of the ancient world, the majuscule and the minis-cule. Majuscules are the letters of antiquity, familiar to us through architectural inscrip-tions and the typefaces based on them, such as Adobe's Trajan. Miniscules are a sort of shorthand letter, handwritten forms indirectly descended from the majuscules and akin to our modern lowercase. Jenson successfully reconciled these two different alphabets by rendering the shapes of the miniscule in the style of the majuscule, taking written forms and remaking them in an eloquent vocabulary borrowed from inscriptions featuring stems, hairlines, and serifs. In so doing, Jenson and his Venetian cohorts cemented a typo-graphic relationship which persists as a familiar if invisible dichotomy, that of the upper-case and lowercase. A broader discussion of Jenson's innovations would include a survey of how inscriptional lettering changed under the Roman Republic and how changes in media forced the evolution of these letters into the quadrata, rustica, and uncial scripts which ultimately informed the Carolingian miniscule—but this is really the province of epigraphers, paleographers, and semioticians.

And so it goes, proceeding in many directions at once. Even in its infancy, type history is the confluence of many histories, and cross-pollination between these different areas of development only multiply as history advances. By the nineteenth century, when the dom-inant letter styles appear in many media, the lines of influence become impossible to chart. In *Nineteenth Century Ornamented Typefaces,* Nicolete Gray discusses lettering of a style she terms "English Vernacular," describing not only printing types but painted letters on shop fasciae, incised letters on monuments, and cast-iron letters on gravemarkers—never con-cluding that any of these examples is singularly supreme. By the twentieth century, when the design of typefaces is commonly informed by literary and artistic influences, which are decidedly outside the realm of typography, it becomes impossible to classify typefaces by their historical position alone. Type history invariably demonstrates that its exemplars, if not all of its participants, occupy the crossroads of many historical themes, none of which are fully within the scope of the study of printing types. The problem of when history begins is thus complicated by the larger question of what history includes.

One Man's Language

With the understanding that typographic history is more than the history of type, we may better appreciate the approach taken by the Central Lettering Record, which pre-sents a holistic view of lettering by making frequent excursions into related fields. Although this approach presents a more integrated view of type history, it is not without its own difficulties.

The technical terms specific to any area of study are likely to evidence their own bias-es, and the collision of many disparate vocabularies inevitably introduces ambiguities. A term as seemingly neutral as *roman,* for example, even divorced from its geographical, national, historical, and political meanings, is fraught with ambiguity: to a typographer it means "upright types," but in orthography it denotes the Latin alphabet, and to calligraphers it describes a style of lettering peculiar to the fifteenth century. Sometimes terms specific to typography have multiple or even contrary meanings, leading to such delightful oxymoron's as Serif Gothic and Times Roman Italic. The terms *antique, gothic,* and *old english* are among typography's most widely used and, entertainingly, also the most convoluted: *antique* can mean a slab serif (Antique No.3), a sans serif (Antique Olive), a humanist book face (Zapf Antiqua), or simply anything that looks old (Caslon Antique). Similarly, *gothic* can refer to a sans serif (Franklin Gothic), or a blackletter (Totally Gothic), or occasionally both (Gothic Gothic). *Old english* is a hornet's nest, best avoided altogether.

Terminology also shows its roots. The very words used to describe the inscription on the Trajan Column might betray the concerns of a stonemason, an architect, a geologist, a lapidary, or a type designer, since the specialized vocabulary used by any profession is inevitably colored by particular areas of interest. The language typographers use to discuss non-typographic artifacts is no exception, as seen in the terms adopted by the Central Lettering Record: for example, *augustan, rustic, tuscan,* and *wedge* are among the stylistic groupings used to organize Its collection of inscriptional photographs. Although these terms were developed to highlight a specific area of interest, even they are prone to confusing many lines of inquiry: *Augustan* is a historical marker, indicating those letters made in the style popularized under Caesar Augustus (27 BC–AD 14); *rustic,* divorced from its adjectival meaning, is a paleographic term which describes a particular style of handwriting; *tuscan* is a term coined by 19th-century typographers to describe several genera of ornamented printing types; *wedge,* though the least colorful of the lot, is the only term to describe letters on a purely visual level.

Apples, Oranges

The conflation of historical, technical, and formal terms is a common problem with typeface classification systems, seen especially in the scheme adopted by the British Standards Institute in 1958, and revised in 1967. For instance, while its *slab serif* and *lineale* categories are purely visual, *garalde* is a historical denomination (a synthesis of Garamond and Aldus), and its *script* category takes into account the intention of the design, for it includes only "typefaces, which imitate writing." Other systems muddle things further by expanding their criteria to include usage, such as the DIN (Deutsche Industrie Norman) classification which subdivides *classical styles* into four sub-sections, three of them chronological (early, late, and modern) and the fourth reserved for typefaces designed for newspapers. The situation gets worse with systems that include geographical designations, like those which maintain a distinction between *dutch old styles* and *english old styles,* without ever elaborating on these groups' taxonomic differences. Much of this is sheer jingoism and can be largely attributed to Daniel Berkeley Updike and his seminal *Printing Types: Their History, Forms, and Use,* a standard desk reference on type history since its publication in 1922. Despite its usefulness, Updike's scholarship is marred by extraordinary prejudices at every turn. Without exception, every achievement in three centuries of Dutch typefounding is somehow ascribed to the influence of the French (with whom Updike is inexplicably enamored), while the Dutch are portrayed in shockingly racist stereotypes: Plantin, Van Dijck, and the Elzevirs are commended for their shrewdness, their diligence, their thrift. Updike spits about the mediocrity of "a rugged little Dutch type," a typeface which is praised earlier in the edition where it is properly identified as the work of Frenchman Robert Granjon. This is par for the course in Updike.

Most typeface classification systems attempt a purely historical approach, categorizing typefaces according to the time of their genesis. The eighteenth-century types of Van Dijck and Caslon share many characteristics and are commonly collected as *old styles*. Bodoni and Didot's types of a century later are distinctly different and are designated *modern*. Between these extremes are the types of John Baskerville and others, conveniently labeled *transitional*. Aside from the obvious problem that compartmentalized systems demand *rigidity*, such classifications distort the historical record by equating chronology with typographic style. This becomes especially awkward in a discussion of nineteenth-century types, when entire categories of type develop coevally. Immediately following the period during which the modern style flourished, a number of styles developed simultaneously, including sans serifs and slab serifs. The category that is lifted directly after modern in a classification system might understandably be mistaken as the next evolutionary step, even if this is not really the case.

Assigning types to discrete time periods also intimates that historical styles are visual explorations that have long since been completed. As a result, such systems are utterly unable to cope with typefaces of the late twentieth century, which are only incidentally related to historical styles. This invariably leads to confusion: typefaces of vastly different construction are corralled under a single heading (*slab serif* includes nineteenth-century egyptians as well as 1974 Lubalin Graph), modern designs not explicitly designed in any historical style are grouped with the oldies (Gerard Unger's Swift typeface of 1985 is considered a *Garalde*), and designs which don't fit any of the molds are summarily expelled. Not all the exiles are freaks, as can be gathered from any type specimen book that includes special designations like *twentieth-century romans,* a questionable grouping usually included for the express purpose of accommodating Times Roman.

Much of the scramble to organize typefaces has come from type manufacturers, since commercial typefounding brings a special urgency to the question of how typefaces are listed. No discussion of classification would therefore be complete without at least a little review of some of the more colorful developments in the private sector. Bitstream's approach is rather ecumenical, giving equal weight to sans serifs and "typefaces adapted from typewriters and daisy-wheel printers," among other comprehensive categories (although things take a turn for the worse in category 15, where "typefaces outside the typographic norm" are ghettoized as *exotic.*) Letraset forecloses the discussion with their *graphic* category, which warehouses some two-thirds of the faces in its library. The FontShop's FontFont range has recently been reorganized along conceptual lines, bringing to typography an updated version of the nine muses: *Amorphous, Destrudive, Geometric, Handwritten, Historic, Intelligent, Ironic, Pi & Illustrations,* and *Typographic*. (Note that a typeface cannot be both Historic and Intelligent, and that only some typefaces get to be Typographic.) Perhaps it was inevitable that the beloved Dewey decimal system would be interpreted typographically, as David A. Mundie has done with *A Field Guide to Type Classification,* published on the Internet. Beginning with standard morphological differences (serifs vs. sans), Mundie provides subdivisions for progressively subtler typographic distinctions, right on past several decimal points to an almost fractal level of refinement. The result is that Universe Black, which Adrian Frutiger outfitted with the workaday number 75, is designated: "14.4.3.4.1.2.2.2.2.2, R flag roman [498]."[1]

Horizons

In *The Elements of Typographic Style,* Robert Bringhurst outlines an interesting approach to type classification, which lays the foundation for a more sensitive conservancy of type history. Recognizing that the period of a typeface's development will reflect not only its style but its manufacturing process, Bringhurst introduces two complementary scales for classifying type. The first is a series of artistic movements, borrowed from the fine arts: Renaissance, Baroque, Neoclassical, and so on. These labels ignore the vagaries of x-heights and serif designs, and instead attempt a reference to the artistic circumstances relevant to each period in typographic history. Intersecting this system is a second scale, which indicates the original form of a typeface: foundry type for hand composition, hot metal type for machine composition, phototype, or digital fonts. By classifying typefaces under both methods, a system emerges which allows for the comparison of visually related designs without overtly suggesting relationships between them. Therefore Fournier's types of the 1740s might be stylistically grouped with their 1926 interpretation for machine casting, Monotype Fournier, as well as Fleischman's No. 65 (1738), not to mention more recent designs that are only arguably their descendants, such as Matthew Carter's Charter (1987). By locating history along perpendicular axes denoting artistic and technological concerns, Bringhurst dispenses with the usual laundry-list approach and hints at something far more compelling to emerge.

Since typeface classification systems are rarely constructed with concern for the needs or interests of their users, let alone anticipating their level of sophistication, they rarely raise the question of who might benefit from their use. Mundie's *Field Guide to Type Classification,* for all its obscurity, is one of few systems that directly confronts the question of readership. Presenting his system as a field guide rather than a comprehensive taxonomy, Mundie makes a clear distinction between handbooks for beginners and reference works for the proficient. His botanical parallel is a good one: "[A] field guide is free to use categories such as 'pink flowers,' while the taxonomic botanist is apt to concentrate on whether the pistils are adnate to the perianth." The student learning to recognize typefaces undoubtedly has different concerns from those of the art director who is likely to be more interested in the stylistic and cultural references of a particular font, as well as its location in a catalog. The historian's interests are different still, as are those of the bibliographer, the cultural anthropologist, and the increasing number of nonprofessionals who have discovered an interest in type through their font menus.

A New Reference

Questions about organization and audience amount to curatorship, an aspect of type classification that has never really been articulated. "Lettering is often interesting from many points of view," wrote Leonora Pearse about the Central Lettering Record, "so to make a classification according to one aspect of style may in fact prove more restricting than helpful." Mindful of the fact that classification systems inevitably leave an editorial imprint on the material they organize, the research group at Central Saint Martins has allowed their system to evolve with the understanding that when complete, it will serve as only one of many means for navigating the history of typography.

Although rooted in the archival resources of the Record, the CD-ROM has evolved in an atmosphere which strongly reflects the human resources of the college. Under the stewardship of Jesse Collins, Herbert Spencer, Anthony Froshaug, and most recently, Phil

Baines, the College has engendered an interest in typography, perhaps overshadowing the other lettering arts. Despite the CD's focus on printing types (especially those of the past fifteen years), it shares with the Record an approach to type history integrating the new and the old. "Our first thought," says editor/designer Eric Kindel, "was to provide the students with an overview that incorporates the familiar with the obscure, such as historical background material."

The CD consists of four basic sections. The first is an electronic specimen book which contains more than 150 fonts (recorded as anti-aliased bitmaps) whose characters can each be fully displayed at enlarged scale and alongside the same characters in other typefaces (as many as eight at a time). In the second section, most of these faces are presented in the context of original use, i.e., in books and ephemera gathered from the Record. Included as high-resolution scans, these examples come from a variety of sources, including type specimen books and typefoundries' promotional material, as well as posters and ephemera. A split-screen interface allows both sections to be viewed at once; thus a reader might examine Monotype Bembo alongside its historical progenitor, a type used by Aldus in the Renaissance novel *Hypnerotomachia Polophilii,* which is shown as a striking enlargement. A third section contains historical synopses of all the typefaces included on the CD (provided as searchable text), and the fourth and most comprehensive section contains an elaborate timeline of type designers. The CD also offers various other materials, such as QuickTime animations (no CD is complete without them), which generally support the larger reference work.

The job of distilling half a millennium of type history down to 150 typefaces is an unwelcome task, but one that has been skillfully handled by Kindel and Dixon. Among the typefaces chosen are not only those which have enjoyed commercial success, but those which represent significant developments in technology. The technological front represented by Monotype Imprint (the first custom-designed typeface for machine composition) continues with Apollo, the first face explicitly designed for photocomposition, and on to Adobe Minion, the first Multiple Master. Other aspects of the relationship between design and technology are introduced through the inclusion of machine-readable fonts such as OCR-A and OCR-B, and machine-inspired fonts such as Citizen and Beowolf. Still other typefaces are included as examples of different perspectives on a historical model, such as the three Bodoni revivals, the early Bauer Bodoni, the more recent ITC Bodoni, and the "bastardization," as Kindel puts it, Monotype Bodoni. Typefaces which are crucial to the discussion but remain unavailable digitally are illustrated in the first image section, such as the generous number of Garamond revivals which are shown as foundry specimens.

Unlike digital publications which are fundamentally books or educational films, the appeal of the Central Lettering Record CD is that it is presented not as a story, but as a database. Unlike conventional type histories in which typefaces are arranged chronologically, gathered stylistically, or merely listed alphabetically, the materials on the CD are not offered in linear order. The hypertext structure of the CD requires that the reader leap from font to font in pursuit of points of comparison, and the narrative about type history that emerges does so not on the screen but in the user's mind. "Our hope was to put in as much as possible," says Kindel, "and to allow the connections to form for themselves. There are certain ideas we're hoping to draw out—namely the context in which the types have evolved, the technology and influences underlying them, what predecessors' types represent, and what they themselves were based on—but I'd argue that we ultimately take no opinion about the merits of the material included." This approach is less laissez-faire than it sounds, for included with the CD may be a series of scholarly essays that will refer to the material on the disc in different ways. These routes through a common terrain might be thought of as typographic travelogues, and their parity with the user's journey serves to remind that the hierarchies posited by any type history, and every type classification system, are highly subjective.

A New System

With the imperative to present contemporary and historical material in the same source, chief content researcher Catherine Dixon set about developing a classification system as a supplementary means of accessing the material on the CD-ROM. Since its conception, the system has undergone a number of changes, many of which are a response to the research team's own explorations of their CD, explorations which continue to suggest new ways of organizing material. Many of the original categories which reflected typefaces' formal qualities have been discarded in favor of more abstract terms which take into account their intentions. The *industrial vernacular* class, represented by Erik van Blokland's Trixie typeface, has since been absorbed into a new category, *emulative,* which is less wedded to a particular fashion. "Categorizing Trixie as an emulative typeface suggests that it employs strategies that may have been tried before," says Dixon. "There are countless Letraset faces which are emulative—all those LCD types, for instance—but if you think about it, Gutenberg's type is really emulative, as well." The *sampled* category has been similarly redefined, no longer referring only to typefaces made from other typefaces, but now encompassing designs that "take an aggressive stance towards history," as Dixon puts it. Whether it will be possible to uncouple *sampled* from a larger cultural ethos has yet to be seen; like *industrial vernacular,* it connotes strong existing cultural and temporal associations. And the part of the project that involves determining conceptual underpinnings remains slipppery, as Dixon is quick to point out: "It's a major trap, talking to designers about what they've done. The hype is largely after the fact."

The latest iteration of the system calls for a plane, formed by the intersection of a timeline on the one axis, and a list of identified typographic models on the other axis. Like Bringhurst's approach, typefaces are evaluated according to multiple criteria, but the CD's system takes a unique approach to how they are plotted on the grid. Historical sources might be represented by a single point on the grid—a foundry type made by William Caslon, for instance, might be at the intersection of AD. 1732 and Garalde—but later designs that refer to historical material in different ways might be represented by a range encompassing a number of points, each of them a typographic reference. The corner of 1732 and Garalde might find itself a part of many neighborhoods, appearing in the profiles for not only explicit revivals like Adobe Caslon and Caslon No. 540, but more ironic interpretations like Mark Andresen's Not Caslon—and, even more unexpectedly, the Kennerley typeface which Frederic Goudy claimed as his homage to Caslon. The system becomes especially interesting when these sorts of unforeseen patterns emerge.

As the system continues to evolve, it threatens to become increasingly difficult to represent visually. Recent review suggests the need for a way of displaying non-visual references, which the team now hopes to incorporate as a listed appendix—time permitting, as the project's funding expires this summer. What happens then remains uncertain, but the team hopes to develop subsequent releases of the CD, some of which might be necessitated after the profession has had a chance to respond to the classification system. "In conversation with type designers," notes Dixon, "it has become clear that they aim for the cracks between categories within type design, combining elements of this with elements of that and so on." In spite of its flexibility and openness, perhaps this classification system is raising the bar, encouraging today's samplers and emulators to find new ways of hacking the system tomorrow. In addition to thriving on challenge, type designers are, to a person, smart alecks: the chance to have an entire category named after them in version 2.0 may prove irresistible.

---

[1] http://ivory.lm.com/~mundie/Typography/Faces.html

From *Emigre,* no. 42 (Spring 1977).

Type Is to Read

By William Golden

f there is such a thing as a "New American Typography" surely it speaks with a foreign accent. And it probably talks too much. Much of what it says is obvious nonsense. A good deal of it is so pompous that it sounds like nonsense, though if you listen very carefully it isn't . . . quite. It is just over-complicated. When it is translated into prewar English it is merely obvious.

I don't know what it is that impels so many designers to drop their work to write and speak so much about design.

Is it the simple (and perfectly justifiable) instinct for trade promotion? Or have we imported the European propensity for surrounding even the simplest actions with a *gestalt?*

Perhaps the explanation is simpler. The kind of effort that goes into graphic expression is essentially lonely and intensive, and produces, at its best, a simple logical design. It is sometimes frustrating to find that hardly anyone knows that it is a very complicated job to produce something simple. Perhaps we want them to know that we've gone through hell, sweating out a job to reach what seems to be an obvious solution.

And since our professional medium of communication is not verbal, designers don't seem to be lucid writers or speakers on the subject of design.

I have been frequently stimulated by the work of most of the people on this panel, but only rarely by what they have said about it.

While it must be assumed that these endless discussions have values that I am blind to, I am more acutely aware of the dangers they hold for the young. If you have recently interviewed a crop of young designers—the New Renaissance Man in a hurry—applying for their first or second staff job, you will know what I mean.

I was forced to part with one such man on my staff a while ago. He was pretty good, too. But he was another victim of the overseriousness of graphic arts literature. He had all the latest and obscure publications from here and abroad (mostly in languages he couldn't read). He attended all the forums. He would argue endlessly on theory . . . and he was just paralyzed with fright at the sight of a blank layout pad. He could spend as much as a week on a fifty-line newspaper ad. His trouble was, that no matter how he tried, an ad looked very much like an ad, and not any of these almost mystical things he had been reading about.

If there were some way to fix an age limit for attendance at these conferences, in the way that minors are forbidden to attend over stimulating movies, I think they would be relatively harmless, and it might even be pleasant to chew our cud together.

For it has all been said, and said many times, and in a most confusing way and almost none of it is new. Even the insistence on newness at any cost is in itself familiar.

Perhaps it would be useful for a conference like this to sort it all out. Not merely to summarize this conference, but all of them. If it could be done without padding, I imagine that what is valid about typography would be very brief and relatively simple.

What is right about current typography is so apparent when you see it that it requires no explanation. What is wrong is a little more complex.

It is not as difficult to define what is wrong as it is to find how we got there.

I have my own notion of how we got where we are, and though I have neither the competence nor the ambition to be a typographic historian, this is roughly how it looks from one viewpoint.

Some thirty years ago the rebellious advertising and editorial designer in America was engaged in a conspiracy to bring order, clarity, and directness to the printed page. He fought against the picture of the factory, the company logotype, and the small picture of the package that invariably accompanied it. He protested that the copy was too long, and that he was obliged to set it so small that no one would read it. He argued that the normal ad contained too many elements. (He even invented the "busy" page in some effort to accommodate himself to it.) He insisted that this effort to say so many things at once was self-defeating and could only result in communicating nothing to the reader.

He was essentially picture-minded, and only reluctantly realized that he had to learn something about type. It was and still is a damned nuisance, but when he realized how thoroughly its mechanical and thoughtless application could destroy communication of an idea, he had to learn to control it—to design with it.

More and more typography was designed on a layout pad rather than in metal. Perhaps the greatest change in American typography was caused by this simple act—the transfer of the design function of the printer to the graphic designer.

The designer was able to bring a whole new background and a new set of influences to the printed page. He could "draw" a page. There was more flexibility in the use of a pencil than in the manipulation of a metal form. It became new medium for the designer.

Under the twin impact of the functionalism of the Bauhaus and the practical demands of American business, the designer was beginning to learn to use the combination of word and image to communicate more effectively.

Under the influence of the modern painters, he became aware (perhaps too aware) of the textural qualities and color values of type as an element of design.

And surely a dominating influence on American typography in the prewar years was exerted by the journalists.

Newspapers and magazines were the primary media of mass communication. The skillful development of the use of headline and picture was a far more prevalent influence than the European poster. The newspaper taught us speed in communication. Everyone knew instinctively what the journalists had reduced to a formula: that if you read a headline, a picture, and the first three paragraphs of any story you would know all the essential facts.

The magazine communicated at a more leisurely pace and could be more provocative since it addressed a more select audience. Because the magazine dealt more in concepts than in news it was far more imaginative. There was more opportunity here, to design within the framework of the two-page spread. But still, the device that bore the main burden of interesting the reader, was the "terrific headline" and the "wonderful picture."

Perhaps it was the growth of radio, a rival medium, that hastened a new effort on the part of the magazine.

Certainly the new technical developments in photography increased the range of its reportage.

But what gave it a new direction and style was not so purely American. I think it was men like Agha and Brodovitch. These importations from Europe set a pace that not only changed the face of the magazine and consequently advertising design, but they changed the status of the designer. They did this by the simple process of demonstrating that the designer could also think.

The "layout man" was becoming an editor. He was no longer that clever, talented fellow in the back room who made a writer's copy more attractive by arranging words and pictures on the printed page in some ingenious way. He could now read and understand the text. He could even have an opinion about it. He might even be able to demonstrate that he could communicate its content better and with more interest than the writer. He could even startle the editor by suggesting content. It wasn't long before he began to design the page before it was written, and writers began to write to a character count to fit the layout.

Whatever successes this revolution achieved were accomplished by demonstration—by individual designers proving to their clients and employers (by solving their problems) the validity of their point of view and the value of their talents. It was accomplished without a single design conference in New York or in Colorado or anywhere else in America.

There were, of course, exhibitions and award luncheons. But the exhibitions were an extension of the process of demonstration, and the arrangers of the award luncheons by some lucky instinct seldom permitted the designer to speak about his work, but rather forced the businessman to discuss it.

But more than any other single factor, I believe the designer won his new status in the business community because he had demonstrated that he could communicate an idea or a fact on the printed page at least as well, and often better, than the writer, the client, or his representative. And he could demonstrate this only if he was at least as faithful to content as he was to style.

During the war and for some time afterward, American typographers made great strides in relation to the Europeans, for the simple reason, I suppose, that there was not only a shortage of paper in Europe but there was a shortage of design. The printers and designers were in foxholes, concentration camps, or dead, and presses and foundries were being bombed.

There was a long period when the bulk of the world's graphic material was being produced in America. Though there was something approaching a paper shortage here, too, there was an excess of profits available to spend on advertising. There were few products to advertise and therefore very little to say about them. But since it was relatively inexpensive to keep a company name in print, it didn't matter too greatly what or how it was said. We produced such a volume of printed material for so long a time, that we were able to assimilate a vast amount of prewar European design, and adapt it to our own language and uses. It had become such a familiar idiom with us that it is now hardly surprising that the announcement of this conference can call contemporary typography purely American.

My first look at postwar typography was fairly bewildering. I had seen and applauded the prewar work by Burtin and Beall. They were developing newer graphic forms, and using words and images on the printed page to communicate. In their hands these images were employed to make a statement clearer, faster.

The new avant-garde was saying nothing and saying it with considerable facility. They could say in their defense that the world was more chaotic than ever, that nobody was saying anything very rational, and that their need to make some kind of order was satisfied to some extent, by creating it on the printed page. It was, largely, an order without content.

There was precedent for this point of view. The determined sales promotion campaign of the abstract expressionist painters was in full swing in America. That it could have been so successful so quickly must surely be due, in part, to its absence of content. In a curious way this revolution was a remarkably safe one—it was so noncommittal.

I have no quarrel with the abstract movement—except with its vociferous intolerance of any other school. But I think the effect on the minds of young designers is a matter of concern. To regard the blank rectangle on a layout pad with the same attitude that the abstract painter confronts his blank canvas is surely a pointless delusion.

The printed page is not primarily a medium for self-expression. Design for print is not Art. At best it is a highly skilled craft. A sensitive, inventive, interpretive craft, if you will, but in no way related to painting.

A graphic designer is employed, for a certain sum of money, by someone who wants to say something in print to somebody. The man with something to say comes to the designer in the belief that the designer with his special skills will say it more effectively for him.

It sometimes develops that as a result of this hopeful transaction, the statement becomes an advertisement for the designer rather than his client. And should there be any doubt about the designer's intention, he will sign it—just as the easel painter does.

Logically enough, this attitude toward design is only tolerated when the client has nothing to say. When his product is no different than anyone else's, and no better. When his company has no "personality"—he borrows the personality of the designer. This is rarely permitted in the mainstream of advertising, but only in the "off-Broadway" arenas.

The immature avant-garde designer seems bitter about the mainstream of American advertising. He hates the "hard sell" and avoids clients who interfere with his freedom. He believes that the role of business should be one of patron of the Arts, and insists that his craft is art.

I do not argue for the return to any form of traditionalism. I do argue for a sense of responsibility on the part of the designer, and a rational understanding of his function.

I think he should avoid designing for designers.

I suggest that the word "design" be considered as a verb in the sense that we design something to be communicated to someone.

Perhaps it would help to clear the air a little if we were conscious that printing and advertising cost a great deal of money. If a designer could pretend that the money to be spent to reproduce his design was his own, I suspect he would subject himself to far more rigid disciplines.

When he examines his work with relation to its function, he wouldn't bury the text and render it illegible on the ground that it is inferior anyway. He will insist, instead, that it be better. If no one will write a better text, he will have to learn to write it himself. For having become, in effect, his own client, he will want to be sure that what he has to say will be clearly understood—that this is his primary function.

He will find that the most satisfying solutions to a graphic problem come from its basic content. He will find it unnecessary and offensive to superimpose a visual effect on an unrelated message.

He might even find that writers, too, have a certain skill, and he might enjoy reading them, and making their work legible.

Perhaps the most important thing that would happen is that all those pointless questions about tradition and modernism, whether our typography is American or European, will become properly irrelevant. All of these influences, and many more, will have become part of the designer's total design vocabulary.

If he applies it successfully, the end product will show no traces of having been designed at all. It will look perfectly obvious and inevitable.

If he is more concerned with how well his job is done than he is about whether or not it is "new," he will even win awards for his performance.

But no matter how many honors are bestowed on him throughout his career, he will never mistake the printed page for an art gallery.

At your conference last year, the most stimulating speaker for me, was not a designer at all. He was a semanticist—Dr. Anatol Rapoport of the University of Michigan's Mental Health Research Institute. In trying to analyze our profession, he was pretty close, I think, when he thought of us as intermediaries. He likened us to performers. Actors who speak other people's lines. Musicians who interpret what composers write.

Though he plucked us from the stratosphere and put us in our proper place, he also soothed our ruffled egos by gently suggesting that some performances could be superb.

To the extent that his analysis is correct, it might be useful to quote an old "square" writer on the subject.

I happen at the moment to be working on a reprint of *Hamlet*. Here is what the author demanded of performers:

"Speak the speech, I pray you, as I pronounce it to you . . . For if you mouth it, as many of your players do, I would as leif the town crier spoke my lines.

"Nor do not saw the air too much with your hand, thus; but use all gently. For in the very torrent, tempest, and as I may say, whirlwind of your passion, you must acquire and beget a temperance that may give it smoothness.

"Be not too tame, neither. Suit the action to the word, the word to the action . . . For anything so overdone is from the purpose of playing, whose end is, to hold, as 'twere, the mirror up to nature.

"And let those who play your clowns speak no more than is set down for them. Go make you ready."

From an address to the Type Directors Club of New York, "Typography—U.S.A.," New York, April 18, 1959. Published in *The Visual Craft of William Golden,* edited by Cipe Pineles Golden, Kurt Weihs, and Robert Strunsky (New York: George Braziller, Inc., 1962).

Typography—"The Eye Is a Creature of Habit"

By David Ogilvy

ood typography *helps* people read your copy, while bad typography prevents them doing so.

Advertising agencies usually set their headlines in capital letters. This is a mistake. Professor Tinker of Stanford has established that capitals retard reading. They have no ascenders or descenders to help you recognize *words,* and tend to be read *letter by letter.*

The eye is a creature of habit. People are accustomed to reading books, magazines, and newspapers in *lower case.* . . .

Another way to make headlines hard to read is to superimpose them on your illustration.

Another mistake is to put a period at the end of headlines. Periods are also called full stops, because they stop the reader dead in his tracks. You will find no full stops at the end of headlines in newspapers.

Yet another common mistake is to set copy in a measure which is too wide or too narrow to be legible. People are accustomed to reading newspapers which are set about forty characters wide.

Which typefaces are easiest to read? Those which people are *accustomed* to reading, like the Century family, Caslon, Baskerville, and Jenson. The more outlandish the typeface, the harder it is to read. The drama belongs in what you say, not in the typeface.

Sans serif faces like this are particularly difficult to read. Says John Updike, "Serifs exist for a purpose. They help the eye pick up the shape of the letter. Piquant in little amounts, sans serif in page-size sheets repels readership as wax paper repels water; it has a sleazy, cloudy look."

Some art directors use copy as the raw material for designing queer shapes, thus making it illegible.

In a recent issue of a magazine I found forty-seven advertisements with the copy set in reverse—white type on a black background. It is almost impossible to read.

If you have to set *very long* copy, there are some typographical devices which increase its readership:

1. A subhead of two lines, between your headline and your body copy; heightens the reader's appetite for the feast to come.
2. If you start your body copy with a drop-initial, you increase readership by an average of 13 percent.
3. Limit your opening paragraph to a maximum of eleven words.
4. After two or three inches of copy, insert a cross-head, and thereafter throughout. Cross-heads keep the reader marching forward. Make some of them interrogative, to excite curiosity in the next run of copy.

5. When I was a boy, it was common practice to square up paragraphs. It is now known that widows—short lines—increase readership.
6. Set key paragraphs in bold face or italic.
7. Help the reader into your paragraphs with arrowheads, bullets, asterisks, and marginal marks.
8. If you have a lot of unrelated facts to recite, don't use cumbersome connectives. Simply number them—as I am doing here.
9. What size type should you use?
<small>This is 5-point and too small to read.</small>

This is 14-point, and too big.

This is 11-point, and about right.
10. If you use leading (line-spacing) between paragraphs, you increase readership by an average of 12 percent.

You may think that I exaggerate the importance of good typography. You may ask if I have ever heard a housewife say that she bought a new detergent because the advertisement was set in Caslon. No. But do you think an advertisement can sell if nobody can read it? You can't save souls in an empty church.

As Mies van der Rohe said of architecture, "God is in the details."

From *Ogilvy on Advertising* (New York: Vintage Books, 1985).

Reflections: Type and Passion

I Am Type

By Frederic W. Goudy

 AM TYPE! Of my earliest ancestry neither history nor relics remain. The wedge-shaped symbols impressed on plastic clay in the dim past by Babylonian builders foreshadowed me. From them through the hieroglyphs of the ancient Egyptians, the lapidary inscriptions of the early Romans, down to the beautiful letters by the scribes of the Italian Renaissance, I was in the making. John Gutenberg was the first to cast me in metal. From his chance thought straying through an idle reverie—a dream most golden—the profound art of printing with movable types was born.

Cold, rigid, implacable I may be, yet the first impress of my face brought the Divine Word to countless thousands. I bring into the light of day the precious stores of knowledge and wisdom long hidden in the grave of ignorance. I coin for you the enchanting tale, the philosopher's moralizing and the poet's visions. I enable you to exchange the irksome hours that come, at times, to every one, for sweet and happy hours with books—golden urns filled with all the manna of the past. In books I present a portion of the eternal mind caught in its progress through the world, stamped in an instant and preserved for eternity. Through me, Socrates and Plato, Chaucer and the bards become your faithful friends who ever surround and minister to you. I am the leaden army that conquers the world: I AM TYPE!

From a pamphlet published by the Village Press, 1931. Reprinted in *A Bibliography of the Village Press,* by Melbert B. Cary, Jr. (New York: The Press of the Woolly Whale, 1938) and in *Looking Closer 3,* edited by Michael Bierut, Jessica Helfand, Steven Heller, and Rick Poynor (New York: Allworth Press, 1999).

I Am Type! Revisited

By Philip B. Meggs

bring into the light of day the precious stores of knowledge and wisdom long hidden in the grave of ignorance. I am the leaden army that conquers the world: I am type!" proclaimed a 1933 broadside designed and written by the great typeface designer Frederic Goudy. Were he alive today, Goudy would probably be alarmed at the turn American type design has taken a half century after his death: His army of lead soldiers has been transformed into a fusillade of electronic bits, bytes, and pixels. Today's computer-based technology permits designers to extend the visual range of type into new directions that Goudy could hardly have foreseen.

Typography is no longer just a craft used to give visual form to the spoken language, for contemporary designers have reconstituted type into symbolic icons and expressive visual forms undreamed of by Goudy and his contemporaries. A number of significant changes in our modern culture have caused this revolution in the noble art of alphabets. In earlier times, the spoken word was ephemeral but the printed word remained fixed on carved stone or printed page. Electronic technology now makes possible the recording of speech, permitting the spoken word to survive just as the printed word does. Typography has thus been freed from a mindset that viewed it as the sole documentary record of human thought.

The kinetics of film, video, and animation have greatly influenced print graphics, resulting in a new emphasis on movement and energy. The ability of type to literally march across the video screen, zoom back into infinity, or rush forward until the dot of a lowercase *i* fills the screen has not been lost on graphic designers working with a static printed page. Capturing the vitality of kinetic energy and freezing it in printing inks is now commonplace.

Visual art has been redefined, and twentieth-century artists and designers have proven that colors, textures, and shapes—including letterforms—have lives of their own apart from their representational or symbolic meaning. In typographic design, this non-verbal level of expression can be teamed with the verbal meaning of words to intensify or enhance the message.

For over five hundred years, type marched in horizontal rows dictated by the relentless constraints of typesetting technology. Today, flexibility abounds. Technology places unprecedented control of space and scale in the hands of the designer. Both enormously large and minutely small sizes of type operate at extremes of scale that disregard the limitations of traditional technology. Spatial configurations warp, bend, fracture, and separate, defying the regimen of Goudy's leaden army. Type can run over, around, and through images with any desired degree of transparency. All of these new possibilities can be accomplished with the click of a mouse. Tracking of letterspacing in measurements of 1/20,000 of an em, using negative line spacing, stretching type, bending it back in space, and setting type in circles, ovals, and any configuration devised by the designer's imagination becomes routine.

Technology alone cannot fully explain the creative freedom of contemporary graphic design. Art moves forward by action and reaction, and many designers seem to be challenging the ease and conformity permitted by computer technology. Some are experimenting with spontaneous—and even crude—yet beautifully designed hand lettering and writing. Collage is used to combine unlike and unexpected shapes, color, and texture. Many designers are fabricating words as solid dimensional objects, capable of being constructed from substances ranging from Plexiglas to cake icing or discarded pieces of wire or metal; anything that can make an image becomes a potential tool for the designer seeking to imbue words with expressive form.

An element of play has entered typographic design, pushing at the seams of conventional wisdom and traditional practice. Designers sometimes propel their work toward the outer limits of legibility, almost as if they were daring the client to reject it or defying the reader to decipher it. Although failures abound, many of the works included here proved that risk-taking can avert disaster and result in graphic design which fascinates the eye with new visions and experiences.

Each of the 175 designs selected for this book appeared in the 1992 edition of *Print's Regional Design Annual*. They are presented much larger and in a more detailed form than is possible in the Annual, and in a context that emphasizes their typographic distinction. The work ranges over the entire spectrum of print communications, and if Goudy were here to review it, he would doubtless amend his broadside to read: "I am the liberated letters that bring into the light of day the precious duality of form and message, freed from the grave of tradition and rigid technology. I am the electronic army that flows around the global village; I am type!"

From the Introduction to *Print's Best Typography* (New York: RC Publications, 1994).

The Dog of Alcibiades: Being a Brief History of Modern Typography or, for That Matter, of Everything Else

By M. F. Agha

nce upon a time, in Ancient Greece, there lived a young man named Alcibiades. He craved affection, but nobody loved him. He craved popularity, but nobody paid any attention to him. So he cut off his dog's tail—and became famous overnight. The whole of Athens talked of nothing but the tailless dog of Alcibiades.

All this is a matter of historic record and a little hard for us to believe. We have seen so many different kinds of dogs, with and without tails, that a tailless dog is no treat to us, but Greek taste was apparently less jaded than ours. A dog's tail was more than just a tail to them; it was a symbol of everything that is wholesome, sound, and Republican. So Alcibiades' little joke assumed the proportions of a refreshing gesture of creative protest against academic routine and aesthetic stagnation. He had many followers.

It soon became evident to these followers that it was a crime to allow any dog to keep his tail. They argued that a tail is nothing but an atavism with hair on; a leftover from the Dark Ages when dogs were lizards and leaped from tree to tree, using their tails as stabilizers; that Man and the better grade of Apes have, in course of Evolution, succeeded in replacing the tail by the coccyx, and that it is our duty to help man's best friend to reach the same civilized state through a little surgical intervention.

They also pointed out that, beside being correct from a cultural viewpoint, a tailless dog would fit much better into the streamlined surroundings created by modern decoration and architecture; that people who live in glass houses should not have dogs with tails.

All this sounded very convincing, and a great many dogs lost their tails and their masters attracted a lot of attention, but the doctrine of Alcibiades was not without opposition. The opposition was formed mainly by people who did not need or want to attract attention: solid citizens with established reputations, merchants with conservative investments, publishers commanding large circulations. Some of them were as violent as the friends of Alcibiades. "We have grown up with our dog's tail," said they. "It guided our first tottering steps. Our habits are formed under its aegis. We will not give it up." Others argued that the roots of the dog's tail go deep down into history. "Our dog's tail was designed by Goudy," said they. "He saw pictures just exactly like it in the Old Dutch manuscripts at the Morgan Library."

The theorists of the opposition submitted that a dog without a tail has no means of expressing an emotion and is apt to alienate the affection of the public by his cold and forbidding appearance; that he looks more like a bear than like a dog, and that any man with a rifle would shoot him on sight.

"Display is a matter of contrast," said they. The dog's tail, this slender, dynamic curve, offers a sharp contrast to the static body of the animal. Cut it off and what is left? Nothing but a dull, gray mass, uninviting to the eye—practically invisible. Why, a dog without a tail would be run over by a chariot in no time at all."

But the Alcibiades movement was spreading, in spite of all opposition. Little by little the conservatives began to feel that no reputation is so well established as to be able to ignore the spirit of the time—no matter how decadent. Timidly, at first, they tried to join the movement. Some of them felt that it is perhaps safer and also more humane to cut the dog's tail not all at once but little by little—an inch a month.

Others thought that, while cutting off the dog's tail is unavoidable if one is to keep up with competition, a dog without a tail looks too angular and geometric, and that a little ornamentation would improve greatly his appearance without destroying the principle. They invited a lot of tail designers and put the problem squarely before them. "Can we," said they, "have a dog which has no tail but looks exactly as though he had one?" The designers offered several solutions.

The most popular one was to supply the tailless dog with an artificial tail made out of chromium and bakelite. A tail was designed somewhat along old Greek lines and was called neoclassic.

Soon, however, sabotage reared its ugly head among tail designers. Some of them, in their heart of hearts, were contaminated by the teachings of Alcibiades; they introduced a new tail made of Nylon and Lucite. Being transparent, this tail was invisible. It was there and could be shown to the auditors, if necessary, but, to the casual observer, the dog with a Lucite tail looked completely tailless.

However, neither the dog with a tail, which looked tailless, nor the tailless dog, which looked as though he had a tail, had a very lasting vogue. The compromise dogs had no news value and, therefore, an urgent need was felt for a further remodeling of the dog.

Strange as it may seem, attempts in this direction were not made by the left wing of the Alcibiades school, but rather by that branch of conservatives which had to deal with the ever-changing and jaded tastes of women. They felt that their license to use imagination and fantasy could be applied to dogs as well as to togas and chitons. They found that an entirely new kind of dog can be produced by plastic surgery, lavishly applied. Soon their dogs were so far removed from the original species that they could hardly be recognized as mammals. In the most advanced form, they had five legs and three tails—all of different lengths, and pointing in all possible directions.

The further progress of this idea, however, was impaired by the discovery of the so-called primitive dog. This dog, which was found painted on the wall of a cavern, had a tail. It was such a nice simple, bucolic tail—neat, but not Gaudy—that it gave complete aesthetic and moral satisfaction to both the partisans of Alcibiades and their enemies. At the same time, the research people, who were checking up on the manufacturing, operating, and maintenance costs of dogs' tails and on their distribution, discovered that the great controversy about dogs' tails did not reach further than the outskirts of Athens and that the rest of the country still had their dogs in their natural state, which was so much like the primitive dog in the cavern you could not tell them apart.

It was an easy matter thereafter for Alcibiades and his friends to procure several country dogs and to lead them triumphantly on the leash along the main street of Athens—the dogs' tails waving like banners in this parade which opened a new era. The parade was a sensation. All of Athens talked of nothing but the dogs of Alcibiades and their wonderful natural tails.

From *Print* 2, no. 1 (May/June 1941).

The Trouble with Type

By Rudy VanderLans

n the article "Decay and Renewal in Typeface Markets," published in *Emigre* no.42, Alan Marshall addresses the age-old complaint of people in the type industry that piracy will ultimately kill the industry. Marshall counters by stating that "Type markets are conditioned by a complex set of economic factors whose force lies in their ability to evolve in the light of social and cultural changes."

Being a relative newcomer in this industry, I can't help but notice that this "evolution" is marked by an increasing lack of respect for the artistic product itself. With the passing of each of the giants of type manufacturing, a new company takes its place selling mostly derivative typefaces, spending fewer dollars on the development of original designs and more dollars on marketing and selling fonts. With a few exceptions, the bulk of the new or surviving foundries and distributors have only one goal: to sell as much type as cheaply as possible without concern for the quality, use, conservation, or development of typefaces. Despite his own accounts on the demise of such influential companies as Monotype and ATF, Marshall, throughout the article, remains steadfast and writes "Total industrial chaos seems just about as unlikely as the threatened collapse of the quality typeface market." He points out, like others before him, that type is really only half the story and that how type is used is what really counts. One solution to type piracy and the preservation of quality type is through education. Educate users about type, and crummy rip-off versions will simply disappear.

While there is much merit in this solution, it is difficult to ignore that the type companies that *did* educate, such as ATF and Monotype, are the ones that have fallen by the wayside or are struggling to survive. Few type companies today invest in the education of type usage and the heritage of type design the way that Monotype or ATF did in the first half of the twentieth century. Compare the Image Club catalog with, let's say, the *ATF Type Specimen* book, or Agfa's printed materials with the *Monotype Recorder*, and you'd have to be blind not to see the obvious difference in quality, both visually and in terms of content. Where are the Stanley Morisons, the Beatrice Wardes, the Jan van Krimpens, the Frederic Goudys, and the Morris Fuller Bentons of today?

Perhaps this is simply a transitional period, and perhaps Marshall is right and ultimately the cream rises to the top. Currently, however, things look rather bleak. One reason why we see ever more companies selling cheap derivatives by the CD load and fewer companies genuinely involved in the design of new typefaces is that the United States, one of the largest typeface markets in the world, continues to deny copyright protection to typeface designs.[1] While there are other methods to protect typeface designs, none is as effective as copyright. Patent protection, for instance, is limited both in terms of time and territory since it is granted for only fourteen years and it is not universally accepted by other countries, as is copyright protection.

The idea behind a copyright is to provide protection to encourage the development of new and innovative work, ultimately for the benefit of society. Without this protection, there is less incentive for individuals or companies to create new work, as it can be copied by anyone the moment it is made public. While copyright protection does not automatically stamp out piracy or infringement, it does give artists the opportunity for legal recourse in the event their work is copied without permission. In the absence of proper protection methods and with copying extremely easy with today's digital technology, companies investing in quality type will continue to disappear, and with them the heritage of five centuries of typeface development. These losses will definitely not benefit anybody.

Typeface piracy has always existed, but it is obvious that with each new technology the act of copying has become easier and that copies have become increasingly indistinguishable from originals. Today it requires literally no expertise of any kind to make a perfect copy of a typeface. Without proper protection, typefaces have become easy targets for opportunists eager to bank on the public's desire for typefaces.

The United States is one of the few, if not only, industrialized nations in the world that does not extend copyright protection to typeface designs. The reason for this comes from the old copyright doctrine that typefaces, like most industrial designs, are considered to be utilitarian and that they exhibit insufficient original authorship. In general, such articles are not copyrightable, unless they contain artistic features capable of existing separately and independently of the overall utilitarian shape. Furthermore, the courts that have upheld the Copyright Office's decision regarding typefaces have also expressed other concerns. By granting copyright protection to typefaces, the court has argued, the freedom of the press might be impeded. But typeface designers do not seek to claim ownership of the alphabet; they seek protection for the various expressions of the alphabet. Designers recognize that as an idea, the alphabet should remain unprotectable, since it is part of the public domain. Typeface designs, on the other hand, are the expressions of that idea. And as expressions of an idea, they constitute original works of authorship.

The Copyright Office's decision to bar all typeface design from copyright protection intrigues me for two reasons. First, it goes to the very core of what a typeface is, a debate that has occupied many pages in *Emigre*. Second, this argument cuts to the very center of our livelihood: the design, manufacture, and distribution of original typeface designs. The Copyright Office's decision, which dates back to 1978, is outdated. The typeface industry has changed significantly since this decision. The postmodern and deconstructivist theories that circulated throughout art schools in the '80s and '90s had a profound influence on the design of typefaces and typography, ultimately freeing them from the restrains of functionality. Coupled with new methods of creating type facilitated by the personal computer, a renaissance in typeface design has taken place that has no precedence in its 500-year history. This fact has been duly noted by curator Ellen Lupton who, in the recent show *Mixing Messages, Graphic Design and Contemporary Culture* at the Smithsonian's Cooper-Hewitt Museum, gave singular attention to typeface design, and reflected upon font production as "a new form of underground publishing."[2]

In today's image-conscious information era, type is taking up an increasingly prominent role in giving shape to the world around us. As such, typeface design is now regularly discussed in the mainstream press, is shown in major museums, and is the topic of countless anthologies, annuals, how-to, and other design books. Typeface design was even the topic of a recent television program on MSNBC's *The Site*. Writer Neil Feineman, quoted in an article about typeface design in the *Los Angeles Times*, reflects upon this recent phenomenon. "Quirky type and page design," he says, "have come to be harnessed simply for their trendiness, not because they blend to create meaning."[3] While trendiness is a description not all type designers like, Feineman's statement does underline how typefaces have moved from being simple carriers of linguistic meaning to expressions of entire trends. Or, as design critic Michael Rock puts it ". . . [typefaces] document and codify the 'current,' generating the artifacts that will serve to frame our own generation."[4] It is this particular quality of secondary meaning and expressivity that has earned the new crop of fonts such high acclaim and exposure, and demonstrates that there is ample original authorship in typeface design.

The Beauty of Type

There are at least two separate aspects to a typeface. First, there is the utilitarian/alphabetic aspect, which allows it to create linguistic meaning when letters are combined into words and words into sentences, etc. The other is the artistic aspect, the different type designs that express the alphabet visually in myriad ways. It is the latter that makes type so desirable because type users recognize the value of differentiation that a particular typeface design brings to their message. This is why they pick one typeface over another with such determination.

Obviously, type is functional as well, but not intrinsically so. First, the individual letters have to be arranged so that they make sense. Context is everything. Once this is accomplished, a typeface can make the spoken word and ideas visible, but it can do so in many different ways. In that respect, a typeface functions much like a photograph or a painting. Just as you can represent a tree differently by photographing or painting it in a variety of styles, so you can represent a text differently by setting it in a number of type styles and sizes.

There are many typefaces that have artistic features that far outweigh their ability to communicate linguistic messages. In fact, there are typefaces that have artistic features that diminish and sometimes render the linguistic utility of the typeface completely useless, making it "illegible." Take the initial caps used in illuminated manuscripts, for instance. While they were considered to be the visual expression of the word of God, much of the verbal meaning was derived from the context in which they were used. It is not the individual letters that are functional. The utility of a typeface also heavily depends upon the intention of the user. Arrange letters arbitrarily and no linguistic meaning is generated; yet the visual, artistic qualities of the typeface remain and can easily be incorporated into all kinds of visuals.

This raises some obvious questions; if a typeface is considered illegible, is it still a typeface? And where exactly does one draw the line between legible and illegible, or, for that matter, between typeface and picture? Take, for instance, the letters created by the artist William Wegman, which are made up of his dogs laid out on the ground to form letter shapes. Are they pictures of dogs, or pictures of alphabetic characters? Is this a typeface, or is this a photographic illustration? Probably all of the above, but what makes them so original is their distinct visual features, not their alphabetic utility.

Regardless of the level of artistic authorship in a typeface, the fact remains that a typeface has a certain level of utility, which is exactly why it is considered unprotectable. What is problematic with this assessment is that all things visual have some level of utility; yet photographs, illustrations, and most other visual expressions are usually granted the copyright protection that is denied to typefaces. What is the intention of the photographer when s/he takes a picture, and what is the intention of the painter when s/he sets out to do a painting, and the illustrator when doing an illustration? Isn't that communication, too? Aren't we asked to "read" a photograph much like we read a text? Take the photographs "utility" as a container of meaning away and what is left? The illustrations in an airline safety guidelines booklet, too, function much like letters. By arranging the separate pictures in a particular order they create meaning—how to jump out of a plane, how to put on an oxygen mask, etc. Or, take a series of panels in a comic strip. Don't these pictures also function much like type? Take the utility of these images away or rearrange the pictures, and little is left. Yet somehow such illustrations seem to be considered by the Copyright Office to be without utilitarian function and are fully copyrightable, as are photographs, paintings, and almost any other kind of visual art.

This exception of excluding typeface designs from copyright protection becomes particularly problematic in relation to typefaces that are pictorial. Regardless of William Wegman's status as a world-renowned artist whose dogs are the subject and object of thousands of pieces of visual art, the moment they laid down on the floor to create letters, according to the Copyright Office's ruling, they lost their status as dogs and became utilitarian objects whose shapes were in the public domain.

Similarly, it would be interesting to hear Disney, a company that rigorously protects its intellectual property rights, argue against anyone taking Mickey Mouse and manipulating him into a twenty-six-letter alphabet. Of course, Wegman and Disney would make the argument that the parts that make up the letters, the photographs of the dogs and drawings of Mickey Mouse, are themselves copyrighted and trademarked icons. But what are most letters but shapes made up of various parts similarly copyrightable? There are typefaces that are made up out of tree parts; some are made out of intricate geometric shapes. BitPull, an electronic typeface designed by the Dutch type laboratory LettError, literally pulls together bits of images of any shape to form letters. I can create copyrightable art by combining any abstract or non-abstract element into infinite variations unless I arrange them such that they become recognizable as letters, at which point they fall in the public domain. An odd idea, don't you think?

The alphabet is a system, but it's an idea that exists without a single fixed expression. It materializes only after the letters have been fully rendered. This can be done in infinite ways, with each interpretation representing an original work of authorship containing significant expressive and artistic qualities. Typefaces, as I've pointed out, can even exist separately and independently of their utility. These are all characteristics that make most forms of art qualify for copyright protection. Therefore, to exclude all typeface designs across the board from copyright protection, simply because of their utilitarian aspect, seems arbitrary, particularly in light of the fact that most forms of art contain utilitarian functions. To exclude typefaces simply because it would be difficult to discern between what some perceive to be the existence of many look-alikes is also moot, since this problem is not unique to typeface design. Thousands of records, books, paintings, and illustrations are produced each year, and each person has the opportunity to register his or her work with the Copyright Office. In case of a dispute, it becomes the court's decision to determine who may claim the work. Typeface designs, on the other hand, are simply not considered worthy.

If there is a positive side to the growing number of companies selling knockoff typefaces by the thousands, it must be that it indicates that the public has an insatiable appetite for type. While it might seem that the pirates are fulfilling a yeoman's job feeding the masses with inexpensive typefaces, it must not be forgotten that the fonts they sell are usually copied from others. Without copyright protection, however, little incentive exists for the companies and individuals who actually produce these typefaces to continue to invest in the development of new typefaces or the adaptation of existing typefaces to emerging technologies. Instead, we will be left with dozens of companies selling knockoff fonts, run by individuals who feel it is within their legal right to copy any typeface the minute it comes out. None has an interest in typefaces beyond their profitability, which is obvious by the complete absence of product source information. While their CDs often boast the inclusion of award-winning "designer" fonts, we are usually left guessing who these designers are. No design methods are discussed, and no references are ever made as to the source material of the typeface designs. While they might brag that we all stand on the shoulders of giants, they never disclose who these giants are, since historical references are never mentioned. Thus the anonymity of both typeface origin and designers is perpetuated, and little by little, with each supersaver release, the heritage of typeface design is erased.

Typeface design is a living and breathing art form which, as Paul Elliman points out, imbues its models with attributes that "convey the dynamics of history, anthropology, linguistics, political science, sociology, economics, and so on."[5] It is a sad fact that we allow the people who are the least interested in typeface design, the knockoff companies who are tripping all over themselves to release poor quality derivatives, to benefit the most from it. I guess those typefaces, too, tell us something about our culture, but it's hardly something to be proud of. I would like to believe that Alan Marshall is right, and that the type industry and quality typefaces will survive. Copyright protection would greatly serve this ideal, but it's something that needs to be actively pursued. This article is one of my contributions to a much larger effort by type aficionados from around the world who are determined to win copyright protection for typeface design in the United States.[6]

227

---

[1]Before you run off and start copying all your friends' typefaces, beware that certain parts and functions of the font software are copyrightable, and that certain typefaces also have design patents, trademarked names, licensing restrictions and other forms of protection.

[2]Ellen Lupton, *Mixing Messages: Graphic Design in Contemporary Culture.* New York: Cooper-Hewitt National Design Museum and Princeton Architectural Press, 1996.

[3]Irene Lacher, "The Difficult Type," *Los Angeles Times,* June 28, 1993.

[4]Michael Rock, "Typefaces Are Rich with the Gesture and Spirit of Their Own Era," *I.D,* (May/June 1992).

[5]Paul Elliman, "Reading Typography Writing Language," *Fuse 10, Freeform* (Summer 1994).

[6]A diverse collective of type designers and specialists has formed an advocacy group determined to win copyright protection for font designs in the United States. TypeRight is an independent organization devoted to education and informing the public about why copyright is needed for fonts and encouraging members of the digital design community to urge their Congressional representatives to amend U.S. law to protect typeface designs. Central to this effort is TypeRight's Website, at *http://www.typeright.org.*

From *Emigre,* no. 43 (Summer 1997).

Experiments in Type Design

By Tobias Frere-Jones

he design of my own typefaces is often punctuated by questions. For the last six years or so, any free time has been spent delving into various questions regarding type design—how these forms behave on a page, how we pull meaning from text, the limits of legibility, the role of context, and so on. These are more trains of thought than typefaces, and I will present them as I worked on them. None of these are really finished: there are no conclusions here, only a progress report of what I've found. For this collection, I have selected a few of the more complete efforts.

This is not meant as a definitive statement of a typographic philosophy, nor is there necessarily any link from one design to the next. Each font is a catalyst, not necessarily an end product. A font is made, and the process continues, perhaps to another font later on.

Cassandra

If we have all the ingredients, do we need the same recipe?

Some time ago, I was thinking about what makes one character different from another. On each character there is a structure which makes it distinct from all others, an event or a detail that will make it completely *A,* undeniably *R,* and so on.

I remembered the numbered dials of gas pumps and odometers, spinning around and stopping between one character and the next. I remembered seeing the pump attendants jigger the pump so that it read exactly ten gallons or fifteen dollars or whatever was appropriate. What was the point? If you can see all of a one, a five, a zero, and part of another zero, then it must be fifteen dollars. (The value of gasoline was foreign to me; I thought the only reason was to make a neat and tidy display on the gas pump.) I realized that if you see half of a zero, you must also be seeing half of a nine, and both would probably be legible. The display could conceivably read fifteen dollars and nine cents.

Fiddling with these wheels some sixteen years later, the question resurfaced. Given half a nine and half a zero, what conclusion would we draw? Choosing between nine and zero is actually a question of context, and what concerned me was: If we need only a part of a character to recognize it (usually the top), would we be confused by seeing the rest somewhere else? If a character were split horizontally, and the upper and lower halves were switched, could we read it? All that would change would be arrangement: no elements would be added or subtracted.

If an *H* is two verticals and one horizontal, do we need anything else? Or, more interestingly: If an *H* is two verticals and one horizontal, does the order of those parts matter? If we have all the necessary ingredients, do we need the same recipe?

THE QUICK BROWN FOX JUMPS OVER
THE QUICK BROWN FOX JUMPS OVER
A LAZY DOG PACK MY BOX WITH FIVE
DOZEN LIQUOR JUGS THE QUICK BRO
DOZEN LIQUOR JUGS THE QUICK BRO

Now it was time to make some tests. Garage Gothic, a typeface I had designed the previous summer, was used as grist to rearrange and consider. In any typeface, each character
is placed within a blank rectangle called the body. When text is set, these boxes are
stacked up next to each other, just as though it were metal type. The relation of a character to the sides of the body will determine its standard spacing. The relation to the top
and bottom of the body effects line spacing; "solid leading" would mean that these boxes
are stacked directly atop each other. To investigate the effects of the window in the original gas pump, the type body itself could serve as a surrogate. Once the characters were
cut apart, the fragments were put flush to the edge of the body, like the numbers being
cut off by the window. With the characters pushed to the edges of the body (quite rare in
any conventional font), some interesting situations would occur when setting text. If no
leading were introduced, the half-characters would recombine into new (and probably
unintelligible) characters.

I had put the edges of each character fragment flush to the edges of the body, making
for some unexpected results with solid leading:

Proximity grouping is the tendency to read objects near each other as one unit, and
subjective contour is the perceived completion of an implied form. Proximity grouping
pushes us towards the conclusion that these half-characters must be full characters,
because their parts seem to connect and relate. The way that they don't quite line up (in
most cases) creates a subjective contour that redirects us towards the "real" characters.
Running through each combined character is the suggestion of a line, which is the edge
of the body itself, revealing where each character really begins and ends. The role of
white space is inverted here: where it usually separates one form from the next, its function here is to connect the two character fragments.

What I had created was a conflict between perception and experience, based in the
reader's assumptions of completeness. It is a natural tendency to seek the simplest possible
structure, and here, it leads to confusion; the path of least resistance becomes a dead end.

As in the cryptic speech of a prophet, meaning is lost in a straightforward interpretation;
the reader must take a circuitous route in exhuming content from this unfamiliar structure.

Illinois

During the first semester of my junior year, I was designing a typeface named Evangelica,
loosely based on the Nicholas Jenson type of 1470. In the process, my attention was
drawn to a decision that faces any designer using a letterpress font as a model. Were the
forms cut in metal the intended design, or the image printed on paper? Although I never
completed Evangelica, this question in a more general form came back to me later as I

a a

The quick brown fox
jumps over the lazy dog?
PACK MY BOX WITH FIVE
DOZEN LIQUOR JUGS!

read a description of Stempel Garamond. It was said that this version, in opposition to most others, took the punch-cut, not the printed, character as its model. The question here is whether the original or the copy is the true "typeface."

Is the "typeface" what the designer makes, or what the reader sees?

Technology soon becomes important, because copying a set of forms and disseminating them implies the use (and influence) of technology. What then, is the role of the technology in determining the identity of a font? With all these different Garamonds now being spit out of laser printers and Linotrons, the question is only more urgent. Does the "typeface" appear at the beginning or the end of the production cycle?

The original or the copy? The means or the end?

I needed a piece of concrete evidence to consider. I chose the most chunky of digital faces, Chicago, for my experiment. I made a metal printing plate of the Chicago character set, and printed it on a letterpress.

Chicago is a typeface originally designed for screen displays on the Macintosh system, and its appearance reflects this original purpose. I created a zinc plate of the Chicago character set, allowing me to print it as though it were lead type, reversing the normal

The quick brown fox
jumps over the lazy dog?
PACK MY BOX WITH FIVE
DOZEN LIQUOR JUGS!

process of technical translation. This new metal type was then printed on a letterpress, with an effort to exaggerate the effects of this process (too much ink, too much pressure, all on cheap paper). The resulting prints were digitized as the basis of a new typeface, Illinois. The printed copy became the original for the new digital font. The questions can now be more specific: What is its identity? It's possible to call it a computer font, because that's where it began and ended, but it visibly carries the influence of the letterpress.

How does Illinois differ from Chicago? Is it really different? What is a typeface, anyway? How do we define it?

Based on the instinct which guides all this research in the first place, and not on any empirical proof, I have a guess. During the design of a typeface, the designer creates a set of rules and algorithms that dictate the total effect of the final product, from details like serif brackets to generalities like character spacing. We react to the total effect of these original rules and not to individual form changes precipitated by a technology.

Our first example may serve to clarify. Is the "real" Garamond in metal or on paper (or in binary, for that matter)? It doesn't matter, because the form changes from one technology to another are essentially irrelevant. Those decisions that made these characters Garamond characters are still in evidence. While those decisions may be influenced by the potential of a specific medium, the typeface, in its purest sense, is completely independent of the supporting technology.

What is so "Garamond" about Garamond is a specific procedure.

The typeface is a mechanism, designed to take an input (the Latin alphabet, in this case) and spit out a product (a character set). We can only recognize this procedure from its result, so it's easy to think that Garamond is just a set of characters, when, in fact, the Garamond procedure could be applied to anything from life drawing to automotive design, because of its inherent abstraction. How else could dingbats and fleurons ever relate to a specific typeface, as they are often meant to? The font-logic has no relation to the alphabet, either. "Garamond" is abstract, and its only recognized application is in type design.

Echo

As suggested by Oliver Selfridge's "Pandemonium" model of recognition, we assign meaning to forms through comparison—not to the images of what we've seen before, but to a list of their attributes.

To take the example of a capital *A,* this list may call for something triangular (usually), some kind of horizontal element, and an open base. We're all familiar with the forms that can satisfy these criteria, and therefore be recognized as *A.*

But are these the only approaches to the problem? Could the list of requirements be satisfied with different methods? Could a new approach deliver the same effect?

We reach the next project, called Echo. It begins with a basic sans serif, which follows a very straightforward model of character structure. The contour of these characters was then cut apart and looped back on itself, to deliver the same image in an unfamiliar way.

After several cycles of feedback and distortion, I still had the right recipe, but entirely different ingredients. Because it depends on a perception of area rather than edge or line, it has the unusual effect of being more legible the smaller it is set.

Microphone

A short time ago, I was asked to make a contribution to the fifteenth issue of *Fuse,* with the theme of cities. I considered working with surveillance, crime, mass transit, urban planning, and so on. What came to mind, though, was the line that used to introduce an old

AN'T DO ANYTHING WE FORGOT

I SCHEDULE he'll get o
RIGHT IN THE MIDDLE OF THE STREET WI
I st hope what are you looking at? I CAN'T
you're looking for a pistol, right?

o you know what she said? it's so beaut RIGHT NOW he
n-sixteen
hello
e not going to do that are you?
HEY TRICKED you just take it hello
DON'T ASK ME OK YOUR ATTE
RUNNING AWAY FROM SOMETHING st how they rea

American TV show: "There are six million stories in the naked city." I decided to approach this theme from a social angle, focusing on how its inhabitants talk to each other.

I walked around Boston, eavesdropping on people's conversations as they passed by. I kept notes of what I heard, and used the text for a typeface called Microphone.

In the Microphone character set, these fragments of conversation were used in place of individual letters. A single character in Microphone will trigger an entire phrase.

The style, size, and spacing of each phrase were chosen to reflect the different voices I heard.

Rather than leave each phrase carefully clear of its neighbors, each one is spaced so it overlaps the others, like the simultaneous and confusing sounds of the city.

Microphone does not treat text as content to be rendered and presented as any other typeface would. Instead it treats text as a sequence of "plot" generator. Text set in Microphone becomes a ready-made recording of conversations in the street.

More than anything else, Microphone is a short story, which uses the digital font format for its ability for rearrangement.

Sum of the Parts

While I was a student at the Rhode Island School of Design, I had an argument with another student. He had dreamt up a system that he thought would be the ultimate scientific measure of legibility. You would begin by placing each character on a grid, which would create an image of pixels.

You then compare that bunch of pixels to all the other images you could make from the same grid, thereby finding its position in the spectrum from most legible to the least. From its position on that scale, you could prove that Garamond rates an 82 on the legibility scale, and Caslon rates an 87, and so on. I thought it was a nice idea and all, but it would never work correctly, because it ignores context. He seemed confused, and said that if we can read a letter in a sentence, and in a paragraph of text, we must be able to read it on its own. I told him no, no, no. It doesn't work that way. Context is too important. I don't know how or when, but I will draw a typeface that proves you wrong.

I believe that you can learn a lot about how something works by figuring out how to make it stop working. Watching a system struggle and collapse can tell you about what that system needs and what it doesn't. With that in mind, I made an approach to proving my friend wrong about context.

After examining some truly illegible handwriting samples, I began this face, called Sum of the Parts. It uses its sloppy, handwritten origins as a guise for its real purpose: to blur character identities. Although there appear to be twenty-six distinct characters here, there are only eleven. Each form represents at least two other letters, and context will tell you which role a letter is playing at any given moment.

It functions, then, as a potentially effective code (for a typeface, at least), because the identity, or key, to the system is always in flux. In drawing a form and calling it *a*, we submit to the established system of character shape and identity. A necessary part of that system is that character shapes are mutually exclusive. A successful *a* and *d* look nothing alike.

Here was the device for me to tamper with. What would happen if I removed the quality of mutual exclusivity? How could I introduce this kind of confusion? Legibility is normally a responsibility shared by form, context, and experience. The goal of this "exercise in obscurity" was to shift all of the responsibility to context and experience. The characters of this face were drawn to rest on the borderline between two or more identities, leaving the reader to push them into or the other. With context being the key, the face was named "Sum of the Parts." But because you only get eleven characters instead of twenty-six, it has the alternate name "Some of the Parts."

Conclusion

As I said, there are no conclusions here, but only what I've found so far. If you agree with what I've found, that's terrific. If you don't, that's even better, because then we can argue and find more answers and, more importantly, more questions.

From *AIGA Boston Journal* 2 (1999).

Electronic Typography

By Jessica Helfand

n 1968, Mattel introduced Talking Barbie. I like to think of this as my first computer. I remember saving up my allowance for what seemed an eternity to buy one. To make her talk, you pulled a little string; upon its release, slave-to-fashion Barbie would utter delightful little conversational quips like "I think mini-skirts are smashing" and "Let's have a costume party."

If you held the string back slightly as she was talking, her voice would drop a few octaves, transforming her from a chirpy soprano into a slurpy baritone. What came out then sounded a lot more like "Let's have a cocktail party."

I loved that part. What I loved was playing director—casting her in a new role, assigning her a new (albeit ludicrous) personality. I loved controlling the tone of her voice, altering the rhythm of her words, modulating her oh-so-minimal (and moronic) vocabulary. I loved having the power to shape her language—something I would later investigate typographically, as I struggled to understand the role of the printed word as an emissary of spoken communication.

Twenty-five years later, my Macintosh sounds a lot like my Barbie did then—the same monotone, genderless, robotic drawl.

But here in the digital age, the relationship between design and sound—and in particular, between the spoken word and the written word—goes far beyond pulling a string. The truth is that the computer's internal sound capabilities enable us to design with sound, not just in imitation of it. Like it or not, the changes brought about by recent advances in technology (and here I am referring primarily to interactive media) indicate the need for designers to broaden their understanding of what it is to work effectively with typography. It is no longer enough to design for readability, to suggest a sentiment, or reinforce a concept through the selection of a particular font. Today, we can make type talk: in any language, at any volume, with musical underscoring or sci-fi sound effects or overlapping violins. We can sequence and dissolve, pan and tilt, fade to black, and specify type in sensurround. As we "set" type, we encounter a decision-making process unprecedented in two-dimensional design: unlike the kinetic experience of turning a printed page to sequence information, here, time becomes a powerful and persuasive design element. Today, we can visualize concepts in four action-packed, digital dimensions.

Interactive media have introduced a new visual language, one that is no longer bound to traditional definitions of word and image, form and place. Typography, in an environment that offers such diverse riches, must redefine its goals, its purpose, its very identity. It must reinvent itself. And soon.

Visual language, or the interpretation of spoken words through typographic expression, has long been a source of inspiration to artists and writers. Examples abound, dating as far back as the incunabula and extending upwards from concrete poetry in the '20s to "happenings" in the '60s to today's multicultural morass of pop culture. Visual wordplay proliferates, in this century in particular, from F. T. Marinetti's *Parole in Libertà* to George

Maciunas' *Fluxus* installations to the latest MTA posters adorning New York subway walls. Kurt Schwitters, Guillaume Apollinaire, Piet Zwart, Robert Brownjohn—the list is long, the examples inexhaustible. For designers there has always been an overwhelming interest in formalism, in analyzing the role of type as medium (structure), message (syntax), and muse (sensibility). Throughout, there has been an attempt to reconcile the relationship between words both spoken and seen—a source of exhilaration to some and ennui to others. Lamenting the expressive limitations of the western alphabet, Adolf Loos explained it simply: "One cannot *speak* a capital letter." Denouncing its structural failings, Stanley Morison was equally at odds with a tradition that designated hierarchies in the form of upper and lowercase letterforms. Preferring to shape language as he deemed appropriate, Morison referred to caps as "a necessary evil."

Academic debate over the relationship between language and form has enjoyed renewed popularity in recent years as designers borrow from linguistic models in an attempt to codify—and clarify—their own typographic explorations. Deconstruction's design devotees have eagerly appropriated its terminology and theory, hoping to introduce a new vocabulary for design: it is the vocabulary of signifiers and signifieds, of Jacques Derrida and Ferdinand de Saussure, of Michel Foucault and Umberto Eco.

As a comprehensive model for evaluating typographic expression, deconstruction has ultimately proved both heady and limited. Today, as advances in technology introduce greater and more complex creative challenges, it is simply arcane. We need to look at screen-based typography as a new language, with its own grammar, its own syntax, and its own rules. What we need are new and better models, models that go beyond language or typography per se, and that reinforce rather than restrict our understanding of what it is to design with electronic media: what Wendy Richmond has called "extreme and unusual metaphors."

Learning a new language is one thing, fluency quite another. Yet we've come to equate fluency with literacy—another outdated model for evaluation. "Literacy should not mean the ability to decode strings of alphabetic letters," says Seymour Papert, Director of the Epistemology and Learning Group at the MIT Media Lab, who refers to such a definition as "letteracy." And language, even to linguists, proves creatively limiting as a paradigm. "New media promise the opportunity to offer a smoother transition to what really deserves to be called literacy," says Papert. Typography, as the physical embodiment of such thinking, has quite a way to go.

The will to decipher the formal properties of language, a topic of great consequence for communication designers in general, has its philosophical antecedents in ancient Greece. "Spoken words," wrote Aristotle in *Logic,* "are the symbols of mental experience. Written words are the symbols of spoken words." Today, centuries later, the equation has added a new link: What happens when written words can speak? When they can move? When they can be imbued with sound and tone and nuance and decibel and harmony and voice? As designers probing the creative parameters of this new technology, our goal may be less to digitize than to dramatize. Indeed, there is a theatrical component that I am convinced is essential to this new thinking. Of what value are typographic choices— bold and italics, for example—when words can dance across the screen, dissolve, or disappear altogether?

In this dynamic landscape, our static definitions of typography appear increasingly imperiled. Will the beauty of traditional letterforms be compromised by the evils of this new technology? Will punctuation be stripped of its functional contributions, or ligatures their aesthetic ones? Will type really matter?

Of course it will.

In the meantime, however, typography's early appearance on the digital frontier doesn't bode well for design. Take e-mail, for example. Gone are the days of good handwriting, of the Palmer Method and the penmanship primer. In its place, electronic mail, which despite its futuristic tone, has paradoxically revived the antiquated art of letter writing. Sending e-mail is easy and effortless and quick. For those of us who spend a good deal of our professional lives on the telephone, it offers a welcome respite from talking, and, consequently, bears a closer stylistic resemblance to conversational speech than to written language. However, for those of us with even the most modest design sense, it eliminates the distinctiveness that typography has traditionally brought to our written communiqués. Though its supporters endorse the democratic nature of such homogeneity, the truth is, it's boring. In the land of e-mail, we all "sound" alike: Everyone writes in system fonts.

E-mail is laden with such contradictions: ubiquitous in form yet highly diverse in content, at once ephemeral and archival, transmitted in real time yet physically intangible. E-mail is a kind of aesthetic flatland, informationally dense and visually unimaginative. Here, hierarchies are preordained and nonnegotiable: passwords, menus, commands, help. Commercial services like America Online require that we title our mail, a leftover model from the days of interoffice correspondence, which makes even the most casual letter sound like a corporate memo. As a result, electronic missives all have headlines: Titling our letters makes us better editors, not better designers. As a fitting metaphor for the distilled quality of things digital, the focus in e-mail is on the abridged, the acronym, the quick read. E-mail is functionally serviceable and visually forgettable, not unlike fast food. It's drive-through design: get in, get out, move on.

And it's everywhere. Here is the biggest contribution to communication technology to come out of the last decade, a global network linking some 50 million people worldwide, and designers—communication designers, no less—are nowhere in sight.

Typography, in this environment, desperately needs direction. Where to start? Comparisons with printed matter inevitably fail, as words in the digital domain are processed with a speed unprecedented in the world of paper. Here, they are incorporated into databases or interactive programs, where they are transmitted and accessed in random, nonhierarchical sequences. "Hypertext," or the ability to program text with interactivity—meaning that a word, when clicked upon or pointed to will actually do something—takes it all a step further: By introducing alternate paths, information lacks the closure of the traditional printed narrative. "Hypertextual story space is now multidimensional," explains the novelist Robert Coover in a recent issue of *Artforum,* "and theoretically infinite."

If graphic design can be largely characterized by its attention to understanding the hierarchy of information (and using type in accordance with such understanding), then how are we to determine its use in a nonlinear context such as this? On a purely visual level, we are limited by what the pixel will render: the screen matrix simulates curves with surprising sophistication, but hair-lines and serifs will, to the serious typophile, appear inevitably compromised. On a more objective level, type in this context is both silent and static, and must compete with sound and motion—not an easy task, even in the best of circumstances. Conversely, in the era of the handheld television remote, where the user can—and does—mute at will, the visual impact of written typography is not to be discounted. To better analyze the role(s) of electronic typography, we might begin by looking outside: not to remote classifications imported from linguistic textbooks, or even to traditional design theories conveniently repackaged, but to our own innate intelligence and distinctive powers of creative thought. To cultivate and adequately develop this new typography (because if we don't, no one else will), we might do well to rethink visual language altogether, to consider new and alternative perspectives. "If language is indeed the limit of our world," writes literary critic William Gass in *Habitations of the Word,* "then we must find another, larger, stronger, more inventive language which will burst those limits."

In his book *Seeing Voices,* author and neurologist Oliver Sacks reflects on the complexity of sign language, and describes the cognitive understanding of spatial grammar in a language that exists without sound. He cites the example of a deaf child learning to sign, and details the remarkable quality of her visual awareness and descriptive, spatial capabilities. "By the age of four, indeed, Charlotte had advanced so far into visual thinking and language that she was able to provide new ways of thinking—revelations—to her parents." As a consequence of learning sign language as adults, this particular child's parents not only learned a new language, but discovered new ways of thinking as well—visual thinking. Imagine the potential for interactive media if designers were to approach electronic typography with this kind of ingenuity and openmindedness.

William Stokoe, a Chaucer scholar who taught Shakespeare at Gallaudet College in the 1950s, summarized it this way: "In a signed language, narrative is no longer linear and prosaic. Instead, the essence of sign language is to cut from a normal view to a close-up to a distant shot to a close-up again, and so on, even including flashback and fast-forward scenes, exactly as a movie editor works." Here, perhaps, is another model for visual thinking: a new way of shaping meaning based on multiple points of view, which sees language as part of a more comprehensive communication platform—time-sensitive, interactive, and highly visual. Much like multimedia.

From *Six Essays on Design and New Media* (New York: William Drenttel, 1995).

238

A Face by Any Other Name Is Still My Face:
A Tale of Type Piracy

By David Pankow

n June 1929 a passionate complaint by Rudolf Koch, the great German type designer was published in the magazine *Gebrauchsgraphik; International Advertising Art*. Titled "Geistiger Diebstahl/Intellectual Theft," Koch's article castigated the American Type Founders Company for appropriating his Koch Antiqua typeface (called Eve for its release in the U.S.) and issuing it with slight design modifications under the name Rivoli. ATF was accused in no uncertain terms of "committing highway robbery of German intellectual property." Before the controversy faded from view, a number of the major printing periodicals of the day and many influential figures in the graphic arts industry had been drawn into the fray. It was from the beginning a conflict which stirred up strong emotions and prompted an escalating series of charges and counter-charges.

Since the early sixteenth century, type designers have fought the misappropriation of their faces, but rarely has such a dispute been aired as thoroughly and publicly as this one. And even though it took place some seventy years ago, the perplexing problem it raises— that of what confers originality upon a type design—is as immediate and thought-provoking as ever. Moreover, because there is still no copyright protection for type designs in the United States, the issues raised by Koch and his adversaries continue to be relevant and worth re-examining.

The story begins in late 1925, when a former executive for the Remington Typewriter Company, Melbert B. Cary, Jr. established the Continental Typefounders' Association in New York City, with himself as president and Douglas C. McMurtrie as vice-president. The Continental, as it came to be known, aimed to provide American printers and advertisers with a series of dashing, provocative, and, most importantly, novel types. Most of these were manufactured by European foundries, cast or machined to American standards, and imported into the U.S. by Continental. Melbert Cary neatly stated the objectives of his company in the introduction to his first specimen book:

> A few of the most enterprising typographers in the larger cities have enriched their cases, at considerable trouble and expense, with some of the many strikingly attractive type faces produced by the foreign foundries. But the difference in the point system and height-to-paper of continental type; the distance from the source of supply; the expense of transportation in small quantities, the customs duties, and the difficulty of negotiating satisfactorily in a foreign language by mail, all have combined to make these famous foreign typefaces practically inaccessible to the progressive American printer.
>
> The Continental Typefounders Association has been organized to put at the disposal of printers and typographers in the United States a careful selection from the wealth of beautiful faces produced by the French, Dutch, English,

TYPE DESIGNS
that are well=drawn

DEMANDS
particular set=up

German, and Spanish typefoundries, . . . all cast to American height-to-paper and standard body size; at prices which will enable high class printers and typographers to offer their customers an entirely new face whenever the distinctiveness of an old one has become dulled by constant repetition.[1]

Among the European and English foundries whose types appeared in that first specimen were Deberny & Peignot (represented by Astrée), Klingspor (Narcissus), and Richard Gans (Greco), as well as decorative material from the R. H. Stevens foundry. The new types soon began appearing in the advertising of such department stores as B. Altman, Franklin Simon, and Macy's. By 1927, Le Mercure, Caslon Old Face, Lutetia, Eve (Koch Antiqua), and Neuland were added. Eve soon became one of the most popular types in Continental's inventory.

Its name notwithstanding, Continental also negotiated a distribution agreement with Frederic Goudy to handle the faces produced in the U.S. at his small by influential Village Letter Foundry, thereby relieving Goudy of having "to tie up with his own fair hands a half pound of type telegraphed for by a printer in Oklahoma."[2] This arrangement secured the popular types Kennerley, Goudy Modern, Hadriano, and Forum. Goudy himself was then in the interesting position of owing allegiance to three different American typeface suppliers: He had an agreement to design several new faces a year for American Type Founders; from 1920, he was the art director for the Lanston Monotype Company; and, around 1927, he replaced Douglas McMurtrie as vice-president of Continental Typefounders. He soon discovered the complications that came with simultaneous allegiances to increasingly contentious rivals.

Melbert Cary was indefatigable in promoting the interests of his firm. Cary of the Continental, as he became known, was a familiar and ubiquitous guest speaker at Craftsmans' Club luncheons and various typographic and advertising society meetings throughout the country; he also received generous press coverage in American printing trade journals. Continental was aggressive in its advertising, distributing thousands of beautifully printed, striking specimens of its typefaces, usually free for the asking.

**HEN** we discover here and there a printer wasting his energies and abilities in the vain endeavor to execute printing to the satisfaction of his clients with type lacking in originality, in art, and devoid of the life that can only be imparted by a genius in designing, we are reminded of the cruel task allotted to the Hebrews by the old Egyptians. There is neither profit nor pleasure in trying to impart an artistic effect with inartistic type. It is a question whether the durability of such type is not an added injury to the unfortunate printer who uses it. Pound for pound the type of the American Type Founders Co. costs no more than type unenlivened by artistic merit; but in its true value it surpasses all other type as the masterpieces £376

See Index for Jenson Initials and Jenson Embellishments suitable for use with above Series

AMERICANS have realized within recent years that there are some provinces by the sea, located as the mariners would say nor'-nor'east of us, which for wholesome climate and varied sights offer a greater wealth of attractions during summer days than is possessed by any other nearby region. Geographers have given to them the name of Maritime Provinces

Above: ATF's Jenson Oldstyle, based on William Morris's Golden type; below: ATF's Satanick type, based on Morris's Chaucer type.

As the supply of foreign types increased in the U.S., there was bound to be a vigorous reaction from the American Type Founders Company, by far the largest manufacturer of foundry type in the U.S. ATF had been incorporated in 1892 as an amalgamation of some twenty–three foundries, largely in response to the withering, long–standing competition between these foundries and the looming menace presented by the composing machine manufacturers, principally Mergenthaler Linotype and Lanston Monotype. The early years of ATF were spent in consolidating resources and imposing a central authority over the company.

Many of the bizarre and eccentric types developed during the nineteenth century were purged from the ATF's specimen books and the company embarked on a program of introducing sensible new designs and reviving old classics. Its first great successes were Jenson Oldstyle and Satanick, both modeled on the private types of William Morris. Under the design leadership of Morris Fuller Benton, more blockbuster sales followed the release of the Cheltenham and Century families, followed by the ATF revivals of Bodoni and Garamond designs. Despite its impressive sales of body types and the very real talents of Morris Benton and his assistants, ATF seems to have been caught a little offguard by the 1920s craze for modernist types. There were very few stylistically daring typefaces in ATF's massive 1923 specimen book, except perhaps for faces like Hobo and Souvenir, both Benton designs. However monolithic and conservative it was at first, ATF was not unaware of new European designs and, as Cary acknowledged,

the beginning of the importation of foreign faces and the start of new designing in this country was pioneered by the American Typefounders Co.
Association, who brought Nicolas Cochin from France. This was followed
closely by the Linotype interests who used Narcisse, making their first big display in the advertisement of Altman's department store of New York City.[3]

Broadway appeared in 1926 and was a genuine success, but ATF struggled to produce
equally striking advertising faces to blunt the impact of the dynamic foreign types. Later
in the '20s, ATF tried to catch up with advertising faces like Benton's quirkily charming
Novel Gothic. Barnhart Bros. & Spindler, one of ATF's satellite foundries, released Japanet
as one of its contributions to the modernistic craze, but it was nothing more than a
warmed-over reissue of Wedge Gothic, a BB & S face from 1893. Cary seemed unconcerned by these or any of the other new types, dismissing them as the work of "so-called
designers [who] started to work in America, producing such short-lived faces as Nubian,
Gallia, Parisienne, Sheik, Cubist, Modernique, and many others of little note."[4]

In September 1927 an International Graphic Arts Exposition was held in New York
City to which the Stempel Typefoundry of Frankfurt came with a carefully prepared
exhibition of German printing, as well as settings in English of Stempel typefaces.
Members of the Stempel delegation included David Stempel, one of the founders of the
firm, and Dr. Rudolf Wolf, Stempel's director of typeface development, who also wrote
an account of their visit.[5] The exposition presented an opportunity to gauge at first hand
the American reactions to the latest in German typography, determine export potentials

for Stempel types, and provide an excuse for making diverting sidetrips to celebrated
American printing plants like R. R. Donnelley and William Edwin Rudge. Stempel and
Wolf were encouraged by the enthusiastic responses to their firm's exhibit and by what
they perceived as a strong interest in German type design, especially Lucian Bernhard's
vastly popular Bernhard Cursive (originally, Bernhard Schönschrift), marketed by the rival
Bauer foundry through its recently established sales office in New York City. As for ATF's
type display, Wolf was not impressed:

> In its type policy ATF seems to go from one extreme to the next, a strictly
> conservative attitude to extreme modernism. The amazing thing is that these
> new creations do not even correspond to the graphic lettering on posters and
> advertising pieces [presumably ATF's] and also are not a good expression of
> contemporary forms. In Germany, we could not afford such types where one is
> used to a more daring originality.[6]

During its visit to the U.S., the Stempel delegation was approached by Melbert Cary,
who hoped to represent Stempel interests in the United States. After consulting with
Harry Gage, an executive with Mergenthaler Linotype, David Stempel was persuaded that
an alliance with Continental might cause offense and was urged instead to seek a collaborative arrangement with ATF through a meeting with its president, Frank B. Berry. At a
subsequent conference, ATF insisted on obtaining the matrices for Stempel types so that
it could cast as well as distribute these faces in the U.S. This was an intolerable condition
for the Germans, and the negotiations never went further than this preliminary discussion. Shortly thereafter, Rudolf Wolf met with Melbert Cary and, after some considera-

AN ADVANCED TYPE STYLE NOW OFFERED IN
THIRTEEN SIZES FROM SIX TO SEVENTY-TWO POINT

NOVEL GOTHIC

Modernism in typography came in response to a widespread desire for striking new type designs that would be more expressive and typical of the current development in architecture, industry, commerce and, of course, in advertising

AMERICAN TYPE FOUNDERS COMPANY

ATF's Novel Gothic typeface, originated by Charles H. Becker of ATF's matrix department and completed by Morris Fuller Benton for release in 1928.

tion, settled on the Continental Typefounders' Association as its exclusive American sales representative.[7] Wolf knew that such an alliance would not come without cost. He wrote in his report that, in transferring its agency to Continental, Stempel would have to "support this company with samples and promotion material of the most excellent quality in the most generous way, as it is clear that the development of an extensive business in America is not possible without spending great resources." He also realized that there were risks other than financial, noting that "it must also be brought to attention that in America there is no legal protection for artistic products."[8] Nonetheless, a deal was struck, under which Adastra, designed by Herbert Thannhäuser, became one of the first typefaces made available in the U.S.

Continental continued to prosper, and the introduction to its 1929 specimen book bubbled over with enthusiasm: "In the following pages are shown great types, great because it has been possible to pick and choose from the trials and failures of a dozen great foundries, leaving aside the poor and the merely good and importing only the best."[9] Among the dynamic new display faces were Stempel's Metropolis, by Willy Schwerdtner; Gloria, from the Gans foundry in Madrid; and Deberny & Peignot's Bifur, by A. M. Cassandre. Continental's most popular European import, however, was still Rudolf Koch's Eve type. One contemporary analysis of Eve was written in a style very much like a wine review:

> [Eve] seems more typical of the American spirit than any American-designed face we have; individual, lively, crisp even to the point of brittleness, clean-cut—and yet evincing a flash of crudeness from time to time . . . which perhaps emphasizes its vitality.[10]

Such lavish praise for a foreign type could hardly have failed to gall the executives at ATF. No longer a minor irritant, Continental had in three short years expanded from a small selling house in New York City to a nationwide network of outlets, with type stocked in Boston, Detroit, Cleveland, and San Francisco. Troubled by the increasing competition in its domestic markets, ATF responded with a strategy designed to undercut its rivals. Early in 1929 it released the typeface Rivoli in roman and italic versions. Rivoli was a thinly disguised interpretation of Eve drawn by Willard T. Sniffin, an ATF staff designer. Sniffin was an old hand at such work, having in 1927 "designed" Liberty, ATF's close copy of Bauer's Bernhard Cursive, the very type whose success David Stempel had so much envied on his American visit.

The message was unmistakable: ATF regarded its foreign competition as decidedly unhealthy to its own best interests and had begun to fight back. One indication of its resolve was the circulation of a broadside on which a long-standing policy statement was set in the Rivoli and Liberty series. In it ATF avowed its intention "to discourage unhealthy competition and encourage such trade methods as will increase prosperity in existing plants."[11]

Then, on January 18, 1929, Cary made a stupendous mistake. Knowing that various congressional committees were revisiting the tariff rates on imported goods for the Smoot-Hawley tariff revision bill, Cary submitted a request asking that the rates on imported type be reduced from 20 percent to 15 percent ad valorum—that is 15 percent of the declared value. Hearing of this, ATF immediately protested, asking that the tariff

MODERN

Modern type faces are created primarily to attract the attention and hold the eye of the general reader ✰ We are living in a fast moving age and catering to the most exacting and discriminating people in the history of the world ✰ *Modern advertisers fully appreciate the importance of the new movement* ✰ They understand its progress. Old styles of type display are outmoded, and advertising has gained in effectiveness

✰

American Type is Strictly Modern

A specimen setting of ATF's Rivoli typeface.

245

instead be raised to a staggering thirty cents per pound, or about a 500 percent increase. The gauntlet had been thrown and ATF now needed to produce its champion, a spokesman who would tirelessly fight for the interests of the company.

It surprised no one at ATF when Henry Lewis Bullen was chosen for that role and proved to be a formidable opponent. Where Cary was young, urbane, cultured, and charming, Bullen was a larger-than-life, irascible seventy-year-old printer who had worked his way up in the ranks of the ATF to a lofty management position and then, in a brilliant crowning achievement, formed ATF's world-famous Typographic Library and Museum. He was blunt, fearless, and steadfastly loyal to ATF. Bullen often enlivened the pages of trade magazines like the *Inland Printer* and *American Printer* with essays on printing history as well as pungent criticism on issues of the day. He was a master at making a quick jab to the chin with one hand and then considerately sponging up the blood with the other. Writing about Fred Goudy in 1923, for example, he slyly noted:

> Notwithstanding his unfortunate tendency toward megalomania, I recognize Mr. Goudy's unusual ability as a designer (and advertiser). He has made more good type designs than any other man since type designing began . . . I trust and hope that he will in due time give the printers a really great type design.[12]

Most importantly, Bullen knew the typefounding business inside out. His first task was to prepare all of ATF's arguments against a reduction of the tariff. In fact, Bullen later confessed, ATF's decision to ask for an increase in the tariff was made out of "pure cussedness." The issue of type piracy was also raised.

Cary rejoined with a supplemental brief and also testified in person before the committee. The first part of his argument dealt with the dominance of ATF in the American type market. Cary compared relative sales of domestic versus foreign manufactured type and noted that an increased tariff would "crush any shadow of foreign competition." Cary also answered ATF's piracy complaints by charging them with the piracy of the Bernhard Cursive, as well as two other unnamed faces, probably the roman and italic versions of Eve. The battle was now joined in earnest, and ATF countered with a detailed response that included the company's position on the type-piracy issue: "The latest specimen book of the American Type Founders Co. shows its type products, and there is not a design in it which infringes any ethical, financial, or legal right of any person or typefoundry anywhere."[13]

Listed in Appendix B of the brief, however, was a list of thirty-seven typefaces ATF claimed had been pirated by German founders from American sources. The Stempel firm alone was charged with fourteen instances of plagiarism, including Morris-Gotisch (based on Satanick), Tasso (Houghton), Amerikanisch Altgotisch (Ihlenberg), Union (Cheltenham Oldstyle), Halbfette Romanisch (De Vinne), and Freie Romanische (Childs). By 1929 these faces, with the possible exception of Cheltenham, had long been out of fashion, but whether the congressional committee knew that or not is irrelevant; the list itself was damning. The charge that ATF had copied Bernhard Cursive was dismissed with the declaration that "Professor Bernhard's design may be traced to letterings under copperplate engravings of the early eighteenth century, the designs of which letterings have become the property of the art."[14] By the end of July, the tariff revision bill had passed the House of Representatives with the duty on foreign type fixed at 30 percent. It was then remanded to the Senate. The dispute now shifted to a more public forum, the printing trade journals.

Rudolf Koch's article in the June 1929 *Gebrauchsgraphik* leveled a direct, indignant charge of plagiarism against ATF. The typeface Rivoli, said Koch, was "nothing more nor less than a shameless imitation of the Koch-Antiqua and must be designated as such . . . That the free mobility of the original has been transformed into a piece of dry, academic pedantry cannot be recognized as an essential difference, for it is nothing more than the mark of the mere mechanical imitator." Acknowledging that there was no legal protection for typeface designs in the U.S., Koch concluded by making a moral appeal for "an awakening of the public conscience."[15]

Reprints of Koch's article were circulated in the U.S. and there is little doubt that Melbert Cary played a role in ensuring that influential figures in the graphic arts community were informed of the injuries that Koch felt had been inflicted on him. Bullen, of course, regarded Cary as a troublesome meddler and reacted to Koch's intellectual-theft charges by sending the firm's managers and salesmen a "General Letter" over the signature of ATF's Typographic Department. A copy of the letter was also made available to selected printing trade magazines, and its text appeared more or less in its entirety in the December 7, 1929, issue of *Printing*. It is a brilliantly crafted letter, a "retort courteous," as Bullen privately described it, by a company which claimed to have always been in full and active sympathy with the just desires of artists of all sorts, especially the type designers, for adequate legal protection."[16] Indeed, ATF had spent sizeable amounts of money creating designs or purchasing them without ever having any guarantee that they wouldn't be copied. Bullen's letter further claimed that ATF had frequently prosecuted infringements on its type designs, but without a single success. Readily admitting that Rivoli was a copy of Eve, ATF asserted that this was the only effective reprisal it could make. As Bullen put it, "a slight dose of their own medicine has caused the actual offenders to see the light of fair business methods."[17] Though Eve was made by the Klingspor Foundry in Offenbach, and though Bullen admitted to never having examined one of their specimen books for imitations of American types, he insisted they were a fair target. His reasoning was simple: the Stempel foundry owned a controlling interest in Klingspor, and Stempel could be charged with fourteen specific instances of piracy. "[I]f the Klingspor Foundery is guiltless of plagiarisms of American type designs, it shares the odium attaching to an association of which it is a member . . ." No longer would ATF observe the "Messianic precept of 'turning the other cheek,'" but rather would test the effectiveness of the "Mosaic law of 'an eye for an eye and a tooth for a tooth.'"[18]

This was exceptionally blunt language but not as strong as the letter's original draft, which included charges of plagiarism not only against Stempel but also against the Bauer and Berthold foundries. However, Lucian Bernhard, one of Bauer's most important designers, had just been recruited to work for ATF and, as Bullen confided in a letter to J. H. Phinney, manager of ATF's Boston branch, "it was thought politic not to stir them up."[19] Meanwhile, Bullen continued to hear reports that Cary was orchestrating a series of pesky maneuvers, including the appointments of investigative committees by the American Institute of Graphic Arts and the Boston-based Society of Printers. Phinney, writing from Boston, alerted Bullen to the fact that Cary was criss-crossing the country making speeches, his objective being "an appeal for the crumbs from the big Type Trust's table, and he gets more of these than he deserves."[20] Bullen was not worried. The General

Letter was his "opening gun," he wrote to Harvey Best, president of Lanston Monotype, and "our biggest shells are yet to come."[21]

Even as the inflammatory *Printing* article was being readied for publication, Bullen wrote a conciliatory letter to Koch on November 29, 1929. After sympathizing with Koch's desire to have his designs protected, Bullen adopted a decidedly condescending tone: "I assure you, dear Professor, that I have long been a admirer of your type designs, though of the opinion that they are better adapted to German taste than to the America[n]—there is a marked difference." Nonetheless, he suggested that ATF might be interested in purchasing any new Koch types "adapted to typographic taste in the United States." Bullen also urged him to help lobby for an international agreement protecting type designs, though in the absence of such an agreement ATF was not willing to "waive its right of reprisal."[22] Finally, Bullen enclosed a copy of a letter he had written the same day to Hugo Steiner-Prag, president of the Verein Deutsche Buchkunstler in Leipzig. In it, he complained that much of the publicity attaching to the type piracy issue was "done at the instigation of certain agents for the sale of German types in the United States, who have very foolishly and futilely adopted a policy of personal antagonism to the American Type Founders Company."[23] He was clearly referring to Melbert Cary.

Koch held his ground in his reply of December 21, 1929. Referring to what he considered Klingspor's blamelessness in the matter of plagiarism, he wrote that he could not understand "that you[r] company believes to get rid of one wrong by committing another one. Or should it be the custom in your country that somebody who has been robbed is going to any a third person entirely innocent to rob him with the argument that by doing so he wishes to frighten the first robber from repeating."[24]

A separate printed complaint, set in the Eve type and dated December 30, 1929, was circulated by the Klingspor foundry in the form of an open letter to ATF and was published in *Printing*'s issue of February 8, 1930. Klingspor reiterated that it saw itself as the injured third party and claimed that ATF was unfairly focusing on piracies of American types that had taken place decades before. "Do you really intend to make people believe that in 1929 you have imitated our type as an "admonitory reprisal" because German firms imitated yours a quarter of a century and more ago?" asked Klingspor. "These are threadbare subterfuges. You have made your imitation because you have seen how important a success we have had in America with our Eve series (Koch Antiqua) and the Bauer foundry with their Bernhard Schoenschrift. You have made your imitation because the competition of the German foundries was irksome to your monopoly."[25]

This unrepentant posture was exactly what Bullen had been waiting for. He had been holding a bombshell in reserve for some time and he was ready to use it. On February 22, 1930, *Printing* published ATF's response under the headline " 'Intellectual Theft' Claim False—Eve Design 400 Years Old." The March 1930 *American Printer* carried the same article in slightly modified form.

Though signed by ATF president Joseph F. Gillick, the letter and an accompanying addendum were almost certainly ghost-written by Bullen and betray his typically aggressive style. Bullen delivered what seemed to be a devastating accusation, namely that Rudolf Koch had directly based the design of Eve type on a model taken from *Libellus valde doctus,* the 1549 calligraphic writing book of Urbanus Wyss of Zurich. He revealed that the Klingspor foundry had already been confronted with the same accusation in

1926 during the course of a lawsuit brought by Klingspor against the Vienna foundry of Karl Brendler & Sohne.

The Brendler foundry had issued a direct copy of Eve type under the name Radio-Antiqua and was promptly sued by Klingspor. According to Bullen, who was relying on what he called a "reliable Austrian source," Klingspor was defeated based on evidence that "Gebruder Klingspor and Karl Brendler & Sohne had both derived the design in litigation from a design of Urbanus Wyss in the Lombardic style of calligraphy printed in Zurich in 1549, and therefore the design was the common property of the art of lettering, and therefore available to all who practice that art."[26] In addition, wrote Bullen, Klingspor subsequently paid Brendler "a sufficient sum to discontinue the manufacture of the Radio-Antiqua type family, which in my opinion [rubbing it in a little] is superior to the Koch-Antiqua (Eve) type family."[27] Accompanying the article were reproductions of pages from the Wyss writing book and specimens of the typefaces Eve, Radio-Antiqua, and ATF's Rivoli shown in comparative displays. Bullen had thus deftly swept away the one seemingly impregnable argument that Koch had made—namely, that Koch and Klingspor were innocent victims of a piracy controversy between two giant typefoundries.

Bullen had already confronted Koch himself in a January 6, 1930, reply to Koch's letter of December 29, 1929. Among other things, Bullen delivered a sharp Biblical rebuke: "I expected from you an admission, an apology and not a repetition of your hypocritical attacks . . . Your answer is a shameless disregard of the facts and apparent in the written assumption that we are not interested in the facts. You hypocrite, first cast out the beam out of thine own eye; and then shalt thou see clearly to cast out the mote out of thy brother's eye."[28]

The balance of the *Printing* article was devoted to ATF's rebuttals of various points raised in the Klingspor "Open Letter," primarily concerning the fourteen imitative faces marketed by Stempel. Though ATF, so far as I know, had no significant type sales to speak of in Germany at the time the piracies took place (or even in the 1920s), and even though the faces in question, except possibly for Cheltenham and De Vinne, could hardly have been big sellers, ATF's complaints of plagiarism were very persuasive. Finally, Klingspor's "Open Letter" was none too subtly (though probably correctly) attributed to Melbert Cary: "Another surmise is that this propaganda, though ostensibly created in Germany, and mailed from there, actually had its origin in New York with an importer of European types, whom, I am informed, has very limited experience and an imperfect knowledge of the subject."[29] Together with the visual evidence indicating that the Eve design was indeed in the so-called domain of art, ATF had apparently won the day. But all was not what it seemed.

Re-examining the Evidence

It seems only fair, seventy years later, that the record should be set straight. A cursory and uncritical examination of the evidence presented by Bullen in his article tends to support his claim that the Wyss original and Eve are very similar. A closer look, however, suggests otherwise.

In comparing Eve with details from the Urbanus Wyss writing-book page alleged to be the model for Koch's type, it is clear that there are certain general similarities. Eve's tall, swelled ascenders, the oblique stress of the letterforms, and the influence of a humanistic writing style are consistent with the Wyss exemplar. An analysis of the lowercase letter-

abcdefghijklmnopqrſstuvwxyz ckſchfftiflſtſſſiltſſ a ꜩ&

Above: Eve roman; below: the roman alphabet of Urbanus Wyss, as it appears at the bottom of the lii recto page in his writing manual.

forms, however, brings out a considerable difference between many of the characters in the two designs.

- ❖ The Wyss *a* has a definite vertical stem, while the Eve *a* stem curves leftward up from the baseline.
- ❖ The Wyss *c* is fairly upright in appearance, but the Eve *c* with its oblique stress appears to lean backward.
- ❖ The Wyss *e* has a small counter with a moderate pitch to the bar, while the Eve *e* has a large counter with a pronounced pitch.
- ❖ The Wyss *g* is substantially different from the Eve *g*. Note the ear on the Eve *g* and the unusual construction of the lower bowl. The Eve *g,* along with the *a,* might be considered signature letters of the design.
- ❖ The Wyss *k* has a closed upper counter; Eve's does not.
- ❖ The Wyss *l* has a flat bottom serif, while the bottom serif of Eve's curves up to the right.
- ❖ The Wyss *p* and *q* have long descenders terminating in horizontal serifs, but Eve's have short descenders with oblique terminations.
- ❖ The Wyss *t* has a stem which above the bar leans very distinctly to the right. The Eve *t* has an entirely vertical stem.
- ❖ Finally, Wyss dotted his *i*'s while Eve has oblique slashes.

The *b*'s are, in fact, quite similar, particularly since a bottom spur is absent in both—a fairly unusual type design detail, and one Bullen was quick to point out. Nonetheless, the differences noted above (and others) leave little doubt that Eve is an original typeface. As for the capital letterforms, there are no likely models anywhere in the Wyss writing book, despite Bullen's assertions to the contrary.

Had Koch seen the Wyss manual before he designed Eve? Bullen certainly thought so. Koch, on the other hand, had stated in print as early as 1921 that the roman and cursive forms of Eve were based on two calligraphic broadsides he had created in 1915. At the urging of Dr. Karl Klingspor he refined these designs into the typeface Koch Antiqua, subsequently issued in 1922 by the Klingspor foundry. In a March 7, 1930, letter to the type designer Emil Rudolf Weiss, Koch wrote that he had not seen an original copy of the Wyss writing manual before 1918. A facsimile edition was not published until 1927, but a copy of it was acquired by Bullen for ATF's Typographic Library and consulted by him in his exposé of what he believed to be Koch's deceit. Koch also noted in his letter

The calligraphic broadside by Rudolf Koch, originally created in 1915, which later served as the model for his 1922 Koch Antiqua typeface.

to Weiss that Klingspor had lost its lawsuit against Brendler & Sohne, the manufacturer of Radio Antiqua, because Austrian law required proof that willful infringement of ownership rights had taken place, proof which the court decided had not been furnished to its satisfaction by Klingspor. Yet, according to Koch, Radio-Antiqua had been produced from electrotyped matrices of Koch-Antiqua! Nevertheless, Koch continued, Brendler was directed by the court to cease its manufacture of Radio Antiqua.[30] This is quite a different account than that provided by Bullen for readers of American printing periodicals.

Even if Koch had somehow consulted a copy of the original edition of Wyss before 1915 (the date of his calligraphic broadsides), the influence of this sixteenth-century writing master on the extraordinarily original and gifted Koch would have been general at best. Koch Antiqua, as the comparative illustration clearly shows, was an original typeface.

Bullen's illustrations for the *Printing* article, however, seem to tell a different story. The most important of them, labeled figures A and B, appeared on a special insert supplied by ATF to *Printing*. In figure A, Bullen reproduces the purported model from the Wyss manual. Figure B, directly below, is captioned as "a tracing from the original wood engraving (Fig. A), in which the flourishes and the swashes and extensions of certain characters, impracticable to the typefounder, have been eliminated, as a preliminary to redrafting for type making purposes."[31] The apparent similarity is startling. To drive the point home, Bullen's figure 3, appearing elsewhere in the article, shows three lowercase alphabets. The first shows much of the same alphabet already seen at the bottom of Bullen's figure B and is described as being reproduced from a "tracing in exact register with the original Wyss design of 1549." The alphabet on the second line is Eve, and the third is ATF's Rivoli. If Eve appears to look more like the so-called Wyss than Rivoli looks like Eve, that is doubtless what Bullen hoped to suggest.

The similarities are remarkable—and confusing: note the *a*'s, *e*'s, and *g*'s. Yet a study of [these two typefaces illustrated above] clearly proves that these and other characters are not as alike in Wyss and in Eve as Bullen would have the reader believe. The apparent contradiction is easily explained. The captions describing the letterforms in Bullen's

SUPPLEMENT to the Reply of the American Type Founders Co. to an Open Letter of the Klingspor Type Foundry of Offenbach-am-Main, relating to an alleged "Highway Robbery of German Intellectual Property." [This supplement is supplied by the American Type Founders Company and inserted by the courtesy of the Editor of PRINTING.]

Nihil es t amabilius uirtute, nihil quod magis al; liciat homines ad diligendum. Quippe cum prop; ter uirtutem Xpbitatem, etiam quos nunq uidi mus, quodammodo diligimus. Cuius ea uis es t, ut eam, quod maius es t, in hos te etiam diligamus. A a b c d e fff g h ik l m n o p q r ſſs t u x y z.

Fig. A.—Reproduction, in exact size of original, of a page of a text book of calligraphy by Urbanus Wyss, printed in Tigurinum (Zurich, Switzerland) in 1549. This is the original from which the design of the type faces Eve (Koch-Antiqua), Radio-Antiqua and Rivoli was derived. The original was printed from a wood engraving. The title of Wyss' book is *Libellus Valde Doctus, elegans et utilis, multa et varia, scribendarum literarum genera complectens*.

252

Nihil es t amabilius uirtute, mhil ouod magis al; liciat hommes ad diligendum. Quippe cum prop; ter uirtutem O pbitatem. etiam quos nunq uidi; mus ouod ammodo diligimus. Cuius ea uis es t ut eam quod maius es t.m hoſ te etiam dilioamus. A a b c d e fff g h ik l m n o p q r ſß t u x y z

Fig. B.—Reproduced from a tracing from the original wood engraving (Fig. A), in which the flourishes and swashes and extensions of certain characters, impracticable to the type founder, have been eliminated, as a preliminary to re-drafting for type making purposes. This reproduction is in exact register with the original wood-cut engraving shown in Fig. A, above. The above characters have a closer resemblance to Eve Heavy than to Eve.

Figures A & B from Bullen's article in *Printing* (February 22, 1930).

ALPHABET REPRODUCED FROM TRACING IN EXACT REGISTER WITH THE ORIGINAL WYSS DESIGN OF 1549 SHOWN IN
FIGS. A AND B IN INSERT

abcdefffghiklmnopqrtux

ALPHABET OF KOCH ANTIQUA (EVE), CLAIMED BY GEBRUDER KLINGSPOR TO HAVE BEEN ORIGINATED BY PROF. KOCH
IN 1916-1922

abcdefffghiklmnopqrtux

ALPHABET OF RIVOLI ISSUED BY THE AMERICAN TYPE FOUNDERS COMPANY, IN 1929, IN RETALIATION FOR THE APPRO-
PRIATION BY GERMAN FOUNDERS OF MANY OF ITS ORIGINAL DESIGNS

abcdefffghiklmnopqrtux

Fig. 3.—Miniscule alphabet designed by Urbanus Wyss of Zurich, Switzerland, in 1549, compared with the type faces Eve and Rivoli. See also Figs. A and B in insert

Figure 3 from Bullen's article in *Printing* (February 22, 1930).

figures A, B, and 3 are extremely misleading, not to say wrong. The figure B alphabet and the top line of figure 3 were not produced by tracing over the original Wyss engraving; they are, in fact, the Radio-Antiqua types arranged in the text of the Wyss original, print- ed onto a soft card stock with a heavy impression so as to make them heavier in weight, and then reproduced for these illustrations! (Note also that the *p* and *q* are actually an upside-down *b* and *d*.) Thus, the apparently amazing resemblance between Eve and the Wyss alphabet "tracing" is attributable entirely to the fact that the text of the so-called tracing is actually set from the Brendler foundry's faithful copy of Eve. There can be no doubt that these mis-labeled examples were set using Radio-Antiqua, because the origi- nals still exist in the ATF archives at Columbia University, where they were carefully laid years ago—the inside front cover of copy no. 238 of the 1927 facsimile edition of Urban Wyss's 1549 writing manual.

Somehow, the resourceful Bullen had managed to obtain some of the actual pieces of evidence used in the Klingspor-Brendler lawsuit,. On the back of the evidentiary exhibit reproduced by Bullen as figure B in his *Printing* article is the signed statement of Adalbert Carl Trupp, the Viennese printer who prepared it: *"Umseitiger Druck wurde in meiner Druckerei, in meinem Beisein hergestellt. Der Satz bestand aus neuen unbeschädigten Lettern der Radio-Antiqua"* ("The printing on the other side was produced in my presence in my printing shop. The composition consisted of new, undamaged letters of Radio-Antiqua.") For some reason, the ATF insert containing Bullen's figures A and B was not bound into the version of his article in the March 1930 *American Printer*. That Bullen considered this a crucial piece of evidence is revealed in his complaint about its omission to Frederick C. Kendall of the *American Printer:* "Cary's fool partisans will not be able to see the relation- ship between Fig. A and the typefaces involved."[32]

One question begs to be answered. Was Bullen being deliberately deceptive in his article, or did he really believe that Koch's Eve was a frank and unabashed plagiarism? Support for the latter view came in a letter written to H. L. Koopman, librarian at Brown University, in December 1929:

> Koch-Antiqua is an almost exact copy of a design used by Urban Wyss . . . Koch deceived the German foundry that bought his "design." When the Germans and Cary have exhausted their abusive propaganda we will reprint Wyss' design and the German and American copies. There will be fun. P.S. When I say "almost exact" I mean perfectly copied except the exclusion of the flourishes common enough in calligraphy but impracticable in typemaking."[33]

Yet if all Koch had done was to remove the flourishes, the resulting letterforms would have varied considerably from the "perfectly copied" alphabet shown in Bullen's illustrations. Koch addressed this issue in his March 7, 1930, letter to Weiss. Referring to the same court exhibits that Bullen later acquired, Koch wrote that Brendler based its assertions on prints that "were calculated to deceive" and showed Koch's type *"ganze verquetscht,"*—"totally squashed." Even the court-appointed experts, Rudolf Junk and Rudolf von Larisch, were temporarily startled by the putative similarities, wrote Koch, but eventually declared that Koch's type was original enough to warrant copyright protection.[34]

Despite the enormous good Bullen did for the printing industry by writing lucid and engaging articles on the history of printing, he occasionally perverted his own cause with tainted scholarship. More than once Bruce Rogers, for example, pointed out inaccuracies that had crept into Bullen's writings. It seems most likely that Bullen's loyalty to ATF, his enmity against Melbert Cary stemming from their import tariff confrontation, his belief that Klingspor had lost its plagiarism lawsuit, his blatant anti-German feelings, and, finally, his fierce, implacable stubbornness, led him to a mean-spirited misinterpretation of the facts. There may even have been a hidden agenda. There is evidence in the ATF archives to suggest that by bringing the deficiencies of the American copyright law out into the open, ATF hoped to staunch the murderous piracies it was suffering in the U. S. at the hands of the machine-composition companies.

Seventy years ago ATF came out as the clear winner of a trial conducted very much in the court of public opinion. In March 1930, Frederic Goudy resigned as vice-president of Continental Typefounders, claiming disagreements with the firm's policies. In April, a letter from Wilhelm Cunz of the Stempl Type Foundry was published in *American Printer.* Arguing that ATF's reprisals against a Koch face would only have been reasonable if made in response to copies made in Germany of a contemporary Goudy design, Cunz nevertheless offered to withdraw all of the faces in Stempel's inventory which ATF claimed were piracies. Subsequent Stempel specimen books do not show these faces.

Despite its seeming financial health, ATF went into bankruptcy in 1933, was rescued, and continued to offer Rivoli until the 1950s. Rudolf Koch died in 1934, Bullen in 1938, and Cary in 1941.

In the end, little changed. Despite repeated efforts to persuade legislators, the absence of a type-design copyright law in the U.S. continues to confound and distress all type designers who might reasonably desire some measure of security for their work. Recent court rulings have at least permitted the descriptive code for digital faces to be copyrighted, though the designs themselves remain fair game.

Despite these gains, an abstract sense of intellectual property may be all the designer will ever have to claim as his or her own. What is an original type design, anyway? As Frederic Goudy once put it, a type designer is someone who "thinks of a letter and draws a line around it." He also said, "The old guys stole all our best ideas."

---

[1] Melbert B. Cary, Jr., "Introduction," *Specimen of Types from European Foundries* (New York: Continental Typefounders Assoc.), 1926, pp. 3–4.

[2] Art Center, New York, *Bulletin* (March 1927).

[3] Melbert B. Cary, Jr., quoted in Carnegie Institute of Technology, *Newsletter* (March 6, 1931).

[4] Ibid.

[5] Wolf's thirty-two-page manuscript account, titled "Bericht über die Amerikareise," provides a fascinating glimpse through German eyes of the exposition and the booming American printing industry of the 1920s. It is now part of the Stempel archive at the Technische Hochschule in Darmstadt, Germany. I am indebted to Lili Wronker for providing me with a complete translation, portions of which are used in this article.

[6] Rudolf Wolf, "Bericht über die Amerikareise," manuscript account dated October 31, 1927, p. 4, Stempel archive, Technische Hochschule, Darmstadt.

[7] Ordinarily, David Stempel would have conducted these negotiations, but he was forced by illness to cut short his American trip and return to Frankfurt. He died on November 1, 1927, after an unsuccessful operation.

[8] Wolf, 31.

[9] Continental Typefounders Assoc., *Specimen Book of Continental Types*, 4th ed. (New York: CTA), 1929, p. 8.

[10] Kent D. Currie, "The Foreign Invasion," *Printed Salesmanship* (April 1928), p. 116.

[11] American Type Founders Co., "Our Policy" (Jersey City, N.J.: ATF), 1929, Broadside.

[12] Henry Lewis Bullen, "Observations on Type Designs and their Press Agents," *Inland Printer* 71 (September 1923), p. 835.

[13] U.S. Congressional Hearing. Tariff Act of 1929. "Metals and Manufactures of" (Washington, D.C.: GPO), 1929, pp. 1088–89.

[14] Ibid., 1089.

[15] Rudolf Koch, "Geistiger Diebstahl," *Gebrauchgraphik* 6 (June 1929): 54–56. Koch's outrage is perhaps best explained by the following description of him by Fritz Genzmer: "He was a stranger to any kind of arrogance; till the end of his days he remained what he had become on the basis of his origin and development: a humble, quiet worker, whom success did not make arrogant but, on the contrary, brought to an ever deeper degree of humility." In "The Type Designer Rudolf Koch," *Archiv für Druck und Papier* No. 4 (1956).

[16] [Henry Lewis Bullen], "American Type Founders Co. Replies to Attacks," *Printing* 50 (December 7, 1929), p. 23.

[17] Ibid.

[18] Ibid.

[19] Henry Lewis Bullen to J. H. Phinney, 30 November 1929. Typographic Library Manuscripts, Rare Book and Manuscript Library, Columbia University. Ironically, it was Phinney who first approached William Morris in the 1890s about making a commercial copy of Morris's Golden type, but he was rebuffed. As Bullen later recounted in one of his "Discursions" for the *Inland Printer* (June 1907), p. 354, "Morris did not want to popularize [the Golden type] or make its reformatory influence available in general typography, but rather to keep it for the narrow purpose of enhancing the value of his limited publishing business. Mr. Phinney, therefore, felt himself absolved, and proceeded under his legal right to cut the design in a magnificent series of fourteen sizes . . ."

[20]J. W. Phinney to H. L. Bullen, 5 December 1929, Typographic Library Manuscripts, Rare Book and Manuscript Library, Columbia University.

[21]H. L. Bullen to Harvey D. Best, 6 December 1929, Typographic Library Manuscripts, Rare Book and Manuscript Library, Columbia University.

[22]H. L. Bullen to Rudolf Koch, 29 Nov. 1929, Koch archive, Klingspor Museum, Offenbach am Main.

[23]H. L. Bullen to Hugo Steiner-Prag, 29 Nov. 1929, Koch archive, Klingspor Museum, Offenbach am Main.

[24]Rudolf Koch to H. L. Bullen 21 Dec. 1929, Koch archive, Klingspor Museum, Offenbach am Main.

[25]Gebr. Klingspor, "Open Letter to the American Type Founders Co." (Offenbach am Main: Klingspor, December 30, 1929). Broadside.

[26]Joseph F. Gillick [i.e., H. L. Bullen], "Intellectual Theft Claim False—Eve Design 400 Years Old," *Printing* 51 (February 22, 1930): 17.

[27]Ibid.

[28]H. L. Bullen to Rudolf Koch, 6 Jan. 1930. Koch archive, Klingspor Museum, Offenbach am Main. I have not come across the original English text of this letter. The portion quoted here was translated back into English from a German translation made for Koch from Bullen's original.

[29]Gillick, 17.

[30]Rudolf Koch to E. R. Weiss, 7 March 1930, Klingspor Museum, Offenbach am Main, Koch archive. In this letter, Koch also complained of piracies made by Lanston Monotype of his Kabel type design. Referring to Bullen's letter to him of January 6, Koch believed that not only he but Germans in general had been insulted.

[31]Ibid., 18A.

[32]H. L. Bullen to Frederick C. Kendall, 10 March 1930. Much of the letter is given over to charges that Laurance Siegfried, editor of the *American Printer,* showed too much partiality toward Melbert Cary. Bullen was also critical of an article by Paul Johnston—"Modern Fine Book Printing in America"—that appeared in the same issue (March 1930) and which was devoted to the work of Updike, Roberts, Rollins, Goudy, and Dwiggins. "Mr. Siegfried's virtue of boosting his friends is also observable in . . . an article written by a facile writer with a shallow background of knowledge of his subject, and a penchant for over praising the playboys of typography."

[33]H. L. Bullen to H. L. Koopman, 19 December 1929, Typographic Library Manuscripts, Rare Book and Manuscript Library, Columbia University.

[34]Rudolf Koch to E. R. Weiss, 7 March 1930.

Bad Credit

By Zuzana Licko and Rudy VanderLans

his article is about an unpopular subject, namely giving credit where credit is due in graphic design annuals. With design being an inherently collaborative process the question as to who should take or deserve full credit for the final product has always been a matter of contention.

In the past, it was common practice to simply attribute the entire work to the star designer, the head of the company, or simply to the company itself. Over the years, perhaps as the result of disgruntled employees and other contributors who felt that their contributions deserved perhaps at least a modicum of acknowledgement, things have changed. It became clear that the anonymous assistants in many cases did much more than simply realize the ideas of the great "conductor." This must have caused the editors of design annuals to start listing a hierarchy of contributors including art director, designer, photographer, or illustrator.

For one reason or another, these lists of contributors have continued to grow, to include printers, paper manufacturers, copywriters, clients, even film separators. When the personal computer was introduced and graphic designers took control over typesetting and other production functions previously left to others, certain design annuals added software programs and computer models to credit listings. In the introduction to one design annual it was even suggested that the person filling out the credit questionnaires and competition submission forms is as much a part of the collaborative effort as anybody involved in the creation of a design. It will only be a matter of time before the person making sure there's coffee in the morning, or the cleaners who come in on the weekend, will receive credit.

All of this, I believe, is a good thing. Comprehensive credit listings function both as a nice gesture to thank the people involved in the realization of a design, and they inform us, to an extent, about how a design was created. However, among the ever growing lists of credits, there remain two absentees: names of typefaces and typeface designers. With a few exceptions, the bulk of the design annuals published today do not list what is often one of the most significant building blocks of any design, namely the typeface and, by extension, the typeface designer. This one piece of software, the font, that can contribute the most to the look and feel of a design, is usually not mentioned, even in cases when type is the only visual ingredient of a design.

Type designers invest their artistic skills in their creations. And while most design professionals regard type design as a valuable, creative activity, it has suffered in the public eye because of a lack of recognition. As a result, the works of type designers are often pirated—something that has become easy with digital fonts—with no reward for the author who often has invested months, if not years, to create them. The anonymity of typeface origins and their designers is an unfortunate situation that has become increasingly detrimental to the field of typeface design.

Before the democratization of type, which resulted from the introduction of personal computer technology, just over a decade ago, there existed an established collection of typefaces and foundries that were familiar to graphic designers, typesetters, and others who worked with type. The introduction of new typefaces in those days was a slow process that allowed ample time for the type community to become accustomed to the new designs. Because everyone in the industry could identify typefaces, graphic designers and typesetters had grown accustomed to leaving out credits for the typeface names or typeface designers. Today, however, typefaces are being introduced into the marketplace faster than anyone can keep up with the selection. One way to keep the design community informed would be to credit typeface names and their designers, whenever practicably possible.

Having witnessed, over the years, the list of credit lines in design annuals and publications grow to include many peripheral professions of graphic design, we took the initiative to approach publishers of design annuals with a petition outlining our thoughts regarding credits. The basic request was for publishers to add the categories of "type design" and "type designer" to the credits listed in design competition submission forms. The petition was signed by more than thirty fellow type designers and foundries and sent to some ten publishers in the U.S. and abroad.

Although the response to the petition has been positive, publishers agreed in principle with the idea that the type designer and the font should be credited, many raised questions regarding the practicability and logistics of doing this. Following are some of the objections brought up by the *Print* magazine editors. Our reply follows each point.

❖ Designers can use four of five fonts—maybe even more—in one design. Crediting all of them would take up too much space.

If space is a consideration, then we would ask to list only the two most prominent fonts.

❖ Designers often submit work to competitions and/or publications months after it has been designed and printed. In the case of work submitted to a magazine for publication as part of a profile of the designer, or a historical survey, the work may have even been done years before. It is unlikely that the designer will remember what specific typefaces he or she used.

First, our request focuses primarily on design annuals that solicit comprehensive design credits in their Call for Entries mailers.

Second, it is difficult to imagine that a designer would forget the typeface that he or she used in a particular design, especially for a design they deemed worthy of submitting to a design competition. Designers spend much time studying and picking fonts, and many designers use only four or five fonts during their lifetime.

To solve this problem entirely, we suggest that designers credit the fonts in the design piece along with their other credits. This is not at all uncommon in book design, and makes it easy to identify which fonts were used, no matter how much time passes since its publication.

❖ While it is illegal to borrow fonts, designers, unfortunately, do borrow fonts, and as might be expected with designers who engage in this practice, they don't always know exactly what they have borrowed.

It is difficult to see this as a reasonable excuse since it is in principle illegal to "borrow" fonts. Perhaps the designer who "borrows" fonts should simply fill out the form stating: "stolen." It stands to reason that this "borrowing" is somewhat the result of the anonymity of typefaces. It's easier to steal from someone you don't know. By repeatedly crediting fonts, and by attaching the name of the designer to the font, awareness and knowledge will be raised, hopefully resulting in an increased respect for the intellectual property invested in the design of a typeface.

❖ Even if a designer knows, for example, that he or she has used an ITC Garamond, how does s/he know who designed it? In a sense, that particular Garamond is like a stock photo that belongs to a stock house rather than to a photographer: It belongs to ITC rather than to the designer.

While I understand the skepticism, I'm optimistic about designers being able to identify typefaces. Designers are very passionate, picky, and therefore quite knowledgeable about the typefaces they use. Also, designers now buy their fonts directly from the manufacturers, which adds to their awareness of the origins of the fonts. And when it comes to the classics, designers have always been specific, to the point of snobbism, about choosing one version of a particular font over another.

For those designers that are unfamiliar with the names of the designers of the fonts they use, there's all the more reason to try and raise their awareness. I should also note here that many typefoundries can do a much better job than they do currently in identifying the type designers from whom they license their fonts.

In response to the question of whether the foundry or the designer deserves credit, I would like to ask; should illustrators forego credit when their work is done "for hire"?

❖ What if the designer uses an identifiable font and then manipulates it? Does the original designer want to be recognized?

Here, too, I need to respond with a question; should the photographer forgo credit when his or her photos are being cropped, or should the writer relinquish ownership when the designer manipulates the writing? These questions run to the very center of the discussion regarding who deserves credit for what.

All we ask in our petition, since there seems to exist a definite tendency to list ever more credits, that design annuals also solicit credit information for fonts used. There will always be situations, such as the one described above, that are not clearcut. How to resolve this? There is such a thing as a code of ethics in every profession. If graphic designers enjoy the continuing influx of new type designs, and their usage shows us that they do, it becomes simply a matter of decency that they acknowledge and credit the fonts they use, just as they acknowledge the work of the illustrators, photographers, copywriters, printers, etc., who make their work possible. In the end, however, it is up to each individual designer to decide how much of the spotlight they are willing to share.

From *Print* 51, no. 2 (March/April 1997).

The Land of Dancing Serifs

By Peter Hall

hough many a great pop song incorporates a well-written lyric rendered inaudible by a cavalcade of electronic noise, few artists have made use of the written word in their music videos. This is now in stark contrast with video's close cousin, the TV commercial, where bouncing, bowling ad copy has become a staple of the little screen. Those inspired few who have experimented with type and tune, however, have uncovered a realm of semantic possibilities.

The first apparition of musical typography was arguably director D. A. Pennebaker's enduring opening sequence to the 1967 documentary *Don't Look Back,* featuring a young Bob Dylan standing in a back alley tossing flashcards to the ground to the tune of "Subterranean Homesick Blues." The sequence didn't set any technological precedents in special type effects, but it inspired a handful of imitators decades later and touched on a kinetic word-image game with a great future. Dylan's quirkily scrawled flashcards added a second, mischievous voice to the song. At first, the words on the cards appeared simply to correspond with certain words in the rambling "keep a clean nose" hymn to the beat generation. But by the end of verse one, the flashcards were beginning to show discrepancies, as the sound track Dylan sang "Eleven dollar bills," while the nonchalant on-screen Dylan, mouth shut, held up a card marked "$20." By the end of the song, the willful cards began delivering their own version of the lyrics, punctuated at the end by a flashcard marked "What?" that slipped from Dylan's fingers as he ambled off camera.

As a designer Emily Oberman puts it, on-screen type adds a "subliminally suggested voice" to a soundtrack. Working with M&Co's founder Tibor Kalman and David Byrne of the Talking Heads, Oberman helped create a memorable addition to the nascent typokinetic genre with the band's "Nothing but Flowers" video. "I hesitate to say that it was the bouncing ball idea," says Oberman. "The song itself was very metaphorically lush. We wanted to create a pristine thing out of it, where you had to work with your imagination. The type didn't create a story you had to follow." In the video, words from the song appear on the minimal stage set, framing the members of the band, mocking them, and even projecting themselves over Byrne's face as he tells of his former guise "as a billboard." There is an undercurrent of semiotic sports in the relationship between the sung words and the moving words, as if the signifier were being physically separated from the signified.

"Nothing but Flowers" scattered seeds of typokinetics all over the screen. Type charged through music videos and commercials, even onto poetry programs. Some applications were quite inventive. In the video for REM's "Everybody Hurts," directed by Jake Burns, lines of type played the role of subtitles, revealing the thoughts of drivers stuck in an apocalyptic traffic jam. The MTV pioneer Mark Pellington, who had previously experimented with all-caps treatments of polemical messages rapid-fired on-screen in *Buzz TV,* applied similar techniques to the safe-sex messages of the "Red Hot and Dance" video and—with Oberman again—to the PBS poetry series *United States of Poetry*. On-screen text also began to echo trends in print design, and degraded and dimensional type began to wander around in front of the action.

Designer P. Scott Makela, an inventor of futuristic and dimensional type particularly well suited to the screen, supplied illustrative letters to Mark Romanek (in Michael and Janet Jackson's "Scream") and to Jeffrey Plansker, who added flashes of twisted ad copy to videos by Urge Overkill and 10,000 Maniacs. Other bands and directors paid direct homage to the aphorism art of Jenny Holzer, hurling pithy maxims on-screen, often regardless of their pertinence. In Van Halen's "Right Now," directed by Mark Fenske and Scott Burn, the type provided an ongoing commentary, a melee of meaningless trivia, self-parody, and shock statistics (a device also used in "Nothing but Flowers").

Oddly, however, the flurry of activity never made musical type an on-screen regular. "Videos really go through movements," says Plansker, "and it's almost as though type on-screen was a movement in a weird way. You don't see that much happening now, probably because there aren't that many opportunities for it in videos, whereas in advertising, there's always some kind of message they're laying down."

Though viewers would hardly wish for typographic "Buy this record" messages in the middle of their favorite videos, the lack of inventive on-screen graphics is surprising. For the good stuff now, viewers need to go underground, late night, or overseas. Graphic design's newfound ghetto is MTV's hour-long late-night show *Amp*. Broadcast at 1 AM on Friday and Saturday nights, *Amp* melds together four segments of ambient, dance, drum and bass, and techno music videos with a graphic identity that feeds off the rich imagery around it. "We pride ourselves on our design ethic," says producer Todd Mueller, who sees the oscilloscope-inspired interstitial effects and type as an evolving and changing organism. "It seemed good to represent the [dance] genre in the most eclectic way possible," he says. Footage scoured from various archives is reduced to kinetic outlines in green, blue, and white light on a black background. The *Amp* logo frequently appears, revolving in 3-D, and occasionally the screen dissolves into digital ripples and ambient sand.

In the graphically driven videos featured on *Amp*, Mueller notes a shift in pop iconography away from live action. "I like to think that the graphics are replacing the outfits and personalities that people are more familiar with," he says. "It's the long-hair, plaid-dress-code, spitting-on-the-camera ethic revised." A piece for the Japanese artist Towa Tei, directed by Hiroyuki Nakano, is an impressive 3-D computer-animated sequence of the artist cloning himself and his dog to the bouncing beat and occasional typographic slogans like "wired world" and "peace delivery." Other bands have on-board designers who provide an integrated visual accompaniment to the music. A designer by the name of Buggy G. Riphead is a member of the band the Future Sound of London. Riphead's trademark image of alien, amorphous Day-Glo blobs floats through the city in FSOL's "Dead Cities." The band Underworld, meanwhile, forms part of the hugely influential design collaborative Tomato, whose Graham Wood created what might be the closest thing to a type-only video, for the band's song "Cowgirl." A high-velocity montage of textures and words with dancing serifs, including a line or two from a philosophical treatise by Ludwig Wittgenstein, the eight-minute sequence is mind-bogglingly addictive. Ironically, most of these type-driven dance videos are for songs with very little lyrical content.

If anything, *Amp* anticipates a future TV world in which computer-generated programming is as prevalent as live action. When interactive TV rolls into our homes with clickable messages and scrolling type, the days of music video's angst-ridden singer hugging the walls of a small room will be over. We'll look back at these early days of the music video genre and recognize that a few pioneering typokinetic gems lurked amid the trash. Then again, we might also long for the days of single-image TV, uncluttered by on-screen verbiage.

From *AIGA Journal of Graphic Design* 15, no. 3 (1997).

[The Authors]

M.F. Agha (1896–1978) was the art director for Conde Nast's *Vanity Fair* and *Vogue* and introduced a modern typographic sensibility to these magazines. He was also a frequent contributor to *Print, PM,* and other trade magazines.

Otl Aicher (1922–1991) was a founder and teacher at Hochschule für Gestaltung in Ulm from 1954–1966 as well as a typographer and designer of corporate identities for Braun Elektrogeräte, Deutsche Lufthansa, ZDF, ERCO-Leuchten, Flughafen Frankfurt, Westdeutsche Landesbank, Dresdner Bank, and Severin and Siedler Verlag.

Herbert Bayer (1900–1985) was a Bauhaus member from 1921–1928. From 1925 on he headed the workshop for "Printing and Advertising." In 1938 he immigrated to New York, where he continued to design and paint. As consultant for the Container Corporation of America, he designed the landmark book, *The World Geo-Graphic Atlas.*

John D. Berry was the editor of *Upper and Lower Case.* He is a typographer, book designer, and writer who lives in Seattle.

Charles Brodie was the president of the Advertype Company, Incorporated.

Kees Broos is an art historian, in Arnhem, The Netherlands. His books include *De Nieuwe Fotografie in Nederland* (with Flip Bool), *Grafische Vormgeving in Nederland, Een eeuw* (with Paul Hefting), *Dutch Graphic Design, Mondriaan, De Stijl en de Nieuwe Typografie,* and *Piet Zwart (1885–1977).*

Matthew Butterick is president of Atomic Vision, an Internet development company in San Francisco that has built websites for CNET, Excite, and *Wired* magazine.

Moira Cullen is a design writer, educator, and strategist whose career spans the worlds of dance, photography, fashion, marketing, and design. The former chair of the Communication Arts Department of Otis College of Art & Design and past president of the AIGA Los Angeles Chapter, she currently manages the design studio at Hallmark Cards, Inc.

Eugene M. Ettenberg was a type director for advertising and commentator in printing trade magazines of the typographic scene from the 1930s to the 1950s. He was the author of *Type for Books and Advertising.*

Peter Fraterdeus *(peter@designonline.com)* founded Alphabets, Inc., in Evanston, Illinois, and designOnline, Inc., where he helps corporations develop Internet strategies.

Tobias Frere-Jones was born in 1970 in New York. He graduated from Rhode Island School of Design in 1992 and began full-time work for Font Bureau as a Senior Designer. In 2000, he began work with Jonathan Hoefler in New York. He teaches a type design course with Matthew Carter at Yale School of Design.

William Golden (1911–1959) was the creative director of advertising and sales promotion for the CBS television network and responsible for the creation of its early visual identity, including the CBS Eye. *The Visual Craft of William Golden,* edited and designed by Cipe Pineles, was published after his death.

Frederic W. Goudy (1865–1947) founded the Village Press in Park Ridge, Illinois in 1903 with Will H. Ransom. In 1908, he created his first significant typeface for the Lanston Monotype Machine Company, Goudy Light. In 1911, he produced Kennerly Old Style for an H.G. Wells anthology published by Mitchell Kennerly. His most widely used type, Goudy Oldstyle, was released by the American Type Founders Company in 1915. In addition to designing typefaces he was devoted to writing, teaching and lecturing.

Peter Hall is a journalist and design critic based in New York. He wrote and co-edited the book *Tibor: Perverse Optimist* and coauthored *Pause: 59 Minutes of Motion Graphics.* He writes regularly for *Metropolis, Guardian, I.D., Men's Journal, Print, Architecture and Interiors,* and has contributed essays to the books *Sex Appeal* (Allworth Press) and *Architecture and Film.*

Jessica Helfand is a partner of William Drenttel/Jessica Helfand, a multimedia and print media company. She is the author of *Six Eassys (to 12) on Design and New Media* and *Paul Rand: American Modernist.*

Steven Heller is the art director of the *New York Times Book Review* and cochair of the MFA/Design department of the School of Visual Arts. He is author of eighty books on graphic design, including *Typeplay; Faces on the Edge; Typology; Letterforms: Bawdy, Bad, and Beautiful; Design Literacy* (Allworth Press); and *Graphic Design Time Line* (Allworth Press).

Jonathan Hoefler is the director of *The Hoefler Type Foundry,* a design studio specializing in the development of typefaces in the Proto-Hoeflerist style.

Karrie Jacobs is the editor-in-chief of *dwell,* a San Francisco-based magazine about modern residential design and architecture. In the recent past, she was *New York Magazine's* architecture critic. She still knows a thing or two about type, but she knew a lot more back in the 1980s, when she worked at *Metropolis.*

Alastair Johnston is a partner in Poltroon Press in Berkeley, California and is the author of *Alphabets to Order,* a study of nineteenth-century typefounders' specimens.

Mr. Keedy is a designer, writer, type designer, and educator who has been teaching in the Graphic Design Program at California Institute of the Arts since 1985. His designs and essays have been published in *Eye, I.D., Emigre, Critique, Idea, Looking Closer* and *Looking Closer Two, Faces on the Edge: Type in the Digital Age, New Design: Los Angeles,* and *The Education of a Graphic Designer.*

Jerry Kelly is a designer, calligrapher, and printer in New York City. He has also written numerous articles and lectured and taught widely. He has designed books for various publishers and institutions, including the Morgan Library, The Grolier Club, Little Brown and Company, Columbia University, Callaway Editions, and St. Martin's press. His publications have won awards from AIGA, Type Directors' Club, Felice Feliciano (Italy), Society of Typographic Arts (London), and others.

Zuzana Licko, a type designer, is the cofounder of Emigre, a digital typefoundry and publisher of graphic design related software and printed materials based in Northern California. Founded in 1984, coinciding with the birth of the Macintosh, Emigre was one of the first independent typefoundries to establish itself as centered on personal computer technology.

Ellen Lupton is adjunct curator of contemporary design at Cooper-Hewitt, National Design Museum, Smithsonian Institution in New York. She is chair of the graphic design department at Maryland Institute, College of Art in Baltimore. She is the author of numerous books, including *Design Writing Research: Writing on Graphic Design,* coauthored with J. Abbott Miller.

Rauri McLean, a type scholar, now partially retired, lives in Scotland. His *Manual of Typography* (originally published in 1980) has been translated into Spanish, Greek, and Serbo-Croatian. His most recent books are *How Typography Happens* and *Time to Type: A Typographical Autobiography.*

Douglas C. McMurtrie (1888–1944), a Chicago-based type designer and graphic arts historian, was known for his research on the legacy of type and paper.

Philip B. Meggs is School of the Arts Research Professor at the Virginia Commonwealth University School of the Arts, where he teaches design history, typography, and graphic design. His book, *A History of Graphic Design,* has been translated into Chinese, Japanese, Korean, and Spanish. It received an award for excellence in publishing from The Association of American Publishers. *Typographic Design: Form and Communication,* written and designed with Rob Carter and Ben Day, was selected as one of the best designed books of the year in the annual AIGA book exhibition. Meggs's most recent book is *Revival of the Fittest: Digital Versions of Classic Typefaces,* edited with Roy McKelvey. This book was a collaborative project, with sixteen faculty and graduate students contributing to the writing and design. Currently, Meggs is working on a Third Edition of *Typographic Design: Form and Communication.*

Laszlo Moholy-Nagy (1895–1946) was the founder of the typography workshop at the Bauhaus. In 1937 he emigrated to America to direct the New Bauhaus, an experimental school in art and design in Chicago. A prolific writer, as well as one of the most fertile experimental artists of his time, Moholy-Nagy was a painter, photographer, filmmaker, builder of light-space machines, teacher, and philosopher of new aesthetics.

Stanley Morison (1889–1967) was a typographer and journalist. He served as typographical consultant to Cambridge University Press and to the English Monotype Corp. He was editor of the *Fleuron* from 1926–1930. From 1929 to 1944 he was typographical advisor to the *London Times* and designer of a new format for the newspaper and of the typeface Times Roman. In 1945, Morison became editor of the *Times Literary Supplement*. His major writings on type are *Four Centuries of Fine Printing* (1924) and *First Principles of Typography* (1936).

Josef Müller-Brockmann (1914–1996) was pioneer of Swiss typographic design and the author of *Grid Systems in Graphic Design: A Visual Communication Manual* and *A History of Visual Communication*.

Alexander Nesbitt was a calligrapher who taught the subject at the Cooper-Union. He wrote *The History and Technique of Lettering*, and he edited *Decorative Alphabets and Initials* and *Two Hundred Decorative Title Pages.*

David Ogilvy (1911–1999) founded, in 1948, the agency that would become Ogilvy & Mather. Starting with no clients and a staff of two, he built his company into one of the eight largest advertising networks in the world. He was one of the most famous names in advertising and one of the handful of its "Big Idea" thinkers (Raymond Rubicam, Leo Burnett, William Bernbach, Ted Bates) who shaped the business after the 1920s.

David Pankow is the curator of the Melbert B. Cary, Jr. Graphic Arts Collection at Rochester Institute of Technology in Rochester, New York. The Cary Collection is one of the country's premier rare book libraries on the history and practice of printing and also includes holdings on papermaking, bookbinding, typefounding, and the art of the book. He is a professor in the graduate program of RIT's School of Printing, where he teaches courses on the history of the book and is currently the editor of *Printing History,* the scholarly journal published by the American Printing History Association.

Rick Poynor writes about design, media and visual culture for *Eye, Print, Metropolis, Frieze, Artbyte,* and many other publications. His books include *Typography Now, Design Without Boundaries, Vaughan Oliver: Visceral Pleasures,* and *Typographica,* a study of the post-war design journal.

Paul Rand (1914–1996) was a pioneer American Modernist graphic designer and author. His books include *Thoughts on Design, Paul Rand: A Designer's Art, Design Form and Chaos,* and *From Lascaux to Brooklyn.*

Talbot Baines Reed (1852–1893) was a typefounder and typefounding historian. He authored "A History of Old English Letter Foundries."

Emil Ruder (1914–1970) was a typographer and exemplar of the Swiss Style. He was the founder and directed the Typography class at the Basle School of Design, in Switzerland. He wrote that "typography has one plain duty before it and that is to convey information in writing. No argument or consideration can absolve typography from this duty."

L. Sandusky was a type director, writer on type history, and contributor to *PM* (Production Manager).

Paul Shaw is a calligrapher, type designer and design historian. For the past twenty years he has taught at various New York City design schools. Currently he is teaching typography at Parsons School of Design and graphic design history at the School of Visual Arts. Since 1994 he has been a partner with Garrett Boge in LetterPerfect, a digital typefoundry. With Peter Bain he co-curated the exhibition "Blackletter: Type and National Identity." His writings have appeared in *Print, Baseline* and *Letter Arts Review.*

Stefan Themerson (1910–1988), with his wife Franciszka, ran the Gaberbocchus Press in London. Gaberbocchus, known for experimental typographic books, published both Kurt Schwitters and Bertrand Russell—and these extremes unite in Themerson's uniquely individual brand of philosophical Dadaism.

Jan Tschicold (1902–1974) was exposed to typography at the Leipzig Akademie, where he studied under the type designer Walter Tiemann. His enthusiasm for avant-garde was sparked by a visit to the 1924 Bauhaus exhibition. In 1928, he published *Die neue Typographie,* in which he advocated the use of sans serif typefaces and asymetric layout. By 1935 he had reconsidered many of his earlier ideas, and in his *Typographische Gestaltung,* he called for a more traditional approach to typographic design.

Rudy VanderLans is the editor and designer of the quarterly design journal *Emigre* and author of two books of photographs, *Palm Desert* and *Cucamonga.*

Beatrice Warde (1900–1969) was a typographer, writer, and scholar who spent much of her working life in England. She was educated at Barnard College, Columbia, where she developed an interest in calligraphy and letterforms. From 1921–1925 she worked as assistant librarian with the American Type Founders Company, pursuing her research into typefaces and the history of printing. She was also a contributor to the printing journal *Fleuron,* edited by Stanley Morison.

Hermann Zapf is the designer of Palatino, Melior, Optima, Hunt Roman, Linofilm Medici, Digiset Marconi, Comenius, ITC Zapf International, Digiset Edison, and ITC Zapf Chancery.

[Acknowledgments]

The editors want to thank all the authors and their representatives for allowing the work herein to be republished in this anthology. Through their generosity designers and design students will have unprecedented access to important writings on type and typography.

We are particularly indebted to the following people for their support: Manuel Aicher, Carol Burtin Fripp, Hattula Moholy-Nagy, Martin Fox, Rick Poynor, John Walters, Ric Grefe, and Marion Rand.

Thanks again to James Victore for his fine cover and format design, and to Jennifer Moore for her page design. Finally, but definitely not least, we gratefully acknowledge our editorial team at Allworth Press—Nicole Potter, editor; Jamie Kijowski, associate editor; Elizabeth Van Hoose, editorial assistant; Bob Porter, associate publisher; and Tad Crawford, publisher—for their hard work and continued support.

[Index]

Books from Allworth Press

Graphic Design Time Line: A Century of Design Milestones by Steven Heller and Elinor Pettit (softcover, 6¾ × 9⅞, 256 pages, $19.95)

Graphic Design and Reading: Explorations of an Uneasy Relationship edited by Gunnar Swanson (softcover, 6¾ × 9⅞, 240 pages, $19.95)

Design Connoisseur: An Eclectic Collection of Imagery and Type by Steven Heller and Louise Fili (softcover, 7 × 9⅜, 208 pages, $19.95)

Design Literacy (continued): Understanding Graphic Design by Steven Heller (softcover, 6¾ × 9⅞, 296 pages, $19.95)

Design Literacy: Understanding Graphic Design by Steven Heller and Karen Pomeroy (softcover, 6¾ × 9⅞, 288 pages, $19.95)

The Education of a Graphic Designer edited by Steven Heller (softcover, 6¾ × 9⅞, 288 pages, $18.95)

The Swastika: Symbol Beyond Redemption? by Steven Heller (hardcover, 6 × 9, 176 pages, $21.95)

Sex Appeal: The Art of Allure in Graphic and Advertising Design by Steven Heller (softcover, 6¾ × 9⅞, 288 pages, $18.95)

Design Culture: An Anthology of Writing from the AIGA Journal of Graphic Design edited by Steven Heller and Marie Finamore (softcover, 6¾ × 9⅞, 320 pages, $19.95)

Looking Closer 3: Classic Writings on Graphic Design edited by Michael Bierut, Jessica Helfand, Steven Heller, and Rick Poynor (softcover, 6¾ × 9⅞, 304 pages, $18.95)

Looking Closer 2: Critical Writings on Graphic Design edited by Michael Bierut, William Drenttel, Steven Heller, and DK Holland (softcover, 6¾ × 9⅞, 288 pages, $18.95)

Looking Closer: Critical Writings on Graphic Design edited by Michael Bierut, William Drenttel, Steven Heller, and DK Holland (softcover, 6¾ × 9⅞, 256 pages, $18.95)

AIGA Professional Practices in Graphic Design, The American Institute of Graphic Arts, edited by Tad Crawford (softcover, 6¾ × 9⅞, 320 pages, $24.95)

Business and Legal Forms for Graphic Designers by Tad Crawford and Eva Doman Bruck (softcover, 8½ × 11, 240 pages, includes CD-ROM, $24.95)

Please write to request our free catalog. To order by credit card, call 1-800-491-2808 or send a check or money order to Allworth Press, 10 East 23rd Street, Suite 510, New York, NY 10010. Include $5 for shipping and handling for the first book ordered and $1 for each additional book. Ten dollars plus $1 for each additional book if ordering from Canada. New York State residents must add sales tax.

To see our complete catalog on the World Wide Web, or to order online, you can find us at *www.allworth.com*.